COMMANDO CLASSICS

A Field Manual for Helping Teens Understand (and Maybe Even Enjoy) Classic Literature

DARIA PLUMB

VOYA Press

an imprint of E L Kurdyla Publishing, LLC

Bowie, Maryland

ISBN 978-1-61751-008-3

Published by VOYA Press, an imprint of E L Kurdyla Publishing LLC

LCCN: 2012935468

The paper used in this publication meets the minimum requirements of the American National Standard for Information Sciences-Permanence of Paper for Printed Materials, ANSI Z39.48-1992.

Printed in the United States of America

This book is dedicated to my mom, Pam, who served as my model for what a smart and motivated woman can do, and to my dad, John, who served as my model for what an enthusiastic teacher looked like.

Contents

PART 2
COMMANDO CLASSICS

Acknowledgements

I would like to extend my most sincere thanks to:

My family, who knew long before I ever did that I could do anything I put my mind to and whose unconditional love and support have allowed me to have a life and career that I love.

My awesome friends, who keep me sane, make me laugh, and are the best cheerleaders a girl could ever ask for.

All of my students, past and present, who make me work really hard, but who also teach me something new every day and provide me with *all* of my best material.

My editor and fairy godmother, RoseMary Honnold, who not only helped me realize that I just might have a book in me after all, but who also contributed some of her own programming ideas.

Librarians extraordinaire, Mary Arnold and Diane Tuccillo, for taking time out of their busy schedules to share their fantastic programming ideas with me.

My local "rockstar" librarians—Jennifer Grudnoski, Sheree Beaudry, Amber Reed, Kelli Venier, and Jadin Howton—who have given me innumerable suggestions and incredible support.

My coworkers (current and retired) at Riverside Academy—Tom Walentowski, Mindy Bailey, Jan Smith, Darlene Baldwin, and Helen Nabozny—who fill(ed) every work day with moomba!

Teri Lesesne, Bonnie Kunzel, CJ Bott, Don Gallo, Wendy Glenn, and Patrick Jones, who have been extremely generous with their time and advice and who have truly become mentors to me.

My colleagues (and family) from the Assembly on Literature for Adolescents of the NCTE (ALAN) who continually teach me, inspire me, support me, and open innumerable doors for me.

Dr. Susan Groenke, who attended my ALAN breakout session about *Commando Classics* and invited me to submit it as an article to *English Leadership Quarterly*.

Dr. Gilbert Cross and Dr. Sheila Most, professors emeritus from Eastern Michigan University, who encouraged my first forays into the worlds of academia and presenting.

The staff at the Dundee Public Library, who are always friendly, helpful, supportive, and who will do darn near anything to help me turn my students into readers.

Preface

I was a fresh-faced twenty-one-year-old, straight out of college, when I began teaching at Dundee Alternative High School (now called Riverside Academy). The job was a perfect fit for me, despite the fact that four years earlier I would never have predicted I would end up there. I had been a good student in high school and English had been my favorite subject—I loved memorizing authors and the titles of the books they'd written, I wanted to read Shakespeare, and I liked poetry, writing, and theater. I desperately wanted to be cultured and smart. I couldn't wait to become an English teacher so I could teach advanced placement English and have intellectual discussions with smart, motivated students about classic literature.

Imagine my surprise then when I began my student teaching experience in a British Literature class filled with bright, college-bound juniors who had educated, professional parents—students who actually did the writing assignments, read the material, and wanted me to tell them everything they would need in order to succeed in college—only to discover that I was miserable. It wasn't the fault of the students or my supervising teacher, all of whom were wonderful to me. It's that, in between graduating from high school and beginning that student teaching assignment, I had done most of my classroom observations and was also doing part of my student teaching in a school-within-a-school program specifically designed to catch the students who were falling between the cracks. It was there that I found my niche. Those teens needed me, not to tell them what they were going to need to know for college (most of them were not headed down that path), but to care about them and to interact with them on a personal level. So, upon my graduation from college, I found myself returning to my hometown and accepting a job at Dundee Alternative High School.

The students at Dundee Alternative High School/Riverside Academy are similar to the students you'd find in most alternative high school programs. They range in age from fourteen to nineteen. Most were in jeopardy of dropping out (and some had been thrown out) of their home high schools because of poor attendance, discipline problems, bad grades, or a combination of the three. Most would be labeled "at-risk," which means that they come from homes with single or step-parents; are teen parents; are not living at home; are abusing drugs and/or alcohol; have a parent who has died; have been involved with the court system; have depression or bipolar disorder; have a learning disability; and/or have gone to numerous schools. Most of them (probably 70-80 percent) are boys. They come to our program because it's their last chance at a high school diploma. Some do not come willingly (their parents or the courts have demanded that they attend school) and some choose to come because they have reached the conclusion that they need a diploma in order to get ahead in life.

Because our program tends to attract teens who hate to read and who would do wonderfully well in a hands-on, vocational education program, most of them have very little use for or interest in "LITERATURE." I can understand why. Many will be the first in their family to graduate from high school. Their parents generally don't have a post-high-school education and most of these teens don't plan on attending college either;

some will enter the military or go to a technical school, but most will head directly into the workforce after they graduate. They aren't going to need to know Shakespeare while roofing houses and poetry isn't going to be all that important while working the line in a factory. So why (and maybe more importantly, how) do I teach them the classics? Let's first address the why. The rest of this book will address the how.

First, I teach all of the English classes in our school. This set-up doesn't allow me to teach the same thing year after year, so I teach a rotation of General English, World Literature, American Literature, and British Literature. I am responsible for meeting state standards and benchmarks and for preparing students to take the same tests all students in the state take. While I do believe we need to drastically rethink the language arts curriculum to include more high-quality young adult literature (more on this in Chapter 1), the reality is that classic literature still has an extremely strong toe-hold in the secondary curriculum.

Second, I like the challenge of getting alternative ed students to understand (and maybe even enjoy) literature, be it young adult or canonical. My students have been told so often that they're "not smart enough," either at home or at school, that their self-esteem is in the gutter. Most of the teens I've worked with over the years didn't come to alternative school because they weren't smart enough to do regular high school work; in fact, I've had some downright gifted young people over the years. The problem is that their lives outside of school—their family troubles, their habits, their lack of problem-solving skills, and their addictions— have kept them from being successful. It's my job to teach them that they are smart and are capable of learning the same things the teens at the "regular" school learn. I like Shakespeare and I believe that, given the chance and the right teaching techniques, my students will like him, too.

Third, references to classic literature are everywhere—from our vernacular to children's cartoons to satirical television shows to music to movies. Maybe the quote, "Something is rotten in the state of Denmark" won't be on a job application for an electrician's apprentice, but you can almost guarantee that most people will hear it at least once in their adult lives. I don't want my students walking around in the "real world" asking, "What's Denmark got to do with anything?" Speaking of *Hamlet*, Disney's *The Lion King* is loosely based on the plot, *South Park's* Terrence and Phillip do the final death scene, singer Mary Prankster has a song titled "Green Eggs and Hamlet," and *Renaissance Man* (starring Danny DeVito) features army recruits reading the play. As Mitch pointed out after we completed our Shakespeare unit, "That Shakespeare stuff is everywhere!" He's right; there are references to Shakespeare everywhere, as well as references to *Frankenstein*, *A Christmas Carol*, *The Scarlet Letter*, *The Raven*, *Moby Dick*, and "The Road Not Taken," to name just a few.

* * *

The real perk of teaching in an alternative school is that I have the opportunity to use creative and non-traditional methods. When I started, I did what so many of us do—I repeated the methods my teachers had used. There's nothing fundamentally wrong with this, but it wasn't working for the students I was teaching. As I got more comfortable, and because my boss was willing to let me try pretty much anything I wanted, I gained the confidence to step out of the box and try different things.

The first thing I realized is that the students I was working with were not great readers. I would give them an assignment to read a short story or a chapter from a novel, but even if they tried to read it (and most of them didn't), they were only reading the words; they weren't putting the words and sentences and paragraphs together to *hear* the story. Also, only about half of them knew what I meant when I asked, "How many of you *see* the story in your head while you're reading it?" So, I started reading the assignments out loud—all of them, every day—with the students following along so they can see the words while they listen to me reading them "the right way." I give them participation points for this. This way I can stop to describe the scene and they can start to envision what is happening in the story. We can also stop to discuss, predict, and/or clarify what's going on.

Next, because my anthology didn't have enough selections to keep us busy every day for an entire school year, I began to experiment with supplemental materials. The Internet has made this especially easy—just point, click, cut, and paste and suddenly you can have the text of an entire short story or epic poem at your fingertips. At first, I looked for supplements to the readings in the anthology, usually just other poems or stories by the authors already in the textbook. In doing this, I began to find other materials that I either liked better than the selections in the anthology (like the medieval ballads "The Unquiet Grave" or "The Cruel Mother") or other stories or poems that were left out of the anthology (like "The Highwayman" by Alfred Noyes or *The Monkey's Paw* by W.W. Jacobs). Now I rarely use the anthology for anything more than a jumping off point and most of what we read in class is supplemental. I also bring in other materials that reference the story we're studying, like newspaper articles, picture books, art, music, or folklore.

Finally, I started to break away from the original text and use alternative texts. When possible, I do use the original text, especially with shorter poems, ballads, or short stories in which the language isn't too difficult and the plot is pretty straightforward. I don't hesitate to substitute with a graphic novel, film, picture book, or summary though, if I think the students are going to get bogged down by the language or if we don't have enough time to read the whole story. I found that these formats enabled me to present the basic story in its entirety, which I liked much better than reading a scene here and a chapter there. It seemed as if the students liked it, too, because suddenly the plot was accessible to them.

I knew I had finally hit upon the right method when, after reading a summary of *Paradise Lost*, I asked my students, "What other story have we read in which one character is jealous because he wasn't chosen to be second-in-command to a powerful man?" and they knew the answer was *Othello*. I hadn't known that when I was in high school—in fact, I hadn't read *Othello* or *Paradise Lost* in high school. Now, my students hadn't read the *original* versions of either story, but here they were comparing *Paradise Lost* and *Othello*. It told me that they had a basic understanding of both stories. Did it matter that we hadn't read the original versions? I didn't think it did, and so the commando idea was born.

References

The Lion King. Walt Disney Home Video: Buena Vista Home Video, 1995.

Prankster, Mary. "Green Eggs and Hamlet." *Blue Skies Forever*. Palace Coup Records, 1998.

Renaissance Man. Touchstone, 1994.

"To Be or Not To Be Buddy?" *South Park*. Aired: July 17, 2001.

PART I

THE COMMANDO APPROACH

What Is the Commando Approach?

Shakespeare and *poetry*—probably two of the most reviled words in the English language. Why do these words engender fear and loathing in a large percentage of the population today? Because they are seen as subjects that are irrelevant and inaccessible to all but the most highly educated people; in fact, even well-educated adults have been known to groan and shiver at the very mention of these words. This reaction becomes generalized and gets associated with everything literature-related. When I meet someone and tell them that I am an English teacher, they cringe and either comment, "Oh, I guess I better watch my grammar," or they regale me with horror stories about reading some classic novel in high school. I'd be willing to bet that it's not that different for librarians. And dentists think they have it bad? At least they make a lot of money and get some respect!

The fear of classic literature is widespread and many students enter high school already dreading the assigned reading. Who can blame them? They've heard about Shakespeare—he's that old dude who wears tights and talks funny—and the joy they once experienced reading Shel Silverstein and Jack Prelutsky has been replaced by training in how to "tie the poem to the chair with a rope and torture a confession out of it (Collins 58). They have also been trained to believe that only the teacher really knows what a story or poem is about. We probably all remember playing this game in school:

> Teacher: What does the rose in this poem symbolize?
>
> Student 1: Something that smells good?
>
> Teacher: Wrong.
>
> Student 2: Something that's red?
>
> Teacher: Wrong. The rose symbolizes (*youth, beauty, love, etc.*)
>
> Student 3: How do you know that's what the rose symbolizes? Were you there when he wrote it?
>
> Teacher: I know because I'm the teacher.

Reading stops being a fun activity and becomes work. Not only that, it becomes a game students can't win.

If I could, I'd use all young adult literature all the time; I think many of us would. I like the classics (in fact I've come to appreciate them more now that I'm an adult), but I'm not 100 percent sure they're what all high school students should be expected to read. As Don Gallo points out in his article "How Classics Create an Aliterate Society":

The classics are not about TEENAGE concerns! They are about ADULT issues. Moreover, they were written for EDUCATED adults who had the LEISURE time to read them. They were also, not incidentally, written to be ENJOYED—not DISSECTED, not ANALYZED, and certainly not TESTED. (34)

Gallo makes the argument that, by subjecting young people to books that aren't written for them and by using outdated methods to teach these books, we are causing teens to become aliterate—they can read, but choose not to. I agree with Gallo. We need to completely rethink HOW and WHY we teach the classics in high school. What are we really trying to give students? As the classics are being taught right now, the objective doesn't seem to be to teach students to enjoy good literature. In fact, it seems to be much the opposite; it seems as if we are sending the message that the only good literature is literature that is painful to read and/or difficult to understand. That's the reason we hear so many students say they hate reading. They don't hate reading. They hate reading and dissecting books that don't seem the least bit relevant to their own lives. Most people do not become English teachers so they can make kids hate reading, but that is exactly what ends up happening. Dusty, a student of mine, said about the classics, "That's the kind of stuff that pulls kids away from reading because they think that's all there is."

However, the reality of most school districts is that administrators and parents believe students must be taught the classics. One argument is that students need to read the classics in order to prepare for college. Another argument is that the classic canon has always been taught in high school and we should continue that tradition. Another argument is the ever popular, "School isn't supposed to be fun—sometimes you just have to do things you don't want to do." Finally, some might argue that, if we want students to have a well-rounded education and become culturally literate, then they should be reading the classics.

Take heart. A 2006 thread on the yalsa-bk listserv (an email discussion list hosted by Young Adult Library Services Association), titled "Books Teens Hate," may offer us a way to please everyone. Though it was hard for people to agree on *which* books teens hate, the general consensus among the librarians, teachers, and professors who responded was that the *way* in which the material is presented makes a huge difference. While we may not always be able to select the books we want for our classrooms, we *can* make an effort to present the books in the most engaging and interesting manner. Even Mark Twain, a now-classic author himself, defined a classic as, "Something everybody wants to have read but nobody wants to read." Aye, there's the rub. We want to know what the story is about, but we want to be able to gain that knowledge without having to slog through hundreds of pages of difficult and often tedious text. That's where the commando idea comes in.

It's All about the Plot!

Mary Ann Tighe and Charles Avinger say a classic meets three criteria: (1) it stands the test of time; (2) it addresses universal dilemmas and concerns; and (3) it has a "unique beauty of style and structure that causes it to endure." While I think the first and third criteria are important, my commando approach is based largely on the second. Many classic stories have great plots, but the language and/or the length of the original make them inaccessible to today's teens. I often tell my students, "People are people. No matter where or when they live, they experience the same emotions and have the same hopes and dreams as you do. The reason _____ is still being read today is because it's about things we're still interested in today—love, jealousy, revenge, fears, and so on."

In order to get my students on board with the idea of reading the classics, I employ what I call a "commando" approach. I sneak in, hit them with the *basic plot* of the story, and get out before they realize what happened. Once I've breached their defenses, I pepper them with many plots so they can see and begin to appreciate the similarities between stories. To do this, I will use any means necessary—graphic novels, picture books, movies, summaries, and more—to help me present the story in a way they can understand. Though I do realize that alternative materials do not always contain secondary characters and plot lines, I am willing to sacrifice some of those things in order to get my students to the basic plot. Believe me, after reading *The Scarlet Letter* aloud three times a day and stopping after every sentence to explain in "real English" what I'd just read, I learned the value of getting to the plot in an expedient manner. I found that my students liked trying to sort out the mystery behind Pearl's parentage, but they couldn't follow the story as it was written. Should they be robbed of a good story because they're not ready for mid-nineteenth-century language? I don't think so. I think that students will be more likely to return to the classics as adults if their experiences with them in high school are not completely frustrating.

With the commando method, students don't have to dig through layers of difficult language, symbolism, and metaphor in order to get to the plot. I give them the plot and let *it* become the springboard for our discussions and activities. This changes our roles. It takes the power out of my hands and places it in theirs. I am no longer the only person in the room who is "smart enough" to understand the story—we all know it, therefore we can all talk about it. They don't have to worry about being wrong. They don't have to feel stupid because they don't understand symbolism. They don't have to struggle to understand the language.

When these roadblocks are removed, they can see the work for what it is—a great story. When students are able to see the connections between stories and to compare them, they start to see that the plots and themes found in classic literature are repeated in all other art forms, past and present. For example, when we were about halfway through our reading of a prose version of *Beowulf*, Marvin said, "This story is just a *Lord of the Rings* rip-off." "Wait a minute," I said, "*when* was this written?" His response was, "OK, *Lord of the Rings* is just a *Beowulf* rip-off." And, once they understand that these themes are repeated because they speak to what makes us human, then students can see how these stories are relevant to their own lives.

Think Outside the Anthology

By definition, an anthology is a collection of works. Expecting an anthology to offer numerous pieces by one author would be unrealistic and would make for a large, unmanageable tome. So, in order to present an overview, editors are forced to offer only portions of longer works, select only one or two of an author's most famous works, or select works that demonstrate or represent a particular literary era or element. As a result, anthologies aren't always filled with the best reading choices for teens. My student Dale pointed out, "I think there should be a rule that you should be interested in a book before you're interested in [literary] terms."

This is a good point. We should never select a story or poem for the sole purpose of teaching literary elements; if it's a true classic, as defined by Tighe and Avinger, its style and structure should enable us to teach just about any literary element we want. We should look for good stories that will engage our students first and worry about the literary elements second. This is why I'm always on the lookout for good supplemental materials.

Here's a perfect example. The only William Wordsworth poem in my anthology is "Daffodils." When we read it, my students' first (and often only) question is, "Was he gay?" I can see why they ask—it doesn't seem terribly masculine for a guy to write about his heart filling with pleasure at the memory of daffodils—and this isn't what I want them to take away from their only reading of Wordsworth. This poem also doesn't show readers that the Romantic poets "were the rebels of their time [whose] poetry, when it first appeared, received the same kind of reaction accorded rock and roll when it burst upon the music scene," as it says in the Teacher's Edition of my book (Potter and McCubbrey). So, I supplement with: "She Dwelt Among the Untrodden Ways," a poem mourning the death of the speaker's love; "Simon Lee: The Old Huntsman," a poem about a man who has grown old and is unable to perform his household duties; "There Was a Boy," a poem about a boy who goes out in the evening and calls to the owls and communes with nature only to die before he turns twelve; "To Sleep," a poem begging sleep to come and refresh the speaker who has had insomnia for three nights; and the students' favorite, "We Are Seven," a poem about an argument between the speaker and a young girl who disagree about the number of people in her family because two of her siblings have died (see More William Wordsworth Poems in The British Literature Arsenal). These poems are a better representation of Wordsworth's and the early Romantic poets' interest in nature, love, death, and spirituality.

Here's another example. My literature anthology has only one hundred twenty-three lines from the epic poem *Beowulf*—and that's one hundred twenty-three lines out of the *middle* of the poem. Starting in the middle of a 3,182 line poem makes it difficult for students to get a feel for what is actually an exciting story. So, I use Kevin Crossley-Holland's prose version of *Beowulf*, which is accessible and can be read and discussed in two class periods. Shortly after reading it in class, Lauren told me about a friend from "regular" school who complained about being completely lost while reading *Beowulf*. Lauren was able to explain the story to her. The friend's response was, "You read *Beowulf* at alternative school?" Lauren's analysis of why she understood it and her friend did not was that I "know how to teach it." Now, we can use the animated movie *Beowulf* and Gareth Hind's awesome graphic novel *The Collected Beowulf* to help generate even more interest in this one-thousand-year-old poem.

Introducing (drum roll, please)... the Text Set

Whenever possible, I try to build a unit or a text set around a central literary work or theme. ReadWriteThink defines text sets as:

> …collections of resources from different genre, media, and levels of reading difficulty that are designed to be supportive of the learning of readers with a range of experiences and interests. A text set collection focuses on one concept or topic and can include multiple genres such as books, charts and maps, informational pamphlets, poetry and songs, photographs, non-fiction books, almanacs, or encyclopedias.

I like to think that a text set allows me to provide students with a three-dimensional or well-rounded view of the novel or theme we are studying. Here's a diagram that illustrates the concept:

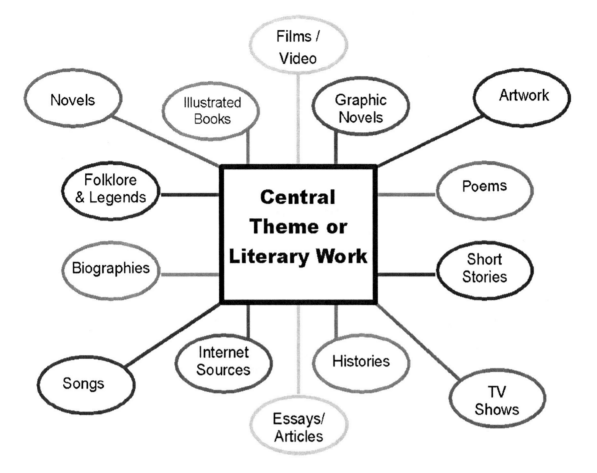

All of the materials in a text set do not need to be brought into the classroom, but they can be mentioned in the class discussion or lecture. If you can pull three or four, you'll have the making of a good text set. If the focus is on a broader theme, such as heroes, it may be easier to draw together more than that.

COMMANDO LIBRARIANS

All of the text sets included in this book can be adapted to help you create themed displays. Also, offer to help teachers create text sets for books they are teaching.

Using the text set and the idea that the plot is of utmost importance, I try to expose students to anything that will connect to the story we're reading. Here's an example of my three-day unit for *The Hound of the Baskervilles* by Sir Arthur Conan Doyle. First, we read the folklore surrounding black dogs. These dogs are often found wandering the deserted roads of the moors at night and are described as being "as big as a calf with red eyes." They generally appear out of nowhere and are thought to bring bad luck or to be omens of death. In order to show that the folklore of the black dog is still very much alive in pop culture, we discussed J.K. Rowling's use of this same black dog lore in *Harry Potter and the Prisoner of Azkaban* and looked at a copy of the Goosebumps book, *The Barking Ghost*, which even features a main character named Cooper Holmes. Then we segue into Sherlock Holmes, the character. I print a biography of the character from *The Sherlock Holmes Museum* website (*http://www.sherlock-holmes.co.uk*) and give the students the "Sherlock

Holmes Quiz" (eleven logic problems) from the same website. I also mention to students that the character Artie in the movie *Shanghai Nights* (starring Jackie Chan and Owen Wilson), was Arthur Conan Doyle, the creator of Sherlock Holmes. After that, we read the illustrated classic of *The Hound of the Baskervilles*. We then finish up with an article titled "The War of the Baskervilles" by Guy Saville, which was released in conjunction with the 100th anniversary of the book, and examines the claim that Doyle may have "stolen" the plot line of *The Hound of the Baskervilles* from a friend. All of this is done in class and, in that short period of time, the students are able to understand the basic plot of the entire story; read some of the folklore that may have inspired Doyle; learn a bit about the famous character Sherlock Holmes; and see how the folklore continues to appear in literature today. We could also have watched clips from one of the old versions of the movie, watched "Ghostly Creatures: Black Dogs" from *Animal X Natural Mystery Unit*, or explored the websites for the *Baskerville Hall Hotel* (*http://www.baskerville.co.uk*) or *Yorkshire Moors and Coast Travel and Tourism* (*http://www.yorkshiremoorsandcoast.com*). For the complete text set for *The Hound of the Baskervilles* see the The British Literature Arsenal.

Once the idea of creating a text set is understood, it's not too difficult. My first stop is usually the county library website, mainly because I know I'll be able to get my hands on most of the materials I find in a timely manner. Once there, I search first the title and then the author's name. This brings up a plethora of novels, nonfiction books, movies, and picture books loosely connected to my central literary work. I pick and choose the ones that seem most appropriate for my students and add them to my list. My second stop is usually *Wikipedia* (*http://www.wikipedia.com*). Though not considered a valid source for research projects, *Wikipedia* is a great place to find out about movies, TV shows, and other books in which a specific book, character, and/ or author appear. My third stop is the *Internet Movie Database* (*http://www.imdb.com*) to search the title to find any relevant movies. Finally, I do a *Google* (*http://www.google.com*) search to find anything else I might have missed, like websites, web quests, artwork, or lesson plans.

Students can also be a source of information for text sets. Students often point out to me that one story or another was featured on *The Simpsons* or *South Park* or they bring in songs that correspond with the unit we are studying. It was through my students that I learned that *South Park* had featured part of the final scene of *Hamlet*. A student named Brandon told me about the song "Kenji" by Fort Minor, which is about the Japanese internment camp Manzanar. Asking students to create their own text sets can help to bring more pop culture references into the classroom and will allow students to discover that references to these classic stories are indeed everywhere. If the school has the technology, students could also put together movie clips featuring some of the more memorable scenes from the novel the class is studying or show the different ways a famous character, like Hamlet, Dracula, Hester Prynne, or Tom Sawyer, has been depicted on film over the years.

COMMANDO LIBRARIANS
Text Set in a Tub

Build themed collections (i.e., portable text sets) for the classroom that a teacher can check out for an entire unit. Many libraries offer special extended loan periods for educators. For example, collect young adult fiction with Shakespearean plots, Shakespearean plays, and nonfiction books about the Globe Theatre and life in the Middle Ages. Maps, DVDs, and other materials can complement the collection. Create a guide with helpful websites, a pathfinder list of resources available in your library on the topic. Collect all in a plastic tub with a list of the contents for easy transport to and from the library.

A Text Set Planner

CENTRAL LITERARY THEME OR WORK

NOVELS

ILLUSTRATED BOOKS

FILMS/VIDEOS

GRAPHIC NOVELS

ARTWORK

POEMS

TV SHOWS

INTERNET SOURCES

SONGS

BIOGRAPHIES

FOLKLORE & LEGENDS

HISTORIES

MISCELLANEOUS

ESSAYS / ARTICLES

SHORT STORIES

Calling for Reinforcements

Every good English teacher needs a partner to help plan and execute her/his attack. The ideal person for this job should be focused on getting teens to become lifelong readers; have excellent research skills; have access to and knowledge of lots of books, videos, and other media; and be willing to come into the classroom from time to time to talk to the students. Believe it or not, there is one person who fulfills all of these requirements; s/he is often overlooked by teachers as a source of support and is probably "hiding in plain sight" in the building. It is, of course, the librarian. Unfortunately, during this time of deep educational budget cuts school librarians are being eliminated at alarming rates. This means that teachers may need to go outside of their buildings and seek out help from the librarian(s) at their local library branches. These librarians are also willing and able to help, and they may have access to resources and funding that school librarians do not. And, if you let them, they are happy to come to schools. As my friend and former youth services librarian Mary Arnold once explained, the patrons of a youth services librarian are a captive audience between the hours of 8 a.m. and 3 p.m., which justifies a youth librarian spending at least some of her/his work week making contacts at and visiting the local junior high schools and high schools.

WHY A COMMANDO TEACHER NEEDS A COMMANDO LIBRARIAN

I posed the question, "What kinds of programs can a librarian design for a teacher?" to my local librarian friends Jennifer Grudnoski, Sheree Beaudry, Amber Reed, Kelli Venier, and Jadin Howton. They outlined many ideas, but the main takeaway for me was that the possibilities are literally limited only by the teacher's and librarian's imaginations. Here are just a few of the things they are available to do:

- Organize and provide the materials for craft projects.
- Bring in "live acts" (i.e. musicians, actors, authors, etc.) to talk to or perform demonstrations for students.
- Show movies that coincide with classroom curriculum.
- Host programs in which students can make and/or sample different types of food.
- Give booktalks to students.

COMMANDO LIBRARIANS

Lunch Time Book Club

Get permission from the administration to start a book club during lunch in the school library or in the corner of a cafeteria or in a room where the students can bring their lunches.

Partner with the school librarian to alternate days or share the discussion. While the librarians must read the featured title, often the students will do well discussing the book on their own. Prepare a few leading questions as prompts to use if the conversation lags.

Bring multiple paperback copies of a title that will appeal to girls and boys. Seek funding for book discussion books from community foundations and chain discount stores, such as Wal-mart or Target. Many of these stores do matching grants which will double the money you have to spend.

Please believe me when I say that librarians are eager to get into our classrooms. They want to give book talks to students. They want to talk to students about the educational and fun programming their libraries have to offer. They want to help students with their research projects. They want to make their libraries teacher and teen friendly. And, they are baffled by the fact that more teachers don't ask for their help.

Here is just one of the many, many examples I can give to illustrate why teachers should befriend as many librarians as possible. When I was preparing to write this book I was talking to my local librarian, Jennifer Grudnoski, about developing a text set based on mad scientists in literature. She told me about the nonfiction book *Guinea Pig Scientists: Bold Self-Experimenters in Science and Medicine* and said that it would

---

COMMANDO LIBRARIANS AND TEACHERS

Assignment Alerts are helpful communications between teachers and librarians. A ready-made form that can be filled in online and submitted to the librarian will help the librarian prepare resources for the students. The librarian can collect materials or create a bibliography of titles and Internet resources for the class. The librarians can use the many lists in this book to get started. Repeated assignments from school to school or year to year are great suggestions for building themed collections.

COMMANDO LIBRARIANS AND TEACHERS

The school librarian (AASL), children's (ALSC), and young adult (YALSA) divisions of American Library Association share many successful partnerships between school and public libraries at *http://www.ala.org/alsc/externalrelationships/coopacts/schoolplcoopprogs*.

---

be a perfect addition to my list. Since we were at a meeting at a coffee shop, I thanked her for the suggestion and made a note to look for the book. When I checked my patron record online less than a week later, however, the book had already been requested and was waiting for me at my local library branch! This is not the first time this has happened; there have been numerous times when I've mentioned a project to the wonderful people who work at the Dundee Branch Library only to find books waiting for me that I haven't requested, but that are nonetheless a perfect fit for my project.

Because I always hear teachers complain that they don't have enough time to do everything they need to do (and it is a legitimate complaint), every teacher should run to the nearest library and introduce him/herself to the librarian and exchange e-mail addresses and phone numbers. Then they should schedule a meeting to sit down and talk about what the class is working on and find out what the librarian can offer in the way of help. It is amazing to see the lengths a librarian will go to in order to help—designing displays, scheduling programs, creating book lists, and more. You can help her/him out by encouraging students to go to the library and to attend programs by offering extra credit; you can probably even ask the librarian to verify student attendance for you. I guarantee that the amount of time spent making this connection will be dwarfed by the amount of time and effort the librarian will put forth once s/he is in your corner, so get to it (I'll wait)!

COMMANDO LIBRARIANS
Literature Comes Alive!

(Courtesy of Diane Tuccillo, Poudre River Public Library District, Fort Collins, CO)

We have been discussing the idea of doing special Literature Comes Alive! programs at the library starting in the fall that we would promote through the schools and encourage teachers to give extra credit to their students for attending. This would be a joint effort between adult and teen services at our library. We are hoping to help teachers tie-in to classics through these programs.

One of our main sources for "character" performers is the Chautauqua Speakers Bureau. The Chautauqua and other programs of this type involve people learning great details about their characters, figuring out what costumes they would have worn, and creating performances where the characters come alive. This could be done for the writers themselves, as we are planning to do, but it could also be done with book characters if teachers and librarians wanted to do something really innovative with this idea.

- "Chatauqua Speakers Bureau Roster," Colorado Humanities (*http://www.coloradohumanities.org/content/ chautauqua-speakers-bureau-roster*)
- "Young Chatauqua," Colorado Humanities (*http://www.coloradohumanities.org/content/young-chautauqua*)

COMMANDO LIBRARIANS AND TEACHERS
Meet Mark Twain

(Courtesy of Mary Arnold, Maple Heights Branch, Cuyahoga County Public Library, Maple Heights, OH)

The ninth graders at our local high school alternate between reading *The Adventures of Tom Sawyer* and *Adventures of Huckleberry Finn* each year. I worked with the teachers on an introductory presentation, not on the books themselves, but on Mark Twain/Samuel Clemens as presented by Huck. I would actually dress in a plaid shirt, red suspenders and a straw hat and quote the first line of the book "You don't know about me…a book written by Mr. Samuel Clemens, a right interesting fellow."

I'd give a brief biography of Twain: his several careers and travels; the origin of his pen name; the fact that his image became so recognizable that he was one of the first "celebrity spokespersons" (I printed out and mounted pictures of his blurbs for everything from cigars, a brand of flour, Oldsmobile cars to shaving soap). Twain was also a big self-promoter, using his trademark humor to sell tickets to his travel lectures. I put together a facsimile placard for one I found in a biography. There's even an online link now (*http://www.fastcompany.com/node/59875/print*).

We'd also show a clip of Hal Holbrook as Mark Twain from the VHS/DVD—but now there are *YouTube* clips that would work as well, and that demonstrate his political and social activism stands.

We ended by making origami jumping frogs (*http://www.howcast.com/videos/310-How-To-Make-an-Origami-Jumping-Frog*) and staging a contest. I borrowed a cool frog hand puppet from the Children's Department as a prop.

You could also include the quote on "classic literature" from Mr. Twain. The presentation serves to humanize and modernize Twain for 21st century readers.

For Commando Librarians ONLY (Teachers, Look Away)!

I am not just kissing up when I say that I love librarians—some of the people I respect and idolize the most are librarians or are people who teach librarians. I do realize and appreciate the fact that this book will find its way into most teachers' hands because of the librarian reader. And it is my most sincere hope that this book will lead teachers back to the librarian. For many teachers, the commando approach I am outlining will require time (which they don't feel they have), research (which may be overwhelming), and support (which they may not get from their peers). This is where the librarian (who can provide all of these things) comes in. It would be almost impossible for a teacher to become a true commando teacher without the librarian's help.

It probably seems like a "no-brainer" that English teachers and librarians go together like peanut butter and jelly, but please don't take offense at the fact that many teachers forget what a valuable resource a great librarian can be. It's not personal; once we get into our classrooms, we often lose touch with the outside world. Please, keep trying to make connections with the teachers in your area. If just one makes the connection—maybe start with a new teacher who will need all the help s/he can get—word will spread that the librarian is a priceless asset.

> **COMMANDO LIBRARIANS**
>
> Most school districts hold teacher in-services before the school year begins and periodically throughout the year. This is a ready audience for school and public librarians to show what they have to offer in services and resources that will enhance the curriculum. This is a great time to explain the benefits of mixing pop culture with classic literature. Do book talks, give booklists, and/or create a handout with the services you can provide.

> **COMMANDO LIBRARIANS**
>
> Book deliveries to schools via a courier will reach more students. Students can place holds on titles using the online catalog and the teacher or media specialist's special loan card. The items are checked out using that card number and collected for delivery. Many schools already utilize a courier among the schools. The books are delivered to the media specialist or teacher (one contact person per school keeps it simple), who uses the school library's system with temporary barcodes to keep track of the books.

Today the Classroom, Tomorrow the World!

So, who is this book really written for? Well, since I am an English teacher, that's obviously the angle I bring and most of the ideas are intended for classroom use. I hope that the vignettes about my students will help to convince the reader of the efficacy of this method. I have also written with librarians in mind. The goal of this book is that teachers and librarians will team up to help make students into lifelong readers (not just of classic literature, but of *all* literature).

> **COMMANDO LIBRARIANS**
>
> September is Library Card Signup Month! The American Library Association provides free promotional tools at *http://www.ala.org/conferencesevents/celebrationweeks/card* to help you reach students, teachers, and parents to remind them that a library card is the most important school supply of all!

References

Beowulf. Paramount Home Entertainment, 2008.

Collins, Billy. "Introduction to Poetry." *The Apple That Astonished Paris*, Second Edition, p. 58. University of Arkansas Press, 2006.

Conan Doyle, Arthur. *The Hound of the Baskervilles.* Pendulum Press, 1977.

Crossley-Holland, Kevin. *Beowulf.* Oxford University Press, 1982.

Dendy, Leslie and Mel Boring. *Guinea Pig Scientists: Bold Self-Experimenters in Science and Medicine.* Henry Holt and Company, 2005.

Fort Minor. "Kenji." *The Rising Tied.* Warner Brothers, 2005.

Gallo, Donald R. "How Classics Create an Aliterate Society." *English Journal.* January 2001, 33-39.

"Ghostly Creatures: Black Dogs." *Animal X Natural Mystery Unit.* Series 1, Episode 1. *http://www.animalx. net/ghostly_creatures.html*

Hind, Gareth. *The Complete Beowulf.* Candlewick Press, 2000.

Potter, Robert and Ruth D. McCubbrey. *Globe Literature: Gold Level.* Globe Book Company, 1990.

ReadWriteThink. "Creating Text Sets for Your Classroom." National Council of Teacher of English/ International Reading Association, 2004.

Rowling, J.K. *Harry Potter and the Prisoner of Azkaban.* Scholastic, 1999.

Saville, Guy. "The War of the Baskervilles." *The Independent*, July 11, 2001.

Shanghai Knights. Touchstone Home Entertainment, 2003.

Stine, R.L. *The Barking Ghost.* Scholastic, 1995.

Tighe, Mary Ann and Charles Avinger. "Teaching Tomorrow's CLASSICS." *The ALAN Review.* Volume 21, no. 3. Spring 1994.

"To Be or Not To Be Buddy?" *South Park.* Aired: July, 17, 2001.

Defending Your Choices

Before we plunge headlong into the commando approach, I would issue this warning: for some readers, some of what I'm going to talk about might be out of the comfort zone. It might be startling. Blasphemous, even. Despite what it might sound like, I'm not anti-rigor. I'm not anti-classics. I'm not anti-original texts. I am, however, anti-readicide. I am passionately and whole-heartedly against creating readers who have no desire to pick up a book once they leave high school (and in many cases, who won't pick up a book even while they're *in* high school). What's the good in that? I didn't become an English teacher so I could make students hate reading.

Teachers have a couple of options. We can keep presenting the classic canon in a traditional way. Parents and administrators won't complain; in fact they'll probably love it because it's exactly the way they were taught and, in education, we often live by the, "If it ain't broke . . ." mantra. Along the way, we'll continue to lose more and more students because they won't be willing and/or able to make the connection between these texts and their real lives. We'll keep bemoaning the fact that, "Kids today just don't read." *Or* we can rethink the way we teach because we have to, because it *is* broken. Because having five students out of twenty-five who've actually done the reading assignment each day shouldn't be an acceptable option for any English teacher.

I know it's scary to think outside the box, but I don't have a choice; outside the box is where I *have* to teach if I want any chance of connecting my students to literature. My students aren't in the business of playing along like good, meek little students; they will call me on the carpet anytime and anywhere (and sometimes even when I think I've delivered a damn good lesson) if I fail to make my course content relevant to them. I can't go in there with the old, "This book/poem/story is a classic. We're going to analyze it and dissect it and find all of the symbolism in it, and you will love it because it is great literature" routine, it just won't fly. I tried it for the first couple of years, and it's a wonder anyone survived to tell the tale. In fact, I should probably apologize right now to all of the students who had me in the first five years of my career when I was learning how to be a teacher . . . and I should also thank them for turning me into one.

Building Your Arsenal

When a teacher chooses a text for the classroom, she/he goes through a process: weighing its literary value; determining how and where it aligns with the standards and benchmarks; considering optional texts that could be used, should a parent request one; reading journal articles, reviews, and consulting other teachers; and considering the maturity level, reading ability, and prior knowledge of the students. Depending on the school district's policies, this process may occur mentally, or it may be required to write and submit it. Always, always, always be sure to C.Y.A. (cover your, ahem, *ass*-ignments). Have an article or book (or a list of them) on hand to support the choices and teaching techniques. Nearly every chapter in this book will direct the reader to several articles from professional journals, books, and/or websites that will provide not only support for using these particular methods but more great teaching ideas as well.

There is one document that will support virtually every aspect of the commando method; this is the kryptonite to all of the nay-sayers. It is the National Council of Teachers of English/International Reading Association's *Standards for the English Language Arts* (the entire document is available at *http://www.ncte.org/standards*). Every idea discussed in the upcoming chapters can be justified with this single document. I would particularly like to point out the frequency with which these standards mention utilizing a variety of print and non-print texts from a variety of genres and time periods for a variety of purposes (including pleasure, which let's face it, is always the toughest thing to justify in the classroom—if it's fun, it can't be learning, right?). Several of the standards also call our attention to using texts to help students better understand themselves and the world around them and to allowing students to respond to texts in a variety of ways. So when selling this method to colleagues and administrators, start and end with this document. Keep it handy. Post it in the classroom. Memorize it. Chant it when meditating. Sleep with it under the pillow. Seriously, how many mere mortals will argue with both the International Reading Association *and* the National Council of Teachers of English? Exactly.

Finally, document the things that work well and that will be continued in future classes. This doesn't have to be super scientific, but make note if there are fewer disciplinary problems, higher test scores, positive student responses, etc. Keep copies of particularly good student projects or writing assignments. Share successes with colleagues, administrators, and the school board. As classroom teachers, I think we're often hesitant to believe that we are capable of being the "experts" about what works best in the classroom, but, despite the very best efforts of some politicians to prove otherwise, we are the ones who know what works and doesn't work in our classrooms. Besides, you never know when you might want to write a book of your own.

Yeah, But...

Before attempting to implement the ideas in this book, be warned that there are people who will question this approach to teaching literature. A lot of ivory tower academics don't understand what the reality is for those of us who are working in the trenches. Even some of your colleagues won't get it (maybe ever). I've heard this line plenty of times from other English teachers, "Well, that's fine for you. You teach at an *alternative* school. I can't use this with *my* students, they're going to college." I'm always tempted to whisper back, "Well, make sure to tell them that *Hamlet* wasn't actually a comic book and they should be just fine." It often makes me wonder where they think my students came from. My students came from their classrooms, and plenty of students like mine are still in their classrooms. Alternative schools aren't the only places where there are reluctant and resistant learners.

I'm not willing to concede that this method isn't effective for the students who are going to college. Will it hurt college-bound kids to have a solid understanding of the entire plot of a difficult text like *Beowulf* or *Hamlet*? Will it be detrimental to their college careers if they are knowledgeable about how a classic novel or poem can be linked to other art forms (films, paintings, songs, other literature, etc.), past and present? Will it hinder their analytical abilities if they are asked to compare characters and themes of classic stories? Is asking them to engage with and respond to literature in a thoughtful and creative manner, rather than regurgitating notes from our daily lectures back to us on an essay test, going to turn them into poor students? It just sounds downright silly when put like that, doesn't it?

Next, I'll go point-by-point through some of the criticisms I've heard over the years and address each of them individually.

Alternative Texts

In my experience, the part of the commando method that makes people the most uncomfortable is the idea of replacing original texts with alternative texts. If I had a better background in literary and social criticism, I might argue that some people might not want everyone to have access to classic literature; that they want to keep the classics for the well-educated only, but that's a book for someone else to write. On the other hand, I have also talked to people who think I'm underestimating my students by not asking them to read original texts, that I'm "dumbing down" my curriculum, so to speak. So, let me be clear. I'm not suggesting that I never use original texts. For example, in my British Literature class we read original poetry by Chaucer, Shakespeare, Wordsworth, Byron, Keats, Shelley, etc. (pretty much all of the big names), as well as many short stories. I want my students to hear the author's voice when we're studying a piece of literature. I want them to know that people talked differently in different time periods, and to be able to "translate" and understand what an author is saying. I'm not suggesting that we take that away, and I'm certainly not suggesting that we replace all classic literature with comic books.

I am suggesting, however, that we carefully consider *what* we choose to present in its original form. If a text is so difficult that we have to explain every sentence or line before our students can even begin to understand it, then what's our rationale for teaching it? Is it dictated by the curriculum or by the state's standards and benchmarks? If it is, then get creative and figure out a way to meet that requirement without totally losing the students in the process, i.e. present the story in an alternative format. If it's not, then think about replacing it with something more relevant by the same author or that touches on the same themes.

Remember, when using an alternative text (a graphic novel, film, picture book, etc.) in place of an original text, the literary elements of the original story can be taught, and the class can also discuss and analyze the format of the alternative text. When using a graphic novel to teach *Othello*, talk about the plot points, the character development, and setting of the play and also analyze how these elements are presented in the graphic novel format. Think of it as a two-for-one deal; more bang for the educational buck.

The "Easy Button"

Some people suggest that I choose to teach in this manner because it is easier. For whom is it easier? Let's examine that question. It's definitely not easier for the teacher. It takes a lot of prep work to go outside the comfort zone of the anthology and to sort through and find works students can relate to (and maybe even enjoy), to create new assignments to accompany the new readings, and to devise new ways of evaluating and assessing students' knowledge and understanding. The teacher who is looking for easy will simply pull out the anthology, use the prepackaged worksheets, assign the questions at the end of each reading selection, and give the tests that come with the teacher's guide. This approach should not be chosen because it might be easier. It isn't. Even with the help from this book, there will still be a lot of legwork to do based on the needs of the students and the curricular requirements.

So, maybe they think it's easier for the students? I think the answer to that is that it *is*, and it *isn't*. Getting through the actual text might be easier if students are given an alternative version of the story, for example. However, it also forces students to become active and engaged members of the classroom community. They no longer need to depend upon the teacher to interpret the language and/or plots; everybody in the room knows what the story is about, so everybody can talk about it. This means that classroom time isn't necessarily dominated by the teacher who is lecturing and explaining the story or by the "smart kid" who is answering all of the teacher's questions so no one else has to pay attention or think. They will be asked to think critically about, interact with, and respond to the texts in new and creative ways—ways that will often push them out of their comfort zones—and, as teens are creatures of habit, this is one of the most difficult things we can ask them to do. So, it's not easier for them, either.

The F-Word

For some people, the idea of making "serious literature" fun is blasphemous. I agree that we shouldn't feel like we *have* to make everything in school fun for students (there are plenty of times when I tell my own students, "Sorry, it's not going to be fun today, so just suck it up."), but if it *can* be fun and they still learn, why not do it as often as possible? Besides, if it's more fun for them, it will probably also be more fun for the teacher. Have you ever felt energized and excited after teaching poetry to high school students? How long has it been since you looked forward to teaching Shakespeare to your general English class? When was the last time your students discussed anything you've done *in* class outside of the classroom? If the answer to these questions is, "Never," or, "It's been so long I can barely remember it," then you're doing yourself and your students a disservice. When my students say to me, "You always have the best stories" (not *reading assignments*, but *stories*), when they show me that they've made a connection between what we've studied in class and their everyday worlds, or when they win bets with detention center guards about Edgar Allan Poe (more on this in Chapter 4), that's when I know that fun *can* be effective.

Let's not forget about allowing students to respond to literature in fun ways. I'll admit it, I'd rather poke myself in the eye repeatedly with one of those four-color pens than read a bunch of book reports. Students feel the same way about writing them. So why do we keep assigning them? Can't we assess the same learning with a collage and a written piece that explains it? Can't we ask students to imagine that they're the defense attorney for the villain in a story? Can't we let our teens who are good with their hands build something that represents the story? I've seen some unbelievably cool projects over the years that have demonstrated more understanding of a story or a character than a book report can, especially when students are using *Sparknotes* (*http://www.sparknotes.com*) instead of actually reading the book in the first place.

This Can't Be Considered "Teaching Literature"

This is the criticism that bothers me the most, and it practically turned me into the Tasmanian Devil cartoon character when I read a similar comment from a reviewer after I submitted a journal article on the commando approach. I could live with not being published, but this one comment undermined my confidence and made me question what I do every day in my classroom. Was I a sham of a teacher? Was I failing to understand what my job was? Was I doing a disservice to my students? My heart said, "No," but my head wasn't sure. Maybe I really didn't understand what it meant to "teach literature." Maybe ten years (that's how long I'd been in the classroom at the time) in an alternative high school setting hadn't made me a better teacher as I believed; maybe it had just lowered my standards.

Then I thought about what takes place in my classroom on a regular basis. My students interact with literature they would otherwise sleep through or not understand if it were presented differently. They discuss literary elements, such as plot, setting, and characters. They explore themes and talk and write about how and why these themes continue to appear in literature and popular culture today. They learn about the beliefs, personal experiences, and cultural factors that influenced famous writers. They make predictions, compare texts, and respond personally to what they've read. Last time I checked, that *is* teaching literature.

Since then, I've learned a couple of things. I learned that there were plenty of people who did believe in what I was doing. In August of 2007, *English Leadership Quarterly* published "New Rules for Old Literature: Connecting At-Risk Kids to the Classics 'Commando Style,'" and it was named honorable mention for the Best Article of the Year. I've presented on the commando approach at both the Assembly on Literature for Adolescents of the NCTE (ALAN) Workshop and Michigan Council of Teachers of English Autumn Assembly. A post I made on a listserv provided a book editor with a link to my webpage, which led to this book.

Most importantly, though, I learned to trust my instincts. I'm the one who is in my classroom every day. I'm the person who has to deal with it if a lesson crashes and burns (and, boy oh boy, sometimes they really do). I know my students. As teachers, we take a risk every day that what we try won't work, that students won't respond, and that we'll have to go back to the drawing board. It's not a job for the faint of heart. It's a job for the commando teacher.

References

National Council of Teachers of English/ International Reading Association. *Standards for the English Language Arts. http://www.ncte.org/standards*

Plumb, Daria. "New Rules for Old Literature: Connecting At-Risk Kids to the Classics 'Commando Style.'" *English Leadership Quarterly.* August, 2007.

Generation Y—The Visual Generation: Incorporating Visual Media and Texts

The students entering classrooms today are extremely visually oriented. They are not the MTV generation; they are the *children* of the MTV generation. They have grown up in a world where advanced technology allows them to be constantly connected to the world at large for virtually every second of every day. They grew up with the DVD player as a babysitter/teacher and they do not remember (nor can they conceive of) a time without the Internet, high-resolution video games, one-hundred-fifty TV channels, and cellular phones. As a result, they interact with the world differently from any other generation. We must remind ourselves that different is not always bad. True, their attention spans are shorter, but they are also able to multi-task a way that makes my head spin—they can play video games, IM their friends, listen to music, and talk on the phone all at once—and they have unparalleled visual literacy. We can choose to either bemoan this fact or embrace it. If we hold onto the "old school" belief that students should conform to our notions of what the world and education should be, then we risk losing them before we even open our anthologies. This isn't to say that we have to design media-driven lessons or use visual texts each and every day, but it doesn't hurt to put forth a little effort to hook students.

The main reason I incorporate visual texts is because they allow me to quickly and easily expose students to the basic plot of a story. In less time than it would take to read the novel *Dracula,* we can read the illustrated classic and watch movie scenes from the classic Bela Lugosi *Dracula* film on YouTube or DVD, view "Forget *Twilight,* Here's the Real Dracula" (*60 Minutes Overtime*, Oct. 31, 2010. *http://www.cbsnews.com/8301-504803_162-20021189-10391709.html*), and read the illustrated book *Vampires* by Stephen Krensky to learn about vampire folklore and vampires in pop culture. Not only do students gain the knowledge of the plot of *Dracula,* they also have a well-rounded experience with the book; it's not just a story anymore, it's been brought into their worlds and made relevant and (hopefully) memorable.

Another reason I use visual texts is because it helps students to *see* the story. A lot of people are not aware that a startling number of poor readers do not see "movies in the mind" when they read. So, when they read a story the words are just words; the words aren't creating any images in their minds. In fact, many of them don't even know that that's what happens for people who are readers. It's hard for most of us to imagine that. What's the point of reading a story if the reader can't visualize what's happening? Exactly—now it is understandable why these students don't want to read anything. When they read the story in a graphic novel or picture book format, they can start to make the connection that the words in books are supposed to conjure images for them. My theory is that the biggest reason they don't already make this connection is because they weren't read to often enough as children, so maybe we need to backtrack for them a little bit and introduce (or reintroduce) this concept to them.

Finally, visual texts can enable students to learn numerous concepts. Graphic novels, picture books, and films can all be analyzed in the same way as literary texts; students can diagram plot sequence, discuss character development, look for symbolism, etc. In addition to studying the literary elements, students can also study the art of illustration and design. Mark Gonyea's *A Book about Design: Complicated Doesn't Make It Good* and *Another Book about Design: Complicated Doesn't Make It Bad* discuss line, color, perspective, contrast, shapes, symmetry, and so on and can quickly provide students with the proper terminology to discuss artwork. Check out the National Council of Teachers of English resource "Engaging Media Savvy Students Kit" and the Fall 2005 special issue of *The Wisconsin English Journal* devoted solely to the topic of Visual Literacy for more ideas.

Graphic Novels

Many people misspeak and call the graphic novel a genre when, in fact, the graphic novel is a format. What's the big deal what we call it? Well, it's important to understand that, because it is a format, the graphic novel can and does cover every genre of literature: nonfiction, historical fiction, fantasy, realistic fiction, mythology, and more. This important fact will hopefully help debunk the common misconception that all graphic novels are just comic books about superheroes. Though even the study of superheroes can be appropriate in the literature classroom (see the Heroes Text Set in The World Mythology and Folklore Arsenal), this association with comic books and superheroes usually holds a negative implication about quality. For my purposes, I will use the terms *graphic novel* and *comics* interchangeably to refer to stories that have text and illustrations presented in sequence. Be aware that there are many divergent opinions on whether there is a difference between a comic book and a graphic novel.

There are a couple of misconceptions about graphic novels I would like to clear up. The first is that many people assume this format will automatically appeal to reluctant readers, which has simply not been my experience. In fact, I often have better luck selling a graphic novel to my better readers. For some students, the graphic novel format is too visually stimulating and for some it's just plain confusing. It takes

COMMANDO LIBRARIANS

The graphic novel is a format that may be unfamiliar to teachers. Make arrangements to speak at a staff meeting or English Department meeting about the wide variety of graphic novels that will work well in the classroom.

Present teachers with books and articles supporting the use of this format in the classroom and bring copies of some of the books so they can look at them. Also, give them suggestions and examples about how to use graphic novels to teach both literary and artistic concepts.

skill to read a graphic novel and students (and maybe even some teachers) may need to be coached on just what to do. They need to:

- know how to progress through the frames and which items to read first;

- be instructed to pay as much attention to "reading" the illustrations as they do to the written text;

- be able to differentiate between spoken text and thought bubbles;

- be able to tell the characters apart.

Don't assume that all students will figure these things out. Create a book mark or a cheat sheet for them to keep nearby when they're reading so they won't feel embarrassed if they become confused. It's also a good idea to model by reading some of the story out loud before turning them loose on their own.

The second misconception is that the graphic novel is only useful as a bridge to "more legitimate" literature. The graphic novel *is* a legitimate form of literature in its own right and can be taught as such in the language arts classroom; in fact, a graphic novel, *American Born Chinese* by Gene Luen Yang, won the 2007 Michael L. Printz Award, which selects books on the basis of literary merit. Consider teaming with social studies teachers and using Marjane Satrapi's *Persepolis* and Art Speigelman's *Maus: A Survivor's Tale* when teaching World Literature/History, or George O'Connor's *Journey into Mohawk Country* when teaching American Literature/History. An interesting and fun literary twist can be seen in Alan Moore's comic book series *The League of Extraordinary Gentlemen*, which features famous literary characters such as Allan Quatermain (from H. Rider Haggard's *King Solomon's Mines*), Dr. Jekyll and Mr. Hyde (from Robert Louis Stevenson's *The Strange Case of Dr. Jekyll and Mr. Hyde*), Captain Nemo (from Jules Verne's *20,000 Leagues Under the Sea*), Mina Harker (from Bram Stoker's *Dracula*), Rodney Skinner aka the Invisible Man (from H.G. Wells' *The Invisible Man*), and more, as a "Justice League of Victorian England" (*http://en.wikipedia.org/wiki/Characters_in_The_League_of_Extraordinary_Gentlemen*). See Stephen Weiner's book *The 101 Best Graphic Novels* for help selecting graphic novels for classroom use or for collection development.

Teachers should be prepared for criticism if they are going to utilize graphic novels or comics in the curriculum. Comics are generally not viewed as typical educational fare and the catch-22 is that the very thing that will help hook the students is likely to be a turn-off for colleagues and/or for parents. Many uninformed educators (maybe even some in the English department) will argue that the graphic novel is not an appropriate medium for the literature classroom. Parents may see their children reading graphic novels as schoolwork

---

FOR AN INTRODUCTION TO GRAPHIC NOVELS, CHECK OUT THESE RESOURCES

- Scott McCloud's *Understanding Comics: The Invisible Art* (HarperPerennial, 1993)

- Paul Gravett's *Graphic Novels: Everything You Need to Know* (Collins Design/HarperCollins, 2005)

- Robin Brenner's website *No Flying, No Tights* (© Robin Brenner, 2002-2012) *http://noflyingnotights.com/index2.html*

COMMANDO LIBRARIANS

Create a bookmark for students and teachers about graphic novels. On one side include instructions on "How to Read a Graphic Novel." On the other side, include the most recent list of great graphic novels from the American Library Association (*http://www.ala.org/yalsa/ggnt*).

and jump to the conclusion that the educational system really has gone to "H-E-double hockey sticks in a hand basket." Be prepared to confront these fears and prejudices with the same type of rationale you'd use for any other challenge about materials or content—in other words, be able to articulate why graphic novels were chosen. James Bucky Carter has edited a CD-Rom titled *Rationales for Teaching Graphic Novels* that is an invaluable resource. There are numerous articles to support the use of graphic novels in the classroom, such as Katherine Bucher and M. Lee Manning's "Bringing Graphic Novels into a School's Curriculum," Gretchen Schwarz's "Graphic Novels for Multiple Literacies," and Stephen Weiner's "Show Don't Tell: Graphic Novels in the Classroom." Also, take a look at the book *Building Literacy Connections with Graphic Novels: Page by Page, Panel by Panel* edited by James Bucky Carter, which features articles about pairing graphic novels with classic literature, as well as using graphic novels as stand alone literature. Another valuable resource is Scott Tingley's website *Comics in the Classroom http://comicsintheclassroom.net/*), which features reviews, lesson plans, and many links, all geared specifically for teachers. As the academic world "discovers" graphic novels as an effective teaching tool, more publishers are marketing graphic novels to teachers, raising the quality of the offerings.

Graphic novels are also useful for presenting the entire plot of a classic story. Comic books have offered abridged, illustrated versions of classic works since the 1940s and have provided many people (including me) with their first experiences with classic literature in a non-threatening and easy-to-understand format. Publisher Papercutz is reissuing the Classics Illustrated series from the mid 1900s and is also adding new adaptations with cutting-edge illustrations in its Classics Illustrated Deluxe series (Kean). Read about the history of this format in *Classics Illustrated: A Cultural History, with Illustrations* by William B. Jones Jr. I often use selections from the series *Now Age Illustrated Classics* and *Lake Illustrated Classics*. These retellings are about sixty pages long and are available in a variety of stories. I find them especially useful because they are written in modern English. I also like them because they are short enough to be read in one or two class periods. This trend has recently begun to resurface. Puffin Books (*http://www.penguin.co.uk/static/cs/uk/0/aboutus/publishingstructure.html*), Eureka Productions' Graphic Classics (*http://*

MORE RESOURCES TO SUPPORT THE USE OF GRAPHIC NOVELS IN THE CLASSROOM

- McTaggart, Jacqui. "Using Comics and Graphic Novels to Encourage Reluctant Readers." *Reading Today*. October/November 2005, p. 46.

- Mendez, Teresa. "*Hamlet* Too Hard? Try a Comic Book." *The Christian Science Monitor*. October 12, 2004.

- "Using Comics and Graphic Novels in the Classroom." *The Council Chronicle*. September 2005, pp. 2, 8.

- Versaci, Rocco. "How Comic Books Can Change the Way Our Students See Literature: One Teacher's Perspective." *English Journal*. November 2001, pp. 61-67.

COMMANDO LIBRARIANS

Order and display eye-popping graphic novels based on classic works in areas where teen patrons can see them.

See the List of Illustrated Classics at the end of this chapter or see these websites: *http://www.classicalcomics.com, http://www.mangashakespeare.com,* or *http://www.us.penguingroup.com/nf/Theme/ThemePage/0,,1292267,00.html*

www.graphicclassics.com/), Stone Arch Books' Graphic Revolve (*http://www.stonearchbooks.com/aspx/pDetail.aspx?EntityGUID=ef179cf8-e5b8-47f3-8055-30ef51aa45b7*), and Sterling Publishing's All-Action Classics, for example, have created new versions of illustrated classics that include artwork by contemporary artists (*http://www.sterlingpublishing.com/catalog?series=All-Action+Classics&limit=10*).

Picture Books

Like *graphic novel*, the term *picture book* also describes a format, rather than a genre. Also like the graphic novel, the picture book deals with every genre of literature. This makes them wonderful tools for use in the classroom. As mentioned earlier with graphic novels, picture books can be used to discuss plot and literary elements (for example, use Jon Scieszka's *The True Story of the Three Little Pigs* to highlight point of view and parody; David A. Johnson's *Snow Sounds: An Onomatopoeic Story* to teach onomatopoeia; or Chris Van Allsburg's *Bad Day at Riverbend* to teach postmodernism), as well as artistic elements, such as line, shading, contrast, and shape.

Recently, picture books have begun to be recognized by teachers at all grade levels (yes, even high school) as a valid and legitimate way of presenting information. In my experience, the key to using picture books with high school students is to explain *why* they are being used—otherwise you risk alienating teenagers who resent feeling that they're being treated like babies. While some picture books are geared for a very young audience, there are many gorgeously illustrated and sophisticated picture books that lend themselves to use in the high school curriculum. For example, Dr. Seuss's *The Butter Battle Book*, *The Lorax*, and *The Sneetches* comment on war, the environment, and conformity, respectively. Many fiction and nonfiction picture books deal with mature themes such as war, death, the Holocaust, slavery, and other topics.

A picture book is also a great way to quickly present background information about an era being studied—*Pink and Say* by Patricia Polacco and *Henry's Freedom Box* by Ellen Levine, for example, both help

---

COMMANDO LIBRARIANS

Picture books aren't just for the elementary classroom anymore. While you may already know this, many high school teachers aren't accustomed to looking at picture books as a curriculum resource. Refer them to these articles:

- Brandt, P. "Picture Books for Secondary Students." Curriculum Library, University of Iowa. September 2000.

- Carr, Kathryn S., Dawna L. Buchanan, Joann B. Wemtz, Mary L. Weiss, and Kitty J. Brant. "Not Just for the Primary Grades: A Bibliography of Picture Books for Secondary Content Teachers." *Journal of Adolescent & Adult Literacy*. Vol. 45, No. 2. 2001.

- Fingerson, Julie, and Erlene Bishop Killeen. "Picture Books for Young Adults." *Teacher Librarian*. April 1, 2006.

- Giorgis, Cyndi. "The Power of Reading Picture Books Aloud to Secondary Students." *Clearing House*. Vol. 73, No. 1, pp. 51-53. Sep-Oct 1999.

- Brodie, Carolyn S., and Mary Anne Nichols. "Picture Perfect: Picture Books for Teens." *VOYA*. December 2011.

Also, offer to gather a stack of picture books that complement teachers' lessons.

**TEACHING POSTMODERNISM WITH
PICTURE BOOKS**

- Antsey, Michele. "'It's Not All Black and White': Postmodern Picture Books and New Literacies." *Journal of Adolescent & Adult Literacy.* Vol. 45, No 6, pp. 444–457. March 2002.

- Goldstone, Bette P. "Whaz Up with Our Books? Changing Picture Book Codes and Teaching Implications: Children's Books Change with the Culture around Them. Understanding Postmodern Picture Books Helps Children Make Sense of a Complex World." *The Reading Teacher.* Vol. 55, No. 4. 2001

- Henry, Julie. "Postmodern Picture Books in the Middle School." *ReadWriteThink.* (http://www.readwritethink.org/lessons/lesson_view.asp?id=66)

personalize the Civil War era. Picture books can be used to introduce historical characters, both famous—Leonardo Da Vinci is featured in books by both Diane Stanley and Maria Teresa Leoni Zanobini—or lesser known—African American opera singer and civil rights activist Marian Anderson's life is detailed in Pam Munoz Ryan's *When Marian Sang: The True Recital of Marian Anderson.* Picture books featuring authors are also available—for example, Henry David Thoreau appears as a bear in D.B. Johnson's books *Henry Hikes to Fichtburg, Henry Climbs a Mountain,* and *Henry Builds a Cabin.*

Picture books also offer adaptations of classic works for younger readers, once again allowing us to present the basic plot of a story quickly and in an easily accessible way—check out Robert Sabuda's intricate pop-up adaptation of Lewis Carroll's book *Alice's Adventures in Wonderland* or Gris Grimly's delightfully dark *Edgar Allan Poe's Tales of Mystery and Madness* or *The Legend of Sleepy Hollow,* for example. With Brian Selznick's award-winning and groundbreaking book *The Invention of Hugo Cabret* shattering the boundaries between the picture book, the wordless picture book, and the novel, just about anything could be on the horizon for picture books.

Wordless picture books are great for teaching creative writing skills, as well as for teaching/reinforcing the elements of a story. After almost a year of studying folklore in World Literature class, I used a wordless picture book to see how much my students had learned about the structure and motifs of the folktale. I paired the students and gave them copies of the book *The Girl from the Sky: An Inca Folktale from South America* retold by Anamarie Garcia. I intentionally left off the title page and the final page (which gave the text of the story) and asked them to write the text of the folktale based on what they knew about folktales and the arc of a plot. Some students ran with it and others found it incredibly difficult, but they all managed to come up with the basic plot of the story. Wouldn't it also be great fun to let students create a story to accompany David Wiesner's *Tuesday*? Check out the book *Wordless/Almost Wordless Picture Books: A Guide* by Virginia H. Richey and Kathryn E. Puckett to help find wordless picture books that will work (check out the Subject Index in the back of the book).

One of the places we lose a lot of readers is in assuming that all students like fiction. Some readers really prefer reading for the purpose of learning something specific and we should include more of this type of reading in the language arts classroom. While some nonfiction picture storybooks are mentioned above, another type of picture book is the straight nonfiction book. The Dorling Kindersley Eyewitness series is especially fabulous and really appeals to teens. The books in this series are between sixty and sixty-five pages long and use photographs, sketches, and artwork, along with fairly minimal text and captions to give an overview of a particular subject or time period. Some of the books in the series that may be particularly useful for the language arts classroom are: *Ancient Greece, American Revolution, Arms and Armor, Shakespeare, Costume, Knight, Book, Castle, Pirate, Witches and Magic Makers, Medieval Life, Renaissance, Mythology,* and *Wild West.* Another similar series is the Kingfisher Knowledge series, which features books on *Pirates and Smugglers, Castles and Forts,* and *Mythology of the World.* Other great nonfiction picture books are David Macauley's *Cathedral* and *Castle,* Stephen Krensky's Monster Chronicles series (*Bigfoot, The Bogeyman, Creatures from the Deep, Dragons, Frankenstein, Ghosts, The Mummy, Vampires, Watchers in the Woods, Werewolves,* and *Zombies*) and Kathleen Krull's *Lives of the Writers: Comedies, Tragedies (and What the Neighbors Thought).* Also make these types of books available for the fans of nonfiction during sustained silent reading.

Video: Documentaries/*YouTube*/TV Programs/Films

Teens today are accustomed to learning from the television and they are good at retaining information that is presented in this way. They've had years of practice watching Discovery Channel, Animal Planet, History Channel, and more. There's nothing wrong with taking advantage of this tendency. There are actually days when I toy with the idea of videotaping myself teaching a lesson and playing it on the TV, because I think my students would be more attentive if I was on the screen instead of standing in front of them. Videos, films, and video clips can be excellent ways to introduce characters, make students familiar with a setting (for example, like Emily Dickinson, most American high school kids have never seen a moor), provide the basic plot of an entire novel, expose students to background information, or show students that the characters, themes, and plot lines of a story are still relevant today.

Thanks to popular movies, students are already familiar with some famous literary characters before they even enter our classrooms. Most of them can identify the pale man with black hair dressed in the long, black cape (lined in red satin) and white waistcoat and speaking in an Eastern European accent as Dracula; the tall man with the flat, green head, bolts in his neck, too-short pants, and platform boots as Frankenstein's monster; the man in the deerstalker cap and cape, smoking a pipe and carrying a magnifying glass as Sherlock Holmes; and the barefoot, pre-teen boy dressed in overalls and a straw hat carrying a fishing pole as Huckleberry Finn.

The most obvious use of this medium in the classroom is the movie that is based on a novel. Of course, some films are so loosely based on the novel, that the only thing they share is a title and/or the names of some main characters (more on how to use

COMMANDO LIBRARIANS

Some teachers cannot access *YouTube* on their classroom computers. Check with your technology director about software programs that will enable you to copy from your home computer to a disk. Then, offer to help the teachers in your building learn how to do this. Or, if you know that certain texts are always taught each year, burn a disc for each grade level with several basic videos and keep it in the library.

these in Chapter 4), so be sure to choose carefully. The *Internet Movie Database* (*http://www.imdb.com*) is helpful and you can search the keywords "based-on-book." This search will also offer you subcategories such as "based-on-children's book," "based-on-folk-tale," and "based-on-play." Read the plot summary and user comments to help you decide if the adaptation is fairly faithful to the text of the book. The Mid-Continent Public Library has a webpage titled "Based on the Book" (*http://www.mcpl.lib.mo.us/readers/movies/*), which allows you to search by movie title, year, book title, or author. The website *Information Please ® Database's* page "Shakespeare in Film: Film Adaptations of Shakespeare: Best in Show" (*http://www.infoplease.com/spot/shakespeareonfilm.html*) has separated the films into the categories "Relatively Faithful Adaptations," "Looser Adaptations," and "Shakespeare as Launching Pad." However, no matter how much leg work you do, it's very unlikely that even the best book-to-movie movie is going to be 100 percent true to the storyline. So, after you finish the movie, download the summary of the book from *Sparknotes* (*http://www.sparknotes.com*) and read through it with your students. Have students identify the differences between the summary and the film in a Venn diagram. Then, ask them why they think the director made those changes and whether they think it changes the overall mood or theme of the piece. If you don't have time to use the full movie, use clips to highlight important scenes or to introduce setting and characters.

YouTube (*http://www.youtube.com*) is a terrific place to find movie clips and other short videos that will be useful in the classroom. I've only recently started using *YouTube* and I'm finding it to be a really fun and valuable way to connect students to classic literature. Probably the biggest drawback about *YouTube* is that anyone can post almost anything, so it can be difficult to separate the good from the bad. However, if you've got some time to sift through the many video clips, it can be really useful for the classroom. Choose videos that go along (even tangentially) with books or authors you are teaching. Be sure to include serious, funny, and campy videos so you have a variety. See the various text sets in The Commando Arsenals for some ideas for more commonly used texts and/or subscribe to my *YouTube* channel (*http://www.youtube.com/user/daridoo*) for updated lists of the videos that I'm finding and using with my students for all of my literature classes. *YouTube* can also provide a forum for your students to showcase projects they create for your class. FYI: A "spin-off" website, titled *TeacherTube*, focuses more specifically on videos for use in the classroom.

> **HAVING TROUBLE FINDING GOOD *YOUTUBE* VIDEOS FOR USE IN THE CLASSROOM?**
>
> - Team up with the other teachers in your department and work together to find useful video clips on *YouTube*. Create a username for your English Department and save the good videos to the playlists you create.
> - Get your students involved and give them extra credit points for anything they find that you use (or can use) in class.

Another way to utilize video in your classroom is to use educational films to provide background information about an era, an author, or folklore. A&E, The History Channel, Discovery Channel, and PBS have numerous videos you can purchase online. I particularly like A&E's *Biography* and *Ancient Mysteries* series; The History Channel's *Histories Mysteries, In Search of History*, and *MonsterQuest* series; The Discovery Channel's *Unsolved History* series; and TLC and Discovery School's *Great Books* series (see the Educational Videos lists in the various commando arsenals for subject specific titles). Most of the videos in these series have a run time of approximately 45-50 minutes, which makes them perfect for classroom use.

Artwork

Many classic stories were originally published as illustrated books or were later reprinted with illustrations by famous artists. One extremely prolific illustrator of classic works is Gustave Dore, who provided the haunting black and white illustrations for Poe's *The Raven*, Coleridge's *The Rime of the Ancient Mariner*, Tennyson's *Idylls of the King*, Shakespeare's *The Tempest*, Cervantes' *Don Quixote*, and Milton's *Paradise Lost*.

Arthur Rackham also illustrated numerous books that appealed to children, such as Barrie's *Peter Pan in Kensington Gardens*, Carroll's *Alice in Wonderland*, Swift's *Gulliver's Travels*, Shakespeare's *A Midsummer Night's Dream*, and Irving's *Rip Van Winkle*, as did N.C. Wyeth with his illustrations for Defoe's *Robinson Crusoe*, Stevenson's *Treasure Island*, Cooper's *The Last of the Mohicans* and *The Deerslayer*, and Homer's *Odyssey*. Some other well known illustrators and their works include:

> ## COMMANDO TEACHERS
>
> Show students Gustave Dore's illustration "The Ice was All Around" from *The Rime of the Ancient Mariner* (http://www.artpassions.net/cgi-bin/dore_image.pl?../galleries/dore/mariner_ice.jpg) and compare it to Scene 4, chapter 4 (:23:00–:26:10) from *Pirates of the Caribbean: At World's End.*
>
> See if they notice any similarities. Ask if they think it's possible that the director of the movie was familiar with Dore's work. Do they think both the painting and the movie clip evoke the same emotional response?

- Aubrey Beardsley's illustrations for Malory's *Le Morte d'Arthur*

- Walter Crane's illustrations for Gilbert's *King Arthur's Knights: Tales Retold for Boys and Girls* and *Robin Hood and The Men of the Greenwood*, Shakespeare's *The Tempest*, *The Merry Wives of Windsor*, *Two Gentlemen of Verona*, and Spenser's *The Faerie Queen.*

- John Tenniel's illustrations for Carroll's *Alice's Adventures in Wonderland* and *Through the Looking Glass.*

- William Blake's illustrations of his own *Songs of Innocence* and *Songs of Experience*, as well as Milton's *Paradise Lost.*

Visit *Art Passions* (*http://www.artpassions.net*) for examples of many of the works mentioned above.

Emory University literature professor Harry Rusche points out in "The Poet Speaks of Art":

> Painters and illustrators have often been inspired by literature, especially in the eighteenth and nineteenth centuries. The critic Richard Altick says, for example, that between 1760 and 1900, there existed around 2,300 paintings based on Shakespeare's plays alone. These Shakespeare paintings are only one-fifth of the 11,500 paintings on subjects and scenes from literature—and we are talking only about paintings done in England during those years!

Eleven thousand five hundred paintings from England in a one hundred forty year period? That's a lot of art with the paintings *Tristan and Isolde, Thisbe, Juliet, La Belle Dame Sans Merci, Miranda-The Tempest, Gather Ye Rosebuds While Ye May* (from Robert Herrick's "To the Virgins to Make Much of Time"), three paintings of *Ophelia*, and three paintings of *The Lady of Shalott*, as well as many paintings based on mythological characters. John William Waterhouse has been responsible for a strikingly large number of those paintings. Characters from mythology appear in a large number of paintings by other artists as well.

ARTWORK FEATURING MYTHOLOGICAL CHARACTERS

- *The Abduction of Persephone* by Niccolo Dell' Abbate
- *The Birth of Venus* by Sandro Botticelli
- *Daedalus and Icarus* by Charles Lebrun
- John William Waterhouse:
    - *Apollo and Daphne*
    - *Ariadne*
    - *Echo and Narcissus*
    - *Hylas and the Nymphs*
    - *Jason and Medea*
    - *Narcissus*
    - *Nymphs Finding the Head of Orpheus*
    - *Pandora*
    - *Penelope and the Suitors*
    - *Psyche Entering Cupid's Garden*
    - *Psyche Opening the Golden Box*
    - *The Siren*
- *Landscape with Charon's Bark* by Joachim Patinir
- *The Olympus* by Giovanni Tiepolo
- *Orpheus* by Gustave Moreau
- *Perseus Turning His Followers to Stone* by Luca Giordano
- Walter Crane:
    - *Bellerophon Fighting the Chimaera*
    - *Cupid's Dart*
    - *The Fate of Persephone*
    - *Neptune's Horses*
    - *Pandora Opens the Box*
    - *Persephone in Abducted by Hades*

Tragic and tempting female literary characters are also popular subjects, for example: The Lady of Shalott is depicted in paintings by William Holman Hunt, Howard Pyle, Dante Gabriel Rossetti, Arthur Hughes, and G.E. Robertson (see also the "Elaine of Astolat/The Lady of Shalott" page from *The Camelot Project at the University of Rochester http://www.lib.rochester.edu/camelot/elanmenu.htm*) ; Ophelia is depicted in paintings by John Everett Millais, Arthur Hughes, Odilon Redon, Paul Steck, and Meredith Dillman; La Belle Dame Sans Merci is depicted in paintings by Frank Dicksee, Walter Crane, Arthur Hughes, and Frank Cowper; and Guinevere is depicted in paintings by John Atkinson Grimshaw, Marcel LorAnge, and William Morris, as well as many others detailing her relationship with Lancelot (see also the "Guinevere" page from *The Camelot Project at the University of Rochester http://www.lib.rochester.edu/camelot/guinmenu.htm*).

While some art is inspired directly by classic literature, other works of art can be paired with stories in order to provide students with a visual reference. For example, pair: Waterhouse's *Sleep and His Half Brother Death* with the "To be or not to be" soliloquy from *Hamlet*; paintings of fairies by Arthur Rackham with either *A Midsummer Night's Dream* or fairy folklore; *Classical Landscape with a Woman Refusing a Wreath* by Jan Van Huysum with Ben Jonson's "Song: To Celia"; and *The Tiger* by Franz Marc and *Tiger in a Tropical Storm* by Henri Rousseau with William Blake's "The Tyger." *Parrish and Poetry: A Gift of Words and Art*, edited and complied by Laurence S. Cutler and Judy Goffman Cutler, pairs paintings of Maxfield Parrish with famous poems by Marlowe, Shakespeare, Donne, Wordsworth, Byron, Shelley, Blake, Burns, Poe, Tennyson, and many more.

On the flip side of paintings inspired by classic literature is something called *ekphrastic poetry*. Ekphrastic poetry is poetry that is inspired by any kind of art—film, other poems, music, photographs, etc. Probably two of the most famous ekphrastic poems are John Keats' "Ode on a Grecian Urn" and Sir Walter Raleigh's "The Nymph's Reply to the Shepherd." For a description of this art form and more examples visit "Ekphrasis: Poetry Confronting Art" (*http://www.poets.org/viewmedia.php/prmMID/5918*) from the Academy of American Poets or "The Poet Speaks of Art" developed by Harry Rusche of Emory University (*http://homepage.mac.com/mseffie/assignments/paintings&poems/titlepage.html*). ReadWriteThink from the International Reading Association and the National Council of Teachers of English also has an online lesson plan by Ann Kelly Cox titled "Ekphrasis: Using Art to Inspire Poetry" (*http://www.readwritethink.org/classroom-resources/lesson-plans/ekphrasis-using-inspire-poetry-1093.html*) complete with everything necessary to teach students about this art form and to enable them produce their own ekphrastic poetry.

> **COMMANDO LIBRARIANS**
>
> Create a display of ekphrastic poems and the artwork that inspired them. Or pair with English teachers and/or art teachers to display ekphrastic art created by their students.

Assessments/Projects

Because our students are so visual, let's not forget to allow them to respond to their reading assignments in visual ways. Consider asking students to make a collage, PowerPoint, or video presentation featuring art relating to literature. Allow them to make their own comic book adaptation of a novel. Have them make paper dolls of the main characters and create garments for them based on the descriptions given in the book or based on the era of history in which they lived. Ask them to create a "Wanted" poster for the antagonist or villain in the story. Have them compare characters or settings with a Venn Diagram. If you are concerned about the lack of writing in these assignments, ask students to produce a short written piece explaining the significance of the project.

References

Bucher, Katherine T. and M. Lee Manning. "Bringing Graphic Novels into a School's Curriculum." *The Clearing House*. November/December 2004, pp. 67-76.

Carter, James Bucky, ed. *Building Literacy Connections with Graphic Novels: Page by Page, Panel by Panel*. National Council of Teachers of English, 2007.

———. *Rationales for Teaching Graphic Novels*. Maupin House, 2010.

Cutler, Laurence S. and Judy Goffman Cutler, ed. *Parrish and Poetry: A Gift of Words and Art*. Pomegranate, 1995.

Eyewitness Books. Dorling Kindersley.

———. *Ancient Greece* by Anne Pearson, 2000.

———. *American Revolution* by Stuart Murray, 2002.

———. *Arms and Armor* by Michele Byam, 2004.

———. *Book* by Karen Brookfield, 1993.

———. *Castle* by Christopher Gravett, 1994.

———. *Civil War* by John Stanchak, 2000.

———. *Costume* by L. Rowland-Warne, 2000.

———. *Knight* by Christopher Gravett, 2004.

———. *Medieval Life* by Andrew Langley, 2004.

———. *Mythology* by Neil Philip, 2000.

———. *Pirate* by Richard Platt, 2000.

———. *Renaissance* by Alison Cole, 2000.

———. *Shakespeare* by Peter Chrisp, 2002.

———. *Wild West* by Stuart Murray, 2001.

———. *Witches and Magic Makers* by Douglas Hill, 2000.

Garcia, Anamarie. *The Girl from the Sky: An Inca Folktale from South America.* Children's Press, 1992.

Gonyea, Mark. *A Book about Design: Complicated Doesn't Make It Good.* Henry Holt, 2005.

———. *Another Book about Design: Complicated Doesn't Make It Bad.* Henry Holt, 2007.

Grimly, Gris and Edgar Allan Poe. *Edgar Allan Poe's Tales of Mystery and Madness.* Atheneum, 2004.

Grimly, Gris and Washington Irving. *The Legend of Sleepy Hollow.* Atheneum, 2007.

Johnson, David A. *Snow Sounds: An Onomatopoeic Story.* Houghton Mifflin, 2006.

Johnson, D.B. *Henry Builds a Cabin.* Houghton Mifflin, 2002.

———. *Henry Climbs a Mountain.* Houghton Mifflin, 2003.

———. *Henry Hikes to Fichtburg.* Houghton Mifflin, 2000.

Jones, William B., Jr. *Classics Illustrated: A Cultural History, with Illustrations.* McFarland, 2001.

Kean, Benjamin Ong Pang. "Old Is New Again: Talking Papercutz Illustrated Line." *Newsarama.* Posted 10/26/07. *http://forum.newsarama.com/showthread.php?t=134346*

Kingfisher Knowledge series. Kingfisher.

———. *Castles and Forts* by Simon Adams, 2003.

———. *Mythology of the World* by Neil Philip and Nicki Palin, 2004.

———. *Pirates and Smugglers* by Moira Butterfield, 2005.

Krensky, Stephen. Monster Chronicles series. Lerner.

———. *Bigfoot*, 2007.

———. *The Bogeyman*, 2008.

———. *Creatures from the Deep*, 2008.

———. *Dragons*, 2007.

———. *Frankenstein*, 2007.

———. *Ghosts*, 2008.

———. *The Mummy*, 2007.

———. *Vampires*, 2007.

———. *Watchers in the Woods*, 2008.

———. *Werewolves*, 2007.

———. *Zombies*, 2008.

Krull, Kathleen. *Lives of the Writers: Comedies, Tragedies (and What the Neighbors Thought)*. Harcourt Brace, 1994.

"*The League of Extraordinary Gentlemen*." *Wikipedia. http://en.wikipedia.org/wiki/The_League_of_ Extraordinary_Gentlemen*

Leoni Zanobini, Maria Teresa. *Leonardo Da Vinci*. Enchanted Lion Books, 2003.

Levine, Ellen. *Henry's Freedom Box*. Scholastic Press, 2007.

Macauley, David. *Castle*. Boston, MA: Houghton Mifflin, 1977.

———. *Cathedral: The Story of Its Construction*. Houghton Mifflin, 1973.

McCloud, Scott. *Understanding Comics: The Invisible Art*. HarperPerennial, 1993.

Moore, Alan. *The League of Extraordinary Gentlemen, Volume 1*. America's Best Comics, 2000.

———. *The League of Extraordinary Gentlemen, Volume II*. America's Best Comics, 2003.

National Council of Teachers of English. "Engaging Media Savvy Students Kit." National Council of Teachers of English.

O'Connor, George. *Journey into Mohawk Country*. First Second Books, 2006.

Pirates of the Caribbean: At World's End. Walt Disney Home Entertainment, 2007.

Polacco, Patricia. *Pink and Say*. Philomel Books, 1994.

Richey, Virginia H. and Kathryn E. Puckett. *Wordless/Almost Wordless Picture Books: A Guide*. Libraries Unlimited, 1992.

Rusche, Harry. "The Poet Speaks of Art." *http://homepage.mac.com/mseffie/assignments/paintings%26poems/titlepage.html*

Ryan, Pam Munoz. *When Marian Sang: The True Recital of Marian Anderson*. Scholastic, 2002.

Sabuda, Robert and Lewis Carroll. *Alice's Adventures in Wonderland: A Pop-Up Adaptation*. Little Simon, 2003.

Satrapi, Marjane. *Persepolis*. Pantheon Books, 2003.

Schwarz, Gretchen E. "Graphic Novels for Multiple Literacies." *Journal of Adolescent and Adult Literacy*. November 2002, pp. 262-264.

Scieszka, Jon. *The True Story of the Three Little Pigs*. Puffin Books/Penguin, 1989.

Selznick, Brian. *The Invention of Hugo Cabret: A Novel in Words and Pictures*. Scholastic, 2007.

Seuss, Dr. *The Butter Battle Book*. Random House, 1984.

———. *The Lorax*. Random House, 1971.

———. The *Sneetches and Other Stories*. Random House, 1961.

Speigelman, Art. *Maus: A Survivor's Tale*. Pantheon Books, 1986.

Stanley, Diane. *Leonardo Da Vinci*. Morrow Junior Books, 1996.

Van Allsburg, Chris. *Bad Day at Riverbend*. Houghton Mifflin, 1995.

Weiner, Stephen. "Show Don't Tell: Graphic Novels in the Classroom." *English Journal*. November 2004, pp. 114-117.

———. *The 101 Best Graphic Novels*. NBM, 2001.

Wiesner, David. *Tuesday*. Clarion Books, 1991.

Wisconsin Council of Teachers of English Language Arts. *The Wisconsin English Journal: A Wisconsin Resource for Visual Literacy and Visual Materials in the Language Arts Classroom, Special Issue*, Vol. 47, no. 2, Fall 2005.

Yang, Gene Luen. *American Born Chinese*. First Second, 2006.

If You're Smart You Can Get the Jokes: Utilizing Pop Culture

As an English teacher, I am always amazed by how often I see references to famous literature in my everyday life. The more we know, the more we notice. As my student Mitch pointed out, Shakespeare *is* everywhere, and so are many other writers and works of great literature. They appear in TV shows, movies, commercials, and song lyrics, as well as video games, the names of football teams, and nail polish colors (no, I'm not kidding!). If we can make these connections for teens throughout our units of study, then they're more likely to be engaged with and receptive to what we're trying to teach. We can use these examples to further support the argument that great literature has staying power.

For example, the NFL team Baltimore Ravens is named after "The Raven" by Edgar Allan Poe, and the team mascots are three ravens named Edgar, Allan, and Poe. It would only take a minute to introduce that information at the beginning of a lesson on Poe. Will those sports-loving, literature-loathing teenage boys in the back of the room sit up and pay a little more attention after hearing that? Ask *them* to find out how Poe was connected to Baltimore. The good news is they might actually remember it after they exit the classroom. Several years ago, one of my students re-

> **NAIL POLISH BRAND OPI MAKES CLEVER REFERENCES TO CLASSIC LIT IN THE NAMES OF THEIR COLORS**
>
> - Chocolate Shake-Speare
> - Gold Lang Syne
> - Nevermore
> - The Mod Hatter
> - Romeo and Joliet

turned to school from a stint in the county juvenile detention facility. While he was there, he told one of the staff members that the Baltimore Ravens were named after Poe's poem. The staff member didn't believe him (and I suspect found it hard to believe that this teen knew anything about poetry) and bet him a pizza that he was wrong. Thanks to football and Poe (an unlikely combination, to say the least), he ended up winning a free pizza and came away feeling smart because he wasn't supposed to know something like that.

When I'm introducing new literature in class, I often start with what the students know and trace it back to the literary reference, rather than starting with the literature and working forward. Think of it as the hook for the lesson or as accessing their prior knowledge or engaging in an anticipatory set. Once the students see a teacher trying to make connections to their world, they become much more willing to come along for the ride . . . even if they're not 100 percent sure where they are going. When I first started teaching (*way* back in the 20th century), this was much more difficult to do, but now that we've got the Internet (with *YouTube* and i-Tunes) and classroom technology (like computers, SMARTboards, and even iPads), it's become much easier to find and bring these reference points into the classroom and to share them with students. When preparing a unit on Shakespeare's *Henry V*, begin with the 2008 Sony Playstation 3 ad or the scene from the movie *Renaissance Man*, both of which feature the "St. Crispin's Day Speech" from Act IV, scene iii. When teaching *Moby Dick*, start with the Progressive Insurance ad featuring Captain Ahab or the AT&T Blackberry Torch cell phone ad. When teaching Andrew Marvell's "To His Coy Mistress," start the class by playing "Let's Get It On" by Marvin Gaye (you can find all of these and more on my *YouTube* channel: *http://www.youtube.com/user/daridoo*). These quick touchstones reinforce the idea that the characters and themes of literature are still relevant and recognizable in our lives today.

Parody

One thing I often tell my students is, "If you're smart, you can get the joke." What I mean is, while some television shows and movies can be funny to anybody, there is another level of meaning and "in jokes" understood only by those who have the right background knowledge (i.e. if they are smart). This is especially true when it comes to parody. For example, the scene in *Monty Python and the Holy Grail* (Sony Pictures, 1975) in which Galahad is rescued from Castle Anthrax, a stronghold inhabited by "four score young blondes and brunettes" who try on exciting underwear and want to be spanked, is funny on its own. But it's funni*er* when it is understood that Galahad needs to remain a virgin in order to find the Holy Grail; that's why Lancelot keeps insisting that Galahad is in "great peril." *Shrek* (Dreamworks SKG, 2001), the movie about an ogre and his wise-cracking donkey sidekick who set out to rescue a princess, is funny by itself. But it is funni*er* when it is understood that it's taking traditional folktale motifs and characters and flipping them on their heads; the prince is supposed to be the good guy, the ogre is supposed to be the villain, and the princess isn't supposed to be a kick-ass heroine á la *The Matrix*.

Cartoons often provide great examples of parody and allow us to talk to students about different levels of meaning. Most teens have probably had the experience of re-watching a beloved Disney movie or a cartoon from their childhood, only to realize that there are many "adult" jokes that blew right over their heads when they were children. Or, they've come into an English class having seen a *South Park* episode, like "Pip," a parody of *Great Expectations*, (watch it at *http://www.southparkstudios.com/full-episodes/s04e05-pip*) or "Terrance and Phillip: Beyond the

---

MORE FILM PARODIES OF CLASSIC LIT

- *The Adventures of Bob and Doug Mackenzie: Strange Brew* (Metro-Goldwyn-Mayer, 1983) (William Shakespeare's *Hamlet*)

- *The Adventure of Sherlock Holmes' Smarter Brother* (Twentieth Century Fox, 1975) (Sir Arthur Conan Doyle's *Sherlock Holmes*)

- *Hoodwinked* (The Weinstein Company, 2005) ("Little Red Riding Hood" folktale)

- *Robin Hood: Men in Tights* (Brooks Films, 1993) (Robin Hood legends)

- *Young Frankenstein* (Twentieth Century Fox, 1974) (Mary Shelley's *Frankenstein*)

Blow," which wraps with the final death scene from *Hamlet* (watch it at *http://www.southparkstudios.com/full-episodes/s05e05-terrance-and-phillip-behind-the-blow* [8:20-10:08]), only to think, "Oh, I already know this story." *South Park* creators Trey Parker and Matt Stone actually parody classic lit quite a bit, but the content of the cartoon (elementary school-aged kids with potty mouths) makes showing it in class a bit dicey. *South Park* can work its magic without being shown in the classroom, though—it's been my experience that if I so much as mention to a group of high school students that I watch the cartoon, I hear amazed whispers flying around the room, "She watches *South Park*?" . . . and then I'm in.

A safer, though still hilarious and wildly popular, classroom alternative to *South Park* is *The Simpsons*. Although I remember watching shorts of *The Simpsons* during *The Tracy Ullman Show* in the late 1980s when FOX was a new channel, it's still hard for me to believe that this animated program has been on the air for over twenty years. The reason for its longevity is that it's still fresh, timely, and relevant. I can't even count the number of times I've been watching *The Simpsons* only to catch a reference to a literary work; in fact, Matt Groening references classic lit so often in plotlines and episode titles that I think he should make and market a *The Simpsons* DVD specially for English teachers.

Probably the most well-known and popular episode to reference a literary work is from the first ever *Treehouse of Horror* (the annual Halloween episode), in which Bart and Homer act out portions of Poe's poem "The Raven." Several other episodes spoof works of literature, such as *The Odyssey*, *The Island of Dr. Moreau*, and *A Streetcar Named Desire*, to name just a few. These episodes actually base the cartoon's plot on the plot of the literary work. *The Simpsons* also frequently bases the titles of episodes on the titles of literary works.

THINK KIDS CAN'T LEARN ANYTHING FROM WATCHING CARTOONS? CHECK OUT THESE LIT-INSPIRED PLOTS FROM *THE SIMPSONS*

- "The Raven" based on Edgar Allan Poe's *The Raven*
- "A Streetcar Named Marge" based on Tennessee Williams' *A Streetcar Named Desire*
- "Simpsons Tall Tales" featuring the stories of Paul Bunyan, Johnny Appleseed, and Mark Twain's *The Adventures of Tom Sawyer*
- "Tales from the Public Domain: D'Oh, Brother Where Art Thou" featuring Homer as Odysseus
- "Tales from the Public Domain: Do the Bard Man" starring Bart as Hamlet
- "The Devil and Homer Simpson" based on Stephen Vincent Benet's *The Devil and Daniel Webster*
- "Revenge Is a Dish Best Served Three Times: The Count of Monte Fatso" based on Alexandre Dumas' *The Count of Monte Cristo*
- "Bart Simpson's Dracula" based on Bram Stoker's *Dracula*
- "The Island of Dr. Hibbert" based on H.G. Wells' *The Island of Dr. Moreau*
- "Frinkenstein" based on Mary Shelley's *Frankenstein*

Watch full episodes at *http://www.thesimpsons.com/index.html*

THE SIMPSONS SCAVENGER HUNT

The creators of *The Simpsons* have named numerous episodes after famous literary works. Here are some examples:

- "Much Apu About Nothing"

- "Marge Be Not Proud"

- "Bart of Darkness"

- "Homer at the Bat"

- "The Telltale Head"

- "Double, Double Boy in Trouble"

- "The Call of the Simpsons"

- "Homer's Odyssey"

- "The Crepes of Wrath"

- "Lady Bouvier's Lover"

- "The Canine Mutiny"

- "Grift of the Magi"

- "Pygmoelian"

- "The Old Man and the Key"

- "Rome-old and Juli-eh"

- "I Don't Wanna Know Why the Caged Bird Sings"

Give students this list and send them on a scavenger hunt to find the title and author of the classic work that inspired the episode title.

Another cartoon that relied heavily on literary parody is *Steven Spielberg Presents the Animaniacs*. This series, produced by Steven Spielberg and Warner Brothers Animation, ran for five years from 1993 to 1998. Though no longer on the air, the episodes are available on DVD in three volumes. Wikipedia has a brief summary of each episode (*http://en.wikipedia.org/wiki/ List_of_Animaniacs_episodes*). My favorite episodes are those in which Yakko, Wakko, Dot, and their supporting cast (including Hello Nurse, a name that always cracks me up) become Shakespearean characters such as Hamlet, Laertes, Puck, and the three witches from Macbeth, while another character interjects a translation in very funny, yet very accurate, "regular English." It's not just Shakespeare that they poke fun at, many classics and characters from other British and American works also become the butt of the Animaniacs' jokes.

THE ANIMANIACS ON DVD

- *Animaniacs - Volume 1* (Season 1, episodes 1-25)
- *Animaniacs - Volume 2* (Season 1, episodes 26-50)
- *Animaniacs - Volume 3* (Season 1, episodes 51-65; Season 2, episodes 1-4; and Season 3, episodes 1-6)

Amblin Entertainment. (Warner Home Video, c2006)

The Animaniacs Do Shakespeare & Are Even Kind Enough to Translate It for You:

- "A Midsummer Night's Dream" (Puck's Final Speech) *http://www.youtube.com/watch?v=jXMfMID3VaA&feature=related*
- "Alas Poor Skullhead" (*Hamlet*, Graveyard scene) *http://www.youtube.com/watch?v=2KGF3Tap94k*
- "MacBeth" ("Double, double toil and trouble..." scene) *http://www.youtube.com/watch?v=xWQX47spGr0&feature=related*

The Animaniacs Do Brit Lit:

- "Draculee, Draculaa" (*Dracula*) *http://www.youtube.com/watch?v=cdUcnAAjadY*
- "Brain Meet Brawn" (*Dr. Jekyll and Mr. Hyde*) *http://www.youtube.com/watch?v=fBHISdXQ9Po*
- "A Christmas Plotz" (*A Christmas Carol*)
- "Deduces Wild" (Sherlock Holmes)

The Animanics Do American Lit:

- "Moby or Not Moby" (*Moby Dick*) *http://www.youtube.com/watch?v=xyaJcoMFjxc*
- "Mighty Wakko at the Bat" ("Casey At the Bat") *http://www.youtube.com/watch?v=vlnIKk5Pfoc*
- "The Flame Returns, by Henry Wadsworth Longfellow" ("Paul Revere's Ride")
- "Papers for Pappa" (Ernest Hemingway)

Television series also occasionally parody classic literature. One of the more well-known, retro, and campy of these is *The Munsters*, which aired from 1964 to 1966 (seventy episodes) on CBS. This series followed the exploits of a wacky family of monsters, led by Herman Munster (a parody on the Universal Studios version of Frankenstein's monster) and his wife, Lily Munster (whose maiden name was Dracula). The Munster family also included Sam Dracula (aka Grandpa), Herman and Lilly's son, Eddie (who is a werewolf), and their plain (read "non-monstrous") niece, Marilyn, a variety of strange pets, and a cuckoo-clock with a raven in it who repeated the word, "Nevermore" upon the hour. Today's teens might not have grown up watching this show (unless they spent a lot of time watching TVLand with their parents), but it might be fun to show an episode and have them make a list of how many literary references they can catch.

COMMANDO LIBRARIANS

Team with your local English teachers to plan a Retro (Literary) Monster Movie Night at your branch.

Universal Studios' Horror Cycle:

- *Dracula** (1931)
- *Frankenstein** (1931)
- *The Hunchback of Notre Dame* (1923)
- *Dr. Jekyll and Mr. Hyde*
- *The Invisible Man** (1933)

Other films from Universal Studios:

- Edgar Allan Poe's
    - *The Murders in the Rue Morgue* (1932)
    - *The Raven* (1935)
    - *The Black Cat* (1934)
- *Abbott and Costello Meet...*
    - *Frankenstein* (1948)
    - *the Invisible Man* (1951)
    - *Dr. Jekyll and Mr. Hyde* (1953)

There are several movies featuring the spouses and offspring of these characters.

Popular Movies

Lately there has been a slew of popular movies that are loosely based on literary classics, but in many cases they share little more than a title and/or names of main characters. So what can be done with these films? I'm not suggesting showing these movies for in-class viewing (classroom time is precious, as we all know), but they can certainly be used as a way to access students' prior knowledge about the story, to discuss differences and similarities between the original story and the film, and to familiarize students with titles, main characters, and settings of the works upon which they are based. Make a good connection with the local librarian, and s/he may agree to show the film at the library so the students could attend for extra credit.

Here are some examples of recent high profile films that relate to classic lit in some way. *Gnomeo and Juliet* (Miramax, 2011) is an animated movie based on *Romeo and Juliet* with lawn gnomes as the main characters. Jack Black recently starred in a comedic version of *Gulliver's Travels* (Twentieth Century Fox, 2010). King of the strange and gothic, Tim Burton, has presented his own take on *Alice in Wonderland* (Disney, 2010), *Charlie and the Chocolate Factory* (Warner Brothers, 2005), and a loose adaptation of *Frankenstein* in *Frankenweenie* (Walt Disney, 2012). Robert Downey Jr. and Jude Law played Holmes and Dr. Watson, respectively, in *Sherlock Holmes* (Warner Brothers, 2009) and reprised those roles for *Sherlock Holmes: A Game of Shadows* (Warner Brothers, 2011). *Van Helsing* (Universal Pictures, 2004) incorporated characters from *Dracula, Frankenstein,* and *The Strange Case of Dr. Jekyll and Mr. Hyde*, while *The League of Ex-*

traordinary Gentlemen (Twentieth Century Fox, 2003) features characters from *King Solomon's Mines*, *The Strange Case of Dr. Jekyll and Mr. Hyde*, *20,000 Leagues Under the Sea*, *The Invisible Man*, *The Picture of Dorian Gray*, *Moby Dick*, and *The Adventures of Tom Sawyer*.

I often use newer movies that aren't actually based on novels as a hook to generate an interest in classic literature. For example, vampires are hotter than ever these days and a lot of that has to do with the YA lit sensation *Twilight* by Stephenie Meyer (Little, Brown, 2005). Though I'm not a diehard fan (not that there's anything wrong with that), *Twilight* and its subsequent books and movies provide an entry point into *Dracula*, and are also the perfect segue into studying the folklore of vampires and werewolves. For those who don't want their vampire versus werewolf movies tainted with any of that swoony, romantic stuff, check out *Underworld* (Lakeshore Entertainment, 2003) starring Kate Beckinsale.

Coming in a close second to vampires in pop culture popularity are pirates. Facebook has an option to set the language of a page to "pirate" and International Talk Like a Pirate Day (*http://www.talklikeapirate. com/*) is held annually on September 19th (follow the creators on Twitter and Facebook). Though there's probably always been a segment of the population that's been intrigued by these lawless, swashbuckling rogues, there's no doubt that they largely owe their resurgence in popularity to Disney and Jerry Bruckheimer's *Pirates of the Caribbean* films (and there are plans for a total of at least six films in this series, so it will be in the public eye for quite a bit longer). Why not use them as an introduction to one of the most famous pirate novels ever, Robert Louis Stevenson's *Treasure Island*? These films provide a great jumping off point into all things nautical: sea songs and shanties; the real lives of famous pirates; modern day pirates; and the folklore surrounding the sea, including Davy Jones's locker, the Flying Dutchman, the kraken, mermaids, and ghost ships (see the *Treasure Island* Text Set in the British Literature Arsenal).

Many fantasy movie series can provide an opportunity to discuss the elements of high and low fantasy. When looking at the list of high and low fantasy elements, several movies might come to mind (many of which are based on classic children's books, coincidentally) that would fit into each category. For example, *Mary Poppins*, *The Jungle Book*, *Charlie and the Chocolate Factory,* and *Charlotte's Web* are all considered low fantasy, while *Harry*

LOW FANTASY VS. HIGH FANTASY

Low (or Domestic) Fantasy
- Takes place in this world
- Is generally light in tone and theme
- May include magical, supernatural, or fantastical elements
- May feature personified animals and/or toys as characters

High (or Epic) Fantasy
- Set in a different world and/or moves between our world and a fantasy world
- Deals with the theme of good vs. evil
- Draws upon and references mythology
- Often includes a quest or journey
- Reflects and comments upon our world (though it is often set in a different time and/or place)

Potter, *The Lord of the Rings*, *The Golden Compass*, and *The Chronicles of Narnia* are all considered high fantasy. For the secondary classroom, the high fantasy titles will be more appropriate, as they provide for more involved and "meaty" discussion because of their ties to mythology and folklore. The high fantasy examples are based on book series that have either three or seven titles. Ask students to consider the frequency of the numbers three and seven in both Biblical stories, as well as folktales (see Chapter 6 for more folktale motifs). Tolkien's Middle Earth books include many references to Norse mythology, right down to the names of the dwarves who invite Bilbo Baggins on the journey to Lonely Mountain in the prequel to the trilogy, *The Hobbit* (which is scheduled to be released as a two part movie beginning in 2012). In the Harry Potter books, J.K. Rowling references a number of mythological and legendary beasts from many different cultures: Cerberus (a.k.a. Fluffy from *Harry Potter and the Sorcerer's Stone*), centaurs, mermaids, the basilisk, the grim, pixies, elves, and the phoenix. Even the names of characters draw upon famous mythological, legendary, or historical characters (for example, Sirius, Fawkes, Luna, Minerva, and Narcissa) or give insights into a character's inner self (for example, many readers might have known Remus Lupin was a werewolf before it was revealed in the text or the movie). For more specific examples of Rowling's use of mythology, check out *The Magical Worlds of Harry Potter: A Treasury of Myths, Legends, and Fascinating Facts* by David Colbert; *Fantastic Beasts and Where to Find Them by Newt Scamander* by J.K. Rowling; and Priscilla Spencer's website, *What's in a Name?* (*http://www.theninemuses.net/hp/a.html*).

Music Soothes the Savage Beast

Music is a fantastic way to grab teens' attention. Teenagers are so obsessed with music that it often influences large parts of their identity, from their clothes to their attitudes, to the friends they hang out with. Music can be connected to literature in many interesting ways, probably the most obvious of which is to draw parallels between poetry (which teens claim to hate) and song lyrics. Songs and poems are similar entities structurally (both employ rhythm and rhyme), and emotionally (both are immediate and raw), and they both require an efficiency of language (which leads to the use of literary devices). In fact, when the text of an unfamiliar poem is placed next to the lyrics of an unfamiliar song, it is often difficult to tell the two apart. Classic poems sometimes get recorded as songs, like Loreena McKennitt's recording of the Alfred Noyes poem "The Highwayman" (Verve, 1997), and classic songwriters, like Bob Dylan, sometimes get labeled the "Poet of a Generation." We even use the terms *lyric* and *ballad* in both genres, though somewhat differently.

Whether working in the rural Midwest or an urban city on one of the coasts, you can create an immediate in with students by drawing some connections between hip-hop music and poetry. In the African American community, music and poetry are inextricably linked, and when looked at side-by-side, it quickly becomes apparent that they build upon and feed off of one another. For example, the black poets of the Harlem Renaissance used the rhythms and sounds of jazz for their inspiration and, when I'm teaching about this era, I always mention that contemporary hip-hop artists—not the guys with the gold grills and the bouncing cars, but the socially conscious guys like Tupac Shakur, John Legend, Jay-Z, and Kanye West—know about and are familiar with the writing of poets like Langston Hughes, Claude McKay, and Countee Cullen . . . and have been inspired by them. Langston Hughes' poem "Ask Your Mama: 12 Moods for Jazz" has experienced a recent rebirth that is combining the poem with multimedia and music—both Gangsta rapper Ice-T with the Indianapolis Symphony Orchestra and The Ron McCurdy Jazz Quartet, and Questlove, drummer of The Roots, have contributed their talents to versions of this project.

I admit that it's a bit daunting for me to feel current when it comes to hip-hop, and I certainly don't want to seem like one of those old teachers who is trying too hard to be cool. I think the trick here is to let the students lead; they can be the experts and the teacher can be the novice. Just tell them their teacher is "old school"—they'll appreciate the fact that an effort is being made, and the students will do some of the legwork.

A great entry point into the genre is Nikki Giovanni's *Hip-Hop Speaks to Children with CD: A Celebration of Poetry with a Beat.* In the introduction of the book, Giovanni gives a short and succinct history of African American music, poetry, and rap and shows how the three intersect. The book boasts an eclectic collection of fifty-one rhythmic poems and rap lyrics from poets and recording artists like Gwendolyn Brooks, Gary Soto, Maya Angelou, Lauryn Hill, The Sugarhill Gang, and Queen Latifah. It also includes a compact disc with thirty-one of the poems/songs performed either by the original artist, as with Langston Hughes' "The Negro Speaks of Rivers," or by other artists, as is the case with Tupac Shakur's "The Rose That Grew from Concrete" read by Nikki Giovanni.

> ## MORE ABOUT LANGSTON HUGHES' "ASK YOUR MAMA: 12 MOODS FOR JAZZ"
>
> - Melia, Mike. "Jessye Norman, the Roots Team Up for Langston Hughes' 'Ask Your Mama.'" *PBS Newshour Art Beat,* August 27, 2009. http://www.pbs.org/newshour/art/blog/2009/08/jessye-norman-the-roots-team-up-for-langston-hughes-ask-your-mama.html
> - *Ask Your Mama* ©2010 Art Farm West http://askyourmama.com/
> - *The Langton Hughes Project* © 2009, Ron McCurdy http://www.ronmccurdy.com/about_hudges_project.htm

English teacher Allan Lawrence Sitomer has created a book specifically for use in the language arts classroom titled *Hip-Hop Poetry and the Classics*, which is chock full of ready-to-use lessons and handouts on literary elements, writing activities, and even AP Exam prep. This book was published in 2004, so the hip-hop references aren't super current, but the artists will still be familiar to students. For example, one exercise pairs "Do Not Go Gentle into That Good Night" by Dylan Thomas with "Me Against the World" by Tupac Shakur. Another activity pairs Langston Hughes' "Harlem: A Dream Deferred" with the Notorious B.I.G.'s "Juicy."

Possibly the best way to highlight the convergence of these two genres is with spoken word, or slam, poetry. This type of performance poetry is ever-evolving and generally speaks to current and/or political issues. A great way to introduce spoken word poetry is with *Russell Simmons's Def Poetry.* This series aired for six seasons (from 2002 to 2007) on HBO, was hosted by hip-hop MC Mos Def, and showcased well-known poets (like Nikki Giovanni, Jimmy Santiago Baca, and Amiri Baraka) and singers from many genres, including jazz, folk, Motown, rhythm and blues, and hip-hop (like Jewel, Jill Scott, Smokey Robinson, Michael Franti, Alicia Keys, Common, and Kanye West). All six seasons are available on DVD from HBO Home

> ## NEED TO "SCHOOL" YOURSELF ON HIP-HOP?
>
> - *Book of Rhymes: The Poetics of Hip Hop* by Adam Bradley (BasicCivitas, 2009)
> - *The Anthology of Rap* edited by Adam Bradley and Andrew DuBois (Yale University Press, 2010)
> - *Hip Hop World* by Dalton Higgins (Groundwood Books, 2009)
> - *Hip Hop Matters: Politics, Pop Culture, and the Struggle for the Soul of a Movement* by S. Craig Watkins (Beacon Press, 2005)

LEARN MORE ABOUT SPOKEN WORD POETRY:

SpokenOak: The Roots and Branches of Amerikan Spoken Arts – this website provides a definition, a genre list, and genre tree that illustrate how different genres of oral literature and spoken arts—from the traditional (griots, slave songs, jump rope rhymes, etc.) to the modern (slam poetry, rap, urban myths, etc.)—are related. *http://www.spokenoak.com*

Mark Kelly Smith: Founder, Poetry Slam Movement – Smith describes the roots and history of slam poetry. *http://markkellysmith.com*

Spoken Wordz Info: Hot Def Poets and More – a website with downloadable spoken word poems by several poets, including Saul Williams, Mos Def, Nikki Giovanni, and Maya Angelou. *http://www.spokenwordz.info/*

COMMANDO LIBRARIANS

Host an Open Mic Night or Poetry Slam at your library. Don't forget to lure teens with the promise of prizes and free food!

- "Open Mic: The Definitions, Rules, Etiquette, Irony – All About Poetry Open Mics" by Bob Holman and Margery Snyder, *About.com* Guide *http://poetry.about.com/od/livepoetry/a/openmic.htm*
- "How to Host a Poetry Slam Event" by Randi McCreary, *eHow* Contributor *http://www.ehow.com/how_5394360_host-poetry-slam-event.html*

Video (and are probably available through the local library system), but many of the performances can be accessed on *YouTube*. The *Wikipedia* article "Def Poetry" (*http://en.wikipedia.org/wiki/Def_Poetry*) provides an index with a listing of each season's individual episodes and performances. Make no mistake about it, while students may moan and groan when told that a poem will be read to them, they will sit up and pay more attention once they've been introduced to spoken word poetry. For example, during a unit on the Civil Rights Era, we watched a performance of "Coded Language" by Saul Williams. We'd already read and listened to several songs and poems written about topics like lynching, the murder of Emmett Till, and the bombing of the 16th Street Baptist Church, but this spoken word poem had my students riveted. When the video came to an end, they were amazed. When I asked what they thought, they responded with, "What was *that*?" "That was awesome!" and "That was WAY better than the other stuff we've done." The response has been the same with other slam poetry we've watched. This is a genre teens will like and will want to know more about.

On the completely opposite end of the musical spectrum, an art form that has been heavily influenced by literature is the musical. A number of classic novels and/or characters from classic literature have provided the inspiration for musicals over the years: Robert Louis Stevenson's *The Strange Case of Dr. Jekyll and Mr. Hyde* (*Jekyll and Hyde*); the legend of King Arthur (*Camelot*); Victor Hugo's *Les Miserables* (musical of the same name); Miguel Cervantes's *Don Quixote* (*The Man of La Mancha*); T.S. Eliot's *Old Possum's Book of Practical Cats* (*Cats*); George Bernard Shaw's *Pygmalion* (*My Fair Lady*); William Shakespeare's *Romeo and Juliet* (*West Side Story*); traditional folktales *Cinderella, Sleeping Beauty, Rapunzel, Little Red Riding Hood*, and *Jack and the Beanstalk* (*Into the Woods*), and L. Frank Baum's *The Wonderful Wizard of Oz*, which inspired Gregory Maguire's novel *Wicked* (musical of the same name). I find that, although my students aren't big fans of watching musicals in class (in fact, they usually ask me to fast forward through the singing), musicals can help students make a visual connection with texts and provide song lyrics that highlight the major plot points that can be read and examined in class (without the music, if necessary). Just like some students who perk up at the mention of hip-hop, there is also a segment of teens who will respond enthusiastically when they hear about Broadway (I was one of them).

Another great way to make the connection between music and literature is to draw attention to the many times the characters and themes from classic literature appear in contemporary music. For example, Dr. Jekyll and Mr. Hyde are referenced in songs by the punk rock group Devo; the gothic rock band The Damned; the 1980s rock band GTR; classic rockers The Who; alternative band Plumb; and the heavy metal group Judas Priest. Just about every musical preference in the classroom will be hit with those options. I usually discover this kind of information by looking at the *Wikipedia* entry about the novel, or by doing a *Google* search of the character's name and/or song titles and lyrics. There are, however, several fantastic web resources that pair contemporary music and classic literature.

Lit Tunes (*http://www.corndancer.com/tunes/tunes_main.html*), created by Christian Z. Goering, has a downloadable database of classic literary works and the songs that can be paired with them. If a song on the list is starred, then it has been confirmed that the song was actually inspired by the novel, short story, or poem (kind of like ekphrastic poetry). Other songs appear in the database because they share similar themes with the literary work. There are also myriad lesson plans (for things like literary terms, writing projects, theme studies, and even grammar), research to support the use of music in the language arts classroom, and useful links to other web pages.

Another helpful site is the *SIBL (Songs Inspired by Literature) Project* (*http://www.siblproject.org/home.html*), which is hosted by Artists for Literacy. They have a database that is searchable by song title, book title, songwriter, performer, or author. Once an entry is selected, the user is taken to a page that includes the song's lyrics, the names of both the songwriter and the performer, the album title, and links to purchase the book, the album, and the individual song. The *SIBL Project* has also created two benefit CDs, *Songs Inspired by Literature, Chapter One* and *Songs Inspired by Literature, Chapter Two* (2002 and 2003, respectively) that are available for purchase. Each CD contains sixteen songs.

The Rock and Roll Hall of Fame website offers more than fifty ready-to-use lesson plans created by teachers during the Rock Hall's Summer Teacher Institute. The lessons are designed for a variety of subject areas, but many would work well and could be adapted for use in the language arts classroom (*http://rock-hall.com/education/resources/lesson-plans/*). Consider teaming with a music or social studies teacher for some cross-disciplinary projects and/or activities. The Rock Hall also offers field trip opportunities (Cleveland, Ohio) and distance learning opportunities for students through the "On the Road" program (*http://rockhall.com/education/distance-learning/courses/*), as well as classes for college credit and professional development for teachers.

Finally, don't forget to allow students the option of using music as a response to literature. Students might find (or write) "theme songs" for characters from novels. Ask them to choose songs that might become a score for the book; for example, have them select the three most important scenes in the novel and choose the music that might be playing in the background as these scenes unfold. They can choose songs that might illustrate a character's development throughout the course of the story. Or, take a lead from the movie *Dangerous Minds* (remember the Dylan-Dylan contest in which students must find a poem by Dylan Thomas that echoes the theme of a Bob Dylan song?) and give students a classic poem and ask them to find a contemporary song that has the same themes. Any and all of these activities will illustrate a student's understanding of the literature and will be more engaging for the student and more interesting to grade than a book report.

References

Colbert, David. *The Magical Worlds of Harry Potter: A Treasury of Myths, Legends, and Fascinating Facts.* Berkley Books, 2001.

Giovanni, Nikki, Alicia Vergel de Dios, Damian Ward, and Kristen Balouch. *Hip-Hop Speaks to Children with CD: A Celebration of Poetry with a Beat* (A Poetry Speaks Experience). Sourcebooks, 2008.

Rowling, J.K. *Fantastic Beasts and Where to Find Them by Newt Scamander.* Scholastic, 2001.

Sitomer, Allan Lawrence and Michael Cirelli. *Hip-Hop Poetry and the Classics.* Milk Mug Publishing, 2004.

The Simpsons. Fox Broadcasting Company.

———. "Bart Simpson's Dracula." 1993-10-28. Number 86, season 5.

———. "The Devil and Homer Simpson." 1993-10-28. Number 86, season 5.

———. "Frinkenstein." 2003-11-02. Number 314, season 15.

———. "The Island of Dr. Hibbert." *2002-11-03. Number 292,* season 14.

———. "Pygmoelian." 2000 -02-27. Number 242, season 11.

———. "The Raven." 1990-10-24. Season 2, Number 16, season 2.

———. "The Regina Monologues." 2003-11-23. Number 317, season 15.

———. "Revenge Is a Dish Best Served Three Times." 200-01-28. Number 389, season 18.

    "The Count of Monte Fatso" segment

———. "Simpsons Tall Tales." 2001-05-20. Number 269, season 12.

———. "A Streetcar Named Marge." 1992-10-01. Number 61, season 4.

———. "Tales from the Public Domain." 2002-03-17. Number 283, season 13.

    "D'Oh, Brother Where Art Thou?" Homer as Odysseus segment

    "Do the Bard, Man" Bart as Hamlet segment

South Park. Comedy Central.

———. "Pip." 2000-11-29. Number 52, season 4

———. "The Return of the Fellowship of the Ring to the Two Towers. 2002-11-13. Number 92, season 6.

———. "Something Wall-Mart This Way Comes." 2004-11-3. Number 120, season 8.

———. "Terrance and Phillip: Beyond the Blow." 2001-07-17. Number 70, season 5.

Steven Spielberg Presents *The Animaniacs.* Animaniacs. Kids' WB.

————. "Alas Poor Skullhead." 1993-11-11. Number 30, season 1.

————. "Brain Meet Brawn." 1994-02-15. Number 54, season 1.

————. "A Christmas Plotz." 1993-12-6. Number 49, season 1.

————. "Deduces Wild." 1995-09-15. Number 72, season 3.

————. "Draculee, Draculaa." 1993-10-29. Number 29, season 1.

————. "MacBeth" May 3, 1994 1994-05-03. Number 62, season 1.

————. "A Midsummer Night's Dream." 1993-10-19. Number 23, season 1.

————. "Mighty Wakko at the Bat." 1996-09-14. Number 85, season 4.

————. "Moby or Not Moby." 1993-10-26. Number 28, season 1.

————. "Papers for Pappa." 1996-10-19. No. 88, season 4.

————. "The Flame Returns, by Henry Wadsworth Longfellow." 1995-11-11. Number 75, season 3.

Heroes, Fairies, and Ghosts, Oh My: Tying in Traditional Literature

Many years ago, before the ability to read was widespread and when books were accessible only to the wealthy and well-educated, stories were told orally to entertain a wide-ranging audience. Featuring stories filled with tragic love, wars, outlaws, revenge, envy, and superstition, these stories of the folk (legends, folktales, and ballads) appealed to the masses then, and continue to appeal to them today. In fact, many stories and characters of traditional folk literature make frequent appearances in both classic and modern literature and also in movies, which make them the perfect complement when teaching the classics.

In addition to serving as entertainment, folk stories often served as a means of instruction—as a way of warning people to do (or not do) certain things (for example, babies must be baptized lest the fairies come steal them away and replace them with a changeling), or as a model for proper behavior (for example, King Arthur was known for his sense of fairness and chivalry, behaviors held in high esteem in medieval England). Stories like these are recognizable in our modern-day urban legends, but rather than being passed orally, as were the legends of old, urban legends are passed via the Internet. Be sure to make this connection for students; it will help to illustrate the numerous variants of individual stories and will also help them to understand how it was possible that people could believe what today seem like outrageous stories of fairies stealing human babies or mermaids luring sailors to their deaths.

The oldest type of traditional literature is the myth. These stories are different from folktales and legends in that myths are sacred; in other words, myths are believed to be true by the people of the culture from which they come. They are the stories that shape and inform a culture's religious beliefs and address the big questions of life. Because of their importance to a culture, these stories were generally written down long before folktales and legends were.

The following chart illustrates some of the differences and similarities between these types of traditional stories. Notice that the vertical lines separating the genres are not solid. This is because some of these stories cross the boundaries between genres. For example, the Roman myth of "Cupid and Psyche" bears a striking resemblance to and shares many motifs with the folktale "East O' the Sun, West O' the Moon." Depending on the story and the source, King Arthur may be treated as a legendary character, a mythic figure, or a hero.

TRADITIONAL LITERATURE COMPARISON

	FABLES	FOLKTALES	LEGENDS	MYTHS	HERO TALES
Examples	"The Tortoise and the Hare"; "The Boy Who Cried Wolf"; "Ant and Grasshopper"	"Cinderella"; "Three Billy Goat's Gruff"; "The Three Little Pigs"; "Hansel and Gretel"	Tales of Robin Hood; King Arthur; Davy Crockett	Prometheus Steals Fire ; Noah's Flood; Loki Steals the Apples of Youth	Hercules; Theseus; Romulus and Remus; Beowulf; Gilgamesh
Characters	Flat, stock character; Usually a personified animal with only a single trait; Represent human qualities; No names	Flat characters; No variety; Good & bad characters are easily identified; Often common people or animals; Names are either not given, descriptive, or common ; Youngest or weakest character is often on top at the end	Historical figures with fictional traits and situations	Gods with supernatural powers; Semi-divine characters; Sometimes humans	Protagonist is superhuman--usually the son of a god and a mortal woman; Hero embodies the characteristics valued by the society; Most often male; Female heroines are revered for their "male" traits
Plot	Person vs. person (animal vs. animal); Very brief: Usually a single incident; Ends with an explicitly stated moral	Person vs. person; Action moves rapidly to a climax & stock closing ("And they lived happily ever after"); Simple; Punishment is swift & deserved	Any conflict	God vs. god (to establish leadership); God vs. human(s); God vs. supernatural enemy	Hero leaves homeland, initiates self into adulthood, & returns home to reap the rewards; Conflict is usually protagonist vs. monster or person with supernatural powers
Setting	Time and place is unspecified; Setting is merely a backdrop for the story because morals are universal	Time and place is unspecified ("Once upon a time"); Setting is merely a backdrop for the story	Often set in a particular time and place, although it may be fantastic	An earlier world or another world (the home of the gods or the underworld); Time is primeval	Place may be specified, but the time is often unspecified; May be recent or distant past
Theme	Explicit & didactic; Focus is on individual's place in society	Explicit or implicit; Focus on family & justice; Clear; No complexity -- love vs. hate, good vs. evil; Simple, abundant dialogue; Symbolism; Morality is idealized: good is rewarded, bad is punished	Glorification of historical figures in fictional stories; Hero often restores order in the society	Often creation and organization of the universe and humans, but not merely stories of origin; Relationship of humans and gods; The human condition, etc.	Set models for human behavior; Hero fights for good and to restore order
Point of View	Omniscient or dramatic	Usually omniscient or limited omniscient	Usually omniscient	Usually omniscient	Usually omniscient
Style	Terse; Lacks imagery or connotative language	Depends on the culture; Frequent use of motifs; Repetition; Short verses interspersed in text; Short scenes; A lot of dialogue	Frequent use of symbols; Little dialogue; Brief descriptions of action	Symbols are of central significance; Little dialogue; Brief descriptions of action	Symbols are significant; Little dialogue; Brief descriptions of action; More imaginative than myths
Tone	Straightforward; Didactic; Moralizing; Secular	Varies, but not usually didactic; Secular; Reflects the values of the society/group; Not sentimental	Often objective; Secular	Dignified; Sometimes mystical; Sacred; True--articulate a culture's world view	Often objective; Sacred or secular

Adapted from Dr. Sheila Most, Eastern Michigan University, Ypsilanti, MI

Myths

I find that my students are already familiar with (and usually enjoy) Greek and Roman myths, as those tend to be taught in middle school, but that they know little or nothing about the mythology of other cultures. The one conclusion I really want my students to draw from studying mythology (sometimes they do it on their own and sometimes it takes a little nudge from me) is that, no matter how different people may seem on the outside, we all struggle with the same questions on the inside: Where did I come from? Why am I here? What will happen to me when I die? What relationship should I have with my god(s)? What relationship should I have with the world around me? Studying mythology allows me to show this to them. We spend a lot of time studying the similarities between creation myths (more on this in Chapter 6) in order to illustrate this point. Students begin to see that, regardless of whether a culture worships many gods or only one god, the deities and the stories about them generally serve the same purpose: to instruct people about how to behave, to illustrate what is important to a particular culture, and to answer questions about a human being's place in the world.

We can also learn about more than a culture's religious beliefs by studying their myths. We can read between the lines in order to glean information about the day-to-day lives of the people who tell these stories; myths can shed light on everything from the geography of the area in which they live to their rituals, to their diets. If something is important enough to make it into a myth, then it must have been an extremely important part of that culture. If a culture has a flood myth (and most of them do), we can assume that the civilization was located near a body of water that was known to overflow its banks from time to time. (Get students to think about why people tend to settle near water and ask them whether the benefits outweigh the dangers.) If we read a story about a particular game/competition (like the Mayan ballgame of polota) or celebrations/feasts/festivals (like the Roman Bacchanalia), then we can assume that many people traveled to and/or participated in these events. If there is a story about the creation of certain animals (such as the ox in Chinese mythology), then we know that those animals must be native to that area. If a culture has a story explaining where corn came from (as many Native American cultures do), then we can draw the conclusion that corn was an integral part of that group's diet and economy.

Myths also provide us with stories of a culture's heroes. These hero tales can tell us what personality traits and characteristics a culture values. Is the hero known for being: Fierce in battle (like Cuchulain from Ireland)? Exceptionally strong (like Babylon's Gilgamesh)? Resourceful and quick thinking (like Greece's Odysseus)? Loyal (like England's Beowulf)? Kind and selfless (like Palestine's Jesus)? Fair and chivalrous (like Britain's King Arthur)? All of these heroes give us insight into a culture. Though there are some differences between these heroes, there are also many similarities. Heroes are usually male; called to undertake some sort of quest or journey; brave, strong, and honorable leaders; and willing to sacrifice themselves in order to bring justice, peace, knowledge, prosperity, and/or victory to their people.

An added bonus of myths is that they are great stories; in fact, they read a lot like soap operas. There's incest, adultery, fighting, jealousy, murder (especially patricide and fratricide), punishments, etc. that will grab students' attention. Throw in battles with mythical creatures and quests, and there's a lot that students will find exciting. Unlike the other types of traditional literature we'll talk about in this chapter, a culture's myths are often intertwined; there is an assumption that the reader has background knowledge about the creation of the world and the pantheon of gods and goddesses and the relationships between them. So, the more of these stories the students read, the better they will understand the events and the players.

Legends

Legends are often told as true stories. Legends sort of straddle, or bridge, the distance between folktales and myth. They feature people, places, or creatures that were once believed to be real and often identify an actual location and time period in which the story took place. However, because details are added for the purpose of storytelling and the audience's enjoyment, and because the tales change with each retelling (think of it like the game Telephone), these tales are not truly historical, and over the years it becomes increasingly difficult to separate fact from fiction when discussing legends. Legendary characters, places, and creatures occur in stories from all cultures and have also influenced authors from all cultures, so they can be incorporated into

LEARN MORE ABOUT LEGENDARY CREATURES AND PLACES

Here are some reference guides to keep available for students to peruse during Sustained Silent Reading:

- *The Cassell Dictionary of Superstitions* by David Pickering (Cassell, 1995)

- *Cryptozoology A-Z: The Encyclopedia of Lock Monsters, Sasquatch, Chupacabras, and Other Authentic Mysteries of Nature* by Loren Coleman and Jerome Clark (Simon & Schuster, 1999)

- *The Dictionary of Imaginary Places* by Alberto Manguel and Giannin Guadelupe (Harcourt Brace, 2000)

- *Encyclopedia Horrifica: The Terrifying Truth! About Vampires, Ghosts, Monsters, and More* by Joshua Gee (Scholastic, 2007)

- *The Encyclopedia of Ghosts and Spirits, Second Edition* by Rosemary Ellen Guiley (Checkmark, 2000)

- *The Encyclopedia of Vampires, Werewolves, and Other Monsters* by Rosemary Elllen Guiley (Checkmark, 2005)

- *The Illustrated Encyclopedia of Fairies* by Anna Franklin (Vega, 2002)

any literature class. Some famous legendary characters are King Arthur, Robin Hood, Johnny Appleseed, Mulan, and John Henry.

The legend of King Arthur is one of the best examples of a legend with staying power. I spend a number of weeks on the Arthurian legend when I teach British literature because it's got something for everyone—love, betrayal, battles, heroes, villains, knights, magic, and swordplay. The documentary *Arthur: King of the Britons* allows students to learn the history behind the legend and to see where fact and fiction intersect. We then read the legends from the picture books *Tales of King Arthur* and Eyewitness Classic's *King Arthur*. We study medieval life, chivalry, and weapons using the Dorling Kindersley Eyewitness Guides *Knight* and *Medieval Life*. For their culminating project, each student creates her/his own medieval coat-of-arms using a variety of books and Internet sources to research family heritage, crests, and mottoes (more on this in Chapter 8). I then reward the students' hard work with the movie *Monty Python and the Holy Grail* in order to reinforce the idea from Chapter 4 that, "If you're smart, you can get the joke."

The Arthurian legend also provides us with one of the most well-known legendary places, Camelot. This kingdom is so iconic that over seven hundred years after it first appears in the stories of King Arthur, we still use the term to describe a place that is seemingly (and fleetingly) perfect. Other types of legendary places are magical cities (e.g. El Dorado) or sites (e.g. the Fountain of Youth), the land of fairie (e.g. Tir na nOg), the underworld or the land of the dead (e.g. Hades), and sunken or drowned cities (e.g. the Lost City of Atlantis). Though many travelers set out in search of these lands in hopes of gaining the riches and/or knowledge that may be found there, mortals are rarely granted permission to enter. Those who are fortunate enough to be permitted, or those who stumble into one of these lands accidentally, should not accept any food or drink that is offered, as that will render her/him unable to leave. Those who do return home do so only to find that time has passed at a much different rate in the "real world" than in the legendary world—either much more quickly or much more slowly—and they often spend the rest of their lives either pining for the legendary world and trying to find a way to re-enter it, and/or being treated as if they are crazy by their friends and family.

I find that my students also really like studying the legends of creatures such as fairies, dragons, giants, trolls, ghosts, mermaids, black dogs, vampires, and werewolves. The students are often surprised to learn that many people once believed that these creatures were real and that their lore often overlaps. This is when I point out that, though people today don't generally claim to see dragons or fairies, there isn't a shortage of recently documented sightings of Bigfoot, the chupacabra, and aliens.

As my students' knowledge of supernatural creatures grows, they learn a lot about how to "repel" these beings. For example, in British literature we read the ghost story "A Meeting on the Road Home," in which Gabriel Fisher encounters the ghost of a headless woman while walking home from a tavern late one night. My students know that when Gabriel is being pursued by the head, which is "snapping and snarling like some outlandish terrier around his feet" (67), and he happens upon a stream, he should run across it in order to escape the ghost. They are correct. Gabriel does cross the stream because, "The ghost, apparently limited in territory like others of its kind, could not cross running water" (67). Sharing legends with students will also enable them to see how folk beliefs influenced authors, such as Shakespeare in *A Midsummer Night's Dream* (fairies) and *Macbeth* (witches) and Sir Arthur Conan Doyle in *The Hound of the Baskervilles* (black dogs).

COMMANDO LIBRARIANS

Every town and village has a local legend, a ghost, a pirate, a cowboy, a hero... Create a PowerPoint presentation with photos then and now from the local history resources and headlines from newspapers. Invite living history speakers who can bring a character alive to the audience. Display books about the legend.

TIME-LIFE SERIES

Time-Life Books published a twenty-one volume series titled *The Enchanted World*. The titles in this series deal with numerous legends from a variety of cultures and include *Ghosts* (1984), *Dragons* (1984), *Fabled Lands* (1986), *Wizards and Witches* (1984), etc. See the whole list in the "Enchanted World Series" article on Wikipedia (*http://en.wikipedia.org/wiki/Enchanted_World_Series*).

Time-Life Books also published a thirty-three volume series called *Mysteries of the Unknown*. This series focused on the paranormal, examining both the science and folklore behind such things as *Alien Encounters*, *Mystic Places*, and *Mysterious Creatures*. See the whole list titles in the "Mysteries of the Unknown" article on *Wikipedia* (*http://en.wikipedia.org/wiki/Mysteries_of_the_Unknown*).

Though no longer in print, you may be able to find these books in your local library or you may purchase them online from a variety of vendors.

COMMANDO LIBRARIANS

Students can create their visions of Bigfoot or aliens in a fun craft program for an exciting display. Limit the size of their creations to fit in your display area. Use materials around the library: cardboard, paper, packing materials, tape, and glue; add leftover craft materials to add hair, feathers, or scales; paints and markers can add color. Create tent cards for students to write the title of art piece, name of artist, and the source of inspiration.

MORE LEGENDARY CREATURES

- Stephen Krensky's *Monster Chronicles* series (Lerner)

  - *Bigfoot*, 2007.
  - *The Bogeyman*, 2008.
  - *Creatures from the Deep*, 2008.
  - *Dragons*, 2007.
  - *Frankenstein*, 2007.
  - *Ghosts*, 2008.
  - *The Mummy*, 2007.
  - *Vampires*, 2007.
  - *Watchers in the Woods*, 2008.
  - *Werewolves*, 2007.
  - *Zombies*, 2008.

- *When the Chenoo Howls: Native American Tales of Terror* by Joseph and James Bruchac (Walker, 1998)
- *Creatures of the Night* BBC Wildvision for DK Vision and The Discovery Channel, 1998.
- The History Channel's *MonsterQuest* minisite. *http://www.history.com/monsterquest*
- A & E's Biography *Boo-ography* page. *http://www.biography.com/boo-ography*

Folktales

While I find that most of my students don't mind the idea of reading myths and legends too much, I often hear a lot of groans when I mention that we'll be studying folktales (often called fairy tales, though many do not include fairies). That's when I explain that they don't know the *real* versions of the folktales; they only know the sanitized, Disney-ized versions written for children, which include corny songs and happy endings. It is important at this point to explain to students that the idea of childhood as we know it (that children should enjoy a responsibility-free youth and be protected from the harsh realities of the world) is a relatively new idea—in fact it is just over one hundred years old. Prior to that time, children were simply viewed as small adults and the stories that were told in their presence were not altered in any way from the stories that would be told to a strictly adult audience. It's only after I explain this and tell them that the original versions of the folktales were dark and gory that my students actually start to think that studying folktales might be semi-interesting.

They are generally still dubious, though, so I read to them the Grimm brothers' story "Aschenputtel," which couldn't be farther from the Disney version of "Cinderella" that they remember from their childhoods. While this version of the story does still feature a wicked stepmother and cruel stepsisters, there is no horse-drawn, magical carriage, and Aschenputtel's gowns and shoes come from the birds that perch on the tree growing at her mother's grave, rather than from a fairy godmother. Aschenputtel attends the ball three times, each time in a dress more splendid than the last, and on the third night the prince spreads the palace steps with tar so that she cannot escape him. When the prince comes to Aschenputtel's house with the golden slipper, the stepmother orders one step-sister to cut off her toe and the other to cut off her heel in order to fit into the shoe. Both times the prince realizes he has been duped when, thanks to the song of two pigeons, he discovers blood in the shoe. He then returns to the house to find the shoe's true owner. Finally, on Aschenputtel's wedding day, these same pigeons return to peck out the eyes of the wicked step-sisters. That gets their attention. There is justice in this story; there is a happy ending for the people who deserve it and punishment is served swiftly and harshly to those who deserve it. This is typical in folktales. (This version of "Aschenputtel" is in one of my favorite folktale collections, *Grimm's Grimmest*, which was edited by Marisa Bulzone. This collection features nineteen of the Grimm brothers' most disturbing and violent folktales, including my favorite "The Juniper Tree," and has been a big hit in my classroom with some of the most reluctant readers.)

Let's backtrack for more background on folktales. Folktales are different from legends in that they are set in an unspecified time and place (hence the beginnings "Once upon a time" or "Long ago and far away"), and feature characters who have generic names (like Jack, in the English or Appalachian folktales) or names that describe them (like Snow White or Sleeping Beauty). Unlike myths, these stories are meant to stand alone—the reader doesn't have to know the tale of "Snow White" in order to understand the story of "Sleeping Beauty," and the Jack from "Jack and Jill" is not the same Jack from "Jack and the Beanstalk." The youngest character (usually of three siblings) is often most pure of heart and ends up saving the day or winning the prize at the end of the story. As mentioned above, justice is served in folktales, fre-

quently in a quick and harsh manner to those who most deserve it, which serves to teach or convey the values of the society. The audience for these stories was the common folk, who were often illiterate and didn't have the means to purchase books, so these stories were *told*, not read. One of the most important characteristics of a folktale is that there may be many variations (or variants) of the same story. When a story is transmitted orally, rather than being written down, the story undergoes many changes; each storyteller puts his or her own spin on a story, so it's possible that several versions of a story could be circulating in one area at any given time. Once students have been reintroduced to folktales, the lessons can then segue into several different approaches to studying folktale variants or retellings.

One type of folktale retelling involves examining variants of the same tale. I feel that this approach lends the most academic credibility to the study of folktales in the high school classroom. Though the stories were passed orally, authors, folklorists, and historians eventually began to collect and record folktales in an effort to preserve the local heritage and stories of the common people, or the folk. Some of the more famous of these collections were compiled by Charles Perrault (who collected French tales in the late 1600s and coined the term "Mother Goose"), Jacob and Wilhelm Grimm (who collected German tales in the early 1800s), Joseph Jacobs (who collected British folktales in the early 1800s), and Andrew Lang (who collected

British folktales in the late 1800s). Once the stories were written down, other scholars were able to examine and study them.

Two such scholars, Anti Aarne and Stith Thompson, created an index that grouped folktales together based on five tale types. Each group is broken down into numbered subcategories, making it easier to locate and identify a certain type of tale. For example, to study and compare cumulative tales (like "The Old Woman and Her Pig" or "The House that Jack Built"), go to Group IV (Formula Tales), and look for tale numbers 2000-2199. It's incredibly well-organized. D.L. Ashliman of the University of Pittsburgh has created a website titled *Folktexts: A Library of Folktales, Folklore, Fairy Tales, and Mythology* (*http://www.pitt. edu/~dash/folktexts.html*) that is organized alphabetically and also references the Aarne-Thompson tale type numbering system. This site provides a wide variety of stories from all around the globe.

Stith Thompson was a busy guy. In addition to his work with Anti Aarne, he also created an index that examines and classifies twenty-three types of motifs that appear in all types of traditional literature (including folktales, myths, and legends). A motif is an element that appears in many different types of tales, such as R261.1, being pursued by a rolling head (as was seen in "A Meeting on the Road Home" mentioned earlier). This classification system allows searches to find stories that share similar motifs. Visit the website *S. Thompson. Motif-index of Folk-literature: A Classification of Narrative Elements in Folktales, Ballads, Myths, Fables, Mediaeval Romances, Exempla, Fabliaux, Jest-books, and Local Legends* (*http://www.ruthenia.ru/folklore/thompson/index.htm*) to see an online version of the index. In order to help my students better understand motifs, we play a game titled Folktale Motif Bingo, which I'll discuss in depth in Chapter 6.

Many types of folktale retellings have become particularly popular in young adult literature. This generally involves retelling the original tale in the much longer format of the novel.

YA LIT RETELLINGS OF FOLKTALES

Gail Carson Levine:
- *Ella Enchanted* (Cinderella) (Scholastic, 1997)
- *The Fairy's Return* (The Golden Goose) (HarperCollins, 2002)
- *For Biddle's Sake* (Puddocky) (HarperCollins, 2002)
- *Princess Sonora and the Long Sleep* (Sleeping Beauty) (HarperCollins, 1999)
- *The Princess Test* (The Princess and the Pea) (HarperCollins, 1999)

Robin McKinley:
- *Beauty: A Retelling of the Story of Beauty and the Beast* (Beauty and the Beast) (Harper Trophy, 1978)
- *Rose Daughter* (Beauty and the Beast) (Greenwillow, 1997)
- *Spindle's End* (Sleeping Beauty) (G.P. Putnam's Sons, 2009)

Donna Jo Napoli:
- *Bound* (Cinderella) (Atheneum, 2004)
- *Breath* (The Pied Piper) (Atheneum, 2003)
- with Richard Tchen *Spinners* (Rumplestiltskin) (Dutton, 1999)
- *Zel* (Rapunzel) (Dutton, 1996)

ONCE UPON A TIME SERIES
PUBLISHED BY SIMON PULSE

Cameron Dokey:
- *The Storyteller's Daughter* (*The Arabian Nights*) (2002)
- *Beauty Sleep* (Sleeping Beauty) (2002)
- *Sunlight and Shadow* (The Magic Flute) (2004)
- *Golden* (Rapunzel) (2006)
- *Before Midnight* (Cinderella) (2007)
- *Belle* (Beauty and the Beast) (2008)
- *Wild Orchid* (The Ballad of Mulan) (2009)
- *Winter's Child* (The Snow Queen) (2009)
- *The World Above* (Jack and the Beanstalk) (2010)

Nancy Holder:
- *Spirited* (*The Last of the Mohicans* and Beauty and the Beast) (2004)
- *The Rose Bride* (The White and the Black Bride) (2007)

Debbie Vigue:
- *Midnight Pearls* (The Little Mermaid) (2006)
- *Scarlet Moon* (Little Red Riding Hood) (2004)
- *Violet Eyes* (The Princess and the Pea) (2010)

Suzanne Weyn:
- *Water Song* (The Frog Prince) (2006)
- *The Crimson Thread* (Rumpletstiltskin) 2008)
- *The Diamond Secret* (*Anastasia*) (2009)

Tracy Weyn:
- *Snow* (Snow White) (2003)

These novels begin with the familiar folk story and flesh it out. In some of the novels, like the ones from Simon Pulse's Once Upon a Time series, the authors stick fairly close to the original tale, while giving more insight into the characters and their lives. In some cases, authors create a new and/or updated story loosely based on the framework of a familiar tale, like Elizabeth Bunce's *A Curse Dark as Gold* (Rumplestiltskin), Sarah Beth Durst's *Ice* (East O' the Sun, West O' the Moon), Jane Yolen and Adam Stemple's *Pay the Piper: A Rock 'N' Roll Fairy Tale* (The Pied Piper), or Malinda Lo's *Ash* (Cinderella). In other stories, like *Fairest of All: A Tale of the Wicked Queen* by Serena Valentino, *Beast* by Donna Jo Napoli and *Beastly* by Alex Flinn, and *Mirra, Mirror* by Mette Ivie Harrison, tales are retold from the points-of-view of the villain or of secondary characters like Snow White's wicked stepmother, the beast from "Beauty and the Beast," and the witch from the wicked queen's mirror, respectively. In some cases, authors take familiar characters from fairytales and put them into new situations, like Michael Buckley's Sisters Grimm series, *A Tale Dark and Grimm* by Adam Gidwitz, and *Rapunzel's Revenge* by Shannon and Dean Hale.

Another type of folktale retelling is the humorous or "twisted" retelling. These are probably the most fun for teens because the stories they know from childhood often get "flipped." This is a great way to discuss and teach point-of-view, voice, tone, and post-modernism (see Chapter 3 for more on this). Probably the most well-known example is Jon Scieszka and Lane Smith's picture book *The True Story of the Three Little Pigs*, in which Alexander T. Wolf finally gets a chance to tell his side of the story. In the same vein, this duo teamed up for Caldecott Honor book *The Stinky Cheese Man and Other Fairly Stupid Tales,* and Scieszka also wrote *The Frog Prince, Continued.* In *Roald Dahl's Revolting Rhymes,* Dahl retells the folktales "Cinderella," "Jack and the Beanstalk," "Snow-White and the Seven Dwarfs," "Goldilocks and the Three Bears," "Little Red Riding Hood and the Wolf" (my personal favorite), and "The Three Little Pigs" in poem form with some very disturbing and funny twists. For example, "Goldilocks and the Three Bears" is told from the point-of-view of the bears who have had their porridge eaten, chairs broken, and house ransacked by a "nosy thieving little louse," (p. 28) and in "Little Red Riding Hood and the Wolf," when the wolf tries to eat Little Red Riding Hood:

> The small girl smiles. One eyelid flickers
> She whips a pistol from her knickers.
> She aims it at the creature's head,
> And bang bang bang, she shoots him dead. (p. 38)

If fractured fairy tales á la Rocky and Bullwinkle are preferred, they are available in book form (*Fractured Fairy Tales* by A.J. Jacobs) or on DVD (*The Best of Fractured Fairy Tales, Volume 1*). In *Stoopnagle's Tale Is Twisted: Spoonerisms Run Amok*, Keen James tells the stories in spoonerism form, like "Beeping Sleauty" and "Prinderella and the Since." These are really difficult to read aloud, so practice them ahead of time or, better yet, give them to students and have them try to read the stories aloud. In the mid-nineties, when political correctness was still a fairly new idea, James Finn Garner published *Politically Correct Bedtime Stories: Modern Tales for Our Life Times.* These stories, referring to women as "womyn" and dwarves as "height challenged," are a hoot! Pulitzer Prize winning graphic novelist Art Spiegelman and his wife, Francoise Mouly, edited *Little Lit: Folklore and Fairy Tale Funnies*, featuring folktales retold and illustrated by well-known graphic novelists and illustrators, such as "The Sleeping Beauty" by Daniel Clowes and "Jack and the Beanstalk" by David Macauley. Any of these types of retellings can become fun and creative writing assignments; students can write their own fractured or politically correct fairy tales, create a comic book version of a classic tale, write spoonerisms, or retell a folktale from a secondary character's point of view.

Ballads and Narrative Poetry

At one time in their lives, children loved poetry. Bring in a copy of Shel Silverstein's *Where the Sidewalk Ends* and watch how excited students get. Unfortunately, thanks to the way we traditionally teach poetry in schools, this love of words, rhythm, and rhyme often disappears by the time most teens reach high school.

One reason for this downward slide is that, in childhood poems are read simply for enjoyment and pleasure, but by the time teens reach high school, poems have become an alien entity that must be dissected and need a teacher to explain what they "really mean."

I have found that the best way to reintroduce teens to poetry is to focus on ballads and narrative poems. The structure of the ballad is virtually unchanged since traveling bards and minstrels roamed the countryside stopping at gathering halls to tell the tales of heroes, ghosts, love, betrayal, shipwrecks, monsters, demons, fairies, etc. These story poems have a beginning, middle, and end; often have a strong rhythm and rhyme; have repetitive lines or stanzas; and paint a visual picture of the action unfolding (see Medieval Ballads in the British Literature Arsenal). While ballads do employ symbolism, metaphor, simile, alliteration, and onomatopoeia, it is not necessary to understand these literary elements in order to figure out what is happening in the poem. Ballads don't require anything from the reader but imagination. They are fun and easy to understand. Then, if the reader is compelled go back to look for literary elements, these poems are

> ### COMMANDO LIBRARIANS
>
> April is National Poetry month. Create a list or a bulletin board highlighting poems, poets, and novels-in-verse that appeal to teens. Include everything from narrative poems to nonsense poems, as well as poets like Edgar Allan Poe, Sylvia Plath, and Lord Byron who had interesting and controversial lives. Check out the website *Neurotic Poets* (*http://www.neuroticpoets.com*).

> ### FAVORITE POEM PROJECT
>
> Show Favorite Poem Videos from the website *Favorite Poem Project* (*http://www.favoritepoem. org*). Then have students create their own Favorite Poem videos. Allow students to vote for the ten best videos and post the winners on your class/ school website. Offer prizes, if available.

ripe with them. A fantastic resource for ballads is Lesley Nelson-Burns' (aka The Contemplator) website *Folk Music of England, Scotland, Ireland, Wales, and America: Tunes, Lyrics, Information, Historical Background and Tune Related Links* (*http://www.contemplator.com/folk.html*). Not only the text to numerous ballads and sea songs are available here, but also the history of each ballad, a midi file to listen to the music that would accompany the ballad, and variants of the ballads. The ballads can be sorted by country or theme, depending on what is being taught.

Because of the popularity of the story poem, there are some great collections out there to choose from. Kevin Crossley-Holland has edited a fantastic book of illustrated, narrative poems titled *Once Upon a Poem: Favorite Poems That Tell Stories*. This collection includes well-known poems "The Highwayman" by Alfred Noyes, "The Cremation of Sam Magee" by Robert Service, and "Jabberwocky" by Lewis Carroll, which all play particularly well to a high-school-aged audience. After all, who can resist the "landlord's black-eyed daughter," Bess, who shoots herself in order to warn her outlaw lover of the presence of the Redcoats, or Sam Magee's cremation in the boiler of the ice-bound ship, the Alice May, or the brilliant, nonsense wordplay describing a young boy beheading a horrifying creature? William Cole has also edited *The Poet's Tales: A New Book of Story Poems*, which features one hundred fifty narrative poems categorized by the themes: Strange and Mysterious; Characters and Individualists; Birds, Beasts, and Bugs; Adventures and Disasters; Love Stories; Fighting Men; At Sea; and Odd and Funny. *The Oxford Book of Story Poems* is also illustrated *and* features sixty-six modern and classic story poems with a theme index in the back.

Because of the strong visual imagery, narrative poems and ballads lend themselves extremely well to being illustrated. As mentioned in Chapter 3, though written for adults, many longer narrative poems were originally published as illustrated works. Edgar Allan Poe's *The Raven* was illustrated by John Tenniel, Gustave Dore, and Edouard Manet. Samuel Taylor Coleridge's *The Rime of the Ancient Mariner* was also illustrated by Dore. John Milton's *Paradise Lost* was illustrated by both Dore and William Blake. In the case of these more difficult narrative poems, illustrations can help students visualize the action and follow the plot.

VISIONS OF POETRY SERIES
PUBLISHED BY KIDS CAN PRESS, LTD.

- *Lady of Shalott* by Alfred Tennyson and Genevieve Cote, 2005.
- *The Highwayman* by Alfred Noyes and Murray Kimber, 2005.
- *Casey at the Bat* by Ernest Thayer and Joe Morse, 2006.
- *The Owl and the Pussycat* by Edward Lear and Stephane Jorish, 2007.
- *Jabberwocky* by Lewis Carroll and Stephane Jorish, 2004.
- *The Raven* by Edgar Allan Poe and Ryan Price, 2006.
- *My Letter to the World and Other Poems* by Emily Dickinson and Isabelle Arsenault, 2008.

Also by Kids Can Press:
- *The Cremation of Sam Magee* by Robert Service and Ted Harrison, 1983.

Picture book illustrators have also followed in this tradition by adapting classic poems into picture books. Susan Jeffers' versions of Longfellow's *Hiawatha* or Frost's *Stopping by Woods on a Snowy Evening*, Ted Rand's version of Longfellow's *Paul Revere's Ride*, Christopher Bing's version of Longfellow's *The Midnight Ride of Paul Revere*, and George Gershinowitz's version of Christina Rossetti's *Goblin Market* are all beautifully illustrated. There are also several illustrated versions of Lewis Carroll's "Jabberwocky." The Visions of Poetry series published by Kids Can Press also provides illustrated versions of a number of famous narrative poems. In *The Book of Ballads*, Charles Vess teams with other notable writers and illustrators, like Neil Gaiman, Jane Yolen, and Charles de Lint, to present medieval ballads in a graphic novel format. Some of the ballads in this book are typical lit anthology favorites: "Barbara Allen," "Thomas the Rhymer," "Tam-Lin," "The Daemon Lover," and "The Great Silkie of Sule Skerry." Each graphic rendering is followed by the text of the ballad. There is also a discography in the back of the book to play the ballads for the students.

ADAPTATIONS OF LEWIS CARROLL'S "JABBERWOCKY"

- "Alice in Wonderland (1983)-Jabberwocky" recited by Kate Burton *http://www.youtube.com/watch?v=7rpCUZX Luck&feature=PlayList&p=A02304B271D243CB&index=27*
- *Jabberwocky* illustrated by Kate Buckley (A. Whitman, 1985)
- Jabberwocky and More Nonsense illustrated by Simms Taback (Dell, 1964)
- *Jabberwocky: From Through the Looking Glass* illustrated by Graeme Base (Harry N. Abrams, 1989)
- *Jabberwocky* illustrated by Stephane Jorish (Kids Can Press, 2004)
- *Jabberwocky* illustrated by Christopher Myers (Hyperion, 2007)
- *Jabberwocky* illustrated by Joel Stewart (Candlewick, 2003)
- *Lewis Carroll's Jabberwocky: A Book of Brillig Dioramas* illustrated by Graeme Base (Harry N. Abrams, 1996)
- "Jabberwocky" from Once Upon a Poem: Favorite Poems that Tell Stories edited by Kevin Crossley-Holland (Scholastic, 2004)

References

Ashliman, D.L. *Folktexts: A Library of Folktales, Folklore, Fairy Tales, and Mythology.* © 1996-2010. *http://www.pitt.edu/~dash/folktexts.html*

The Best of Fractured Fairy Tales, Volume 1. Classic Media: 2005.

Bing, Christopher. *The Midnight Ride of Paul Revere.* Handprint, 2001.

Buckley, Michael. Sisters Grimm series. (Amulet)

———. *The Everafter War* (2009)

———. *The Fairy Tale Detectives* (2005)

———. *The Inside Story* (2010)

———. *Magic and Misdemeanors* (2007)

———. *Once Upon a Crime* (2007)

———. *The Problem Child* (2006)

———. *Tales from the Hood* (2008)

———. *The Unusual Suspects* (2005)

Bulzone, Marisa, ed. *Grimm's Grimmest.* Chronicle, 1997.

Bunce, Elizabeth. *A Curse Dark as Gold.* Arthur A. Levine, 2008.

Campbell, Joseph. *The Hero With a Thousand Faces.* New World Library, 2008.

Cole, William, ed. *The Poet's Tales: A New Book of Story Poems.* The World Publishing, 1971.

Crossley-Holland, Kevin, ed. *Once Upon a Poem: Favorite Poems That Tell Stories*. Scholastic, 2004.

Dahl, Roald. *Roald Dahl's Revolting Rhymes*. Puffin, 1982.

Durst, Sarah Beth. *Ice*. Margaret K. McElderry, 2009.

Flinn, Alex. *Beastly*. HarperTeen, 2007.

Garner, James Finn. *Politically Correct Bedtime Stories: Modern Tales for Our Life Times*. Maxmillan, 1994.

Gershinowitz, George and Christina Rossetti. *Goblin Market*. David R. Godine, 1981.

Gidwitz, Adam. *A Tale Dark and Grimm.* Dutton, 2010.

Gravett, Christopher. *Knight.* Dorling Kindersley, 1993.

Hale, Shannon and Dean Hale. *Rapunzel's Revenge*. Bloomsbury, 2008.

Harrison, Mette Ivie. *Mirra, Mirror*. Penguin Young Readers, 2004.

Harrison, Michael and Christopher Stuart-Clark, ed. *The Oxford Book of Story Poems*. Oxford University Press, 1990.

Jacobs, A.J. *Fractured Fairy Tales*. Bantam, 1999.

James, Keen. *Stoopnagle's Tale Is Twisted: Spoonerisms Run Amok*. Stone and Scott, 2000.

Jeffers, Susan and Henry Wadsworth Longfellow. Hiawatha, 1983.

Jeffers Susan and Robert Frost. *Stopping by Woods on a Snowy Evening*. Dutton's Children's Books, 1978.

Kerven. Rosalind. *King Arthur*. DK Publishing, 1998.

Langley, Andrew. *Medieval Life.* Dorling Kindersley, 1996.

Lo, Malinda. *Ash*. Little, Brown, 2009.

"A Meeting on the Road Home." *Ghosts.* Time Life, 1984.

Monty Python and the Holy Grail. Columbia TriStar Home Video, 2001.

Napoli, Donna Jo. *Beast*. Simon Pulse, 2000.

Nelson-Burns, Lesley. *Folk Music of England, Scotland, Ireland, Wales, and America: Tunes, Lyrics, Information, Historical Background and Tune Related Links*. Site created: March 1996. *http://www.contemplator.com/folk.html*

Petrich, Loren. *Mythic Heroes. http://homepage.mac.com/lpetrich/www/writings/Mythic_Hero.html*

Raglan, FitzRoy Richard Somerset. *The Hero: A Study in Tradition, Myth, and Drama*. Greenwood Press, 1956.

Rand, Ted and Henry Wadsworth Longfellow. *Paul Revere's Ride*. Dutton, 1990.

Randall, Daniel and Ronne. *Tales of King Arthur*. Armadillo Books, 2002.

Scieszka, Jon. *The Frog Prince, Continued.* Viking, 1991.

Scieszka, Jon and Lane Smith. *The True Story of the Three Little Pigs.* Viking Kestrel, 1989.

———. *The Stinky Cheese Man and Other Fairly Stupid Tales.* Viking, 1992.

Silverstein, Shel. *Where the Sidewalk Ends.* HarperCollins, 1974.

Spiegelman, Art and Francoise Mouly, eds. *Little Lit: Folklore and Fairy Tale Funnies.* RAW Junior, 2000.

"S. Thompson. Motif-index of Folk-literature : A Classification of Narrative Elements in Folktales, Ballads, Myths, Fables, Mediaeval Romances, Exempla, Fabliaux, Jest-books, and Local Legends." Revised and enlarged edition. Bloomington: Indiana University Press, 1955-1958. *http://www.ruthenia.ru/folklore/thompson/index.htm*

Valentino, Serena. *Fairest of All: A Tale of the Wicked Queen.* Disney, 2009.

Vess, Charles. *The Book of Ballads.* Green Man, 2004.

Yolen, Jane and Adam Stemple. *Pay the Piper: A Rock 'N' Roll Fairytale.* T. Doherty, 2005.

PART 2

COMMANDO CLASSICS

The O.C. (Original Classics): Mythology and Folklore

Nothing is more "classic" than traditional literature. In Chapter 5 we defined traditional literature (see the Traditional Literature Comparison Chart) and talked about ways to integrate these stories into any literature class. Traditional literature is invaluable to us for a variety of reasons. It shows us where we came from, and in many ways it also shows us where we are going. Its plot lines and archetypes appear in many stories from classic literature and are still seen in stories that we tell today. Maybe most important, it demonstrates how *all* humans beings are connected by story.

I focus on all of these ideas when I teach world literature (which should probably be renamed comparative mythology and folklore), but the one I believe is most important is the final one. For me, this class is all about drawing connections. Teenagers are at a point developmentally where they are starting to look at the world differently—they are willing to question what they have learned from their parents and society, and they are struggling with and exploring how they are going to fit into the world as adults. If we can get students to make connections between the literatures of different groups of people, then they can start to see that, though people may live in different times and/or places, their hopes, fears, and dreams are very similar. If we can help them make that connection, then we might be able to help them learn to be better global citizens by making them more aware (and maybe even more accepting) of other people's beliefs.

Though it could easily be done, this isn't a class that I teach as a full-on thematic class. I do introductory sections or mini-units on topics like creation stories, flood stories, end of the world stories, heroes, folktales, and legends (for more background on folktales and legends, see Chapter 5 and the Types of Folktales handout in the World Mythology and Folklore Arsenal), in which students get an overview and some background on these different types of tales, but I also like to "tour the world" and focus on different sections of the world for several weeks at a time. My students need this sort of a mixture to keep things from getting too boring. So, we'll do a mini-unit on hero stories, for example, in which we talk about the characteristics of a hero using Lord Raglan's twenty-two archetypal traits, and examine Joseph Campbell's hero's journey and then we'll look at hero stories from each culture when we do our individual units on Africa, Asia, Oceania, Europe, and South America.

In the Beginning ...

In this class the first thing we do is study creation stories from various cultures because I want students to look beyond the surface differences to see the deeper connections and similarities between people from different cultures. Whenever we begin a new unit of instruction, I always begin with that culture's mythology, especially the creation myth. Throughout the year, I continually try to reinforce the difference between the slang word *myth*, which we often use in our culture today to suggest that something *isn't* true, and the word *mythology*, which we use to talk about stories that *are* believed to be true and are sacred to a culture.

We start with the Mythology Introduction handout and the Creation Myths Outline (both of which can be found in the World Mythology and Folklore Arsenal). The Mythology Introduction gives students the idea of the big questions addressed by a culture's myths, provides a definition of *mythology*, and gives brief descriptions of five types of myths (including creation myths). The Creation Myths Outline focuses specifically on two types of creation myths: cosmogonies (which explain how the world and universe are created) and myths of origin (which explain where different features and creatures come from after the creation of the world has taken place). We often find both of these types of stories within a culture's main creation story.

Let's take a look at the outline together. As I get older, the world seems to get smaller, so what interests me most as I look through the outline is the fact that hundreds and hundreds of cosmogonies can generally be distilled down into a handful of features and that each of those features can be broken down into relatively few smaller processes. I want my students to be amazed by this, too, but I prefer to *show* them, rather than tell them, so that they can discover the similarities on their own. The tool I use for this is the Creation Myth Comparison Chart (see World Mythology and Folklore Arsenal). I want to show them how this works with a story that is familiar to them, so we begin by reading the Judeo-Christian creation story from the book of Genesis (Chapters 1 through 3) from the *Bible* (*http://crab.rutgers.edu/~goertzel/genesis.htm*).

I know that some readers will wonder if teachers are allowed to use a *Bible* story in class. Teachers should not preach their personal religious beliefs to students, but they can study religion from a comparative standpoint as a way of examining the beliefs, behavior, and literature of a culture. This is one of those areas, though, where it is necessary to cover all bases well. First, don't assume that everyone in the class is a Christian. I live in an area where most teens who do practice a religion are Christians, but, if I lived in a more diverse area, I would take care to select the creation story(ies) that would be most familiar to my students. Second, be sure to remind students that they are expected to be respectful of other people's beliefs. I'll never forget Larry's reaction to the idea of the cosmic egg when we read the Chinese creation story several years ago: "Cosmic egg? Ha!" I explained to him that people from other cultures might find the idea of an entire world being created in seven days hard to believe, but that it doesn't make it wrong, it just makes it unfamiliar.

Now, back to the Judeo-Christian creation story. We read the story together as a group, and, after we've read through it the first time, we use the Creation Myths Outline to go back through the story and to fill in the Creation Myth Comparison Chart. A couple of tips: 1) Not all creation stories follow the outline in order, so be sure to prep students for the fact that they may not be filling in the boxes from left to right every time; 2) I usually have my students fill in the squares using the terminology from the outline, but they can provide the actual quotations from the text that show how they reached their conclusions.

COMPARING CREATION MYTHS (Sample Answer Key)

Place of Origin	Creator	Vague or Specific Creator?	Image of Pre-creation	World Creation Process	Creator of Humans	Human Creation Process
Judeo-Christian	God	Specific	Nothing; Darkness; Primeval sea	Ordered by creator	God	In the image of God; From part of the earth -- dust
Mayan	Tepeu, the Maker & Gucumatz, the feathered one	Specific	Darkness	Supreme Being orders creation	Tepeu & Gucumatz	From part of the earth: clay, wood, then corn
Incan	Pachacamac, the Sun & Pachamama, the moon	Specific	Nothing; Darkness	Ordered or molded by creator	Pachacama	From part of the earth -- stone
Egyptian	Atum, then Shu, god of the air & Tefnut, goddess of mist and moisture	Specific	Nu -- Darkness; Chaos	Separation of elements -- light and dark; World parent -- Geb and Nut	Atum	Part of god -- tears
Babylonian	Marduk, the sun	Specific	Primeval Sea -- sweet water and salt water	Sacrifice of a primal being -- serpent	Marduk	?? From bones of dead monsters & flesh
Maori	Tane, god of the forest	Specific	Only Rangi, father sky, & Papa, earth goddess	World parent	Tane	?? -- Created Hine, the first woman & mated with her
Inuit	Raven	Specific	?? Not given ??	?? Not given ??	Raven	From part of the earth -- pea-pod
Yoruba	Obatala	Specific	Sky above & water below	Molds creation by hand	Obatala	From part of the earth -- clay
Chinese	Pan- Gu	Specific	Egg containing chaos -- opposites	World egg; Creator molds creation by hand; Sacrifice of primal being -- god's body	Nuwa	From part of the earth -- clay
Norse	Odin and other gods	Specific	Ginnugagap, great emptiness	Sacrifice of a primal being -- giant	Odin	From part of the earth -- ash & elm trees

The creator in this story is God and, because the deity is named, this is an example of II.A.2 "Specific Creator" (this will be the case in most stories—I can't think of one we've looked at over the years that has had a vague creator). Moving to the next box on the chart, we consider the image of pre-creation. In Genesis Chapter 1, verses 1-2 it says,

> ^{1:1}In the beginning God created the heavens and the earth. ^{1:2}Now the earth was formless and empty. Darkness was on the surface of the deep. God's Spirit was hovering over the surface of the waters.

There are two different paths that can be taken here. On one hand, it may be argued that, since the book starts with the creation of the heavens and the earth, we don't know what existed *before* their creation. In this case students could put N/A or "Not given" into the chart. On the other hand, Chapter 1, verse 2 can be used to fill in the chart with II.C. 1, 3, and 5 "Void/Nothingness," "Primeval Sea," and "Darkness," respectively. This is what I've used in my answer key because it fits best with the Creation Myths Outline and will make the most sense as we compare this particular story with other creation stories.

Then, we look at the way in which the creation took place. This story doesn't tell us how the heavens and the earth were created. It does, however, tell us how everything else (from day to night to the features of the earth to animals to humans) was created. Chapter 1, verse 3 says,

> ^{1:3}God said, "Let there be light," and there was light.

Everything that follows (from Chapter 1, verse 3 to Chapter 1, verse 27) is created in this way, so this is an example of I.D.1 "Supreme Being orders creation and it is done." That means that the creator of humans is also God. Finally, we look at the way in which humans were created. Chapter 1, verse 27 says,

> ^{1:27}God created man in his own image. In God's image he created him; male and female he created them.

This is an example of II.A.4 "Humans made in the image of the god(s)." Reading further into Chapters 2 and 3, we read Chapter 2, verse 7,

> ^{2:7}Yahweh God formed man from the dust of the ground, and breathed into his nostrils the breath of life; and man became a living soul.

This is an example of II.A.1 "Humans born from earth or part of the earth," as well. Though we do also get the explanation for the creation of suffering in these first three chapters (II.B.1.a "an instruction, a sin, and the consequence"), the chart doesn't have a space for the creation of suffering because many of the other creation stories we look at don't describe it or it occurs in a different story (as in the Greek myth of Pandora, for example).

Once the class has walked through one example, there are a few ways to proceed, depending on how well the students seem to understand the process: read through several more creation stories as a group and fill in the chart together (which is what I do); group students and give them several creation stories to chart; give each student copies of two to four different stories and have them chart them individually; or give students the assignment to find two to four more creation stories on their own and chart those stories as homework. If the charts are not completed together as a class, I would recommend having students report their findings back to the larger group; students need the chance to see several different creation stories side-by-side in order to highlight the significant similarities between the stories. They *will* see them. I still remember doing this the first time and hearing Sarah say, "Oh, they're all pretty much the same." Though it's the reaction I was going for, I wasn't sure they understood it until that very moment.

CREATION STORIES

Websites

These sites will also be helpful resources for other types of myths.

- *The Big Myth.* © Distant Train 2007 *http://mythicjourneys.org/bigmyth/*
- *Folklore and Mythology Electronic Texts.* © D.L. Ashliman, University of Pittsburgh, 1996-2011 *http://www.pitt.edu/~dash/folktexts.html*
- *Resources for Myths Around the World* at Costume SuperCenter. © *CostumeSuperCenter.com http://www.costumesupercenter.com/csc_inc/html/static/btarticles/resourcesformythsaroundtheworld.html*

Books

- *Beginnings* compiled by Penelope Farmer (Atheneum, 1979)
- *In the Beginning: Creation Stories from Around the World* by Virginia Hamilton (Harcourt Brace Jovanovich, 1988)
- *Primal Myths: Creation Myths Around the World* by Barbara C. Sproul (HarperCollins, 1991)

Once students start to see the connections between these stories, challenge them to think about this question, "How do we explain the fact that people who lived at different times and in different places around the globe (often with very little interaction or travel between cultures) have stories that are so similar?" Possible explanations are that stories are passed through trade and migration. This connection seems obvious when cultures are fairly close to one another geographically, as with the world parent found in Babylonian, Greek, and Egyptian cultures. But, can we explain the fact that people from areas as far apart and as geographically different as Africa, China, and the South Pacific all have stories that feature the world egg, or that the Mayan and Egyptian cultures both share the belief that humans are created from part of a god's body, or that people from Greece, North America (Iroquois), and Australia (Aborigines) all believe that the gods created suffering? This is when I introduce Carl Jung's theory of the collective unconscious and the idea of archetypes. Is it possible that we are all pre-programmed with a shared human memory? Are there certain images that every human sees and responds to in the same way, regardless of culture and era? Are there patterns in stories that are recurring, and therefore universal? This should make for interesting classroom discussion and is a topic to continue to build upon and come back to as more and more layers of stories are added.

COMMANDO LIBRARIANS

After studying a variety of creation myths, students can interpret the stories in the arts. Drawing, painting, dioramas, and sculpture lend themselves well to sharing their visions of how different cultures around the world told the story of how the world began. Use the materials at hand for an onsite project, or invite teens to enter a Creation Myths Art Contest.

MYTHOLOGY TERMS TO KNOW

Collective Unconscious, term introduced by psychiatrist Carl Jung to represent a form of the unconscious (that part of the mind containing memories and impulses of which the individual is not aware) common to mankind as a whole and originating in the inherited structure of the brain. It is distinct from the personal unconscious, which arises from the experience of the individual. According to Jung, the collective unconscious contains archetypes, or universal primordial images and ideas. *http://www.britannica.com/EBchecked/topic/125572/collective-unconscious*

Archetype, (from Greek *archetypos*, "original pattern"), in literary criticism, a primordial image, character, or pattern of circumstances that recurs throughout literature and thought consistently enough to be considered a universal concept or situation. *http://www.britannica.com/EBchecked/topic/32765/archetype*

Another topic to address as these myths are studied is the insight these stories give into a culture's geographical location and surroundings. Let's go back to Larry's reaction to the cosmic egg. An egg could seem like a strange image for the creation of the world, but think about it from the perspective of someone who lives in harmony with the natural world. If a person raises domesticated birds or spends a lot of time in the wild, he might see an animal hatch from an egg. Think of how miraculous that must seem. One minute there is an inanimate object. The next minute, it splits open and there is life. It's pretty amazing, isn't it? So, it's really not that much of a stretch to think that all life began that way. If a culture has a creation story with a world egg or cosmic egg, then that gives us a hint about their relationship with nature. Another creation process that my students tend to have trouble with is the earth diver. It may seem inconceivable that a bird or a turtle could dive to the bottom of a body of water and pull up the earth. It's not as difficult to accept if the culture that tells this story lives near water or on an island and people can watch water fowl and/or turtles dive under water and then return to the surface with food in their mouths. Once the stories are looked at this way—sort of like mysteries with clues to unlock—the different creation processes don't seem so strange after all.

Lastly, we can use these stories to study and explain a culture's relationship with nature, with animals, and with the world around them. If we go back to the Judeo-Christian creation story for an example, in Chapter 1, verses 28 and 29 it says,

> [1:28]God blessed them [man and woman]. God said to them, "Be fruitful, multiply, fill the earth, and subdue it. Have dominion over the fish of the sea, over the birds of the sky, and over every living thing that moves on the earth." [1:29]God said, "Behold, I have given you every herb yielding seed, which is on the surface of all the earth, and every tree, which bears fruit yielding seed. It will be your food."

In this story, God gives man and woman permission to subdue the earth, to hold dominion over the animals, and to use all plants that bear fruit as their food. This puts humans on a level above all other living things and gives them ownership of the earth. This is a very different viewpoint from creation stories in which animals are gods (as in Egyptian mythology) and/or gods are able to shape shift into animal form (as in Greek mythology); the earth is viewed as a "mother" who is to be respected (as with the Incan goddess Pachamama); each human has a spirit animal who acts as a guardian (as in the culture of the Plains Indians of North America); or a god or goddess protects and distributes or releases the earth's animals and/or natural resources for the use of humans (as in the Inuit stories of Sedna).

People who are raised with vastly different creation stories are therefore likely to have a very different regard for the earth and its creatures. Consider what took place during the 19th century in the United States. Land was taken from Native American tribes by a government who believed in Manifest Destiny (the idea that God wanted the United States of America, read *people of Anglo-Saxon descent*, to spread to the Pacific Ocean). Couple this with the fact that many Native American tribes did not believe in "owning" the land (it is not the type of relationship generally dictated by their creation stories and in their religions), and it proved to be a recipe for disaster for the native inhabitants and, many would also argue, for the land and natural resources of North America.

The culminating project for our study of creation myths is a writing assignment in which students create their own worlds (see the Mythology and Folklore Arsenal for the In the Beginning . . . writing assignment). I want them to have a little bit of fun with it, so I intentionally don't put a lot of strict parameters on it. If they want to make it humorous or make themselves or one of their friends the creator, I am okay with that. The purpose of the assignment is for them to show me that they understand the structure of a creation myth. Some students aren't sure what they want to write about, so I print out the images of pre-creation and creation process options and cut them into strips and students who want one can select one of each to help get them started. This will be the first of three stories set in the world they create. In the second story, they will create a cultural hero for the world, and in the third story they will destroy the world. I let students know from the start that these other two stories are coming up and will build upon the first so that they can begin to think the plot line all the way through and to foreshadow future events.

I Need a Hero . . .

As discussed in Chapter 5, a culture's heroes tell us a lot about the behaviors and strengths that are valued in that culture. This is as true today as it's ever been. If a group of people or a cultural group view athletes as heroes, for example, then it suggests that they value talent and physical prowess. If their heroes are people who are successful in the corporate world, then we can guess that they value intelligence, leadership skills, and wealth. If their heroes are philanthropists and humanitarians, then they probably value kindness and altruism. If their heroes are warriors, then they might value strength, courage, and aggressiveness.

When studying the mythic hero, there are two valuable resources that will illustrate the similarities between heroes and hero stories. In *The Hero,* Lord Raglan lists twenty-two archetypal traits often shared by mythical heroes. *The Mythic Heroes* website (*http://homepage.mac.com/lpetrich/www/writings/Mythic_Hero.html*) provides specific examples of how some famous heroes fit into Raglan's formula. In his book, *The Hero with a Thousand Faces*, Joseph Campbell outlines the archetypal hero's journey: the hero at home; the call to adventure; the tests; the helper; the land of adventure; a deathlike experience; the meeting with the goddess; the atonement with the father; stealing or winning the boon; the flight; and the return. Though not every hero undergoes all parts of the hero's journey, many of them can be recognized in ancient and modern hero stories (including J.R.R. Tolkien's *The Lord of the Rings* trilogy, J.K. Rowling's *Harry Potter* series, and George Lucas's *Star Wars* series). Take a look at both Raglan's and Campbell's lists with students and ask them to come up with examples of ancient and modern hero stories that will plug into these formulas.

LORD RAGLAN'S SCALE

1. The hero's mother is a royal virgin.
2. His father is a king and
3. often a near relative of the mother, but
4. the circumstances of his conception are unusual, and
5. he is also reputed to be the son of a god.
6. At birth an attempt is made, usually by his father or maternal grandfather, to kill him, but
7. he is spirited away, and
8. reared by foster-parents in a far country.
9. We are told nothing of his childhood, but
10. upon reaching manhood he returns or goes to his future kingdom.
11. After a victory over the king and or giant, dragon, or wild beast
12. he marries a princess, often the daughter of his predecessor and
13. becomes king.
14. For a time he reigns uneventfully and
15. prescribes laws but
16. later loses favor with the gods and or his people and
17. is driven from the throne and the city, after which
18. he meets with a mysterious death
19. often at the top of a hill.
20. His children, if any, do not succeed him.
21. His body is not buried, but nevertheless
22. he has one or more holy sepulchers.

COMMANDO LIBRARIANS

Teens hanging out in the library will enjoy having drawing paper, pencils, and how to draw superheroes books. Several titles are available, including *Superheroes and Beyond: How to Draw the Leading and Supporting Characters of Today's Comics* by Christopher Hart (Watson-Guptill, 2009), *How To Draw Superpowered Heroes Supersize* by Ben Dunn, Rod Espinosa, and Fred Perry (Antarctic, 2009).

When I introduce this mini-unit in class I ask students to name the characteristics of a hero. Many of them repeat the traits listed above—bravery, intelligence, strength, good leadership qualities, willingness to put him/herself in danger for others, kindness, etc. These are characteristics that apply to both mythic and modern cultural heroes and this reinforces the idea that human beings and their values really haven't changed much over time. Some students list the physical traits of superheroes instead like, "Wears a cape!" or "Can fly!," which isn't exactly what I'm looking for, but does provide a great opportunity to point out the relationship between comic books and classic literature. There are a lot of connections to be made here. Teach about the traits of traditional heroes using Lord Raglan's scale and Joseph Campbell's hero's journey, then ask students to point out the similarities between epic heroes and comic book superheroes. Some traditional heroes have been turned into superheroes, as we see from the Marvel Comics adaptation of Thor and the DC Comics adaptation of King Arthur. Some draw on mythology to create new characters, as we see with DC Comics' Amazonian princess, Wonder Woman. (The Heroes Text Set in the World Mythology and Folktales Arsenal has information and resources that can be adapted to discuss traditional, mythic heroes, superheroes, and/or modern day, real-life heroes.)

In addition to the twenty-two traits listed on Lord Raglan's scale, what are some other traits of a traditional hero? Heroes are usually male. When we do see stories of female heroines, they are generally recognized for qualities that we characterize as being more masculine than feminine—being brave, being skilled archers and/or huntresses, or for being warlike and aggressive, for example. Heroes are often larger-than-life—they may have superhuman strength or be exceptionally good looking or be half divine. They may use magical objects (helmets, shoes, hammers, swords, etc.) to aid and/or protect them. They are often called upon to perform a dangerous task or duty in order to serve their people. They may be or become great leaders.

When the time comes for students to create a cultural hero for the world they created for the "In the Beginning . . ." writing assignment, they are expected to frame their hero's life story around Lord Raglan's scale, but they may include other traits and characteristics, and they are permitted to make their hero a super-hero. They are also asked to select the traits that this hero will model for the people of their world (see the World Mythology and Folklore Arsenal for the I Need a Hero writing assignment).

It's the End of the World as We Know It . . .

Armageddon. The Rapture. Judgment Day. The End Times. Doomsday. The Apocalypse. Whatever term is used to describe it, human beings seem fascinated with the end of the world. Our popular culture even reflects this morbid interest/obsession in the destruction of the world. We see numerous documentaries and movies that speculate about what will happen when the world ends. There are songs about it. End of the world countdown clocks are available. There's an "encyclopedia" titled *A is for Armageddon* that lists in alphabetical order all the ways the world might end. The Center for Disease Control created a zombie apocalypse survival guide.

> **QUIRKY, WEIRD, AND MORE THAN A LITTLE DISTURBING . . .**
>
> - *A is for Armaggedon: A Catalogue of Disasters That May Culminate in the End of the World As We Know It* by Richard Horne (Square Peg, 2009)
> - *End of the World Countdown Timer. http://craziestgadgets.com/2011/06/17/end-of-the-world-countdown-timer/*
> - The Council for Disease Control and Prevention's "Social Media: Preparedness 101: Zombie Apocalypse" by Ali S. Khan, CDC Public Health Matters Blog, May 16th, 2011.

People love to imagine what they would do if they knew the exact date of the end of the world—in some cases they feel it gives them license to do things they wouldn't normally do and, in other cases, they want time to put their "affairs in order" from a moral or religious standpoint. We have a lot of questions about this. What signs will indicate that the end is near? Will the end come by way of water, fire, ice, earthquake, asteroid, plague, or zombie invasion? Who will be saved? Who will be punished? Will another, new world rise from the ashes of the old world? Or will everything and everyone simply be destroyed?

This interest is not a new phenomenon. Throughout history, people from many religions and cultures have questioned how and when the world will end and have told stories and made predictions about this occurrence (see D.L. Ashliman's *Folklore and Mythology Electronic Texts* website for a list of ten world folk stories featuring the end of the world *http://www.pitt.edu/~dash/type2033.html*). Though most of our students probably don't remember worrying that the world would end with the new millennium (many people stocked up on bottled water, canned food, batteries, and flashlights and partied like it was 1999 before Y2K arrived), many probably wondered whether the world would end with the rapture on May 21, 2011 or with the end of the Mayan calendar on December 21, 2012. With the recent spate of horrific worldwide natural disasters—tsunamis, floods, earthquakes, volcanoes, and hurricanes—it's only natural to wonder if the prophesies might actually be true.

FILMS AND VIDEOS ABOUT THE END OF THE WORLD

Feature Films

- *2012* (Sony Pictures Home Entertainment, 2010)
- *Deep Impact* (Paramount Home Video, 1998)
- *Doomsday* (Universal Home Entertainment, 2008)
- *The Day after Tomorrow* (20th Century Fox Home Entertainment, 2004)
- *The Seventh Sign* (Columbia TriStar Home Video, 1998)

Documentaries

- *Apocalypse: The Puzzle of Revelation* (A&E Home Video, 2005)
- *Doomsday 2012: The End of Days* (A&E Home Video, 2007)
- *God vs. Satan: The Final Battle* (A&E Home Video, 2009)
- *Life after People* (A&E Home Video, 2008)
- *Nostradamus: 2012: Hindsight is 20/20, Fore Sight is 2012* (A&E Home Video, 2009)

The History Channel website also has a page of short videos examining different end of the world stories, ranging from the predictions of Nostradamus to the religious beliefs of Christians and Muslims: *http://www.history. com/topics/the-end-of-the-world/videos#armageddon-judaism*

Earlier myths tell us that the world has been destroyed before, often by water. Probably the best known of these stories is the Judeo-Christian flood story of Noah and the Ark (Genesis 6:1 - 9:17). In fact, *Baby SuperMall* (*http://www.baby-supermall.com*) lists Noah's Ark as one of their top twenty popular baby nursery themes (which is sort of creepy and weird, when I think about it). The ancient Babylonians have a very similar (and some claim, older) version of a flood or deluge myth that appears in the epic of *Gilgamesh*. Read both versions and ask students to complete the Comparing Near Eastern Flood Myths worksheet (found in the World Mythology and Folklore Arsenal). B.A. Robinson's "Noah's Ark and the Flood: Comparison of the Babylonian and Noachian Flood Stories" outlines many of the similarities and differences if some guidance is needed. Once students see the similarities between the Old Testament and Babylonian flood stories, give

---

SONGS ABOUT THE END OF THE WORLD

Several songs (including the one that provided the title for this section) reference the end of the world. Ask students to find examples of some of these songs or ask a commando librarian to gather a list for you.

- "May 21st Doomsday Songs: 21 Songs for the Impending Apocalypse" by Dean Praetorius for *Huffington Post.com*, May 19, 2011. *http://www.huffingtonpost.com/2011/05/18/may-21st-doomsday-songs_n_863869.html*
- "The Top Ten Songs about the End of the World" from KROQ 106.7 Radio, May 5, 2011. *http://kroq.radio.com/2011/05/20/the-top-ten-songs-about-the-end-of-the-world/3/*
- "Thirteen Surprisingly Enjoyable Songs about the End of the World" by Rachel Maddux of *Paste Magazine.com*, July 5, 2009. *http://www.pastemagazine.com/blogs/lists/2009/07/fifteen-surprisingly-enjoyable-songs-about-the-end.html*

them the chance to look at flood stories from other cultures.

The website *Flood Legends from Around the World* examines thirty-five flood myths and charts the similarities between them. The most common elements are a warning is given; a god(s) destroys the earth by water; and select humans (and usually animals, as well) are saved by boarding an ark or vessel of some kind. Again, this can raise some interesting discussion questions. Was there one great historical flood that covered the entire earth, thereby causing nearly every culture to have a flood story? Or, do people tell flood stories because most human civilizations are built near a water source that occasionally overflows its banks? Or, do we, as humans, just instinctively understand the force and destructive power of water?

As teenagers are naturally drawn to all things morbid, they will find all of this talk about the destruction of the world very intriguing. That's why it makes sense to wrap up this unit with a creative writing assignment in which students are given free rein to destroy the world they created in their In the Beginning

> **FLOOD STORIES**
>
> - *Flood Legends from Around the World.* http://nwcreation.net/noahlegends.html
> - *Flood Stories from Around the World* by Mark Isaak © 1996-2002. http://www.talkorigins.org/faqs/flood-myths.html
> - "Noah's Ark and the Flood: Comparison of the Babylonian and Noachian flood stories" by B. A. Robinson Ontario Consultants on Religious Tolerance, ©1999-2007. http://www.religioustolerance.org/noah_com.htm
> - "Noah's Ark Found in Turkey? The Expedition Team in '99 Percent' Sure. Others, Well, Aren't," by Ker Than for *National Geographic News*, April 28, 2010. http://news.nationalgeographic.com/news/2010/04/100428-noahs-ark-found-in-turkey-science-religion-culture/

. . . writing assignment (see the World Mythology and Folklore Arsenal for the It's the End of the World as We Know It writing assignment). They will be given the opportunity to be either vengeful or merciful gods. They will choose how the destruction will occur. They will have the power to decide whether everyone will die or whether some will be given the opportunity to live . . . and isn't that just what every teenager wants?

Once Upon a Time . . .

When even a very young child hears the words, "Once upon a time . . . ," s/he understands that a story is about to begin. It doesn't take long for children to figure out how these stories work: they will generally contain a fair amount of adventure, have children (or young adults) as main characters, include some magic and/or some magical creatures, and end with the line, "And they lived happily ever after." For a very long time, folktales were the stories that people of all ages told for entertainment, and, as discussed in Chapter 5, were not the sanitized, politically correct versions with which most children are familiar today. As with myths, these stories also provide scholars with a window into the culture that originally told the tales.

In this class I use folk and fairy tales to show students how people and stories from different cultures can be connected. In order to do this, students need understand the concept of folktale motifs and variants. Even when I taught survey classes in children's literature at the college level, I felt that these concepts were difficult to adequately demonstrate (especially in what was usually only one week of class), so when it came

---

FOLKTALE TERMS TO KNOW

Folkloric Motifs: Recurring patterns of imagery or narrative that appear in folklore and folktales. Common folkloric motifs include the wise old man mentoring the young warrior, the handsome prince rescuing the damsel in distress, the "bed trick," and the "trickster tricked." *http://www.superglossary.com/Definition/Literature/Folkloric_Motifs.html*

Variant: By its very nature, folklore is traditional and its preservation depends upon custom and memory. It is, therefore, subject to all the variations that come from the attempt to repeat exactly the customary action, or to tell or perform that which has been learned from listening to someone else. Every performance of such an act and every repetition of such a tale or song displays differences from all others. *Funk and Wagnall's Standard Dictionary of Folklore, Mythology and Legend* edited by Maria Leach (Funk and Wagnall's, 1949).

---

time to teach these same concepts to fairly reluctant high school students, I wanted a way to *show* them how frequently motifs show up in different folk and fairy tales.

So, I returned to the activity that has become my "old standby" when I'm trying to trick my students into thinking that they're just having fun when they are really learning: BINGO. For Folktale Motif Bingo, I created a list of common folktale motifs (see the World Mythology and Folklore Arsenal for a blank bingo card and the list of motifs) and added to it throughout the year as my students and I noticed motifs that were missing from the original list. Students are given a blank bingo card and the motif list and are told the title(s) of the folktale(s) we're going to read and whether it is a variant of any stories they might already know. They then fill in the spaces on the bingo card with the motifs they think will appear in the story. The goal is to be the first person to get four or five motifs in a row (I usually use the sixteen space card, so there's not a center square to use as a free space, but if the twenty-five space card is used, an option is to give students the center space free). Then, I read the story to them.

I don't give the students their own copies of the story because I don't want them to peek ahead and check off boxes before we get to that part of the story. The challenge here is not only to get the right motifs, but to get them in the correct order, demonstrating that they also understand the plot structure of a folktale. After just a time or two of playing this game, some serious strategizing begins to take place. For example, it's a pretty safe bet that the story will begin with "Once upon a time . . ." or "Long ago and far away . . .," so students often place that motif in a strategic spot, generally towards the center. After that, there is usually a description of the main character. Then, the conflict in the story is introduced. During the climax and the resolution, the youngest/smallest/most mistreated character generally completes the task or overcomes her/his challenge and comes out on top. Although they also know that the story is likely to end with "And they lived happily ever after," we don't usually make it to the end of the story without a winner, so they learn not to rely too heavily on that motif.

I often use the time while the students are filling in their squares to give them hints like, "The title of this story is 'The Princess and the Frog'. What motifs do you think we might see based just on the title?" Then, they might add *princess* and *talking animal* to their cards. Or I say, "This story is a variant of 'Cinderella.' Based on the Cinderella story you know, what motifs do you think we might see?" Then they might add *prince, fairy godmother/magical helper, wicked stepmother*, and *poor or mistreated child* to their cards. When the hint or clue involves a story that is a variant of another, more familiar story, it also illustrates the idea that variants of a tale do not share *all* of the same elements or motifs. For example, the Charles Perrault (French) version of "Cinderella" (which is the basis for the Disney movie, and is therefore the version with which most children are familiar), has a fairy godmother who grants Cinderella's wish to go to the ball in a beautiful dress and an elegant carriage. However, in the Grimm Brothers (German) version, there is no fairy godmother and Cinderella goes to the grave of her mother underneath a hazel tree to ask for a dress and slippers to wear to the ball. Both versions of the story do feature a wicked stepmother and a prince, though. This game reinforces the concepts of motif and variant and illustrates them in very concrete ways, and by the end of the year, I really feel like my students have a strong understanding of both terms.

The great thing about playing this game is that students don't want the other people sitting near them to see what motifs they've put on their cards or where they've placed them, so there's not much chance that they're going to cheat. When we started doing this, I had a bucket of cheap dollar store prizes and candy for the winners to choose from, but eventually the students just wanted extra credit points for winning, so I would give bonus points to the first three people (or groups of people) to get four motifs in a row. This is a great listening exercise and, because there are prizes on the line, students often pay very close attention.

Another way to illustrate the concept of variants is with picture books. With many popular and well-known folktales, there are usually several picture book retellings of the tale—some are very true to the traditional tales and some put a humorous, postmodern spin on them. I generally go to my local library and grab several picture book versions of the same story and put them in sets of three to four books (for a short list of possible titles, see Picture Book Retellings of Folktales in the World Mythology and Folklore Arsenal). I then distribute these sets to pairs (or groups) of students. Each group is given time to read through the three variants and to complete the Comparing Folktale Variants worksheet (see the World Mythology and Folklore Arsenal). Then, each group reports their findings back to the class. If groups share the same basic tale, ask them to combine their data to see if they agree or would like to adapt the list of characteristics for the tale type.

Another activity to consider is called a Shoebox Story (see the assignment description in the World Mythology and Folklore Arsenal). I used this project when I taught a survey course in children's literature at the college level. Though the project was designed with teachers or future teachers in mind (I wanted them to have something they might use in their own classrooms), it can also be used to allow students to demonstrate their understanding of some of the most commonly used folklore motifs. Students work in groups or individually to create a "prop box" filled with items that can be used to act out or illustrate several folktales. Again, there aren't a lot of parameters on this project. I tend to leave my more creative assignments open because I don't want my own lack of imagination to limit what my students might come up with, and I've found that, given some creative freedom, some students will completely knock my socks off. My college students came up with some truly amazing projects—spinning dioramas strung with holiday lights and backdrops that could be folded, changed, and added to depending on the story, just to name a few.

Around the World in 180 Days

Whenever I can, I plan to teach this class at the same time I'm teaching World History and Geography, as it reinforces the content of both classes. Even when it doesn't work out to teach the two at the same time, I still like to follow the same route around the world. We start with Africa, then head east through the Middle East and South Asia, loop down to Australia, then come back north and west to Asia, Europe, then across the Atlantic to the Caribbean and Latin America, and down to South America (see the Around the World Resources in the World Mythology and Folklore Arsenal).

COMMANDO LIBRARIANS

Journey to…

Focus on a place, culture, time in history for a week with presentations, food, film, music, costume, art, and language. Explore your resources in your family, among friends, in the staff and out in the community for people who have lived or traveled to other countries. Invite them to talk about life, school, and work in that country. Serve traditional snacks and listen to traditional music. Invite a dance team to demonstrate traditional dance. Listen to foreign language CDs or ask someone to teach a few introductory words of the language. Show a film that features that country. Display books, audio, and video about the country and post a map of the country. If your library attracts a lot of after school students, adding this dimension to their school day will further impress what they have learned at school. These programs can be presented later in the evening to attract entire families.

As we work our way through the different continents and countries of the world, we begin each unit by exploring the mythology(ies) of the region. *The Kingfisher Book of Mythology: Gods, Goddesses, and Heroes from Around the World* provides a great introductory overview and lists the major deities. *The Illustrated Book of Myths: Tales and Legends of the World* retold by Neil Philip (which groups the stories by the type of myth) and *A World Treasury of Myths, Legends, and Folktales: Stories from Six Continents* (which groups stories by region) as told by Renata Bini provide us with a lot of short versions of the myths.

If we haven't already done so, we take a look at the creation myth(s) and get a brief overview of the pantheon of gods. For some areas, the mythology is more clearly defined than others—for example, Egypt has a very detailed mythology with many easy-to-find stories about the gods and goddesses and their behavior, but the many tribal groups throughout the whole of Africa make it hard to pin down one group of stories to study. In cases where it's harder to find or delineate one mythology or pantheon of gods, we often look at several different myths of origin—stories that explain how certain features of the world were created (fire, for example)—from several different groups.

Then we move on to hero tales and legends. As shown on the chart in Chapter 5, there isn't always a clear line between myths, legends, hero tales, and folklore, so don't worry if it feels a bit inconsistent from unit to unit—that's just the nature of the beast (for another visual representation of the overlap between traditional tales, see Tina Hanlon's "Diagrams of Types of Folktales" at *http://www2.ferrum.edu/applit/studyg/folkdiagram.htm*). Heroes, for example, may be gods or may be semi-divine, which would make them mythological characters, but they may also be legendary characters, as in the case of King Arthur, who is loosely based on a historical person.

ADDITIONAL MYTH RESOURCES

- *A World Treasury of Myths, Legends, and Folktales: Stories from Six Continents* as told by Renata Bini (Harry N. Abrams, 1991)

- *Encyclopedia Mythica* © MCMXCV - MMVII Encyclopedia Mythic *http://www.pantheon.org/mythica*

- *Encyclopedia of Gods: Over 2,500 Deities of the World* by Michael Jordan (Facts on File, 1993)

- *Internet Sacred Texts Archive* ©2011, Evinity *http://www.sacred-texts.com/index.htm*

- *Myth Beasts: Mythical Creatures List* © 2011 MythBeasts: Mythical Creatures List *http://www.mythbeasts. com/index.php*

- *Myths Encyclopedia: Myths and Legends of the World* © 2011 Avdameg *http://www.mythencyclopedia.com/*

- *MythHome* © 1995-2009 Untangle *http://www.mythome.org/mythhome.htm*

- *The Bronze Cauldron: Myths and Legends of the World* by Geraldine McCaughrean (Margaret K. McElderry, 1997)

- *The Illustrated Book of Myths: Tales and Legends of the World* retold by Neil Philip (Dorling Kindersley, 1999)

- *The Kingfisher Book of Mythology: Gods, Goddesses, and Heroes from Around the World* edited by Peter Casterton, Catherine Headlam, and Cynthia O'Neal (Kingfisher, 2001)

- The Minneapolis Institute of Arts' *World Myths & Legends in Art. http://www.artsmia.org/world-myths*

- *The Riverside Anthology of Children's Literature, Sixth Edition* edited by Judith Saltman (Houghton Mifflin, 1985)

When studying legends, don't forget to include legendary creatures (like ghosts, fairies, vampires, genies, dragons, and other assorted monsters) and legendary places (like Atlantis or the land of faerie). Legendary creatures, in particular, are fun for students. First, it's interesting to see how many of these creatures appear in the stories of different cultures—for example, fairy folk are a world-wide phenomena, as are ghosts and vampires. In some cases these creatures are very similar, but in others, the lore surrounding them is very different, as with the European versus the Asian dragon. It's also interesting to read the lore about how to repel or combat these creatures. Here's a fun example: "If an Eastern European vampire is chasing you [this is how I phrase it when talking to my students], and you throw a handful of something, like coins, rocks, seeds, etc., down behind you, the vampire must stop to count the items before it can resume chasing you. Doesn't that sound like something the Count from *Sesame Street* might do?" To continue with the vampire example, it might also be fun to then compare the traditional folklore of vampires with the Hollywood folklore, especially considering the popularity of *The Twilight Saga*. Once in a while when studying these legendary creatures, such as the chupacabra (Latin America) or the Yeti (Nepal and Tibet), I'll throw in an episode of the History Channel's *MonsterQuest*, so students can see that people are still attempting to prove or disprove the existence of these creatures.

We end with the folktales, usually using *The Illustrated Book of Fairy Tales: Spellbinding Stories from Around the World* retold by Neil Philip and *Can You Guess My Name? Traditional Tales from Around the World* retold by Judy Sierra (which groups tales by similar variants) as our primary sources. The more of these students read or hear, the more they will see the overlap of these stories from culture to culture—there are variants everywhere (to do a unit on similar tale types, D.L. Ashliman's *Folklore and Mythology Electronic Texts* website breaks the tale types down alphabetically). In addition to the folktale collections seen in the earlier sidebar, there are plenty of books and Internet sources that focus on certain areas of the world. Because it would take forever for me to list all of the stories we read in each unit, I'll hit some of the highlights from each region below .

FOLKTALE COLLECTIONS

- *A Book of Spooks and Spectres* by Ruth Manning-Sanders (Dutton, 1979)
- *Can You Guess My Name? Traditional Tales from Around the World* retold by Judy Sierra (Clarion Books, 2002)
- *Folklore and Mythology Electronic Texts* ©D.L. Ashliman, University of Pittsburgh, 1996-2011 *http://www.pitt. edu/~dash/folktexts.html*
- *Ghosts and Spirits of Many Lands* edited by Freya Littledale (Doubleday, 1970)
- *Multicultural Folktales for the Feltboard and Readers' Theater* by Judy Sierra (Oryx Press, 1996)
- *Not One Damsel in Distress: World Folktales for Strong Girls* by Jane Yolen (Silver Whistle Books, 2000)
- *Short and Shivery: Thirty Chilling Tales* retold by Robert D. Sans Souci (Yearling, 1987)
- *SurLaLune Fairytales.com http://www.surlalunefairytales.com*
- *The Illustrated Book of Fairy Tales: Spellbinding Stories from Around the World* retold by Neil Philip (D.K. Publishing, 1997)
- *The Oxford Treasury of World Stories* by Michael Harrison & Christopher Stuart-Clark (Oxford University Press, 1998)
- *The Riverside Anthology of Children's Literature, Sixth Edition* edited by Judith Saltman (Houghton Mifflin, 1985)
- *Whistle in the Graveyard: Folktales to Chill Your Bones* by Maria Leach (Viking Press, 1974)

Central and Southern Africa

Africa is such a vast continent with such a variety of cultures and religions that an entire year could be spent studying the mythology and folk literature from this region and still everything would not be covered. With this in mind, I try to hit some of the main points that are fairly common, like the belief in a supreme being, the belief in animism (that spirits exist in natural objects like rocks, trees, and mountains), the belief in magic, and the belief that the spirits of ancestors stay nearby even after death (we'll see this again later in other cultures). It's easier for students to understand these beliefs once we begin reading the myths from this region.

Because West Africa served as the starting point of the slave trade, West African folklore has heavily influenced Caribbean and African American folklore and has therefore worked its way into much of our larger American folklore. Probably the place we see this most is in the storytelling traditions of slaves; the stories they brought with them from Africa were preserved and passed orally from generation to generation. At the end of the 19th century, Joel Chandler Harris captured some of those tales in print with the stories of Uncle Remus, featuring Brer Rabbit (a trickster character in the West African tradition) and Brer Fox whose influence we see today in Warner Brothers' Bugs Bunny and the Coyote.

We also spend a few days comparing folktales using picture books (see the African Folktales list and the African Folktales Comparison worksheet in the World Mythology and Folklore Arsenal). Because this may be the first time students have read picture books in class since elementary school, I want to show them that we'll be looking at picture books in a different, "more scholarly" way. In this case we focus on illustration. Prior to the group work, we read Mark Gonyea's *A Book about Design: Complicated Doesn't Make It Good* (Henry Holt, 2005) so students can be prepared to comment on how illustrations are used to enhance and/or complement the text.

North Africa and the Middle East

Because of its large Muslim population and because it is culturally similar, North Africa gets grouped in with the Middle East, rather than with Central and Southern Africa. When I think of North Africa and mythology, Egypt is the first country that comes to mind. Though Egypt's mythology is generally not as well-known to students as Greek mythology, there are a lot of resources for stories about the gods and goddesses of Egyptian mythology. Students might be interested to note that some of the gods and goddesses are depicted with fully human bodies (like Isis, Osiris, and Amon, for example), while others have human bodies, with the heads of animals (like Horus, Anubis, and Seth).

Maybe I spent too much time as a child watching *Scooby Doo* and *Abbott and Costello,* but I often associate mummies' curses with Egypt. I thought students might enjoy studying the lore surrounding these curses, so we read several stories about people who experienced continued bad luck, and sometimes even death, after crossing paths with a "cursed" Egyptian mummy. *Snopes.com* even refutes a legend that claims that a cursed mummy was aboard the Titanic during its fatal voyage. When we finished the reading, I asked students to imagine being a pharaoh and being able to choose the items that would be buried with them in their tombs. Then, I asked them to write a curse to protect their tomb from grave robbers (see Curse of the Pharaohs Writing in the World Mythology and Folklore Arsenal).

As the Middle East is home to three of the world's major religions—Islam, Christianity, and Judaism—we have a lot to work with as far as the mythology of this region goes. There are also several ancient cultures (Assyrian, Babylonian, Canaanite, Hittite, and Sumerian) whose mythology can be studied. By the time we get to this unit we have already studied creation myths, but I usually save the flood myths for this section, as both the Biblical flood story of Noah and flood story from *Gilgamesh* come from this area. We also read a bit more of the

---

MUMMY'S CURSE

- "Everything But the Egyptian Sinks" by Barbara Mikkelson for *Snopes.com* Jan. 16, 2001. *http://www.snopes.com/horrors/ghosts/mummy.asp*

- "King Tut's Many Curses" by Benjamin Radford Feb. 22, 2010. *http://news.discovery.com/archaeology/king-tuts-many-curses.html*

- "Mummy's Curse: Legend Won't Die" by Brian Handwerk. *http://www.nationalgeographic.com/history/ancient/mummy-curse.html*

- "The Curse of the Mummy." *http://www.kingtutone.com/tutankhamun/curse/*

- "The Curse of the Mummies." *http://www.egyptvoyager.com/features_curseofthemummy.htm*

- "The Unlucky Mummy" © The Trustees of the British Museum. *http://www.britishmuseum.org/research/search_the_collection_database/search_object_details.aspx?objectid=117233&partid=1&searchText=unlucky+mummy&fromADBC=ad&toADBC=ad&numpages=10&orig=%2fresearch%2fsearch_the_collection_database.aspx&currentPage=1*

- "Top 10 Bizarre Curses" Oct. 11, 2007. *http://listverse.com/2007/10/11/top-10bizarre-curses*

Gilgamesh story.

The most famous collection of folktales to come from this region is *The Arabian Nights*. Students will likely be familiar with the tale of Aladdin thanks to the Disney movie (which is not the same version—no Jasmine, sorry), but they probably do not know that the story of Aladdin was one of only many stories told by Scheherezade to her husband to prevent her execution. Also part of this collection are other stories students might already know, such "Ali Baba and the Forty Thieves" (which gives us the phrase "Open Sesame") and "Sinbad the Sailor."

Asia and Oceania

This is a vast and culturally diverse area, so I usually break it down into three, more similar and manageable sections: South Asia; Oceania and Polynesia (despite being part of the United States, Hawaii fits in here);

COMMANDO LIBRARIANS
MEHNDI TATTOOS AND A TASTE OF INDIA

(Courtesy of RoseMary Honnold, Coshocton Public Library, Coshocton, OH)

This is the program that almost didn't happen! I had scheduled a speaker to instruct us on Mehndi and Indian culture four months in advance and she cancelled just two weeks before the program! After discussing it with a couple teens and my daughter who is willing to try new things, we decided to just tweak the program and do it anyway.

I ordered mehndi kits from *http://www.thehennapeople.com* and borrowed all the books I could find in the computer catalog on mehndi and read and experimented on my coworkers! (Update: I now order all my supplies from *http://www.hennapage.com* where there are lots of free downloadable books about henna and all the supplies you would ever need. Check out the glitter tattoos and jewels, very easy to do!)

The program was a hit! The teens went home with tattoos all over them! They stayed almost three hours and didn't want to stop but parents were standing around waiting at that point. The program was on a Saturday morning at 11 a.m. I made chicken curry for lunch and played India travel videos for atmosphere.

If you are a novice as I was, you will find the kits with the premixed henna paste the easiest to handle and easiest for the kids to use. The kits I ordered came with a tube of paste, a tip and three stencils, so even nonartists can make pretty tattoos. My daughter assisted me and purchased the henna powder and mixed her own paste which some of the teens were using later in the program. It can be applied with a paint brush, a tube, toothpicks, fingers, etc.

I collected books with hieroglyphics, Hindi writing, Celtic designs, as well as the traditional Indian mehndi designs for the teens to use for ideas.

Materials:

- Mehndi kits
- Lemon juice
- Toothpicks
- Cotton swabs
- Paper towels
- Hair dryer
- Lemon/sugar glaze (heat lemon juice in microwave and dissolve equal amount of sugar in it)

©2012 RoseMary Honnold (http://www.cplrmh.com/mehndi.html)

and Northern Asia. This area is home to many religions, including Buddhism, Hinduism, and Islam, once again providing us with very rich mythologies to study. What's interesting here is that one of these religions doesn't believe in any gods (Buddhism), one is monotheistic (Islam), and one is polytheistic (Hinduism). This must make for some really interesting interactions in such a densely populated area.

When introducing Buddhism, I show clips from the film *Little Buddha,* which tells the story of Prince Siddhartha. It also explains the concept of reincarnation. The Buddhist Jataka tales, which are stories of the Buddha's earlier incarnations as animals, illustrate to Buddhists the proper way to live. The Hindu Panchatantra animal fables are similar to these tales in many ways as well.

Though haiku aren't considered folk literature, they are traditional Japanese literature, so I do like to squeeze them in as we make our way around the world. Many of my students learned about haiku in elementary school, but I don't think it's a bad idea to give them that exposure again now that they are older and likely to understand them better. After studying the form and reading some examples, I give students the assignment to create their own haiku. In anticipation of the moaning and complaining that always seems to accompany anything poetry-related, I created a pain-free worksheet to help them out (see the Create Your Own Haiku Worksheet in the World Mythology and Folklore Arsenal). I require them to write four haiku of their own. They usually end up using the worksheet for the first one or two and then branch out on their own for the next couple. I've had some really creative haiku on topics like music, trucks, and skateboarding, to name just a few.

Europe

I find that my students already know quite a bit about Greek mythology, so my goal here is just to re-examine it to go along with some of what we've studied about mythology and to compare it to the other myths we've read. We revisit the creation story, review the pantheon of gods, and read about some of the heroes and legends they might not know as much about (see *The Odyssey* Text Set in the World Mythology and Folklore Arsenal). We spend a couple of days on the Lost City of Atlantis, which is a flood story and, like Noah's Ark, is a story scientists and historians are still trying to verify today. It's also a good time to discuss the relationship between Greek and Roman mythology and explain that, when the Romans conquered Greece, rather than introducing a new pantheon of

---

COMMANDO LIBRARIANS

Try an international game and food program for teens. Mancala, Chinese Checkers, Backgammon, Go, Parcheesi, and many other games have interesting beginnings and histories in foreign countries. Accompany the games with a selection of snacks from local restaurants or the freezer section of your grocery. Try snacks like spring rolls, pizza bites, and fruit chunks.

COMMANDO LIBRARIANS

Mandalas are Hindu and Buddhist sandpaintings that are fun and inexpensive to create. Manadalas are traditionally a circle with four gates within a square. They can be quite intricate, but teens can create their own versions with colored sand, glue, and art board or wood. Craft stores will have a variety of boards and many colors of sand. A one-foot square board is large enough for a workshop to make a mandala. Show photos of mandalas you can find on the Internet on a video projector for inspiration. Protractors and rulers are helpful to make a balanced design. Draw the desired design, spread a thin layer of glue in all areas that have the first color of sand. Pour on the sand, and pour off the excess in a pan for that one color of sand. Let dry, using a hair dryer to shorten the drying time. Repeat with the next color until the design is finished. Photos and information to share with students can be found here: *http://en.wikipedia.org/wiki/Mandala.*

gods and goddesses, they simply co-opted the Greek deities and gave them different names (see Greek and Roman Mythology in Picture Books and YA Literature in the World Mythology and Folklore Arsenal).

I prefer Norse mythology to Greek mythology because Norse gods are mortal, which makes it a little darker (I suppose that has something to do with the fact that it comes from such a dark, icy place). Though it is extremely sad, one of my favorite stories is "The Death of Balder," because it really delineates Norse mythology from other mythologies where the gods and goddesses are immortal. There are also some very cool creatures in Norse mythology like Sleipnir, Odin's eight-legged horse; Fenrir, the wolf; and the Midgard serpent that encircles the world. Students who are fans of *The Hobbit* and *The Lord of the Rings* trilogy will notice that Tolkien borrowed from Norse mythology for his stories, right down to the names of the dwarves Bilbo travels with on his way to Lonely Mountain.

European folktales are *the* folktales most of us cut our teeth on as children. These are the tales that are closest to versions of "Cinderella," "Snow White," "Sleeping Beauty," "Beauty and the Beast," and "The Little Mermaid" that our students know from their childhoods spent watching Disney movies. Make it clear to students that Disney has created its own variants of these tales. It is usually during this unit that we use picture books to explore the variants of different tale types mentioned in the "Once Upon A Time . . ." section of this chapter. We also read some literary folktales by Hans Christian Anderson. I give students the Create Your Own Marchen writing assignment (see the World Mythology and Folklore Arsenal) so that they can demonstrate their understanding of the format of a traditional fairy tale. Then we end by having a little fun with traditional folktales by reading some of Roald Dahl's *Revolting Rhymes*.

Latin America, the Caribbean, and South America

In this unit, we study the mythology and folklore of three ancient, native cultures of this area: the Maya, the Inca, and the Aztec. In order to bring things full-circle, point out to students that, like the Egyptians, the Mayans and Aztecs also built pyramids, and discuss the significance of this shape and this structure. We also look at some interesting legends, such as the stories of La Llorona and the chupacabra, which students usually enjoy. One legend that we zero in on in this unit is the Guatemalan Worry or Trouble Dolls. Before going to bed, Guatemalan children tell their worries, troubles, or dreams to these small dolls, then in the morning the magic of the dolls will have made their worries disappear or their wishes come true. Students then create their own Worry Doll. As with the haiku writing, students complain about making Worry Dolls and then really end up loving the activity (in fact they ask me to make them every year). We use small craft clothespins, string, and felt (and anything else the students can come up with) to make the dolls. Over the years I've seen a ballerina, a hula dancer, a smurf, Superman, Spiderman, and even Lil Wayne (complete with a grill made from a foil gum wrapper).

As this unit usually falls at the end of the school year, it's also a good time for me to sort of recap what we've learned. One of the ways we do this is with a wordless picture book called *The Girl from the Sky: An Inca Folktale from South America*. For this activity, the students aren't given any background information on the story (including the title) other than the fact that it's a folktale. I give them copies of the pictures and they write a story to go along with it. By this time we've read several other stories about "star wives" so they are somewhat familiar with this tale type. This assignment also shows whether the students understand the structure of a folktale. After they've written their versions and shared them with the class, I read them the version found at the back of the book.

The World Mythology and Folklore Arsenal

TYPES OF FOLKTALES

- **Marchen/Fairytales** – set in an unreal world, without locality; no definite characters; filled with magic. Humble heroes kill adversaries, succeed to kingdoms, and marry princesses. Ex: Cinderella, Sleeping Beauty, Snow White, Jack and the Beanstalk.

- **Animal/Talking Beast Stories** – not fables (which are didactic and moralistic); animals are the main characters; animals may demonstrate a simple lesson about human nature; little or no magic. Ex: The Bremen Town Musicians, Puss in Boots, The Three Little Pigs, The Three Billy Goats Gruff.

- **Cumulative Tale** – successive incidents with repetition; little magic; simple or absent conflict. Ex: The Old Woman and Her Pig, The Farmer in the Dell, The House that Jack Built, The Gingerbread Man.

- **Drolls** – stories of numskulls and simpletons; give examples of outrageous stupidity; full of exaggerated nonsense. Ex: Jack stories, The Three Sillies, The Husband Who Was to Mind the House.

- **Stories of the Real and Practical World** – characters, plots, and settings that are possible; little exaggeration; no magic involved. Ex: Blue Beard, The Pig-Headed Wife.

- **Porquoi Stories** – explain how or why something is the way it is today; often have animals as main characters. Ex: Why the Chipmunk's Back Is Striped, Why Rabbit Has a Short Tale, Just So Stories by Rudyard Kipling (literary porquoi tales).

- **Literary Fairy Tale or Art Fairy Tale** – a specific author retells traditional tales from a personal perspective and/or creates her/his own original stories using folklore motifs; uses more poetic language; fashions characters who develop and change; introduces literary devices. Some who did this were Hans Christian Anderson ("The Little Mermaid," "The Ugly Duckling," and "The Princess and the Pea"), Howard Pyle, Carl Sandburg, and Isaac Bashevis Singer ("The Devil's Trick"). This has become HUGE in YA lit today. Ex: Robin McKinley, Donna Jo Napoli, and Gail Carson Levine.

- **Trickster Tales** – usually about animals who trick other animals; the trickster usually wins due to his cleverness and some kind of character flaw of his victim. Ex: Brer Rabbit, Anansi, Coyote, Raven.

- **Tall Tales** – about people who (supposedly) really lived and places which really exist; protagonists perform superhuman deeds; especially popular in and often associated with the United States. Ex. Pecos Bill, Paul Bunyan, Davy Crockett, John Henry.

From *Commando Classics: A Field Manual for Helping Teens Understand (and Maybe Even Enjoy) Classic Literature* by Daria Plumb. Bowie, MD: VOYA Press, an imprint of E L Kurdyla Publishing, LLC. Copyright 2012

MYTHOLOGY INTRODUCTION

Who am I?

Where did I come from?

Where am I going?

What do I believe?

How should I behave?

What behaviors are valued by my society?

How do I fit into society?

Why is there suffering?

Does a supreme being exist?

What will happen to me when I die?

- **Mythology** – a collection of related stories that reflect and influence a culture's beliefs.

- **Cosmogonies** – tell how the entire world was created

- **Myths of origins** – explain how features of the world were created. Ex: humans, animals, societies, etc.

- **Myths of culture heroes** – describe the actions and character of beings who are responsible for the discovery of a cultural artifact or technological process. Ex: Prometheus steals fire from the gods (Greek).

- **Myths of birth and rebirth** – tell how life can be renewed, time reversed, or humans transmuted (changed) into new beings.

- **Foundation myths** – creation myths that tell of the foundation of particular cities.

Creation Myths Comparison Chart.

Place of Origin	Creator	Vague or Specific Creator?	Image of Pre-creation	World Creation Process	Creator of Humans	Human Creation Process

From *Commando Classics: A Field Manual for Helping Teens Understand (and Maybe Even Enjoy) Classic Literature* by Daria Plumb. Bowie, MD: VOYA Press, an imprint of E L Kurdyla Publishing, LLC. Copyright 2012

CREATION MYTHS OUTLINE

(to be used with Creation Myth Comparison Charts)

I. TYPES OF CREATION MYTHS

    A. Cosmogonies – how cosmos arose or was created from a primal state.

    B. Myths of Origin – how later features came into being

        1. humans

        2. animals

        3. social order

II. COSMOGONIES

    A. Supreme Being is present

        1. vague

        2. specific (is named)

    B. World in pre-creation was uninhabitable and must be organized

        1. by action of a cosmic force

        2. by all-powerful creator deities

    C. Images of Pre-creation

        1. void/nothingness *(Egyptian, Australian, Greek, Mayan)*

        2. chaos of indistinct elements

        3. primeval sea *(Sumerian)*

        4. cosmic egg containing all things

        5. darkness

    D. Creation Process

        1. Supreme Being orders creation and it is done *(Judeo-Christian)*

        2. Supreme Being molds creation by hand

        3. Supreme Being orders lesser gods to do the work *(Greek, Aboriginal)*

        4. Emergence from lower or higher worlds *(Japanese, Navaho, Hopi, Polynesian, African)*

        5. World egg *(African, Chinese, Indian, S. Pacific, Greek, Japanese)*

        6. World parent *(Babylonian, Egyptian, Zuni, Polynesian, Greek, Japanese, Australian, Iroquois)*

            a. parents beget offspring

            b. offspring live in darkness

            c. offspring desire light

            d. offspring push parents apart

            e. offspring create space for deities to create world

        7. Earth diver *(Siberian-Altaic, Indian, Romanian, N. American, Japanese)*

            a. turtle

            b. bird

8. Sacrifice of a primal being *(Indian, Norse, Babylonian, Hindu)*
    a. giant
    b. serpent
    c. a god's body

9. Struggle between supernatural powers

10. Separation of elements *(Egyptian, Judeo-Christian)*
    a. water & earth
    b. light & dark

11. Uttering of a divine word

12. Self fertilization by a creator deity *(Greek, Egyptian)*
    a. offspring give birth to other gods
    b. pantheon of incestuous family relationships

13. Reflect environmental circumstances of culture

E. Earliest era of world is closest to perfection
    1. Golden Age
    2. Garden of Eden

III. MYTHS OF ORIGIN
A. Humans
    1. Humans born from earth or part of earth *(Yoruba, Norse, Indian)*
    2. Humans born from mating of 2 gods *(Indian, Pawnee)*
    3. Humans born from a part of their god *(Mayan, Egyptian)*
    4. Humans made in the image of the god(s) *(Judeo-Christian)*
        a. by Supreme Being
        b. by child of Supreme Being

B. Suffering
    1. People create suffering *(Greek, Australian, Judeo-Christian, African)*
        a. an instruction, a sin, & the consequence *(Judeo-Christian)*
        b. night, fear, fire, & sin *(Aboriginal, African, Greek)*
    2. God(s) create suffering *(Greek, Japanese, Iroquois)*

SOURCES
• Births. *http://www.cs.williams.edu/~lindsey/myths/myths_1.html*
• Human Creation Myths. *http://library.thinkquest.org/29064/connections/human.html*
• "Mythology," Microsoft Encarta 98 Encyclopedia. 1993-1997, Microsoft Corporation.
• Vawter, Reverend Bruce. "Creation Stories," Microsoft Encarta 98 Encyclopedia. 1993-1997, Microsoft Corporation.

From *Commando Classics: A Field Manual for Helping Teens Understand (and Maybe Even Enjoy) Classic Literature* by Daria Plumb. Bowie, MD: VOYA Press, an imprint of E L Kurdyla Publishing, LLC. Copyright 2012

IN THE BEGINNING . . .

You are a Supreme Being. Though you are all-knowing and all-powerful, one day you realize that you are also lonely and bored, so you decide to create a new world—this world may be one of many or the only one. You will fill this world with humans and animals. You will also decide how big a role you (as the Supreme Being) will take in the day-to-day activities of the people who inhabit your world. (**REMEMBER:** In future writing assignments, you will be creating both a hero story for your world that will show the people of your world how you want them to behave and a story that describes the end of the world, so try to make this world as real and as believable as possible.)

In a 1 ½ page story, and using what you have learned about creation stories this year, describe the creation of this world and its inhabitants. As always, the content of your story must be school appropriate in order to receive credit for the assignment.

Your story should include:

- The image of pre-creation

- The relationship between human beings and the natural world (i.e., the land and the animals)

- Your relationship with the human beings who inhabit this world & how you will communicate with them (if at all)

- The relationship between any other gods (if there are any) and human beings

Also, you must identify the creator of and describe the creation process for the following:

- Any other gods besides yourself (if there are any)

- The earth and the heavens

- Landforms (mountains, bodies of water, deserts, etc.)

- Animals

- Humans (is the first attempt at creation a success?)

From *Commando Classics: A Field Manual for Helping Teens Understand (and Maybe Even Enjoy) Classic Literature* by Daria Plumb. Bowie, MD: VOYA Press, an imprint of E L Kurdyla Publishing, LLC. Copyright 2012

HEROES TEXT SET

May be adapted for use with mythic heroes, classic literary heroes, modern heroes, and/or superheroes

NOVELS
- *Hero* by Perry Moore. Hyperion, 2007.

ILLUSTRATED BOOKS
- *Best Book of Heroes and Heroines* by Pauline Rush Evans. Doubleday, 1964.
- *The Children's Book of Heroes* edited by William J. Bennett. Simon & Schuster, 1997.
- *Star Wars: The Power of Myth* edited by David John. DK Publishing, 2000.

FILMS / VIDEOS
- *The Hero's Adventure.* Mystic Fire Video in association with *Parabola Magazine*, 1988.

ARTWORK
- *How Artists See Heroes: Myth, History, War, Everyday* by Colleen Carroll. Abbeville Kids, 2003.
- *World Myths and Legends in Art: Hero Myths.* The Minneapolis Institute of Arts. *http://www.artsmia.org/world-myths/artbytheme/heromyths.html*

INTERNET SOURCES
- *Hero Machine—Create Your Hero,* UGO Entertainment *http://www.ugo.com/channels/comics/heroMachine.classic.asp*
- "Heroes—The Universal Myth," *Encyclopedia of Myths. http://www.mythencyclopedia.com/Go-Hi/Heroes.html*
- *Hero's Journey,* Maricopa Center for Learning and Instruction. *http://www.mcli.dist.maricopa.edu/smc/journey/main.html*
- *The Museum of Black Superheroes http://bsuperhero.blogspot.com/*

SONGS
- "American Hero" by Bonnie W. Daniels. Bonnie Daniels, 2007.
- "Hero" by Mariah Carey. Sony, 1993.
- "Hero Songs and Lyrics," *PoemHunter.com http://www.poemhunter.com/songs/hero/*
- "I Need a Hero" by Bonnie Tyler. Sony, 1990.

BIOGRAPHIES
- *Akira to Zoltan: Twenty-Six Men Who Changed the World* by Cynthia Chin-Lee. Charlesbridge, 2006.
- *American Heroes* by Marge Ferguson Delano. National Gepgraphic, 2005.
- *Dare to Dream! 25 Extraordinary Lives* by Sandra McLeod Humphrey. Prometheus Books, 2005.
- *Kid Heroes: True Stories of Rescuers, Survivors, and Achievers* by Neal Shusterman. Tom Doherty Associates, 1991.

- *My Hero: Military Kids Write about Their Moms and Dads* by Allen Appel and Mike Rothmiller. St. Martin's Press, 2008.
- *Paths to Peace: People Who Changed the World* by Jane Breskin Zalben. Dutton Children's Books, 2006.
- *Portraits of African-American Heroes* by Tonya Bolden. Dutton Children's Books, 203.

FOLKLORE and LEGENDS

- *American Hero-Myths: A Study in the Native Religions of the Western Continent* by Daniel G. Brinton, M.D. H.C. Watts, 1882. *http://books.google.com/books?id=0dVBAAAAIAAJ&printsec=toc&dq=myth+of+the+hero+in+ya+lit&psp=1&source=gbs_toc_s&cad=1#PPR2,M1*
- *Encyclopedia of Superheroes* by Jeff Rovin. Facts on File, 1985.
- *Fearless Girls, Wise Women, and Beloved Sisters: Heroines in Folktales from Around the World* edited by Kathleen Ragan. W.W. Norton, 1998.
- *Folk Heroes of Britain* by Charles Kightly. Thames and Hudson, 1982.
- *Goddesses, Heroes, and Shamans: The Young People's Guide to World Mythology.* Scholastic, 1994.
- *Gods and Heroes from Viking Mythology* by Brian L. Branston. P. Bedrick, 1993.
- *Gods, Heroes, and Myth. http://www.gods-heros-myth.com/*
- *The Great Comic Book Heroes* by Jules Feiffer. Fantagraphic, 2003.
- *The Great Deeds of Superheroes* retold by Maurice Saxby. P. Bedrick Books, 1989.
- *Greek Mythology: Heroes. Mythweb.com. http://www.mythweb.com/heroes/heroes.html*
- *The Hero Pattern.* from *The Hero: A study in Tradition, Myth and Dreams* by Lord Raglan. *http://department.monm.edu/classics/courses/Clas230/MythDocuments/HeroPattern/default.htm*
- *Hero Tales from Many Lands* by Alice Isabel Hazeltine. Abingdon Press, 1961.
- *The Monomyth http://www.wiu.edu/users/mudjs1/monomyth.htm*
- *William Mayne's Book of Heroes, Stories and Poems* by William Mayne. Dutton, 1967.
- *Women Warriors: Myths and Legends of Heroic Women* by Marianna Mayer. Morrow Junior Books, 1999.

MISCELLANEOUS

- *The Call to Adventure: Bringing the Hero's Journey to Daily Life* by Paul Rebillot with Melissa Kay. HarperSanFrancisco, 1993.
- *Comic Book Character: Unleashing the Hero in Us All* by David A. Zimmerman. InterVarsity Press, 2004.
- *The Comic Book Heroes: The First History of Modern Comic Books—From the Silver Age to the Present* by Gerard Jones and Will Jacobs. Prima Lifestyles, 1996.

HEROES TEXT SET (*Cont.*)

- *The Government Manual for New Superheros* by Matthew David Brozik and Jacob Sager Weinstein. Andrews McMeel, 2005.
- *Hero Myths: A Reader* Edited by Robert Segal. Wiley-Blackwell, 2000.
- *The Hero Myth Revisited* by Michael R. Collins, M.D. Outskirts Press, 2008.
- *The Myth of the American Superhero* by Robert Jewett and John Shelton Lawrence. Wm. B. Erdmans Publishing, 2002.
- *The Hero's Journey: How Educators Can Transform Schools and Improve Learning* by John L. Brown and Cerylle A. Moffett. Association for Supervision & Curriculum Development, 1999.
- *Super Heroes: A Modern Mythology* by Richard Reynolds. University Press of Mississippi, 1994.
- *Superman on the Couch: What Superheroes Really Tell Us about Ourselves and Our Society* by Danny Fingeroth. Continuum International Publishing Group, 2004.

ARTICLES / ESSAYS

- "Heracles: Super Hero" by Linda MacGuire. Yale-New Haven Teachers Institute. Curriculum Unit 84.02.04 *http://www.yale.edu/ynhti/curriculum/units/1984/2/84.02.04.x.html*
- "The Hero Myth in Maya Art and Culture" by Constance Lavender, April 23, 2007. *http://www.opednews.com/articles/life_a_constanc_070423_the_hero_myth_in_may.htm*
- "The Hero's Journey: A Campbellian Look at the Metaphorical Path to Personal Transformation" © 2003, Lynne Millum *Mythichero.com http://www.mythichero.com/what_is_mythology.htm*
- "Myth and the Hero's Journey: Big Screen Blockbusters. Star Wars, Spider-Man – Tell Timeless Tales" by Chris Bergeron. *Daily News*, Framingham, MA. May 5, 2002. *http://www.folkstory.com/articles/spiderman.html*

SHORT STORIES

- *Something Like a Hero: Stories of Daring and Decision by American Teen Writers* edited by Kathryn Kulpa. Merlyn's Pen, 1995.

From *Commando Classics: A Field Manual for Helping Teens Understand (and Maybe Even Enjoy) Classic Literature* by Daria Plumb. Bowie, MD: VOYA Press, an imprint of E L Kurdyla Publishing, LLC. Copyright 2012

I NEED A HERO . . .

For this assignment you will be creating a hero for the world you created for the "In the Beginning . . ." writing assignment. Hero stories are told to show people within a culture which personality traits and characteristics are most desirable, so you will need to decide on a minimum of three characteristics that you would like your hero to embody. Though most heroes are usually male, your hero may be female; however, keep in mind that female heroes traditionally tend to embody more "male" characteristics (strength, bravery, fierceness in battle, etc.).

You will use Lord Raglan's Scale to help you frame the story of your hero's life.
Your story will be at least 1 ½ pages long and will include:

- 3 desirable personality traits that your hero will embody/demonstrate to the people in your world. While you are welcome to give your hero super powers, these are not considered personality traits, so they should be described separately.

- A well-rounded description of your hero. In other words, describe him or her physically and mentally/emotionally (this is where the super powers will come in).

- A minimum of 15 archetypes from Lord Raglan's Scale (see below).

Lord Raglan's Scale

In *The Hero* (1936) Lord Raglan classified the parallel life-patterns of the mythical hero of tradition into twenty-two archetypal incidents, as noted below. The higher a particular hero scores, the closer he is to the archetype of the sacred hero-king of prehistoric religious ritual; a historical hero is likely to share rather few of the mythical characteristics.

1. The hero's mother is a royal virgin.
2. His father is a king and
3. often a near relative of the mother, but
4. the circumstances of his conception are unusual, and
5. he is also reputed to be the son of a god.
6. At birth an attempt is made, usually by his father or maternal grandfather, to kill him, but
7. he is spirited away, and
8. reared by foster-parents in a far country.
9. We are told nothing of his childhood, but
10. upon reaching manhood he returns or goes to his future kingdom.
11. After a victory over the king and or giant, dragon, or wild beast
12. he marries a princess, often the daughter of his predecessor and
13. becomes king.
14. For a time he reigns uneventfully and
15. prescribes laws but
16. later loses favor with the gods and or his people and
17. is driven from the throne and the city, after which
18. he meets with a mysterious death
19. often at the top of a hill.
20. His children, if any, do not succeed him.
21. His body is not buried, but nevertheless
21. he has one or more holy sepulchers (gravesites/tombs).

From *Commando Classics: A Field Manual for Helping Teens Understand (and Maybe Even Enjoy) Classic Literature*
by Daria Plumb. Bowie, MD: VOYA Press, an imprint of E L Kurdyla Publishing, LLC. Copyright 2012

COMPARING NEAR EASTERN FLOOD MYTHS

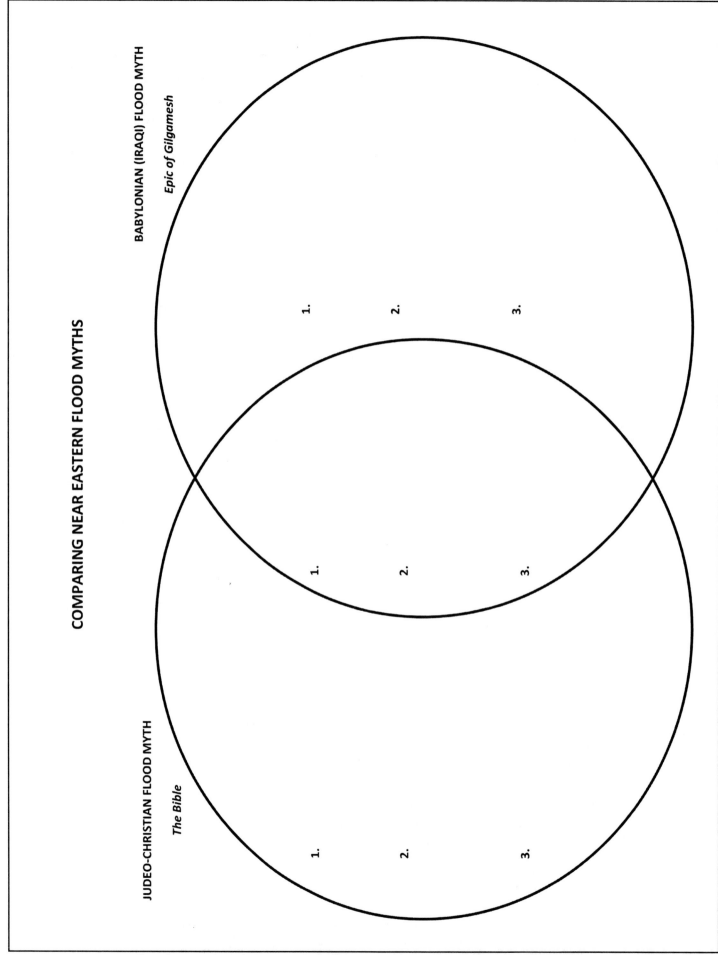

BABYLONIAN (IRAQI) FLOOD MYTH

Epic of Gilgamesh

1.

2.

3.

1.

2.

3.

JUDEO-CHRISTIAN FLOOD MYTH

The Bible

1.

2.

3.

IT'S THE END OF THE WORLD AS WE KNOW IT . . .

In your first two assignments as a Supreme Being you created a world and populated it with human beings, and you sent a hero to guide and instruct your people. But because everything that has a beginning must also have an end, you have known all along that one day it would be necessary to destroy the world you have created. Now that day has come.

You will write a 1 ½ page story that answers the following questions:
- Why are you ending the world?

  - Have people become so sinful that you have no other choice? OR

  - Is it the simply the end of a natural cycle?

- How will people know that the end is near?

  - What *3* warnings/messages/prophecies will foretell the end of the world?

  - Who will deliver these messages?

- What should people do to prepare themselves for the end of the world?

- What will happen to the people who DID NOT follow your instructions/wishes (i.e. the sinners)? How will they be treated?

- What will happen to the people who DID follow your instructions/wishes? Will they face the same end as the sinners or will they be rewarded?

- How will the world end? Be specific.

- Will people experience any kind of rebirth or life after death?

* * *

Eschatology (literally "study of the last") is a part of theology and philosophy concerned with what are believed to be the final events in history, or the ultimate destiny of humanity, commonly referred to as the end of the world. *The Oxford English Dictionary* defines it as "concerned with **'the four last things: death, judgement, heaven, and hell.'**"[1] While in mysticism the phrase refers metaphorically to the end of ordinary reality and reunion with the Divine, in many traditional religions it is taught as an actual future event prophesied in sacred texts or folklore.

(*http://en.wikipedia.org/wiki/Eschatology*)

FOLKTALE MOTIF BINGO

Fill in the squares below with folktale motifs/elements that you think will be found in today's story.

From *Commando Classics: A Field Manual for Helping Teens Understand (and Maybe Even Enjoy) Classic Literature* by Daria Plumb. Bowie, MD: VOYA Press, an imprint of E L Kurdyla Publishing, LLC. Copyright 2012

FOLKTALE MOTIF BINGO

Fill in the squares below with folktale motifs/elements that you think will be found in today's story.

FOLKTALE MOTIFS

- "Once upon a time…" or "Long ago and far away"
- "And they lived happily ever after"
- Handsome, brave prince
- Beautiful, young, and innocent princess
- Use of 3's
- Use of 7's
- Use of 12's
- Wicked stepmother
- Magic item/object
- Magical creatures (trolls, giants, ogres, etc.)
- Magical acts
- Waking from the dead or a long sleep
- An (impossible) challenge or task is given
- A journey
- Remarkable strength
- Disobeying an order/warning
- Riddles
- Dead parent
- Orphan
- Brought back to life with a kiss
- Youngest &/or smallest sibling is successful
- Wishes are granted
- Talking animals
- Use of trickery
- Disguise
- A poor person becomes rich
- Woods = Danger
- Changed into something ugly by a curse
- Breaking a curse

- Rhyming text
- Repeated phrases
- Wise old (wo)man
- Using brains to outsmart the villain
- A wish for a child
- Greed is punished
- Transformation
- Witches/Wizards
- Magical fruits/vegetables
- Villain is punished
- Hero(ine) is rewarded
- Nature &/or animals help the hero(ine)
- Trickster character
- Hero(ine) is helped by a dead relative
- Escape supernatural creature by crossing water
- Hero(ine) is a numbskull (not very smart)
- A (younger) brother/sister who is good
- An (elder) sibling who is mean or evil
- Poor or mistreated (younger) child
- Magical powers
- An incantation/spell
- The power of naming
- Invisibility
- Fairy godmother/magical helper
- Married (engaged to) an undesirable creature/person
- Prediction/prophecy
- Promise/oath
- Enchanted/magical garden

From *Commando Classics: A Field Manual for Helping Teens Understand (and Maybe Even Enjoy) Classic Literature* by Daria Plumb. Bowie, MD: VOYA Press, an imprint of E L Kurdyla Publishing, LLC. Copyright 2012

PICTURE BOOK RETELLINGS OF FOLKTALES

Cinderella

Adelita: A Mexican Cinderella Story by Tomie de Paola (G.P. Putnam's Sons, 2002)

Ashpet: An Appalachian Tale by Joanne Compton (Holiday House, 1994)

Bigfoot Cinderella by Tony Johnston (G.P. Putnam's Sons, 1998)

Cinder Edna by Ellen Jackson (Lothrop, Lee & Shepard, c1994)

Cinderella = Cenicienta by Frances Boada (Chronicle Books, 2001)

Cinderella by David Delamare (Green Tiger Press/Simon & Schuster, c1993)

Cinderella by William Wegman (Hyperion, 1993)

Cinderella Penguin, or The Little Glass Flipper by Janet Perlman (Scholastic, 1996)

Cinderlily: A Floral Fairy Tale in Three Acts by David Ellwand (Candlewick Press, 2003)

Cindy Ellen by Susan Lowell (HarperCollins, 200)

Dinorella: A Prehistoric Fairy Tale by Pamela Duncan Edwards (Hyperion Books for Children, 1997)

The Egyptian Cinderella by Shirley Climo (Crowell, 1989)

Prince Cinders by Babette Cole (Putnam, 1988)

Raisel's Riddle (Jewish/Polish) by Erica Silverman (Farrar, Straus and Giroux, 1999)

Sootface: An Ojibwa Cinderella Story by Robert Sans Souci (Delacorte Press, 1994)

Tam's Slipper: A Story from Vietnam Janet Palazzo-Craig (Troll, 1996)

Tattercoats by Joseph Jacobs (Putnam, 1989)

Yeh-Shen: A Cinderella Story from China by Ai-Ling Louie (Philomel Books, 1982)

The Frog Prince

A Frog Prince by Alix Berenzy (Henry Holt, 1991)

The Frog Prince by Edith Tarcov (Cartwheel, 1993)

The Frog Prince by Kathy-Jo Wargin (Ann Arbor Editions, 2007)

The Frog Prince, Con't by Jon Scieszka (Viking, 1991)

The Frog Princess? by Pamela Mann (Gareth Stevens, 1995)

The Frog Princess: A Russian Folktale by J. Patrick Lewis (Dial, 1994)

The Prince of the Pond: Otherwise Known as The Fawg Pin by Donna Jo Napoli (Penguin Books, 1994)

The Prog Frince by C. Drew Lamm (Orchard Books, 1999)

Little Red Riding Hood

Flossie & the Fox by Patricia C. McKissack (Dial Books for Young Readers, 1986)

Grover's Little Red Riding Hood by Norman Stiles (Goldencraft, 1997)

Little Red Cowboy Hat by Susan Lowell (Holt, 1997)

Little Red Hood: A Classic Story Bent Out of Shape illustrated by Tony Ross (Doubleday, 1979)

Little Red Riding Hood by Jerry Pinkney (Little, Brown, 2007)

Little Red Riding Hood by Andrea Wisnewski (David R. Godine, 2006)

Little Red Riding Hood: A Newfangled Prairie Tale by Lisa Campbell Ernst (Simon & Schuster Books for Young Readers, 1995)

Lon Po Po: A Red Riding Hood Story from China by Ed Young (Philomel, 1989)

OOPS! by Colin McNaughton (Harcourt Brace & Co., 1997)

The Wolf's Story: What Really Happened to Little Red Riding Hood by Toby Forward (Candlewick, 2005)

Yours Truly, Goldilocks by Alma Flor Ada (Atheneum Books for Young Readers, 1998)

Rapunzel

Falling for Rapunzel by Leah Wilcox (Penguin, 2005)

Rapunzel by Paul O. Zelinsky (Dutton Children's Books, 1997)

Rapunzel: A Fairy Tale by Jacob and Wilhelm Grimm (North-South Books, 2005)

Rapunzel: A Groovy Fairy Tale by Lynn Roberts (H.N. Abrams, 2003)

RAPunzel: A Happenin' Rap by David Vozar (Doubleday Books for Young Readers, 1998)

Petrosinella: A Neopolitan Rapunzel by Giambattista Basile (F. Warne, 1981)

Sugar Cane: A Caribbean Rapunzel by Patricia Storace (Jump at the Sun/Hyperion Books for Children, 2007)

Rumplestiltskin

Duffy and the Devil: A Cornish Tale by Carolyn White (Farrar, Straus, Giroux, 1973)

The Girl Who Spun Gold (African American) by Virginia Hamilton (Scholastic, 2000)

Whuppity Stoorie (Scotland) by Harve Zemach (Putnam's, 1997)

Sleeping Beauty

Sleeping Ugly by Jane Yolen (Puffin, 1997)

The Sleeping Beauty = La Bella Durmiente by Miquel Desclot (Chronicle Books, 2003)

Sleepless Beauty by Frances Minters (Viking/Penguin, 1996)

Snoring Beauty by Bruce Hale (Harcourt, 2008)

PICTURE BOOK RETELLINGS OF FOLKTALES (*Cont.*)

Three Little Pigs

The 3 Little Dassies by Jan Brett (Putnam's Sons/Penguin Group, 2010)

The Fourth Little Pig by Teresa Noel Celsi (Raintree, 1992)

OOPS! by Colin McNaughton (Harcourt Brace & Co., 1997)

Tell the Truth by Judy Sierra (Alfred A. Knopf, 2010)

The Three Horrid Little Pigs by Liz Pinchon (Tiger Tales, 2010)

Three Hungry Pigs and the Wolf Who Came to Dinner (Random House, 2005)

Three Little Cajun Pigs by Mike Artell (Dial Books for Young Readers, 2006)

The Three Little Fish and the Big Bad Shark by Ken Geist (Scholastic, 2007)

The Three Little Javelinas by Susan Lowell (Northland, 1992)

Three Little Wolves and the Big Bad Pig by Eugenious Trivizas (Margaret K. McElderry Books: Maxwell Macmillan International, 1993)

Three Pigs by David Wiesner (Clarion, 2001)

The True Story of the 3 Little Pigs by Jon Scieszka (Puffin Books/Penguin, 1996)

Wait! No Paint! by Bruce Whatley (HarperCollins, 2001)

Ziggy Piggy and the Three Little Pigs by Frank Asch (Kids Can Press, 1998)

For detailed lists of folktale variants and retellings, see:

- *Folklore and Mythology Electronic Texts* D.L. Ashliman, University of Pittsburgh, 1996-2011 *http://www.pitt.edu/~dash/folktexts.html*

- *SurLaLune Fairy Tales http://www.surlalunefairytales.com*

- *The University of Iowa's Folk Tales and Fairy Tales: Retellings, Adaptations, Variants and Parodies http://www.education.uiowa.edu/crl/bibliographies/documents/folkandfairytaleindex.pdf*

COMPARING FOLKTALE VARIANTS

BASIC TALE:_____

Provide the following information for each variant:

STORY #1

Title: _____

Author: _____

Illustrator: _____

Country of Origin: _____

STORY #2

Title: _____

Author: _____

Illustrator: _____

Country of Origin: _____

STORY #3

Title: _____

Author: _____

Illustrator: _____

Country of Origin: _____

From *Commando Classics: A Field Manual for Helping Teens Understand (and Maybe Even Enjoy) Classic Literature* by Daria Plumb. Bowie, MD: VOYA Press, an imprint of E L Kurdyla Publishing, LLC. Copyright 2012

COMPARING FOLKTALE VARIANTS (*Cont.*)

Based on the 3 variants you read, list some of the characteristics of this tale type below:

<u>Characters</u>   <u>Setting</u>

<u>Plot</u>   <u>Motifs</u>

Use the diagram below to illustrate the similarities and differences between the 3 variants:

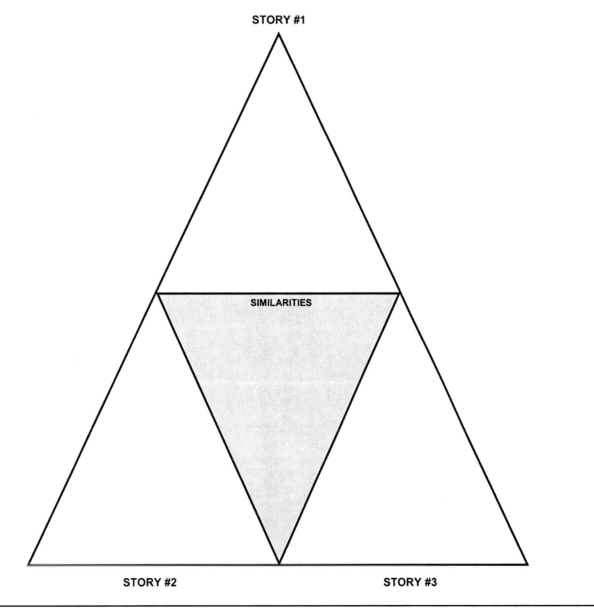

STORY #1

SIMILARITIES

STORY #2   STORY #3

From *Commando Classics: A Field Manual for Helping Teens Understand (and Maybe Even Enjoy) Classic Literature* by Daria Plumb. Bowie, MD: VOYA Press, an imprint of E L Kurdyla Publishing, LLC. Copyright 2012

SHOEBOX STORY

Create a box of props (you must have a minimum of 15 items) that represent the "stock" characters, settings, and situations found in many folktales. They may be puppets, paper dolls, masks, backdrops, etc.—be as creative as you like. You will need to be able to use these props to dramatize the plots of at least *3* different tales. You may choose tales from the *Illustrated Book of Fairy Tales* by Neil Philip (DK Children, 1998) or you may choose from other sources. You do not need to use all of the props for each tale. Be prepared to demonstrate at least one of your tales in class (you will have approximately 15 minutes). Prepare a list of your props and the 3 tales for your classmates.

Examples of Possible Props:
- Prince
- Princess
- Boy
- Girl
- Witch
- Wizard
- Giant
- Ogre
- Troll
- Castle
- Forest/Trees
- Wolf
- Fairy Godmother
- Wicked Stepmother
- Magic Items
- Magic Wand
- Elves
- Fairies
- 3 Siblings
- Barnyard Animals
- Crown
- Cape
- Damsel in Distress
- Frog
- Genie
- Dragon

From *Commando Classics: A Field Manual for Helping Teens Understand (and Maybe Even Enjoy) Classic Literature* by Daria Plumb. Bowie, MD: VOYA Press, an imprint of E L Kurdyla Publishing, LLC. Copyright 2012

AROUND THE WORLD RESOURCES

Central & Southern Africa

- *African Legends, Myths, and Folktales for Readers Theatre* by Anthony D. Fredericks (Teachers Ideas Press, 2008)

- *African Myths of Origin* stories selected and retold by Stephen Belcher (Penguin, 2005)

- *Ashanti to Zulu: African Traditions* by Margaret Musgrove (Puffin, 1992)

- *Bury My Bones But Keep My Words: African Tales for Retelling* by Tony Fairman (Holt, 1992)

- *Hands on Culture of West Africa* by Katie O'Halloran (J. Weston Walch, 1997)

- *Misoso: Once Upon a Time Tales from Africa* by Verna Aardema (Random House, 1994)

- *Nelson Mandela's Favorite African Folktales* by Nelson Mandela (W.W. Norton, 2002)

- *Plays from African Folktales: With Ideas for Acting, Dance, Costumes, and Music* by Carol Korty (Scribner, 1975)

- *A Ring of Tricksters: Animal Tales from America, the West Indies, and Africa* by Virginia Hamilton (Blue Sky Press/Scholastic, 1997)

- *Sundiata: Lion King of Mali* by David Wisniewski (Sandpiper, 1999)

- *Tales from the Story Hat* by Verna Aardema (Coward, 1960)

- *Tokoloshi: African Folk Tales* retold by Diana Pitcher (Celestial Arts, 1981)

North Africa & The Middle East

- *Abu Kassim's Slippers: An Arabian Tale* retold by Nancy Green (Follett, 1963)

- *Aladdin and Other Tales from the Arabian Nights* by Rosalind Kerven (Dorling Kindersley, 1998)

- *Ancient Egypt: The Mythology* (*http://www.egyptianmyths.net/section-myths.htm*)

- *Arabian Nights* (Hallmark Entertainment, 2000)

- *Egyptian Myths* by Jacqueline Morley (Peter Bedrick Books, 1999)

- *Encyclopedia Mythica: Middle East* © MCMXCV - MMVII Encyclopedia Mythica (*http://www.pantheon.org/areas/mythology/middle_east /*)

- *Hands on Culture of Ancient Egypt* by Katie O'Halloran (J. Weston Walch, 1997)

- *Nasreddin Hodja: Tales of the Turkish Trickster* retold by D.L. Ashliman © 2001-2009)(*http://www.pitt.edu/~dash/hodja.html*)

- *Tales of Ancient Egypt* by Roger Lancelyn Green (Puffin, 2004)

- "Top 10 Bizarre Curses" Oct. 11, 2007 (*http://listverse.com/2007/10/11/top-10bizarre-curses*)

- *The British Museum: Ancient Egypt* © 1999 The Trustees of the British Museum (*http://www.ancientegypt.co.uk/menu.html*)

- *The Sultan's Fool and Other North African Tales* by Robert Gilstrap (Holt, Rinehart and Winston, 1966)

- *The Winged Cat: A Tale of Ancient Egypt* by Deborah Nourse Lattimore (HarperCollins, 1992)
- *Turkish Fairy Tales* collected by Selma Ekrem (Van Nostrund, 1964)
- *Zekmet the Stone Carver: A Tale of Ancient Egypt* by Mary Stolz (Houghton Mifflin, 1996)

Asia & Oceania

- *Folktales from Japan* selected and edited by D.L. Ashliman © 1998-2008 *http://www.pitt.edu/~dash/japan.html*
- *Folktales from the Philippines* edited by D.L. Ashliman © 1998-2008 *http://www.pitt.edu/~dash/philippines.html*
- *Hands-on Culture of Japan* by Katie O'Halloran (J. Weston Walch, 1997)
- *Hands-on Culture of Southeast Asia* by Katie O'Halloran (J. Weston Walch, 1998)
- *IndianMythology.com* © 2009 IndianMythology.com *http://indianmythology.com/finish/*
- *Japanese Legends about Supernatural Sweethearts* selected and edited by D.L. Ashliman © 1998-2008 *http://www.pitt.edu/~dash/japanlove.html*
- *The Jataka Tales* edited by D.L. Ashliman © 2002 *http://www.pitt.edu/~dash/jataka.html*
- *Little Buddha* (Buena Vista Home Video, 1994)
- "Ode of Mulan" by Anonymous *http://www.chinapage.com/mulan-e.html*
- *The Panchatantra: A Selection of Tales from Ancient India* edited by D.L. Ashliman © 2002 *http://www.pitt.edu/~dash/panchatantra.html*
- *Panchatantra.org* © 2003 - 2011 HamaraShehar.com Pvt. Ltd *http://panchatantra.org/index.html*
- *Stories from the Billabong* retold by James Vance Marshall (Frances Lincoln Children's Books, 2008)
- *Tales Told in Tents: Stories from Central Asia* by Sally Pomme Clayton (Frances Lincoln Children's Books, 2004)

Europe

- *D'Aulaires' Book of Greek Myths* by Ingri and Edgar D'Aulaires (Bantam Doubleday Dell Publishing Group, 1962)
- *D'Aulaires' Book of Norse Myths* by Ingri and Edgar D'Aulaires (The New York Review Children's Collection, 1967)
- *A Europe of Tales http://www.europeoftales.net/*
- *Favorite Stories of the Ballet* by James Riordan (Checkerboard Press, 1984)

From *Commando Classics: A Field Manual for Helping Teens Understand (and Maybe Even Enjoy) Classic Literature* by Daria Plumb. Bowie, MD: VOYA Press, an imprint of E L Kurdyla Publishing, LLC. Copyright 2012

AROUND THE WORLD RESOURCES (*Cont.*)

- *The Firebird and Other Russian Fairytales* edited by Jacqueline Onassis (Viking Press, 1978)
- *Grimm's Grimmest* by Tracy Arah Dockray (Chronicle Books, 1997)
- *Hands-on Culture of Ancient Greece and Rome* by Katie O'Halloran (J. Weston Walch, 1998)
- *Into the Woods* (Image Entertainment, 1990)
- *Roald Dahl's Revolting Rhymes* by Roald Dahl (Bantam Books, 1988)
- "Satellite Images 'Show Atlantis'" by Paul Rincon, for *BBC News*, June 6, 2004 *http://news.bbc. co.uk/go/pr/fr/-/2/hi/science/nature/3766863.stm*
- *Tradestone Gallery, The Finest Russian Arts and Crafts: Russian Fairy Tales http://www.trade-stonegallery.com/index.php?content=fairytales*
- *Vampire and Ghost Stories from Russia* edited by D.L. Ashliman *http://www.pitt.edu/~dash/ vampire.html*
- *Winged Sandals* ©2003 ABC *http://www.abc.net.au/arts/wingedsandals/default_lowband.htm*

Latin America, the Caribbean, and South America

- *About.com's South America Travel Myths, Folklore, Magic, and Monsters http://gosouthamerica. about.com/od/folklore/Myths_Folklore_Magic_and_Monsters.htm*
- *American Folklore* (includes Mexican folklore) by S.E. Schlosser *http://www.americanfolklore. net/index.html*
- *The Chupacabra Home Page http://www.princeton.edu/~accion/chupa.html*
- *Hands-on Culture of Mexico and Central America* by Katie O'Halloran (J. Weston Walch, 1998)
- *The Girl from the Sky: An Inca Folktale from South America* retold by Anamarie Garcia (Children's Press, 1992)
- "The Legend of La Llorona: The Ghost of the Rio Grande" by Paul Harden for El Defensor Chieftan, Dec. 1, 2007 *http://www.caminorealheritage.org/PH/1207_llorona.pdf*
- *Mayan Trouble Dolls of Guatemala* © 200 Kathy Wirt *http://www.sciencejoywagon.com/kwirt/ mayan/index.htm*
- *A Ring of Tricksters: Animal Tales from America, the West Indies, and Africa* by Virginia Hamilton (Blue Sky Press/Scholastic, 1997)

AFRICAN FOLKTALES COMPARISON

Book Title:_____

Author: _____

Illustrator:_____

Country of Origin (if given):_____

Type(s) of Folktale: _____

Summarize the plot of the story (3 sentence minimum—beginning, middle, & end of story):

_____

_____

_____

_____

_____

_____

_____

Is this story a variant of any other folktales you know? If yes, indicate which one. _____

_____

List 3 folktale motifs found in this story:

    1)

    2)

    3)

How do the illustrations help tell the story?

- Are the colors vibrant or muted?

- Do the illustrations set a certain mood or tone for the story?

- What stands out in the illustrations?

- Do the illustrations have "movement" or are they "still"?

- Do the illustrations reflect the text exactly or has the illustrator added interest to the story with her/his illustrations?

From *Commando Classics: A Field Manual for Helping Teens Understand (and Maybe Even Enjoy) Classic Literature* by Daria Plumb. Bowie, MD: VOYA Press, an imprint of E L Kurdyla Publishing, LLC. Copyright 2012

AFRICAN FOLKTALES BOOKLIST

Picture Books

- *Akimba and the Magic Cow* by Anne Rose (Scholastic, 1976)

- *Bringing the Rain to Kapiti Plain* by Verna Aardema (Dial Books for Young Readers, 1981)

- *The Hunterman and the Crocodiles* by Baba Waque Diakite (Scholastic, 1997)

- *The Lonely Lioness and the Ostrich Chicks* by Verna Aardema (A.A. Knopf, 1996)

- *Mabela the Clever* by Margaret Read MacDonald (A. Whitman, 2001)

- *Mufaro's Beautiful Daughters* by John Steptoe (Lothrop, Lee & Shepard Books, 1987)

- *The Story of Lightning and Thunder* by Ashley Bryan (Aladdin Paperbacks, 1999)

- *This for That* by Verna Aardema (Dial Books for Young Readers, 1995)

- *Too Much Talk* by Angela Shelf Medearis (Candlewick, 1995)

- *Why Mosquitoes Buzz in People's Ears* by Verna Aardema (Dial Press, 1975)

- *Zomo the Rabbit* by Gerald McDermott (Harcourt Brace Jovanovich, 1992)

Anansi (Trickster) Stories

- *Anansi and the Moss-Covered Rock* by Eric Kimmel (Holiday House, 1990)

- *Anansi and the Talking Melon* by Eric Kimmel (Holiday House, 1994)

- *Anansi Does the Impossible: An Ashanti Tale* by Verna Aardema (Atheneum Books for Young Readers, 1997)

- *Anansi Goes Fishing* by Eric Kimmel (Live Oak Media, 1993)

- *Anansi the Spider: A Tale from the Ashanti* by Gerald McDermott (Henry Holt, 1987)

- *Don't Leave an Elephant to Go and Chase a Bird* by James Berry (Simon and Schuster Books for Young Readers, 1996)

- *How Anansi Obtained the Sky God's Stories: An African Folktale from the Ashanti Tribe* by Janice Skivington (Children's Press, 1991)

CURSE OF THE PHARAOHS

The pharaoh was supposedly so much better than ordinary Egyptians that he was actually a god, the son of the Sun-god, Ra. When a pharaoh died, it was believed that he joined Ra in his day boat (the Sun) as he sailed across the sky. The pharaohs built themselves huge burial tombs of stone, the pyramids. Once a pharaoh died, his subjects began a long and intricate process of preserving his body, called mummification. By using the correct chemicals, Egyptians were able to preserve the body of the pharaoh so that it would still be intact in his next life. Mummies that scientists have discovered today are still intact, despite being over 4000 years old!

Pharaohs were buried deep inside the pyramids, surrounded by all of the things that they might need for their next life. These things included food, jewelry, furniture, even beloved pets, and sometimes a favorite servant who died in order to be able to serve his king when the Pharaoh awoke in the afterlife! The huge pyramids could be seen from all over, however, and were easy targets for thieves to break into and to steal all of these riches. Today, many treasures and artifacts are missing from museums as a result of these grave robbers.

from *http://chalk.richmond.edu/education/projects/webunits/egypt/Pharaohs.html*

DIRECTIONS: Make a list of ten things you'd want to be buried with if you were a Pharaoh preparing for the Afterlife. Tell why you'd need each item. Then, write a curse or protective spell that will keep your tomb safe from grave robbers. The items and the curse must be school appropriate.

ITEM	USE IN AFTERLIFE
1) _____	_____
2) _____	_____
3) _____	_____
4) _____	_____
5) _____	_____
6) _____	_____
7) _____	_____
8) _____	_____
9) _____	_____
10) _____	_____

CURSE OR PROTECTIVE SPELL: _____

_____

_____

_____

From *Commando Classics: A Field Manual for Helping Teens Understand (and Maybe Even Enjoy) Classic Literature* by Daria Plumb. Bowie, MD: VOYA Press, an imprint of E L Kurdyla Publishing, LLC. Copyright 2012

CREATE YOUR OWN HAIKU WORKSHEET

Line 1:

Solitary (4)	butterfly (3)	*Select words*
Delicate (3)	daffodil (3)	*that total 5*
Beautiful (3)	volcano (3)	*syllables*
Colorful (3)	flower (2)	
Little (2)	mountain (2)	
Yellow (2)	rainbow (2)	
Angry (2)	leaves (1)	
Purple (2)	lake (1)	
Perfect (2)	cloud (1)	
Quiet (2)	pond (1)	
Strange (1)	moon (1)	
Bright (1)	sun (1)	
Red (1)	frog (1)	
Lost (1)	seed (1)	
Sad (1)	swan (1)	

Line 2:

jumping (2)	among (2)	the flowers (3)	*Select words*
floating (2)	over (2)	the water (3)	*that total 7*
playing (2)	against (2)	the treetops (3)	*syllables*
praying (2)	upon (2)	the snow (2)	
growing (2)	behind (2)	the world (2)	
standing (2)	below (2)	the sky (2)	
looking (2)	under (2)	the wind (2)	
resting (2)	with (1)	the road (2)	
moving (2)	near (1)	the hill (2)	
dancing (2)	through (1)	the mist (2)	

Line 3:

summer (2)	is beginning. (4)	*Select words*
autumn (2)	is over. (3)	*that total 5*
the night (2)	has vanished. (3)	*syllables*
morning (2)	is coming. (3)	
winter (2)	breeze. (1)	
spring (1)	time. (1)	
cold (1)	dream. (1)	

Add or change words wherever necessary to fulfill the syllable requirement. Some things to consider: use adjectives (descriptive words), change the form of the word (from past to present tense or vice versa), add pronouns (he, she, it).

From *Commando Classics: A Field Manual for Helping Teens Understand (and Maybe Even Enjoy) Classic Literature* by Daria Plumb. Bowie, MD: VOYA Press, an imprint of E L Kurdyla Publishing, LLC. Copyright 2012

THE ODYSSEY TEXT SET

NOVELS
- *Adventures of Odysseus and the Tale of Troy* by Padraic Colum. Macmillan Company, 1918.
- *Aleta and the Queen: A Tale of Ancient Greece* by Priscilla Galloway. Firefly Books, 1995.
- *Black Ships Before Troy: The Story of the Iliad* by Rosemary Sutcliff. Delacorte Pres, 1993.
- *Dateline: Troy* by Paul Fleischman. Candlewick Press, 1996.
- *Inside the Walls of Troy* by Clemence McLaren. Atheneum, 1996.
- *Ithaka* by Adele Geras. Harcourt, 2006.
- *Odysseus in the Serpent Maze* by Jane Yolen and Robert J. Harris. HarperCollins Publishers, 2001.
- Tales from the Odyssey series by Mary Pope Osborne.
  - *The Final Battle.* Hyperion Books for Children, 2004.
  - *The Gray-Eyed Goddess.* Hyperion Paperbacks for Children, 2003.
  - *The Land of the Dead.* Hyperion Books for Children, 2002.
  - *The One-Eyed Giant.* Hyperion Paperbacks for Children, 2002.
  - *Return to Ithaca.* Hyperion Books for Children, 2004.
  - *Sirens and Sea Monsters.* Hyperion Books for Children, 2003.
- *The Trojan Horse* by Warwick Hutton. Maxwell Macmillan International, 1992.
- *Troy* by Adele Geras. Harcourt, 2001.
- *The Wanderings of Ulysses: The Story of the Odyssey* by Rosemary Sutcliff. Delacorte Press, 1996.

ILLUSTRATED BOOKS
- *The Adventures of Ulysses: Homer's Epic in Pictures* by Erich Lessing. Doss, Mead, 1970.
- *Cyclops* written and illustrated by Leonard Everett Fisher. Holiday House, 1991.
- *Iliad and the Odyssey: The Heroic Story of the Trojan War, and the Fabulous Adventures of Odysseus adapted from the Greek Classics of Homer* by Jane Werner Watson. Simon, 1956.
- *The Odyssey* by Geraldine McCaughrean. Oxford University Press, 1993.
- *The Odyssey* adapted by Adrian Mitchell. Dorling Kindersley, 2000.
- *The Trojan Horse: The World's Greatest Adventure* by David Clement-Davies. DK Publishing, 1999.
- *The Voyages of Ulysses* by Clifton Fadiman. Random House, 1959.

FILMS / VIDEOS
- *Great Books: The Odyssey.* TLC & Discovery Channel School, 2004.
- *The Journeys of Odysseus.* Top Dog Media, 2005.
- *The Odyssey.* Hallmark Entertainment, 1997.
- *Oh Brother, Where Art Thou?* Artisan Home Entertainment, 2000.
- *Troy.* Warner Brothers Pictures, 2004.

From *Commando Classics: A Field Manual for Helping Teens Understand (and Maybe Even Enjoy) Classic Literature* by Daria Plumb. Bowie, MD: VOYA Press, an imprint of E L Kurdyla Publishing, LLC. Copyright 2012

GRAPHIC NOVELS

- *The Age of Bronze, Volume 1: A Thousand Ships* by Eric Shanower. Image Comics, 2001.
- *The Age of Bronze, Volume 2: Sacrifice* by Eric Shanower. Image Comics, 2005.
- *The Age of Bronze, Volume 3, Part 1: Betrayal* by Eric Shanower. Image Comics, 2007.
- *Odysseus: Escaping Poseidon's Curse* by Dan Jolley. Graphic Universe, 2008.

ARTWORK

- *The Apotheosis of Homer* by J.A.D. Ingres
- *Circe Offering the Cup to Odysseus* by John William Waterhouse
- *A Fantastic Cave with Odysseus and Calypso* by Jan Bruegel the Elder
- Henry Ford:
    - *Calypso and Odysseus*
    - *Circe the Sorceress Turns Odysseus and His Men into Swine and Sends Them to the Styes*
    - *Odysseus Fights a Wild Boar and Gets a Wound in His Thigh*
    - *Odysseus Shoots the First Arrow at the Suitors*
    - *The Shipwrecked Odysseus Meets Nausicca Daughter of King Alcinous*
- *Homer* by Rembrandt
- *Homer and His Guide* by William-Adolphe Bouquereau
- *Homer Blind Greek Poet Singing to the Sailors* by P. Phillipoteaux
- *Odysseus* by Jacob Jordaens
- *Odysseus and Circe* by R. Smirke
- *Odysseus and His Men Poke Out the Eye of Polyphemus*
- *Odysseus and the Sirens, Athenian Red Figure Stamnos Vase by the Siren Painter*
- *Odysseus Finds His Father Laertes* by James Fittler
- *Odysseus Is Recognized by His Dog Argos* by Robert Brown
- *Odysseus Returns to His Wife, Penelope* by Isaac Taylor
- *The Quest for Ulysses* by W. B. Stanford and J. V. Luce
- *Reading from Homer* by Lawrence Alma-Tadema
- *Red-Figure Vase Depicting Odysseus*
- *Relief Depicting Odysseus and Penelope* from Milo, circa 450 BC

TV SHOWS

- D'Oh, Brother Where Art Thou segment from "Tales from the Public Domain." *The Simpsons*. Writ. Andrew Kreisberg, Josh Lied, and Matt Warburton. Dir. Mike B. Anderson. Season 13, episode 283. FOX. 17 Mar 2002.

From *Commando Classics: A Field Manual for Helping Teens Understand (and Maybe Even Enjoy) Classic Literature* by Daria Plumb. Bowie, MD: VOYA Press, an imprint of E L Kurdyla Publishing, LLC. Copyright 2012

THE ODYSSEY TEXT SET (Cont.)

INTERNET SOURCES

- *The Classics Pages: The Odyssey. http://www.users.globalnet.co.uk/~loxias/odchoice.htm*
- *Lesson Plans Library: The Odyssey.* Discovery Education. Summer Productions, Inc. *http://school.discoveryeducation.com/lessonplans/programs/odyssey/*
- *Library Think Quest: The Odyssey. http://library.thinkquest.org/19300/data/odyssey.htm*
- *Mythweb Odyssey* webquest. *http://www.mythweb.com/odyssey/*
- *OdysseusNostos. http://geocities.com/organisedchaosau/OdysseusNostos.html*
- *The Odyssey* at *Sparknotes. http://www.sparknotes.com/lit/odyssey/*
- *WebQuest: The Odyssey. http://coe.west.asu.edu/students/madams/webquest.htm*

SONGS

- "Calypso" by Suzanne Vega on *Songs Inspired by Literature, Chapter 1*. The SIBYL Project, 2002.
- "The Last Temptation of Odysseus" by Justin Wells on *Songs Inspired by Literature, Chapter 1*. The SIBYL Project, 2002.

BIOGRAPHIES

- "The Greek Poet Homer." *Mythography*. June 2, 2008. *http://www.loggia.com/myth/homer.html*
- "Homer." *Answers.com http://www.answers.com/topic/homer*

FOLKLORE and LEGENDS

- *Goddesses, Heroes, and Shamans: The Young People's Guide to World Mythology*. Scholastic, 1994.
- *The Hero Pattern* (from *The Hero: A Study in Tradition, Myth and Dreams* by Lord Raglan). *http://department.monm.edu/classics/courses/Clas230/MythDocuments/HeroPattern/default.htm*
- *The Monomyth. http://www.wiu.edu/users/mudjs1/monomyth.htm*

HISTORIES

- *In Search of Troy: One Man's Quest for Homer's Fabled City* written and illustrated by Giovanni Caselli. P. Bedrick Books, 1999.

MISCELLANEOUS

- *The Classics Pages: The Odyssey. http://www.users.globalnet.co.uk/~loxias/odchoice.htm*
- *The Ulysses Voyage: Sea Search for the Odyssey* by Tim Severin. E.P. Dutton, 1987.

From *Commando Classics: A Field Manual for Helping Teens Understand (and Maybe Even Enjoy) Classic Literature*
by Daria Plumb. Bowie, MD: VOYA Press, an imprint of E L Kurdyla Publishing, LLC. Copyright 2012

GREEK AND ROMAN MYTHOLOGY AND LEGENDS
IN PICTURE BOOKS AND YA LITERATURE

(J) – indicates a juvenile (ages 9-12) book
(YA) – indicates a book written for young adults (ages 13-18)

Arachne
- *Arachne Speaks* by Kate Hovey
- *Why Spiders Spin: A Story of Arachne* by Jamie Simons

Atalanta
- *Atalanta and the Arcadian Beast* by Jane Yolen
- *Atalanta's Race: A Greek Myth* by Shirley Climo
- *Quiver* by Stephanie Spinner **(YA)**

Cupid and Psyche
- *Cupid and Psyche* by M. Charlotte Craft
- *Cupid and Psyche: A Love Story* by Edna Barth
- *Cupid the God of Love* by Frances Winwar
- *The Princess and the God* by Doris Orgel **(YA)**

Demeter and Persephone
- *Demeter and Persephone; Homeric Hymn Number Two* by Penelope Proddow
- *Persephone* by Warwick Hutton
- *Persephone, Bringer of Spring* by Sarah F. Tomaino
- *Persephone and the Pomegranate: A Myth from Greece* by Kris Waldherr
- *Phone Home, Persephone!* by Kate McMullen
- *Song to Demeter* by Cynthia and William Birrer
- *The Story of Persephone* by Penelope Farmer
- *Two Queens of Heaven: Aphrodite and Demeter* by Doris Gates

Hercules
- *Hercules* by Bernard Evslin
- *Hercules* by Robin Moore **(J)**
- *Hercules: The Man, the Myth, the Hero* by Kathryn Lasky **(J)**

King Midas
- *The Adventures of King Midas* by Lynne Reid Banks **(YA)**
- *The Eyes of Kid Midas* by Neal Shusterman **(YA)**

- *King Midas* by Catherine Stoor
- *King Midas and His Gold* by Patricia McKissack
- *King Midas and the Golden Touch* by Charlotte Craft
- *King Midas and the Golden Touch* by Eric Metaxis
- *King Midas and the Golden Touch* by Kathryn Hewitt
- *Max and Ruby's Midas: Another Greek Myth* by Rosemary Wells

The Iliad and The Odyssey

- *Adventures of Odysseus* by Andrew Lang
- *Aleta and the Queen: A Tale of Ancient Greece* by Patricia Galloway (**J**)
- *Black Ships before Troy: The Story of the Iliad* by Rosemary Sutcliff (**YA**)
- *Dateline: Troy* by Paul Fleischman (**YA**)
- *Inside the Walls of Troy: A Novel of the Women Who Lived in the Trojan* War by Clarence McLaren (**YA**)
- *Ithaka* by Adele Geras (**YA**)
- *Odysseus in the Serpent Maze* by Jane Yolen (**YA**)
- *The Odyssey* adapted by Adrian Mitchell (**YA**)
- *The Odyssey* by Geraldine McCaughrean
- Tales from the Odyssey series by Mary Pope Osborn (**J**)
- *The Trojan Horse* by Warwick Hutton (**J**)
- *Troy* by Adele Geras (**YA**)
- *The Voyages of Ulysses* by Clifton Fadiman
- *The Wanderings of Odysseus: The Story of the Odyssey* (**J**)

Medusa

- *The Hero Perseus: A Mad Myth Mystery* by Robyn and Tony Di Tocco
- *Jason and the Gorgon's Blood* by Jane Yolen (**J**)
- *Medusa* by Bernard Evslin (**J**)
- *Perseus* by Bernard Evslin (**J**)
- *Snake Dreamer* by Priscilla Galloway (**YA**)
- *Trap for Perseus* by Ludek Pesek (**J**)

Pandora

- *Max and Ruby in Pandora's Box* by Rosemary Wells
- *Pandora's Box* by Lisl Weil
- *Pandora's Box: The Paradise of Children* by Nathaniel Hawthorne

From *Commando Classics: A Field Manual for Helping Teens Understand (and Maybe Even Enjoy) Classic Literature* by Daria Plumb. Bowie, MD: VOYA Press, an imprint of E L Kurdyla Publishing, LLC. Copyright 2012

Pegasus
- *Pegasus* by Krystyna Turska **(J)**
- *Pegasus* by Marianna Mayer
- *Pegasus, the Winged Horse* by Nathaniel Hawthorne
- *Quicksilver* by Stephanie Spinner **(YA)**

Theseus and the Minotaur
- *Ariadne, Awake!* by Doris Orgel
- *Lost in the Labyrinth* by Patrice Kindl **(YA)**
- *The Minotaur* by Bernard Evslin
- *The Minotaur of Knosses* by Roberto Angeletti **(J)**

Miscellaneous Myths
- *Apollo* by Katherine Miller
- *Arion and the Dolphins* by Lonzo Anderson
- *Cerberus* by Bernard Evslin
- *The Chimaera* by Bernard Evslin
- *The Cyclopes* by Bernard Evslin
- *Cyclops* by Leonard Everett Fisher
- *The Fire Thief* by Terry Deary **(YA)** (Prometheus)
- *The Great God Pan* by Donna Jo Napoli
- *Heraclea: A Legend of Warrior Women* by Bernard Evslin
- *Jason and the Argonauts* by Bernard **Evslin**
- *Perseus* by Warwick Hutton
- *The Prince and the Golden Ax: A Minoan Tale* by Deborah Nourse **(J)**
- *Quicksilver* by Stephanie Spinner **(YA)**
- *The Sirens* by Bernard Evslin
- *Star Boy* by Paul Goble
- *Strangers Dark and Gold* by Norma Johnston (Jason and Argonauts)
- *We Goddesses: Athena, Aphrodite, Hera* by Doris Orgel **(J)**
- *Why Dolphins Call: A Story of Dionysus* by Jamie Simons

CREATE YOUR OWN MARCHEN

So far in class we have read stories that are classified as marchen (or fairytales). Today, you will begin writing your own original marchen. This will be a rough draft, which means you will be getting some ideas and a basic plot structure down on paper. We may revisit these stories and make them into a group project.

Basic Structure of Marchen:

- Are set in an unreal world with a time and place that are not specific
- Have no definite characters—often characters are not named, but instead have names that describe them
- Involve acts of magic and magical characters
- Have heroes who are often humble, young, stupid, and/or small who overcome adversity to win the contest, marry the princess, and/or become rich beyond her/his wildest dreams, etc.
- Often have talking animals as characters
- Fast-paced and simple—less description of characters and setting & more action
- Usually involve good characters being rewarded and bad characters being punished
- Have repeated motifs
- End with the phrase "and they lived happily ever after"

Your story must:

- Follow the basic structure of a marchen (as outlined above)
- Include at least 3 motifs (ooh, hey, isn't THAT a motif?)
- Have a beginning (1 paragraph minimum), middle (3 paragraph minimum), and end (1 paragraph minimum). Each paragraph should have 3-5 sentences, so that means you should write between 15 and 25 sentences.

Outline for Writing a Story:

Most stories share a common organization and progression. Follow this outline as you write your folktale.

I. Beginning:

Introduce the main character.

Describe the setting.

Begin the plot.

II. Middle:

Introduce the character's problem.

Introduce minor characters.

Build toward the point of highest interest, or climax.

III. End:

Reach the point of highest interest.

Wind down the action, and give the final outcome.

From *Commando Classics: A Field Manual for Helping Teens Understand (and Maybe Even Enjoy) Classic Literature* by Daria Plumb. Bowie, MD: VOYA Press, an imprint of E L Kurdyla Publishing, LLC. Copyright 2012

EDUCATIONAL VIDEOS: WORLD LITERATURE

Channel	Series	Title	Length	Unit/Text Set
A & E	MODERN MARVELS	Great Pyramids of Giza and Other Pyramids	50 minutes	Africa
A & E	TIME MACHINE	Strange Egypt	50 minutes	Africa
A & E	UNSOLVED HISTORY	The Assasination of King Tut	42-45 minutes	Africa
A & E	GREAT BOOKS	The Art of War	50 minutes	Asia
A & E	HISTORY'S MYSTERIES	China's Forbidden City	50 minutes	Asia
A & E	IN SEARCH OF HISTORY	Samurai Warrior	50 minutes	Asia
A & E	LOST WORLDS	Pirates of the Caribbean	50 minutes	Caribbean
A & E	ANCIENT MYSTERIES	Ancient Rome and Its Mysterious Cities	50 minutes	Europe
The History Channel	ANCIENT MYSTERIES	Atlantis: The Lost Civilization	50 minutes	Europe
The History Channel	BIOGRAPHY	Hercules: Power of the Gods	50 minutes	Europe
A & E	HAUNTED HISTORY	The Scourge of the Black Death	50 minutes	Europe
PBS Home Video	HISTORY'S MYSTERIES	Vikings: Fury from the North	50 minutes	Europe
Standard Deviants School	IN SEARCH OF HISTORY	Curse of the Gypsies	50 minutes	Europe
The History Channel	IN SEARCH OF HISTORY	Oracle at Delphi	50 minutes	Europe
The History Channel	IN SEARCH OF HISTORY	The Greek Gods	50 minutes	Europe
Standard Deviants School	LOST WORLDS	Athens-Ancient Supercity	50 minutes	Europe
The History Channel	LOST WORLDS	Atlantis	50 minutes	Europe
TLC & Discovery Channel School	LOST WORLDS	Lost City of Aphrodite	50 minutes	Europe
Standard Deviants School	LOST WORLDS	The Pagans	50 minutes	Europe
The History Channel	LOST WORLDS	The Vikings	50 minutes	Europe
The History Channel	n/a	The Dark Ages	94 minutes	Europe
The History Channel	n/a	The Plague	100 minutes	Europe
The History Channel	UNSOLVED HISTORY	The Trojan Horse	42-45 minutes	Europe
The History Channel	SDS FANTASY LITERATURE	Module 1: Intro	26 minutes	Fantasy
The History Channel	SDS FANTASY LITERATURE	Module 2: Heroes and Hocus Pocus	26 minutes	Fantasy

EDUCATIONAL VIDEOS: WORLD LITERATURE (*Cont.*)

Channel	Series	Title	Length	Unit/Text Set
The History Channel	SDS FANTASY LITERATURE	Module 3: Monsters and Myth	26 minutes	Fantasy
The History Channel	SDS FANTASY LITERATURE	Module 4: Grendel, Dragons, & Meanies	26 minutes	Fantasy
The History Channel	ANCIENT MYSTERIES	Dragons: Myths and Legends	50 minutes	Folklore
The History Channel	ANCIENT MYSTERIES	Vampires	50 minutes	Folklore
The History Channel	ANCIENT MYSTERIES	Witches	50 minutes	Folklore
The History Channel	HISTORY'S MYSTERIES	Monsters of the Sea	50 minutes	Folklore
The History Channel	MONSTERQUEST	Giant Squid Found?	50 minutes	Folklore
The History Channel	MONSTERQUEST	Gigantic Killer Fish	50 minutes	Folklore
The History Channel	n/a	Quest for Dragons	50 minutes	Folklore
The History Channel	n/a	Vampire Secrets	100 minutes	Folklore
The History Channel	n/a	Witch Hunt	70 minutes	Folklore
The History Channel	TIME MACHINE	In Search of Christmas	100 minutes	Folklore
The History Channel	IN SEARCH OF HISTORY	Arabian Nights	50 minutes	Middle East
The History Channel	ANCIENT MYSTERIES	The Quest for the Holy Grail	50 minutes	Myth
The History Channel	BIOGRAPHY	Adam & Eve	50 minutes	Myth
The History Channel	DECODING THE PAST	Mysteries of the Garden of Eden	50 minutes	Myth
The History Channel	HISTORY'S MYSTERIES	The Search for Noah's Ark	50 minutes	Myth
The History Channel	IN SEARCH OF HISTORY	The Holy Grail	50 minutes	Myth
TLC & Discovery Channel School	n/a	In Search of Myths and Heroes	240 minutes	Myth
TLC & Discovery Channel School	ANCIENT MYSTERIES	Dreamtime of the Aborigines	50 minutes	Oceania
TLC & Discovery Channel School	GREAT BOOKS	The Odyssey	50 minutes	Odyssey
The Discovery Channel	IN SEARCH OF HISTORY	Prophecies	50 minutes	

What Is an American?
Teaching American Literature Thematically

To be totally honest, American literature had always been my least favorite class to teach. It lacks the sweeping, epic stories of British literature and, though I like Nathaniel Hawthorne and love Edgar Allan Poe and Langston Hughes, the rest of it sort of left me cold (I still shudder when I remember trying to understand Robert Frost's "Birches" as a high school junior). I never felt like I had a good handle on how to hook my students into the class, and even though I implemented my "commando tactics," it didn't really seem to gel. As a result, I never felt like I'd truly put my stamp on it and made it my own. If you are thinking, "Well that's really reassuring, I guess I'll just skip to the next chapter," please read on.

I've frequently toyed with the idea of teaching at least one of my classes thematically. I always figured it would be my young adult literature class because it seemed overwhelming to try to restructure a class that is traditionally taught in a chronological manner, like British or American literature. There is nothing wrong with teaching literature chronologically—it helps students to see how different movements develop in reaction to what came before them, and this is important if we're going to connect classic literature to students' modern lives.

So when the possibility of writing this book arose, I began to think of new and fresh ways to approach American Lit. Once again the idea of teaching a class thematically came to me, but I

COMMANDO LIBRARIANS

AN EVENING WITH EDGAR ALLAN POE

(Courtesy of Diane Tuccillo, Poudre River Public Library District, Fort Collins, CO)

"An Evening with Edgar Allan Poe" was a program hosted by the City of Mesa Library (Mesa, AZ). A local performer traveled around the state doing shows. Teachers assigned students to attend the performances for extra credit, but it didn't matter because they were so popular it was standing room only each time.

The Cherry Hills Library, Albuquerque, NM (http://www.cabq.gov/library/events/traveling-edgar-allan-poe-performance) and the Winterset Public Library, Winterset, IA (http://www.winterset.lib.ia.us/archive/2010/May/duffy-hudson) have also hosted similar programs.

Performers:
- Campbell "Lou" Harmon in *Edgar Allan Poe Live* (Connecticut) http://www.thepoeactor.com/
- David Keltz Appears as Edgar Allan Poe (Maryland) http://davidkeltz.com/
- Duffy Hudson as Edgar Allan Poe (California) http://www.duffyhudson.com/edgar_allan_poe_home.html
- Scott Craig Jones in The Traveling Jones Theater's *Edgar Allan Poe Comes Alive!* (Virginia) http://travelingjonestheater.com/index.htm

wasn't sure how to choose the topics of the units or how to structure them. Then, one summer day an ad came in the mail for a professional book about using questions to guide instruction, and that reminded me of a professional development day in which a literacy consultant and the English teachers in my district brainstormed one big question and several smaller focus questions for each grade level. That's when the light bulb finally came on! It was time to try teaching American literature thematically using questions to guide our units of study (see Guiding Questions and Writing Prompts in the American Literature Arsenal).

Now all I had to do was choose an overarching question. I looked over the materials I already had. There was a protest song unit that I definitely wanted to keep and I had text sets on Japanese internment, *The Scarlet Letter*, Edgar Allan Poe, and the Harlem Renaissance that I also wanted to include, if possible (you'll find the text sets in the American Literature Arsenal). So I paged through my American literature anthology. An

GREAT ALL-AROUND RESOURCES

- *Americans Who Tell the Truth* by Robert Shetterly (Dutton Children's Books, 2005)
- *Colorlines* © 2010. *http://www.colorlines.com*
- *Crossing the Danger Water: Three Hundred Years of African-American Writing* edited by Deidre Mullane (Anchor, 1993)
- *Independent Lens: Community Classroom: Lesson Plans and Film Modules* © 2011 Independent Television Service. *http://www.pbs.org/independentlens/classroom/lesson-plans/*
- *Library of Congress*, For Teachers. *http://www.loc.gov/teachers/*
- The National Archive: Teachers' Resources. *http://www.archives.gov/education/*
- *Poetry Foundation* © 2011. *http://www.poetryfoundation.org/*
- *Poets.org* from the Academy of American Poets © 1997 - 2011. (*http://www.poets.org/*)
- *Rethinking Schools* © 2011. *http://www.rethinkingschools.org*
- *Southern Poverty Law Center* © 2011. *http://www.splcenter.org/*
- *Tapestry: A Multicultural Anthology* edited by Alan C. Purves (Globe Book Company, 1993)
- *Teaching Tolerance: A Project of the Southern Poverty Law Center*. *http://www.teachingtolerance.org*
- *The People Speak* by Zinn Education Project. *http://www.thepeoplespeak.com/home*
- *The Treasury of American Poetry* edited by Nancy Sullivan (GuildAmerica Books, 1978)
- *The United States of Poetry*. *http://www.worldofpoetry.org/usop/*
- *Unsettling America: An Anthology of Contemporary Multicultural Poetry* edited by Maria Mazziotti Gillan and Jennifer Gillan (Penguin, 1994)
- *Us and Them: A History of Intolerance in America* by Jim Carnes (Teaching Tolerance, 1995)
- *Voices of a People's History* © 2011. *http://www.peopleshistory.us/*
- *Words That Built a Nation* by Marilyn Miller (Scholastic, 1999)
- *Zinn Education Project* © 2011 Teaching for Change and Rethinking Schools. *http://www.zinnedproject.org*

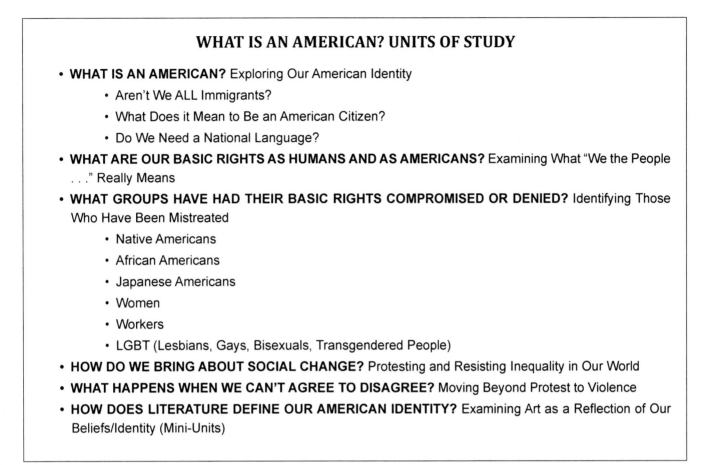

WHAT IS AN AMERICAN? UNITS OF STUDY

- **WHAT IS AN AMERICAN?** Exploring Our American Identity
  - Aren't We ALL Immigrants?
  - What Does it Mean to Be an American Citizen?
  - Do We Need a National Language?
- **WHAT ARE OUR BASIC RIGHTS AS HUMANS AND AS AMERICANS?** Examining What "We the People . . ." Really Means
- **WHAT GROUPS HAVE HAD THEIR BASIC RIGHTS COMPROMISED OR DENIED?** Identifying Those Who Have Been Mistreated
  - Native Americans
  - African Americans
  - Japanese Americans
  - Women
  - Workers
  - LGBT (Lesbians, Gays, Bisexuals, Transgendered People)
- **HOW DO WE BRING ABOUT SOCIAL CHANGE?** Protesting and Resisting Inequality in Our World
- **WHAT HAPPENS WHEN WE CAN'T AGREE TO DISAGREE?** Moving Beyond Protest to Violence
- **HOW DOES LITERATURE DEFINE OUR AMERICAN IDENTITY?** Examining Art as a Reflection of Our Beliefs/Identity (Mini-Units)

(adapted) essay at the beginning of the textbook caught my eye. It was written by Jean de Crevecouer in 1782 and is titled "What Is an American?" I had used this essay in the past, but had never found it to be particularly compelling. This time, though, it seemed like kismet. Here was an essay asking a question that could very well frame an entire school year's study: What *is* an American? It was starting to look as if I had a winner.

I spent a lot of time pouring through anthologies of African American literature, American poetry, American folklore and legends, and multicultural American literature, as well as numerous teaching websites, poetry websites, and the county library website to choose possible readings and videos. Working thematically, rather than chronologically, was a different way of thinking for me. Usually I use one piece of classic literature and build a text set around it. This time I was using a theme and building a large text set around it, which meant that in addition to the usual nonfiction, music, artwork, video clips, movies, and internet resources, etc., I could also have several pieces of both classic and modern literature within one text set—the possibilities were nearly endless (and if you don't believe me, you should see my spreadsheet).

I eventually sorted the results into nine possible units, with the plan that a unit entitled "How Does Literature Define Our American Identity?" could be broken into mini-units on certain types of literature like American Horror (i.e. Edgar Allan Poe), folklore and legends, African American traditional literature, Native American traditional literature, etc., and be inserted between the bigger units. We ended up making it through five of the nine units, and managed to squeeze in a mini-unit on American Horror (featuring Edgar Allan Poe) around Halloween.

The result was a year in which my students and I (wow, did I learn a lot) were asked to really think, talk, and write critically about what it means to be an American. They were interested and engaged learners who asked questions that helped to direct our learning. I asked them to examine big issues like prejudice, racism, equality, and justice in both historical and modern contexts. They read classic and modern works side-by-side. They watched some compelling and heartbreaking documentary films. One of the things of which I am most proud is that, rather than encountering a mostly white curriculum with a few African American authors, a Latino/a author or two, and maybe one Native American author, they read literature written by *many* minority authors—maybe more than they'd encountered in their school careers to that point.

WHAT IS AN AMERICAN?

This is an interesting question and, though we frequently use the term to describe ourselves, we don't often stop to think about what it actually means to be an American. Is anyone living in America an American or does he have to be a citizen? Does it matter how long a family has lived in this country? Are there some people who are "more" or "less" American than others? Are there certain traits that all Americans share or is it impossible to distill it down into one trait or set of traits? Is there an American identity?

Jean de Crevecouer's essay "What Is an American?" kicked off our reading. This essay provides us with one definition of an American, but one that leaves a lot of people out of the mix. While this essay was written when the United States was still a young country (1782), there would have been many groups of non-Europeans (including Native Americans and slaves) in the Americas at that time. Where do they fit into this definition? Or don't they? Jean de Crevecoeur paints a picture of America that, in many ways, fits with the romantic image we have of America. This essay, therefore, makes for a great starting point and raises an interesting question, "How is the reality of America different from the ideal?"

To help answer this question and to highlight the narrowness of de Crevecouer's definition, we then juxtaposed it with modern and classic poems featuring descriptions of America and Americans that don't necessarily fit his vision of America (see the What Is an American? text set in the American Literature Arsenal). Since I tend to think chronologically, it's a bit out of my comfort zone to use group reading materials in any other way, but reading Walt Whitman's "I Hear America Singing" (1860) alongside Langston Hughes' "I, Too" (1925) makes each poem more powerful; it's clear that Hughes' poem is something of a response to Whitman's poem written sixty-five years earlier, and shows Whitman's far-reaching influence as an American poet.

It's also hard for me not to deliberately group the poets by ethnic groups, but looking at the following poems about identity side-by-side, and in no particular order, highlights the fact that minorities in this country face many of the same struggles in defining where they "fit" into America: "Saying Yes" by Diana Chang; "AmeRícan" by Tato Laviera; "Ending Poem" by Aurora Levins Morales and Rosario Morales; "I Am Joaquin" by Rodolfo Gonzales; "Ellis Island" by Joseph Bruchac; and "Cross" by Langston Hughes. We see in these poems a sort of love-hate relationship with America; there is definite pride in being an American, but there is also difficulty being accepted as being fully American.

From there we moved on to explore our immigrant past in a sub-unit entitled, "Aren't We ALL Immigrants?" In response to the recent public outcry surrounding the proposed construction of an Islamic center within blocks of Ground Zero in New York City, *New York Times* op-ed columnist Nicholas D. Kristof wrote a terrific piece entitled "America's History of Fear," an article detailing the way that immigrants and those who have been perceived as "other"—Irish, Germans, Chinese, Italians, Catholics, Mormons—have been viewed with suspicion and marginalized throughout our country's history. Kristof points out that the prejudice we currently see directed towards Muslim Americans is not very different from the prejudice that was directed towards other groups of newcomers to this country. It's important for students to see the parallels between the ways in which their ancestors might have been treated and the way that we treat immigrants today. What if there had been no more room at the inn when our students' relatives had come to America? How might their lives be different today?

During our discussions about immigration, the issue of language came up repeatedly. Students would say things like, "This is America. If you're going to live here, you should have to speak English." When I asked them why they felt this way, the most common answers were that they found it difficult, frustrating, and inconvenient to communicate with the non-English speakers; they assumed the non-English speakers were talking about and making fun of them; or they thought the non-English speakers were simply refusing to learn English. I wanted to give them a sense of how difficult it would be to try to function in a country if you couldn't understand the language. So I went to the U.S. Citizenship and Immigration Services' website and printed the first page of the packet "Welcome to the United States: A Guide for New Immigrants" in several different languages. The next day I gave the students the handouts, asked them to read through the few paragraphs, and to be ready to take a quiz over what they'd read. We also spent time reading articles and writing about whether English should become the national language of the United States (we don't currently have a national language, which is something I never knew).

We concluded with the article "American Identity: Ideas, Not Ethnicity" by Michael Jay Friedman. This brought us full circle as, just over two hundred twenty-five years after de Crevecouer wrote his essay, we see another writer attempting to define what it means to be an American. It certainly suggests that there are no easy answers to this question of American identity. This is the perfect piece to conclude with—not only does Friedman reference de Crevecouer's essay, he also discusses the melting pot vs. salad bowl analogies and ends the article with a quote from Walt Whitman.

What Are Our Basic Rights As Humans and Americans?

In order to prepare for our upcoming third unit on groups whose rights have been compromised or denied in this country, we needed to first define and examine what our basic rights actually are, as both human beings and Americans. We took a look at the thirty-article Universal Declaration of Human Rights that was adopted by the United Nations in 1948. The *Youth for Human Rights: Making Human Rights a Global Reality* (*http://www.youthforhumanrights.org/*) website is the perfect starting place to introduce this document, as it has both the original version and a simplified version of the declaration, thirty PSA videos representing each individual right, and a fantastic (and short) introductory documentary, "The Story of Human Rights." To help students further understand these rights, each student could create a visual representation (collage, poster, diorama, etc.) of one of the thirty rights. We then took a look at the U.S. Bill of Rights and some of the "corrective amendments" (amendments 13, 14, 15, 19, and 24, for example) to the U.S. Constitution,

HUMAN AND AMERICAN RIGHTS

- 1 For All *http://1forall.us/*
- American Civil Liberties Union's Key Issues *http://www.aclu.org/key-issues*
- Bill of Rights, The Charters of Freedom, U.S. National Archives *http://archives.gov/exhibits/charters/bill_of_rights.html*
- *Every Human Has Rights: A Photobiographic Declaration for Kids* (National Geographic Children's Books, 2009)
- "Everybody: We Are All Born Free" video by Amnesty International *http://www.youtube.com/watch?v=x9_lvXFEyJo*
- *First Freedom Center http://www.firstfreedom.org*
- "Human Rights in Action!" by *United Nations' CyberSchoolBus* © 1996-2011 United Nations *http://www.un.org/cyberschoolbus/humanrights/index.asp*
- The National Archive: Documented Rights *http://www.archives.gov/exhibits/documented-rights/*
- The United Nations' *The Universal Declaration of Human Rights* © United Nations 2011 *http://www.un.org/en/documents/udhr/index.shtml*
- The U.S. Constitution FAQ © Craig Walenta 1995-2010 *http://www.usconstitution.net/constfaq.html*

which primarily gave citizenship and voting rights to blacks and to women.

During this unit, we zeroed in on the First Amendment largely because several stories garnering media attention at the time were somehow related to freedom of speech, press, and assembly. We spent a lot of time examining the need for balance and limits where our rights are concerned. Just because a person *can* do something, does it mean that he should? Where do we draw the line? At what point does one person's right to freedom of speech infringe upon another person's right to privacy? When does the right to freedom of speech become dangerous to others? There are a lot of reading (newspaper and magazine articles and blog posts), watching (news reports), writing, and discussion opportunities here, and this is another unit that could probably take up an entire year.

This serendipitously took us into the last week of September, which is when the American Library Association (ALA) annually celebrates "Banned Books Week" (from the outside, it looks like good planning on my part, but it happened totally by chance).

BANNED BOOKS WEEK

(Teachers and librarians prep for this week *all year*, so get one of them into your classroom to talk to your kids about banned books)

- American Library Association's Banned Books Week *http://ala.org/ala/issuesadvocacy/banned/bannedbooksweek/index.cfm*
- "A Guide to Teaching Challenged and Banned Books: Featuring the Novels of Chris Crutcher" from HarperCollins Publishing *http://files.harpercollins.com/PDF/TeachingGuides/0060094907.pdf*
- My *YouTube* playlist for Banned Books Week *http://www.youtube.com/playlist?p=PLA6C3CD4AA9943466&feature=mh_lolz*
- *PABBIS (Parents Against Bad Books in Schools)* website *http://www.pabbis.com*

Because I work at an alternative high school, it probably comes as no surprise that my classroom is filled with reluctant readers. However, my classroom is also filled with amazing YA books, so over the course of their time in our program, most of the students find that they *do* enjoy reading once they have been introduced to the right books. This makes my students rabid supporters of the authors they deem to be their favorites. Because these teens often come from pretty rough backgrounds, they're not fazed by books with what others might term as having "dark" or "tough" content or with "bad language." Many of my students tell stories about how a book not only helped to turn them into readers, but also literally saved their lives, so they don't take too kindly to people trying to remove these books from classrooms or libraries.

> **COMMANDO LIBRARIANS**
>
> During Banned Books Week, create a display of well-known banned or challenged books wrapped in paper. Write a short description of the plot on each book. Teens can guess the title of the book from the plot. If you have a teen advisory board, ask them to wrap the books and write the short descriptions.

We spent time reading materials not only from ALA, but also from Parents Against Bad Books in Schools (PABBIS), as well as news articles and author blogs. We watched online slideshows featuring some of the most surprising banned or challenged books, and video clips of challenged authors talking about and reading from their work. The students became so wrapped up in this issue that they even discussed it outside of school. One day Michael said to me, "So, Plumb, a bunch of us were driving around yesterday . . . and we were talking about banned books and how it pisses us off. Our friends from the other high school were like, 'What are you talking about?' They didn't even *know* about banned books." The culminating project for the unit was to write a letter taking a stand on censorship (see Banned Books Week: Final Writing in the American Literature Arsenal). The audience for the letter could be either the people bringing the challenges or an author of a challenged/banned book. The students were not required to send the letters as part of the assignment, but were given the option to send them or post them to an online blog.

What Groups Have Had Their Basic Rights Compromised or Denied?

This was a doozy of a unit and, as I mentioned earlier, could easily have been our focus for the entire year (which is really sort of unfortunate). I broke this unit into six groups who have had their basic human and/or American rights denied: Native Americans, African Americans, Japanese Americans, Women, Workers, and Gays and Lesbians. It goes without saying that there are many groups not represented here—we simply didn't have the time to get to everybody and it was my hope that, once students became aware of inequities, they'd be more apt to recognize them in their daily lives. I tried to strike a balance between groups that were obvious choices because of our history, groups my students could relate to, and groups against whom my students tend to discriminate. The booklet *Us and Them: A History of Intolerance in America* by Jim Carnes also helped me to frame this unit, as did information from the *Zinn Education Project (http://zinnedproject.org/)*, *Teaching Tolerance (http://www.tolerance.org/)*, and *Colorlines (http://colorlines.com/)* websites ("like" these pages on Facebook and Twitter to receive updates about lessons and resources).

SOCIAL PSYCHOLOGY EXPERIMENTS

- "The Bystander Effect" *http://www.youtube.com/watch?v=OSsPfbup0ac&list=PL27AC941A7215AA83*

- "Learned Helplessness" University of Pennsylvania *http://www.noogenesis.com/malama/discouragement/helplessness.html*

- Milgram's Obedience to Authority Experiment 2009 *http://www.youtube.com/watch?v=3f6LLV3fkXg*

- "Video on the Original Milgram Experiment" from *The Situationist*, April 16, 2010 *http://thesituationist.wordpress.com/2010/04/26/the-original-milgram-experiment-1961-%e2%80%a2-videosift-online-video-quality-control/*

In order to discuss injustice and discrimination, we needed to examine our natural human propensity to focus on the differences between people, rather than the similarities—to label people as either "us" or "them"—and how that distancing allows us to excuse the horrible treatment of people we view as "other." Once distance is created, it is easy to generate fear, and fear is a technique that has been used to successfully control and manipulate people throughout history. Hitler, of course, is one of the first examples to come to mind, but we see evidence of this in many other situations, including the internment of Japanese Americans after the bombing of Pearl Harbor and the lynching of African Americans during the Jim Crow Era. We also focused briefly on the psychology behind learned helplessness (Seligman's shuttlebox experiment), the human response to authority (the Milgram experiment), and the bystander effect.

With this background, we were able to examine the groups whose rights had been denied. Within each individual sub-unit, it was necessary to work chronologically. That didn't mean that the literature we read necessarily had to progress from oldest to newest—for example, Michael Dorris' 1992 young adult novel *Morning Girl* was the first reading for our Native American unit—but we did start at the beginning historically as far as these groups' interactions with Europeans and/or the American government was concerned.

Native Americans

We began with the Native Americans (see the Identifying Those Who Have Been Mistreated: Native Americans text set in American Literature Arsenal). I was surprised to learn that most of my students don't know very much about the people who lived in this country for centuries before the arrival of the Europeans. Nearly every year in elementary school they learned about the first Thanksgiving. Because of our local history, they know about General George Armstrong Custer, who is considered by many to be a "local hero." They know that there are several Native American casinos in Michigan. They believe that if a person has a certain percentage of Native American blood, he can go to college for free. But that's about it.

COMMANDO LIBRARIANS

A craft project can complement a program, class lecture, or booktalks of titles about Native American characters. Beads, feathers, shells, leather cord, and other collected items from nature can make beautiful dream catchers, belts, dolls, and jewelry. Teens like their craft projects to be unique, while younger children want theirs to look like their friends', so a wide assortment of materials will inspire more creativity. Explore books and the Internet for project ideas and how-to videos.

We began this unit by reading selections from the novel *Morning Girl* by Michael Dorris. In the opening chapters we hear about the world from the point-of-view of the title character, Morning Girl, and her brother, Star Boy. We learn about their family, their relationships, and their daily lives. I deliberately don't tell the students that Morning Girl and

Star Boy are Taino Indians living in the Bahamas in 1492 because I want them to relate to these characters as young people who aren't too different from themselves. They need to be in that mindset for the epilogue, which provides us with an excerpt from Christopher Columbus' journal in which he describes these people as simple, poor heathens who will be easy to enslave. We know from reading the early chapters that this isn't true, so how is it possible for Columbus to draw these conclusions mere moments after his arrival in the Americas?

We followed this with "Blankets for the Dead" from *Us and Them: A History of Intolerance in America* by Jim Carnes, which details the forced removal of Native Americans from their homes. This brought us to the question of how it is that President Andrew Jackson, the man who broke treaties and ordered and orchestrated the removal and forced death marches of thousands of Native Americans, is pictured on our $20 bill. This was an issue I'd never thought about until several years ago when Brandon brought in the song "$20 Bill" by Corporate Avenger as part of our protest song unit. The chorus asks the question, "If Hitler was on the $20 bill, how would the Jews feel?" We also read portions of Chief Joseph's famous speech "I Will Fight No More Forever."

Because we talked about the melting pot (assimilation) vs. salad bowl (accommodation) analogies in the opening unit, I wanted to show students the lengths the government took in order to force Native Americans to assimilate. Probably one of the most ghastly ways was through government owned and operated Native American boarding schools. One of the most powerful video clips we watched all year was an excerpt from the 2008 film *Our Spirits Don't Speak English: Indian Boarding Schools* (*http://www.youtube.com/watch?v=qDshQTBh5d4&NR=1*), in which Andrew Windyboy, a Chippewa Cree, describes his experiences as a child in these boarding schools. It is emotional, heartbreaking, gut-wrenching, and difficult to watch and I can't imagine anything that would better drive home the horrors of these schools. When the clip ended, the kids didn't move or speak. Charla Bear's 2008 article, "American Indian Boarding Schools Haunt Many," shows not only the far-reaching effects of these schools on those who attended them, but also includes excerpts from government reports showing the change in attitude towards these schools as investigations took place.

In order to not leave students with the idea that all of this occurred in some far-removed, distant past, we watched the documentary *Broken Rainbow*, which won the 1986 Academy Award for best documentary and shows the government's forced relocation of more than ten thousand Diné (Navajo) in Arizona in 1974 in order to gain the rights to land rich in natural resources. We then ended this unit with several poems, mostly by contemporary Native American poets (including "The PowWow at the End of the World" by Sherman Alexie, "The Never Ending Trail" by Del "Abe" Jones, and "A Tribute to Chief Joseph" by Duane Niatum) and contemporary articles, like Rob Capriccioso's "A Sorry Saga: Obama Signs Native American Apology Resolution; Fails to Draw Attention to It." We also watched the *YouTube* video "How Hollywood Stereotyped Native Americans (*http://www.youtube.com/watch?v=_hJFi7SRH7Q&feature=channel_video_title*) and talked about how these portrayals might have impacted people who believed these images to be reality.

African Americans

Of all the groups we studied this year, this is the one on which we spent the most time. I suppose there are a few reasons for this. First, I would say that my students are more likely to stereotype and discriminate against African Americans than any other group. Second, I was already familiar with a fair amount of African American literature and had a wonderful resource in the anthology *Crossing the Danger Water: Three*

Hundred Years of African-American Writing edited by Deidre Mullane, so finding reading assignments for this sub-unit wasn't as daunting as it was with others. Third, it seems like teens know a lot about slavery because of the Civil War, but they have absolutely no idea what happened *after* the signing of the Emancipation Proclamation. There's another blip on their radar with Dr. Martin Luther King, Jr. They know we have a black president, which they think must prove that everyone is now equal. There are some pretty big holes that need to be filled in (see the Identifying Those Who Have Been Mistreated: African Americans text set in American Literature Arsenal).

We do begin with slavery. There's no way to truly understand the horror of slavery until reading about it from the point-of-view (either real or fictional) of someone who has lived it. Excerpts from Alex Haley's *Roots*, Olaudah Equiano's *The Interesting Narrative of the Life of Olaudah Equiano*, and Paula Fox's young adult novel *The Slave Dancer* took us from life in an African village to the middle passage on a slave ship. The worksheet "The Slave Trade-Capture and Middle Passage" from *History on the Net: Black Peoples in America* (*http://www.historyonthenet.com/Lessons/worksheets/black_peoples.htm*) allowed students to imagine what it would be like to be captured and transported on a slave ship. The opening chapters of Frederick Douglass' *Narrative of the Life of Frederick Douglass: An American Slave* and excerpts from Julius Lester's *To Be a Slave* outline daily life as a slave. Classic poems by African American poets Frances Ellen Watkins Harper ("Bury Me in a Free Land," "The Slave Auction," and "The Slave Mother") and George Moses Horton ("The Slaves Complaint") capture the raw emotions of slavery.

Although I wanted to save slave uprisings for the next unit on protesting, resisting, and bringing about social change, I was a bit unsure about what to do with the Underground Railroad. Escape was obviously the ultimate form of resistance but, for reasons I can't articulate, it felt right to study it in this unit, so we read poems about escape ("Runagate, Runagate" by Robert Hayden and "The Fugitive Slave" by Jones Very), the lyrics to the Negro spiritual "Follow the Drinking Gourd," the picture book *Henry's Freedom Box: A True Story of the Underground Railroad* by Ellen Levine and talked about Harriet Tubman here. As a class we navigated the Underground Railroad via National Geographic's website (*http://www.nationalgeographic.com/railroad/*) and students learned about "Underground Railroad Codes" and "Underground Railroad Messages" from *History on the Net: Black Peoples in America* (*http://www.historyonthenet.com/Lessons/worksheets/black_peoples.htm*).

Much of the content thus far is sort of a recap for my students. They've learned about a lot of this history but that's where their knowledge stops. We started our next section with the reading "A Town Called Rosewood" from *Us and Them: A History of Intolerance in America* by Jim Carnes, in which the primarily black town of Rosewood, Florida, was wiped entirely off the map because a white woman accused a black man of breaking into her home and assaulting her. This story highlights the fact that a black person living in the South was afforded no protection from the police (who were also often the tormentors) or the government. We followed with a bit of background information on lynching. The National Underground Railroad Resource Center's *Without Sanctuary: Lynching Photography in America*, website, and online teacher's guide (*http://freedomcenter.org/without-sanctuary/WithoutSanctuaryTeacherGuide.pdf*) are amazing resources, but do feature some very disturbing images. We also read several poems and songs about lynching. Paul Lawrence Dunbar's "The Haunted Oak," Amiri Baraka's "Biography," and Abel Meerpol's song "Strange Fruit" are particularly poignant.

In order to put a more personal face on the lynching issue, we viewed the amazing documentary *The Untold Story of Emmett Louis Till* by filmmaker Keith Beauchamp. I think teenagers generally have trouble imagining themselves in the shoes of another person (particularly if that person seems very different from them), but this film about a fourteen-year-old black boy who was brutally murdered for whistling at a white woman in Money, Mississippi, in 1955, pulled them right in. No one slept. No one talked. No one complained. When Emmett's mother, Mamie, described going to collect her son's body, girls cried. At the end of each day's viewing, we all sat in the dark in stunned silence. When I asked students later to write about which documentary I should be sure to use the next time I teach this section, this was the overwhelming choice with nearly 70 percent of the votes. Students used words like "haunting" and "it will stay with me forever" to describe their reactions to this film, and continued to reference Emmett throughout the remainder of the school year. It is often said that this particular murder started the Civil Rights Movement, and poets and songwriters like Langston Hughes ("The Money Mississippi Blues" and "Mississippi—1955") and Bob Dylan ("The Death of Emmett Till") memorialized Emmett with their words so that people would never forget what happened.

We moved from Emmett's murder to the equally distressing 1963 16th Street Baptist Church bombing, in which four girls (aged eleven and fourteen) were killed when three KKK members planted a bomb in the church that detonated during Sunday services. We watched the Spike Lee documentary *4 Little Girls*, which not only featured interviews with the families of Addie Mae Collins, Cynthia Wesley, Carole Robertson, and Denise McNair, but also provided quite a bit of background information on the state of race relations in Birmingham at that time. We read Carole Boston Weatherford's picture book *Birmingham, 1963* and read an article following up and giving information about the fates of the bombers. We also read a variety of poems and songs (including "American History" by Michael Harper, "Birmingham Sunday" by Langston Hughes, and "The Ballad of Birmingham" by Dudley Randall) commemorating the deaths of these girls. But, it was the spoken word performance of Saul Williams' "Coded Language" that most captivated the students. Williams dedicates the poem and the future to those who have struggled, fought, and sometimes died for equality, saying,

> Thus in the name of:
>
> ...**four little girls**, Hiroshima, Nagasaki, Keller, Biko, Perone, Marley, Cosby, Shakur, those still aflamed, and the countless unnamed
>
> We claim the present as the pre-sent, as the hereafter.
>
> We are unraveling our navels so that we may ingest the sun.
>
> We are not afraid of the darkness, we trust that the moon will guide us.
>
> We are determining our future at this very moment.

The students were enthralled by the rhythmic, fast, angry, in-your-face slam poetry. They asked, "What was that?" I'd never seen them react so positively to any type of poetry before.

To bring us into the present and to make students aware of the fact that there is still widespread racism in this country, we looked at hate crime statistics for 2009 from the FBI (*http://www2.fbi.gov/ucr/hc2009/data/table_01.html*) and "Active U.S. Hate Groups" from the Southern Poverty Law Center (*http://www.crmvet.org/info/lithome.htm*), watched spoken word performances "Niggas, Niggers, and Niggaz" by Julian Curry (*http://www.youtube.com/watch?v=wD-UpHlB9no&feature=related*) and "Super Negro" by Al B (*http://www.youtube.com/results?search_query=super+negro+al+b.&aq=o*), and watched the documentary *Prom Night in Mississippi*, which details the first integrated prom (in 2008) in a Mississippi high school.

Japanese Internment

It seems as if we spent a lot of time in this unit studying incidents and episodes in our American history that many people know very little about. The internment of Japanese Americans is another such event, and is another example of something that could/should be taught alongside the Holocaust (see the Identifying Those Who Have Been Mistreated: Japanese Internment text set in American Literature Arsenal). Following the 1941 bombing of Pearl Harbor, President Franklin D. Roosevelt issued Executive Order No. 9066, which gave the Secretary of War and the Military Commanders the authority to declare any area a "military area" and to remove from those areas any citizen who might be deemed a threat in the name of "national security." As it turned out, most of the people who were considered threats were Japanese American citizens living on the west coast. These citizens were forced to leave their homes and enter internment camps surrounded by barbed wire and patrolled by armed guards.

Before we even began any reading assignments, we started with a quick write in which I asked students to imagine that for some reason they might not ever see some of their family and/or friends again and then to think about the possessions that they might take with them if they were being forced to leave their homes with only one, small suitcase. Then we read the opening chapters of Jeannie Wakatsuki Houston's young adult novel *Farewell to Manzanar*, in which she describes having many of the same feelings and reactions as the students did in their writing assignments. We followed that by reading factual information on the camps and poems (including "That Damned Fence" by Anonymous, "Manzanar" by Michiko Mizumoto, and "My Mom, Pop, and Me" by Itsuko Taniguchi) that painted a bleak picture of life within the camps, listened to and watched a video for the song "Kenji" by Fort Minor (*http://www.youtube.com/watch?v=3Ckvmc_486U*), and watched a video clip of George Takei of *Star Trek* fame describing his recollections of his own family's relocation (*http://www.youtube.com/watch?v=oUrpIFp7EMA*).

Then, to totally flip things, we watched an "informational"/propaganda film created by the Office of War Information explaining and justifying the relocation of the Japanese (*http://www.youtube.com/watch?v=_OiPldKsM5w*). This video completely contradicted everything we'd read and heard up to that point from real people who experienced it. It would almost be laughable if it wasn't real—it was made to justify the unconstitutional incarceration of over one hundred thousand United States citizens. The focus was on protection and safety for "them" and for "us." Here again was the perfect example of the use of fear to manipulate people.

What struck me most during this sub-unit was how easily all of this could have been repeated following the 9/11 attacks. The "Postwar & Impact Today" page on the website *Exploring the Japanese Internment through Film & the Internet* asks us, "Can it Happen Again?" (*http://caamedia.org/jainternment/postwar/index.html*). This brought us back to a discussion about balance we had during the unit on rights, in which we discussed the fact that some people are willing to give up their rights if they can be convinced that it will guarantee their safety.

Women

Surprisingly, this was the sub-unit that was met with the most resistance by my male students and the most apathy by my female students (see the Identifying Those Who Have Been Mistreated: Women text set in American Literature Arsenal). Many of them agreed that it probably would have been okay if women had never been given the right to vote. Many of them also didn't really seem to have any problems with the fact that, until fairly recently, husbands had complete say over the reproductive rights of their wives. Some students even came in after telling their parents what we were learning about in class and told me that their mothers didn't think women needed the right to vote. As someone who grew up in a household with an educated, professional mother and where I was told I could do anything, this caught me completely off guard.

This radical idea that women should be afforded the same rights as men isn't a new one. To demonstrate this, we started our reading with "Letters between Abigail Adams and Her Husband John" from *The Liz Library* (*http://www.thelizlibrary.org/suffrage/abigail.htm*) and watched a clip of Abigail Adams from the miniseries *John Adams* (*http://www.youtube.com/watch?v=WXQZIo6JN2Q*). The picture books *Patriots in Petticoats: Heroines of the American Revolution* by Shirley Raye Redmond and *Independent Dames: What You Never Knew about the Women and Girls of the Revolution* by Laurie Halse Anderson highlight other outspoken women from early American history.

From there we moved to conferences calling for women's rights, including the first Women's Rights Convention in Seneca Falls, NY (*http://www.youtube.com/watch?v=yXdr7q3jVck*) and an 1851 conference in Akron, Ohio, which brought to the forefront another strong advocate for women's rights, a freed slave named Sojourner Truth. We watched a clip of Truth's speech, "Ain't I a Woman?" (*http://www.youtube.com/watch?v=4vr_vKsk_h8*) from The Zinn Education Project's *The People Speak* (which features celebrities—actors, actresses, musicians—performing/reciting famous speeches, letters, songs, poems, etc. from history).

We also watched the film *Iron Jawed Angels*, which details the suffrage movement led by Alice Paul (the scene in which Alice Paul is force fed, is a "must view" and can be found on *YouTube* if time is an issue). The "Women's History Primary Source Sets: Women's Suffrage" page from the *Library of Congress* website (*http://www.loc.gov/teachers/classroommaterials/themes/womens-history/set.html*) has a collection of maps, photographs, broadsides, political cartoons, etc. from the suffrage movement that can be displayed and shared with students. You could also play the video "Sufferin' Till Sufferage" from *School House Rock* (*http://www.youtube.com/watch?v=3dPF0SGh_PQ*).

We moved from women's suffrage to reproductive rights. As this is often viewed as a moral and religious issue, cover your bases. We read "Body Politics" by Anastasia Higginbotham from *33 Things Every Girl Should Know about Women's History: From Suffragettes to Skirt Lengths to the E.R.A.* edited by Tonya Bolden. We also watched video clips "Roe v. Wade in PBS' The Supreme Court" (*http://www.youtube.com/watch?v=1q5AgCzPIuA*) and "The Birth Control Revolution" (*http://www.youtube.com/watch?v=KmYSNOEsukM*), which addressed issues like abortion and the history of birth control. The op-ed piece "Poor Jane's Almanac" by Jill Lepore for *The New York Times* (which was published after we finished this unit) details the life of Benjamin Franklin's youngest sister and will be included the next time I teach this class.

We concluded this section with the video "This Is What a Feminist Looks Like" (*http://www.youtube.com/ watch?v=3YA13GNT8Mc*) and several songs and poems, including "Still I Rise" and "Phenomenal Woman" by Maya Angelou, "What Women Deserve" by Sonya Renee Taylor (*http://www.youtube.com/watch?v=BoLL6Zqc-Qo*), and "For Women" by Talib Kweli (*http://www.youtube.com/watch?v=0qkjtK3O15Q*).

Workers

Despite the fact that many of my students come from blue collar, working class families, many of them did not know what a labor union was. After seeing the reaction of my students to the story of Emmett Till, I wanted to start our sub-unit on workers' rights with another historical event that involved teenagers in the hope that it would help them better relate to the issues we were going to discuss (see the Identifying Those Who Have Been Mistreated: Workers text set in American Literature Arsenal). We began by studying the Triangle Shirtwaist Fire of 1911 in which one hundred forty-six people (mostly young, immigrant women) died. Cornell University has an absolutely wonderful website commemorating the one hundred year anniversary of the factory fire (*http://www.ilr.cornell.edu/trianglefire/index.html*), which just happened to fall during our study of this event, including a list of those who died, primary source materials, background information, political cartoons, etc. I asked students to read the list of the victims to find the names and ages of the youngest people who died (Katie Leone and Rosaria Maltese, both fourteen) and to count the number of victims who were the same age as they are. We then analyzed some of the political cartoons from the site, read some poems ("Shirt" by Robert Pinsky and "Sisters in the Flames" by Carol Tarlen had a particularly strong impact), read song lyrics ("Ballad of the Triangle Fire" by Ruth Rubin, "Mournful Song of the Great Fire" by Yehuda Horvitz, and "My Little Shirtwaist" by Rasputina), and watched part of the documentary *Triangle Fire*.

After learning of the deplorable working conditions in the Triangle Shirtwaist factory, it was easy to see why there might be a push for legislation and labor unions that would guarantee better, safer working conditions. The "Paying with Their Health" lesson from *Teaching Tolerance* (*http://www.tolerance.org/activity/paying-their-health*) exposed students to the poor working conditions in the food production industry, like food processing factories (included is an excerpt from Upton Sinclair's *The Jungle*) and on migrant farms. We also read *A Picture Book of Cesar Chavez* by David Adler, read Chavez's own writing in "Prayer of the Farm Worker's Struggle" and "Speech to Striking Grape Workers," and listened to songs celebrating Chavez's heroism, including "Corrido de Cesar Chavez (Ballad of Cesar Chavez)" by Rumel Fuentes, "El Corrido de Cesar Chavez" by El Teatro Campesino, and "Si Se Puede" by Linda Allen. We then watched a portion of the documentary "Harlan County, U.S.A," which showed Brookside, Kentucky, coal miners' attempt to form a union in 1973, and finished with several poems ("Forced Overtime" and "What Is a Union?" by David Hurlburt) and songs from *Union Songs...online collection* by Mark Gregory (*http://unionsong. com/*) discussing the need for fair wages and unions.

LGBT

I actually expected this sub-unit on the rights of gays, lesbians, bisexuals, and transgendered people to be the most controversial of this unit (see the Identifying Those Who Have Been Mistreated: LGBT text set in

American Literature Arsenal). Again, some people might make this a moral issue about whether it's right or wrong to be homosexual. I tried to stay away from that particular discussion, although there were times when students brought it up. When that happened, I directed them back to thinking about rights—whether all people (including gays, lesbians, bisexuals, and transgendered people) in this country are entitled to equal rights and protection under the law. We focused on the brutal murders of two, young, gay men which helped it be less about sexual and/or gender orientation and more about whether or not any person has the right to harass, beat, or kill another person.

We began with "A Rose for Charlie" from *Us and Them: A History of Intolerance in America* by Jim Carnes, the story of a young man who was beaten and thrown off a bridge to his death by three teenage boys in Bangor, Maine, in 1984. We read "26th Annual Charlie Howard Memorial Held in Bangor" and "Where are Charlie Howard's Killers?" both by Judy Harrison for *Bangor Daily News* about how the city of Bangor memorialized Charlie and what happened to the three boys who killed Charlie. The poems "Charlie Howard's Descent" by Mark Doty and "Autumn in Maine (for Charlie Howard)" by David E. Patton memorialized Charlie. We also read articles addressing gay rights and discrimination, including "Should *South Park* Get Away with Using the F-Word?" by Michael Jones, "Should Crimes Against Gays Be Considered Hate Crimes?" by Jenny Murphy, and "La. Student Sent Home for Gay T-Shirt" by *Advocate.com* editors.

The murder of Matthew Shepard was the second murder we studied. We watched the film *The Laramie Project*, which was based on a play of the same name examining the impact of the murder of college student Matthew Shepard in Laramie, Wyoming, in 1998. This film doesn't just outline the course of events surrounding Matthew's attack and death, but it also focuses on the reactions of the townspeople to the beating, as well as the amount of media attention it was attracting and how it made the town look to the rest of the world. Many advocates for gay rights—including songwriters Elton John ("American Triangle" with Bernie Taupin), Cyndi Lauper ("Above the Clouds" with Jed Leiber and Jeff Beck), and Melissa Etheridge ("Scarecrow")—had strong personal reactions to Matthew's story and wrote songs about the circumstances of his death. We revisited the FBI's list of 2009 hate crimes (*http://www2.fbi.gov/ucr/hc2009/data/table_01.html*) and watched an interview "10 Years after Matthew Shepard's Murder" (*http://www.youtube.com/watch?v=So5RAanecsg&feature=related*) that Matthew's mother gave to the *Rocky Mountain News* ten years after the death of her son. This interview was strangely reminiscent of Mamie Till Mobley's reaction to her son Emmett's death forty-five years earlier, an observation which brought us nearly full-circle as we finished this unit.

How Do We Bring About Social Change?

As I mentioned earlier, I had difficulty separating the content of this unit from the previous unit. So, when we got to this unit and I looked at my spreadsheet, I found that I still had a big chunk of information left about how African Americans resisted and protested and my sub-unit on protest songs, but that most of the other speeches, songs, and reading assignments I had planned to use for this unit had inadvertently made their way into the unit on denied rights. This leads me to believe that I need to either restructure both units or merge them into one new unit (this is probably the more likely option) the next time I teach this class.

African American Protest and Resistance

When we studied slavery in the previous unit we talked about the Underground Railroad and Harriet Tubman's role as a conductor. We did not, however, talk about other ways that slaves resisted. In this unit we read about some of the major slave rebellions that took place in the United States. We also used a great worksheet, "Slave Resistance" from *History on the Net.com* (*http://www.historyonthenet.com/Lessons/worksheets/black_peoples.htm*), which gave students the opportunity to think about ways that they might have resisted in various scenarios (see the African American Protest and Resistance text set in the American Literature Arsenal).

We then fast forwarded to the Civil Rights Era. *Teaching Tolerance* has a teaching kit available (it comes with a teacher's guide and a forty minute DVD) titled *Mighty Times: The Children's March* (*http://www.tolerance.org/kit/mighty-times-childrens-march*) about the Birmingham Children's March which took place on May 2, 1963. The organizers of the march had used the 16th Street Baptist Church as their rallying place. As we already knew from our earlier unit, the church then became the target of three KKK members just a few months later on September 15, and four young girls died.

We had not really talked about Martin Luther King, Jr. yet, except tangentially in relation to the 16th Street Baptist Church Bombing. We read (and listened via *YouTube*) to parts of King's last speech, "I See the Promised Land" (*http://www.youtube.com/watch?v=x1L8y-MX3pg&feature=related*) which was delivered on April 3, 1968, the evening prior to his assassination. King's speeches are moving and powerful, but knowing that he'll be killed the next day makes the ending of this speech especially poignant. We also watched the CBS news announcement of King's death (*http://www.youtube.com/watch?v=cmOBbxgxKvo&feature=related*) and Bobby Kennedy sharing the news to a crowd in Indianapolis (*http://www.youtube.com/watch?v=MyCWV_N0EsM&feature=related*).

King's influence was obviously far-reaching, but I found that my students had never learned about any other black leaders from this time period. I wanted to give them the opportunity to see that not everyone in the black community aligned themselves with King. The natural counterpoint to King is Malcolm X. We began with a brief biography outlining Malcolm's tumultuous childhood and adolescence. Both Malcolm's background and approach was almost completely opposite King's. We listened to Malcolm's speech, "The Ballot or the Bullet" (*http://www.youtube.com/watch?v=kjEO05mrLdQ&feature=view_all&list=PL27AC941A7215AA83&index=86*). We also watched clips of the hospital scene (*http://www.youtube.com/watch?v=5Uoy6xy5AFM&feature=view_all&list=PL27AC941A7215AA83&index=146*) and the death scene (*http://www.youtube.com/watch?v=53IvBoGf8-s&feature=view_all&list=PL27AC941A7215AA83&index=92*) from Spike Lee's *Malcolm X*. Then we watched an interview clip in which Malcolm is asked about King (*http://www.youtube.com/watch?v=kctEXjAeOKA&feature=view_all&list=PL27AC941A7215AA83&index=84*) and another clip in which King is asked to respond (*http://www.youtube.com/watch?v=MwKIUMbi9Jk&feature=related*).

I wanted to give my students exposure to one more group—the Black Panthers. This was a group I had never known much about until I'd read Kekla Magoon's YA novel *The Rock and the River*. I found the party's "Ten Point Platform" on their website (*http://www.blackpanther.org/index.html*) and shared it with my students. While reading it, we noticed that the "demands" they are making are not outrageous—food, jobs, housing, health care, freedom—in fact, they sound quite a bit like the *Universal Declaration of Human Rights*. We also watched a speech by Bobby Seale in which he outlines the platform (*http://www.youtube.com/watch?v=LPP0hiLuxdQ&fe*

ature=view_all&list=PL27AC941A7215AA83&index=85). After watching this, a student even brought in "Tears of Joy," a hip-hop song by Rick Ross which includes a clip of Bobby Seale speaking. Then I asked the students to choose which group they would have followed. I wanted them to consider not only the different messages, but to also analyze whether they were swayed by the charisma of the leaders. There wasn't one clear favorite, which I found very interesting—I had expected most of them to go with the Black Panthers because they believed in armed resistance, but just as many opted for nonviolent resistance.

There are numerous poems and songs that can be incorporated into this unit. For poetry, check out the *National Humanities Center's* page "African American Protest Poetry" (*http://nationalhumanitiescenter.org/tserve/freedom/1917beyond/essays/aaprotestpoetry.htm*) or "Ballad of the Landlord" and "Dream Deferred" by Langston Hughes and "If We Must Die" by Claude McKay and spoken word poetry "Dreams Are Illegal in the Ghetto" by Twin Poets (*http://www.youtube.com/watch?v=Yj1MNI3Bqoc&feature=view_all&list=PL27AC941A7215AA83&index=103*) and "The X is Black" by Amiri Baraka (*http://www.youtube.com/watch?v=4cOSMGzdZf8&feature=view_all&list=PL27AC941A7215AA83&index=64*). For music, check out the Smithsonian/Folkways CD *Sing for Freedom: The Story of the Civil Rights Movement Through Its Songs*, *Spinner* Magazine's "15 Songs Inspired by Martin Luther King, Jr." (*http://www.spinner.com/2010/01/14/mlk-day-songs/*), Common's "I Have a Dream" (*http://www.youtube.com/watch?v=r_2cwhJndKY&list=PL27AC941A7215AA83&index=89&feature=plpp_video*), and Arrested Development's "Revolution" (*http://www.youtube.com/watch?v=SDF8Evb_jQw&feature=view_all&list=PL27AC941A7215AA83&index=67*).

Protest Songs

I often use music (rather than literature) as an example to drive home the point that all art builds on itself, since many of my students aren't great lovers of literature but most of them are fanatical about their music. So a few years ago I used music as a jumping off point and put together a unit on protest songs from the 1960s.

Over the years, this unit has evolved into one of my personal favorites, and the students really seem to enjoy it, too (see the Protest Song text set in the American Literature Arsenal). This is a unit that changes each time I teach it simply because there is so much music available and the students really direct much of the class activity and discussion. Rather than try to list all of the songs we look at, I'll simply direct

---

PROTEST SONG RESOURCES

- "20 Protest Songs That Matter" for *Spinner* July 13, 2007 *http://www.spinner.com/2007/07/13/20-protest-songs-that-mattered-no-20/*

- "Best Classic Anti-War Protest Songs" by Kim Ruehl, *About.com* Guide *http://folkmusic.about.com/od/toptens/tp/Top10Protest.htm*

- "Best Social & Political R&B/Soul Songs: Sing It Loud!" by Mark Edward Nero, *About.com* Guide *http://randb.about.com/od/top5lists/tp/Protest_Songs.htm*

- "Civil Rights Songs: Some of the Most Notable Songs of the Civil Rights Movement" by Kim Ruehl, *About.com* Guide *http://folkmusic.about.com/od/toptens/tp/CivilRightsSong.htm*

- *Classic Protest Songs.* Washington, DC: Smithsonian Folkways Recordings, 2009.

- My "Protest Songs" playlist on *YouTube http://www.youtube.com/playlist?list=PLBD44DCA0119DF97C&feature=mh_lolz*

- Protest Records *http://www.protest-records.com/index.html#*

- "Strange Fruit", *PBS: Independent Lens* © 2011 Independent Television Service *http://www.pbs.org/independentlens/strangefruit/protest.html*

- "Top 10 Best Labor Songs" by Kim Ruehl, *About.com* Guide *http://folkmusic.about.com/od/toptens/tp/BestLaborSongs.htm*

you to my "Protest Song" playlist on *YouTube* (*http://www.youtube.com/playlist?list=PLBD44DCA0119DF 97C&feature=mh_lolz*). We start with a quick-write about the importance of music in the students' lives. We then read about the history of protest music in "Strange Fruit" from PBS's *Independent Lens* (*http://www. pbs.org/independentlens/strangefruit/protest.html*) which takes us from slavery through the 9/11 attacks. We spend the next few days reading lyrics and listening to songs from the 1960s (which the students complain about because they don't like the music). Then, we move to songs that former students have brought in, and finally, I turn them loose to find their own protest songs to share with the class.

Throughout this process, I ask them to choose and analyze several songs using the Protest Song Analysis worksheet (see the American Literature Arsenal). We also read several articles, including "Why So Few Protest Songs? Chuck D, Tom Morello Have Ideas" by Gil Kaufman, "Rock's Voices of Protest Finally Wake up—And It's About Time" by John Noriss, and "Hip-Hop's Socially Conscious Side" by Jeff Chang and Dave Zirin that debate and explore whether protest songs still exist. The students then write about whether they think the protest song still exists today.

What Happens When We Can't Agree to Disagree?

This unit began as we were wrapping up the school year, so I decided to zero in what happens when disagreements lead to war. As in our first unit, although it goes against my natural inclination, our reading didn't proceed chronologically through the wars of America (see the Moving Beyond Protest to Violence: War text set in the American Literature Arsenal). We went from World War II (excerpt from Harry Mazer's YA Novel *The Last Mission*) to the Civil War (Walt Whitman's "Come Up from the Field Father," Stephen Crane's "War Is Kind," Ambrose Bierce's "A Horseman in the Sky" and "Chapter 5: A Night" from Louisa May Alcott's *Hospital Sketches*) to the Vietnam War (George Bilgere's "At the Vietnam Memorial") and back again. We also listened to the songs "One" by Metallica (the video for this song is powerful) and "War Pigs" by Black Sabbath and looked at the painting "Reflections" by Lee Teter.

This allowed me to illustrate that all wars are the same and have the same impact on those who fight and on those who are left behind. For students who have been raised on extremely violent and realistic video games, that's an important lesson—one boy commented that he'd never thought about how it must affect his grandfather, who is a veteran, to see him playing the video game *Call of Duty*. Randall Jarrell's "The Death of the Ball Turret Gunner" and Kenneth Carroll's "Snookie Johnson Goes Down to the Recruiter's Office Near Benning Road & Starts Some Shit" (which was reminiscent of Phil Ochs' "Draft Dodger Rag" from the protest song unit) were probably the students' favorite poems of this unit. We read "Serving the Country: Military Service around the World" (*http://www.worldatlases.com/gi/cltr_MS.pdf*) and "Military Statistics Service Age and Obligation (Most Recent) by Country" (*http://www.nationmaster.com/graph/mil_ser_age_ and_obl-military-service-age-and-obligation*) about countries in which military service is required. I also asked the students to write about whether military service ought to be required in the United States.

Because we were short on time, we finished the school year with this unit. In the future, I will end this class by asking students to create a culminating project (a definition paper or a PowerPoint presentation, for example), in which they answer the questions that we started the year with, "What Is an American?" It will be interesting for them and for me to see how their definitions and perspectives either change or stay the same as the result of our studies.

The American Literature Arsenal

What Is an American?

Guiding Questions:

- Where does a person's identity come from? Family? Friends? School? Religion? Race? Language?

- Do Americans have a "shared identity" or is everyone's experience different?

- What is the difference between ethnicity, nationality, and race? Is "American" an ethnicity, nationality, or race?

- Is America really a "melting pot"? Or is "salad bowl" a better analogy? What is the difference between accommodation and assimilation?

- How does our past influence our future?

- Where do YOU come from?

Writing Prompts:

- What is an American? What does it mean to you to be an American?

- Write 5 things you think should be required for United States citizenship. Then, number them in order of importance (1=most important).

- Do you think English should be our national language? Explain your answer.

- Melting Pot vs. Salad Bowl. Which term is a better analogy for America? Is it possible to use both terms and have them both be true? Are both realistic or is one more a reality and the other more an "ideal"?

What Are Our Basic Rights as Humans and Americans?

Guiding Questions:

- What is an American? What does it mean to you to be an American?

- Write 5 things you think should be required for United States citizenship. Then, number them in order of importance (1=most important).

- Do you think English should be our national language? Explain your answer.

- Melting Pot vs. Salad Bowl. Which term is a better analogy for America? Is it possible to use both terms and have them both be true? Are both realistic or is one more a reality and the other more an "ideal"?

From *Commando Classics: A Field Manual for Helping Teens Understand (and Maybe Even Enjoy) Classic Literature* by Daria Plumb. Bowie, MD: VOYA Press, an imprint of E L Kurdyla Publishing, LLC. Copyright 2012

Writing Prompts:

- What are the 5 rights you think should be guaranteed to ALL people regardless of race, ethnicity, nationality, religion, etc.? Rate them in order of importance (1=most important).

- "Just because you have the RIGHT to do something, it doesn't mean you SHOULD do it." Agree or disagree with this statement. Explain your answer.

- **"We hold these truths to be self-evident, that all men are created equal, that they are endowed by their creator with certain inalienable rights, that among these are life, liberty and the pursuit of happiness.—*The Declaration of Independence*, Thomas Jefferson**

  What did this sentence mean when it was written in 1776? Who are the "all men" to whom Jefferson was referring? What does this sentence mean to you? Who are "all men" today? How and why has the meaning of this sentence changed over the course of 234 years? Explain.

- When the Constitution was written, what purpose did the first amendment (which guarantees the right to free speech) serve? Should there be a limit to free speech in this country? At what point can/does freedom of speech cross the line and become slander (the act or offense of saying something false or malicious that damages somebody's reputation), harassment, and/or bullying? Should bullies be able to claim protection under the first amendment? What should we do as a community when someone's words "cross the line"?

- Should authors be pressured to write books that don't have any "bad stuff"—swearing, sex, violence, etc.—in them when writing for kids? For teens? Do you think kids and teens are likely to do something bad just because they read about it in a book?

- What do you have to say about book challenges? What should you do when a book is challenged in your own community? What about a challenge in a community far away?

What Groups Have Had Their Basic Rights Compromised or Denied?

Guiding Questions:

- Are there people (or groups of people) who are not entitled to basic American rights? Why or why not?

- What are some groups that have been mistreated or denied basic rights in our country's history?

- Are humans inherently tolerant beings? Explain.

- Whose rights are being compromised today?

- What "hate crimes" do we see today? Are there groups against whom it is still acceptable to discriminate?

GUIDING QUESTIONS AND WRITING PROMPTS FOR EACH UNIT (*Cont.*)

Native American Rights Writing Prompts:

- What things about you define (or help to define) who you are and how you fit into your cultural group—family, religious beliefs, clothing choice, hair style, language, education, etc.? Which of these things is most important to you? Why? How would you feel if someone forced you to change? Would you resist? If no, why not? If so, how?

- What tells you more about a person—her words or her actions? What happens when a person's actions and words don't match? When a person says one thing and does another, how do you decide what to believe?

- What are five things you've learned about the Native American experience? You can write about things from how they interact with the earth to how they are portrayed in history books or how they have been treated by the American government.

African American Rights Writing Prompts:

- Define what the word *lynch* means to you.

- Choose one of the journal prompts from the *Without Sanctuary: Lynching Photography in America Teachers Guide* (link available in "Identifying Those Who Have Been Mistreated: African Americans" text set)

- During the course of this unit we've watched 3 documentaries addressing racism against African Americans in the last 60 years: *The Untold Story of Emmett Louis Till; Four Little Girls;* and *Prom Night in Mississippi*. What did you learn from these films? If I was only able to use one of these movies the next time I teach this class, which one should I use? Why?

Japanese Internment Writing Prompts:

- Write a list of names of all the people you enjoy spending time with or people you see on a regular basis (family, friends, classmates, etc.). How would you feel if you were not able to see any of those special people again? Who would you miss most and why?

- Imagine that a federal agent comes to your home. He tells you that you are going away—he won't say where, for how long, or under what conditions. You are scared and confused. He will only tell you that you have 1 suitcase in which to pack all of your belongings. You will not ever get back the items you leave behind. You **MUST** take the following items: bedding and linens; toilet articles (shampoo, soap, toothpaste, etc.); 1 extra set of clothing; and 1 place setting (fork, spoon, knife, plate, cup). List 10 other items you would take with you (remember, they must fit into a normal-sized suitcase) and rank them in order of importance.

- In your new "home" all of your family must live in 1 room. You have only cots to sleep on. There is no bathroom (it is half a block away) or kitchen in your home. Outside it smells like horses and manure and a barbed wire fence surrounds the buildings you and other people live in. How do you feel about this?

- Do you think that something similar to the Japanese American internment can happen again? Discuss current events - were individuals from the Middle East suspected of espionage and watched closely during the Persian Gulf War, after the September 11th attacks, and now during Operation Iraqi Freedom? Do you think those fears could have escalated and resulted in serious action?

From *Commando Classics: A Field Manual for Helping Teens Understand (and Maybe Even Enjoy) Classic Literature* by Daria Plumb. Bowie, MD: VOYA Press, an imprint of E L Kurdyla Publishing, LLC. Copyright 2012

Workers' Rights Writing Prompts:

- Do you know anyone who is a member of a labor union? What do *you* think is the purpose of labor unions—what do they do for their members? Do you think workers will get better wages and working conditions if they stand up individually or if they stand together as a group? Explain.

- Imagine that you are either: A worker in the slaughterhouse/meatpacking facility described in Upton Sinclair's *The Jungle* **OR** Rosa from *Chicken—'Racing with the Machines'* **OR** Isabel from *Isabel*. Write a letter to your boss describing the dangers of your job (be sure to include not only the working conditions in the fields or factory, but also describe the emotional toll the job takes on you). What could/should be done to improve your working conditions? Why should your boss care about your safety if s/he is making good money? What will you do if s/he does not address some of these issues?

LGBT Rights Writing Prompt:

- **HATE CRIME**—a criminal offense committed against a person or property that is motivated, in whole or in part, by the offender's bias against a race, color, ethnicity, national origin, sex, gender identity or expression, sexual orientation, disability, age or religion.

  Was Charlie Howard's death a hate crime? Explain. Should the punishment for hate crimes be more severe than the punishment for other types of crimes? Explain. Do you think Shawn Mabry, Daniel Ness, and Jim Baines could honestly claim that they didn't intend to kill Charlie Howard? Explain.

How Do We Bring About Social Change?

Guiding Questions:

- Does EVERY American have the right to protest?

- In what ways can someone protest?

- What are the risks of protest?

- Do people today still protest? What are they protesting? How?

Writing Prompts:

- What is one right/cause/issue that you would be willing to fight for? Why? How far would you be willing to go to either gain this right or to keep this right? Would you be willing to be arrested? Go to jail? Be physically tortured? Be mentally tortured? See people you love be harmed? Go on a hunger strike? Die? Explain.

- What are some ways people express their displeasure with or rebel against things, events, governmental decisions, etc. that they feel are unfair? Is the right to protest a right of ALL Americans? What are the risks that someone takes when they choose to protest, rebel, or stand up against inequality?

- "**Returning hate for hate multiplies hate, adding deeper darkness to a night already devoid of stars. Darkness cannot drive out darkness; only light can do that. Hate cannot drive out hate; only love can do that. Hate multiplies hate, violence multiplies violence and toughness multiples toughness in a descending spiral of destruction.**"—Martin Luther King, Jr. How does this quote apply to the Civil Rights Movement? What was Martin Luther King asking people to do? What might Martin Luther King, Jr. expect us to do today?

- After listening to **Dr. Martin Luther King, Jr.** (Southern Christian Leadership Conference), **Malcolm X** (Black Nationalist) and **Bobby Seale** (Black Panther Party), which movement do you think you would have joined? How did you choose who to follow? Did you look for a charismatic leader? The message? The actions? What part(s) of that group's platform do you find most appealing or logical? Is "membership" in one group more or less dangerous? Explain your answer.

- How important is music in your daily life? Can certain songs influence your mood? What about your behavior? Think of some songs that mean something to you. What is it about these songs that you respond to or connect with?

- Do you think the protest song still exists today? Do songs that have socially conscious lyrics motivate teenagers and young adults to act? Do certain genres or styles of music make better/more effective protest songs than others? Explain.

What Happens When We Can't Just Agree to Disagree?

Guiding Questions:

- Can the scars caused by war/violence ever be healed?
- What is the cost of war (in terms of lives, money, and future relationships)?
- Can you solve a conflict with conflict?
- Does war solve anything in the long run?
- Who serves and who dies?
- Is peace possible?

Writing Prompts:

- What happens when protest does not bring about the change people desire? Can you solve a conflict with conflict? Can the scars caused by violence and conflict ever be healed? Explain.

- Many countries require its citizens to serve in the military for a period of time ranging anywhere from 4 months to as many as 2 years. Should the U.S. require mandatory military service? Explain.

  - If so, why do you think this is important? How long should this service last? Should there be any "benefits" associated with service (free education, health care, etc.).

  - If not, why? Is your decision based on economic reasons, safety reasons, religious reasons, etc.? Would you feel differently about it if, for some reason, it didn't apply to you?

From *Commando Classics: A Field Manual for Helping Teens Understand (and Maybe Even Enjoy) Classic Literature* by Daria Plumb. Bowie, MD: VOYA Press, an imprint of E L Kurdyla Publishing, LLC. Copyright 2012

EDGAR ALLAN POE TEXT SET

(Poe's Original Poems and Songs Not Included)

NOVELS

- *The Man Who Was Poe* by Avi. Avon Books, 1991.
- *The Poe Shadow: A Novel* by Matthew Pearl. Random House, 2006.

ILLUSTRATED BOOKS

- *Annabel Lee: The Poem by Edgar Allan Poe* by Gilles Tebo. Tundra Books, 1987.

FILMS / VIDEOS

- *A&E Biography's The Mystery of Edgar Allan Poe.* A&E Home Video, 2004.
- *An Evening with Edgar Allan Poe.* Monterey Video. 2000.
- *Animation—Edgar Allan Poe read Annabel Lee. http://www.youtube.com/watch?v=0qoTH m99jBl&feature=PlayList&p=27AC9417215AA83&index=6*
- *Annabelle Lee. http://www.youtube.com/watch?v=tRhlJB6YD-4&feature=PlayList&p=27A C941A7215AA83&index=7&playnext=1&playnext_from=PL*
- *The Baltimore Ravens and "The Raven." http://knowingpoe.thinkport.org/library/news/ther-aven_ravens.asp*
- *Edgar Allan Poe - 11 Poe Tales Hosted by Christopher Lee.* BFS Entertainment, 2006.
- *The Edgar Allan Poe Collection Volume 1: Annabel Lee and Other Tales of Mystery and Imagination.* Microcinema, 2008.
- *"Edgar Allan Poe" from "Snoopy the Musical." http://www.youtube.com/watch?v=ByZLnPG 0Vkk&feature=PlayList&p=27AC941A7215AA83&index=11*
- *Edgar Allan Poe: Terror of the Soul.* PBS Video, 1997.
- *Edgar Allan Poe's The Pit and the Pendulum.* MGM Home Entertainment, 2001.
- *Edgar Allan Poe's—The Raven* read by Christopher Walken with illustrations by Gustave Dore. *http://www.youtube.com/watch?v=VFy7XidbnKw&feature=PlayList&p=27AC941A72 15AA83&index=8*
- *The Famous Authors Series: Edgar Allan Poe.* Kultur International Films, 2006.
- *Humpty Dumpty by Edgar Allan Poe. http://www.youtube.com/watch?v=xWTZSfFaCck&fe ature=PlayList&p=27AC941A7215AA83&index=9*
- *Masque of the Red Death.* Orion Home Video, 1994.
- *Masters of Horror: The Black Cat.* Starz/Anchor Bay, 2007.
- *Mystery Visitor Misses Poe's Birthday. http://www.youtube.com/watch?v=ebW77CshCg4&f eature=view_all&list=PL27AC941A7215AA83&index=24*
- *The Raven.* Intrepid Pictures, 2012.

EDGAR ALLAN POE TEXT SET (*Cont.*)

- *The Raven-By Edgar Allan Poe http://www.youtube.com/watch?v=EV8BCHIQ2ww&feature =PlayList&p=27AC941A7215AA83&index=10&playnext=1&playnext_from=PL*
- *The Tell-Tale Heart.* Monterey Home Video, 1991.
- *Tim Burton's Vincent featuring Edgar Allan Poe's The Raven. http://www.youtube.com/watc h?v=n0zkFo3lkcY&feature=PlayList&p=27AC941A7215AA83&index=5ature=related*
- *Waiting for the Poe Toaster, 2011. http://www.youtube.com/watch?v=5zUflVx5xkg&feThe Raven-Edgar Allan Poe* performed by Vincent Price. *http://www.youtube.com/watch?v=FID 1CiB4bcU&feature=PlayList&p=27AC941A7215AA83&index=4*

GRAPHIC NOVELS

- *Graphic Classics: Edgar Allan Poe, Fourth Edition.* Eureka Productions, 2010.
- "The Oval Portrait", *Gothic Classics: Graphic Classics Volume 14* edited by Tom Pomplun. Eureka Productions, 2007.
- *The Raven* illustrated by Bill Fountain. *http://www.levelgroundfilms.com/raven.htm*
- "Some Words with a Mummy", *Horror Classics: Graphic Classics Number 10.* Eureka Productions, 2004.

ARTWORK

- Gustave Doré's illustrations to *The Raven. http://www.artsycraftsy.com/dore_raven.html*
- Edgar Allan Poe Photo Galleries. *http://www.poestories.com/gallery.php*

TV SHOWS

- "Lisa's Rival." *The Simpsons.* Season 6, episode 105. FOX. 11 Sept 1994.
- *Poe.* ABC, 2011.
- "The Raven." *The Simpsons' Treehouse of Horror, I.* Season 2, episode 16. FOX. 24 Oct 1990. *http://en.sevenload.com/videos/SCR4nVh-The-Simpsons-The-Raven-engl*

INTERNET SOURCES

- *Maryland Public Television's Knowing Poe. http://knowingpoe.thinkport.org/default_flash.asp*
- *Poe Museum. http://www.poemuseum.org/*
- *PoeStories.com. http://www.poestories.com/index.php*
- *Qrisse's Edgar Allan Poe Pages. http://www.poedecoder.com/Qrisse/*
- "The Raven in Popular Culture" from *Wikipedia. http://en.wikipedia.org/wiki/The_Raven_in_ popular_culture*

From *Commando Classics: A Field Manual for Helping Teens Understand (and Maybe Even Enjoy) Classic Literature* by Daria Plumb. Bowie, MD: VOYA Press, an imprint of E L Kurdyla Publishing, LLC. Copyright 2012

EDGAR ALLAN POE TEXT SET (*Cont.*)

SONGS

- "Annabel Lee" performed by Joan Baez
- "Annabel Lee" performed by Stevie Nicks
- "Edgar Allan Poe" from *Snoopy: The Musical*
- "El Dorado" performed by Donovan
- "Murders in the Rue Morgue" by Iron Maiden
- *The Tales of Edgar Allan Poe: A SyNphonic Collection*
- *Tales of Mystery and Imagination* by Alan Parsons Project

BIOGRAPHIES

- *Edgar Allan Poe: Creator of Dreams* by Russell Shorto. Kipling Press, 1989.
- *Edgar Allan Poe: Tragic Poet and Master of Mystery* by Zachary Kent. Enslow Publishers, 2001.
- "Imp of the Perverse: Edgar Allan Poe." *Lives of the Writers: Comedies, Tragedies, and What the Neighbors Thought* by Kathleen Krull. Sandpiper, 2011.
- *Nevermore: A Photobiography of Edgar Allan Poe* by Karen E. Lange. National Geographic Society, 2009.

MISCELLANEOUS

- "The Baltimore Ravens." *http://knowingpoe.thinkport.org/library/news/ravens.asp*
- Edgar Allan Poe Gifts @ *Shakespeare's Den. http://www.shakespearesden.com/edalpoegi. html*
- "Edgar Allan Poe's Footprints." *http://www.poedecoder.com/Qrisse/footprints.php*
- Edgar Award. *http://www.theedgars.com/*
- *The Incredible Mr. Poe: Comic Book Adaptations of the Works of Edgar Allan Poe 1943-2007* by M. Thomas Inge, The Edgar Allan Poe Museum.
- "The Poe Toaster." *http://knowingpoe.thinkport.org/library/news/toaster.asp*
- "Story of the Birth of the Baltimore Raven Mascots: Edgar, Allan, and Poe." *http://www.baltimoreravens.com/Ravenstown/Mascot.aspx*

ESSAYS / ARTICLES

- "Mystery of Poe Toaster Revealed" Associated Press © 2007. *http://www.cnn.com/2007/ SHOWBIZ/books/08/16/mysteryvisitor.ap/index.html*

LANGSTON HUGHES AND THE HARLEM RENAISSANCE TEXT SET

NOVELS

- *Bronx Masquerade* by Nikki Grimes. Penguin, 2002.
- *Celeste's Harlem Renaissance: A Novel* by Eleanora Tate. Little, Brown, 2007.
- *Harlem Summer* by Walter Dean Myers. Scholastic Press, 2007.
- *Langston: A Play* by Ossie Davis. Delacorte Press, 1982.

ILLUSTRATED BOOKS

- *Jazz on a Saturday Night* by Leo & Diane Dillon. Blue Sky Press. Scholastic, 2007.
- *Langston's Train Ride* by Robert Burleigh. Orchard, 2004.
- *My People* by Langston *Hughes*. Simon & Schuster/Atheneum, 2009.
- *The Negro Speaks of Rivers* by Langston Hughes. Hyperion, 2009.
- *A Song for Harlem* by Patricia C. McKissack. Viking/Penguin Young Readers, 2007.
- *Soul Looks Back in Wonder* illustrated by Tom Feelings. Dial Books, 1993.
- *The Sweet and Sour Animal Book* by Langston Hughes. Oxford University Press, 1994.
- *Visiting Langston* by Willie Perdomo. Henry Holt BYR, 2005.

FILMS / VIDEOS

- *Against the Odds: The Artists of the Harlem Renaissance*. PBS Video, 1994.
- "Danny Glover Reads Langston Hughes' 'Ballad of Roosevelt.'" *http://www.youtube.com/watch?v=HADGKw_wa5E&NR=1*
- *The Great Debaters*. Genius Products, 2008.
- *Harlem Renaissance*. PBS Home Video, 2004.
- *Harlem Renaissance: The Music & Rhythms That Started a Cultural Revolution*. Kultur Video, 2004.
- *Jazz by Ken Burns, Episode Four: The True Welcome*. PBS Home Video, 2001.
- "Langston Hughes' 'Ballad of the Landlord.'" *http://www.youtube.com/watch?v=ylhJnV XQ5nM*
- "The Langston Hughes Project: Ask Your Mama: 12 Moods for Jazz." *http://www.youtube.com/watch?v=wzxff6Nejt0&feature=view_all&list=PL27AC941A7215AA83&index=133*
- *Lullaby of Harlem*. Passport Video, 2004.

ARTWORK

- *The Guide to the Great Art on the Internet: Artcyclopedia Artists by Movement: The Harlem Renaissance Early 1920s to 1930s. http://www.artcyclopedia.com/history/harlem-renaissance.html*
- *Harlem Renaissance: Art of Black America* by Mary Schmidt Campbell. Harry N. Abrams, 1994.
- *Rhapsodies in Black: Art of the Harlem Renaissance* by Richard J. Powell and David A. Bailey. University of California Press, 1997.

From *Commando Classics: A Field Manual for Helping Teens Understand (and Maybe Even Enjoy) Classic Literature* by Daria Plumb. Bowie, MD: VOYA Press, an imprint of E L Kurdyla Publishing, LLC. Copyright 2012

POEMS

- *The Entrance Place of Wonders: Poems of the Harlem Renaissance* selected by Daphne Muse. Abrams Books for Young Readers, 2005.
- *Love to Langston* by Tony Medina. Lee & Low Books, 2006.
- *My Black Me: A Beginning Book of Black Poetry* edited by Arnold Adoff. Dutton Juvenile, 1994.
- *Poetry for Young People: Langston Hughes* edited by David Roessel and Arnold Rampersad. Sterling, 2006.

INTERNET SOURCES

- *Arts Edge: Drop Me Off in Harlem. http://artsedge.kennedy-center.org/exploring/harlem/artsedge.html*
- *Harlem 1900-1940: An African American Community. http://www.si.umich.edu/CHICO/Harlem/index.html*
- *The Langston Hughes Project.* © 2009 Ron McCurdy. *http://www.ronmccurdy.com/about_hudges_project.htm*
- *PAL: Perspectives in American Literature—A Research and Reference Guide—An Ongoing Project* © Paul P. Reuben. *http://web.csustan.edu/english/reuben/pal/chap9/9intro.html*

SONGS

- *Music of The Harlem Renaissance.* Chestnut, 2005.

BIOGRAPHIES

- *Black Troubadour: Langston Hughes* by Charlemae H. Rollins. Rand McNally, 1969.
- *Coming Home: From the Life of Langston Hughes* by Floyd Cooper. Puffin, 1998.
- *I, Too, Sing America: The Story of Langston Hughes* by Martha E. Rhynes. Morgan Reynolds Publishing, 2002.
- *I Wonder as I Wander: An Autobiographical Journey* by Langston Hughes. Hill and Wang, 1993.
- *Jazz Age Poet: A Story About Langston Hughes* by Veda Boyd Jones. Millbrook Press, 2006.
- *Langston Hughes: American Poet* by Alice Walker. Amistad, 2005.
- *Langston Hughes: Poet* by Jack Rummel. Chelsea House Publications, 2005.
- *Love to Langston* by Tony Medina. Lee & Low Books, 2006.
- "The Perfect Companion: Langston Hughes." *Lives of the Writers: Comedies, Tragedies. and What the Neighbors Thought* by Kathleen Krull. Sandpiper, 2011.

LANGSTON HUGHES AND THE HARLEM RENAISSANCE TEXT SET (*Cont.*)

HISTORIES

- *Black Stars of the Harlem Renaissance* by Jim Haskins, Eleanora E. Tate, Clinton Cox, and Brenda Wilkinson. Wiley, 2002.

- *Encyclopedia of the Harlem Renaissance* by Sandra L. West and Aberjhani. Facts on File, 2003.

- *The First Book of Jazz* by Langston Hughes. Ecco, 1997.

- *The Harlem Renaissance* by Veronica Chambers. Chelsea House Publishers, 1998.

- *The Harlem Renaissance: Hub of African-American Culture, 1920-1930* by Steven Watson. Pantheon, 1996.

- *Harlem Stomp!: A Cultural History of the Harlem Renaissance* by Laban Carrick Hill. NY: Little, Brown and Company, 2003.

- *Women of the Harlem Renaissance* by Lisa Beringer McKissack. Compass Point Books, 2007.

MISCELLANEOUS

- *Ask Your Mama. http://www.askyourmama.com/index2.htm*

- *A Harlem Renaissance Retrospective: Connecting Art, Music, Dance, and Poetry* Read WriteThink Lesson Plan. *http://www.readwritethink.org/lessons/lesson_view.asp?id=252*

- *On the Shoulders of Giants: My Journey through the Harlem Renaissance* by Kareem Abdul-Jabbar, with Raymond Obstfeld. Simon & Schuster, 2007.

- *Poetry Speaks: Hear Great Poets Read Their Work from Tennyson to Plath* edited by Elise Paschen & Rebekah Presson Mosby. Sourcebooks MediaFusion, 2001.

- *Rhapsodies in Black: Music and Words from the Harlem Renaissance* [BOX SET]. Rhino/Wea, 2000.

SHORT STORIES

- *Short Stories of Langston Hughes* edited by Akiba Sullivan Harper. Hill and Wang, 1996.

ARTICLES

- "'Ask Your Mama': A Music and Poetry Performance" by Jeff Lunden for *NPR. http://www.npr.org/templates/story/story.php?storyId=101838506*

From *Commando Classics: A Field Manual for Helping Teens Understand (and Maybe Even Enjoy) Classic Literature* by Daria Plumb. Bowie, MD: VOYA Press, an imprint of E L Kurdyla Publishing, LLC. Copyright 2012

THE SCARLET LETTER TEXT SET

NOVELS
- *Angel and Apostle* by Deborah Noyes. Unbridled Books, 2006.
- *Hester: A Novel about the Early Hester Prynne* by Christopher Bigsby. Viking Adult, 1994.
- *Sarah Anne Hartford: Massachusetts, 1651* by Kathleen Duey. Topeka Bindery, 1999.
- *Speak* by Laurie Halse Anderson. Farrar Straus Giroux, 1999.

ILLUSTRATED BOOKS
- *...If You Lived in Colonial Times* by Ann McGovern. Scholastic, 1992.

FILMS /VIDEOS
- *The Scarlet Letter*. Cinergi Pictures, 1996.
- *The Scarlet Letter*. Video Images, 1934.

ARTWORK
- "Images Relating to The Scarlet Letter." *Hawthorne in Salem. http://www.hawthorneinsalem.org/Literature/Hawthorne&Women/ScarletLetter/Images.html*

INTERNET SOURCES
- *Hawthorne in Salem. http://www.hawthorneinsalem.org/Introduction.html*
- *Lesson Plans: The Scarlet Letter. Discovery Education. http://school.discoveryeducation. com/lessonplans/programs/thescarletletter/*

SONGS
- "The Grudge" by Tool
- "High Step" by Sage Francis
- *Scarlet Letter: A New Musical. http://www.thescarletletter.com/home.html*
- "Scarlet Letter Part 2" by Halifax

HISTORIES
- "Anne Hutchinson." *About.com. http://www.answers.com/topic/anne-hutchinson*
- *The Cry at Salem: The Witchcraft Trials of '92* by Jeffrey J. Richards. Paladin House, 1992.
- *In the Days of the Salem Witchcraft Trials* by Marilynne K. Roach. Houghton Mifflin, 1996.
- *The Salem Witchcraft Trials in American History* by David K. Fremon. Enslow, 1999.
- *Understanding the Scarlet Letter: A Student Casebook to Issues, Sources, and Historical Documents* by Claudia Durst Johnson. Greenwood, 1995.

MISCELLANEOUS
- "The Scarlet Letter." *Book-A-Minute Classics. http://www.rinkworks.com/bookaminute/b/ hawthorne.letter.shtml*

WHAT IS AN AMERICAN? TEXT SET

ILLUSTRATED BOOKS

What Is an American?

- *We Are America: A Tribute from the Heart* by Walter Dean Myers. Harper Collins, 2011.

Aren't We All Immigrants?

- *Ellis Island: Doorway to Freedom* by Steven Kroll. Holiday House, 1995.
- *Immigrant Kids* by Russell Freedman. Puffin Books, 1995.

FILMS /VIDEOS

What Is an American?

- "I Am an American" by the Ad Council. *http://www.youtube.com/watch?v=T_5XIOn68Hk&feature=autoplay&list=PL27AC941A7215AA83&index=9&playnext=1*
- "Voices of Lady Liberty" from MSNBC. *http://www.msnbc.msn.com/id/38524096/*

POEMS

What Is an American?

- "A Black American" by Smokey Robinson. *http://www.youtube.com/watch?v=J_KKyw8V-I0&feature=view_all&list=PL27AC941A7215AA83&index=124*
- "Address" by Alurista
- "ALONE/december/night" by Victor Hernandez Cruz
- "America" by Claude McKay
- "AmeRícan" by Tato Laviera
- "Cross" by Langston Hughes
- "Ellis Island" by Joseph Bruchac
- "Ending Poem" by Aurora Levins Morales and Rosario Morales
- "Failure of an Invention" by Safiya Henderson Holmes
- "For My People" by Margaret Walker
- "I Am" by Eric Mata *http://www.youtube.com/watch?v=R8fRVvDhPxY*
- "I Am Joaquin" by Rodolfo Gonzales
- "I Hear America Singing" by Walt Whitman
- "I Too" by Langston Hughes
- "Immigrants" by Pat Mora
- "In the Good Old U.S.A." by Jose Angel Villalongo, Sr.
- "Letter to America" by Francisco X. Alarcon
- "Public School No. 18: Paterson, New Jersey" by Maria Mazziotti Gillan
- "Saying Yes" by Diana Chang
- "When I Was Growing Up" by Nellie Wong

From *Commando Classics: A Field Manual for Helping Teens Understand (and Maybe Even Enjoy) Classic Literature* by Daria Plumb. Bowie, MD: VOYA Press, an imprint of E L Kurdyla Publishing, LLC. Copyright 2012

INTERNET SOURCES

Aren't We All Immigrants?

- Ellis Island website. *http://www.ellisisland.org*

Do We Need a National Language?

- "Do You Speak American?" by Public Broadcasting Service. *http://www.pbs.org/speak/.*
- U.S. English Foundation © 2011. *http://www.usefoundation.org/.*

What Does it Mean to Be an American Citizen?

- U.S. Citizenship and Immigration Services. *http://www.uscis.gov/portal/site/uscis/*
  - Naturalization Self Test
  - Becoming a U.S. Citizen: An Overview of the Naturalization Process video
  - "Welcome to the United States: A Guide for New Immigrants" packet. *http://www.uscis.gov/newimmigrants*

MISCELLANEOUS

Aren't We All Immigrants?

- "The New Americans" Lesson Plans from *Independent Lens. http://www.pbs.org/independentlens/newamericans/foreducators_index.html*
- U.S. Census Bureau's "Ancestry 2000: A Census 2000 Brief." *http://www.census.gov/prod/2004pubs/c2kbr-35.pdf*

What Does it Mean to Be an American Citizen?

- *Becoming a Citizen* by John Hamilton. ABDO Pub. Co., 2005.
- *Citizenship Toolkit* by Office of Citizenship. U.S. Dept. of Homeland Security, U.S. Citizenship and Immigration Services, 2008.
- *U.S. Citizenship Test with DVD* by Karen Hilgeman et al. McGraw-Hill, 2009.
- *Your Road to Passing the U.S. Citizenship Test* [DVD] by US100.org. ECM MultiMedia, 2008.

ESSAYS / ARTICLES

What Is an American?

- "American Identity: Ideas, Not Ethnicity" by Michael Jay Friedman for the U.S. Department of State's Bureau of International Information Programs. February 13, 2008. *http://www.america.gov/st/peopleplaceenglish/2008/February/20080307154033ebyessedo0.5349237.html*

Aren't We All Immigrants?

- "America's History of Fear" by Nicholas D. Kristof for *The New York Times*. Sept. 4, 2010. *http://www.nytimes.com/2010/09/05/opinion/05kristof.html*

Do We Need a National Language?

- "A Modest Proposal: Don't Make English Official, Ban it Instead" by Dennis Baron, March 2, 2007. *http://illinois.edu/db/view/25/1565?count=1&ACTION=DIALOG&sort=ascv*
- "Constitutional Topic: Official Language" The U.S. Constitution Online. © 1995-2011 Craig Walenta. *http://www.usconstitution.net/consttop_lang.html*

BANNED BOOKS WEEK: FINAL WRITING

AS WE WRAP-UP BANNED BOOKS WEEK, YOU WILL WRITE A LETTER TAKING A STAND ON CENSORSHIP

For the purposes of this assignment, you will only be required to turn the letter in to me in order to complete the requirement. However, if you wish to send the letter and/or post it to an online forum, let me know and I will be happy to give you the necessary information.

YOU MAY CHOOSE TO ADDRESS YOUR LETTER TO:

The "Book Banners":

- Dr. Guy Sconzo (Superintendent of Humble ISD, Humble, Texas, who recently disinvited Ellen Hopkins from the Humble ISD Teen Lit Fest)

- Dr. Wesley Scroggins (filed public complaint to Republic School Board, Republic, Missouri addressing content taught in history, government, sex education, science, and English–*Speak*, *Twenty Boy Summer*, and *Slaughterhouse Five*)

- The Stockton School Board (School Board who voted to remove *The Absolutely True Diary of a Part-Time Indian* from both the curriculum and the library of Stockton High School, Stockton, Missouri)

OR

THE AUTHORS:

- Laurie Halse Anderson (award-winning author of many books for children and teens, including *Speak*, *Twisted*, *Prom*, *Chains*, and *Catalyst*)

- Ellen Hopkins (author of novels-in-verse for teens, such as *Crank*, *Glass*, *Fallout*, *Burned*, *Identical*, and *Tricks*)

- Sherman Alexie (award-winning author of *The Absolutely True Diary of a Part-Time Indian*, as well as several well-received novels for adults about the Native American experience)

- Any other author whose book(s) have moved or touched you in some way.

YOU MAY WISH TO COMMENT ON THE FOLLOWING:

- How do you feel about people trying to restrict books that are made available to teens?

- Have any of these books "changed your life", reflected part of your own experience, or helped you to become a better reader?

- Should there ever be restrictions placed on what books should be available to kids? Who should make that decision?

- Is there a better way for teachers, librarians, and parents to deal with books on "tough" subjects or with "tough" language besides banning them?

BANNED BOOKS WEEK: FINAL WRITING (*Cont.*)

HOW TO WRITE A LETTER OR COMMENT TO THESE FOLKS:

- Be respectful. All of these people believe that what they are doing is in the best interest of the children. While you may not agree with them, they don't deserve to be insulted or threatened. Calling people names and bullying is no better than what the book banners are doing. Besides, if you write a letter filled with profanity and threats, it will only make people less likely to listen to what you have to say.

- Make 2 or 3 good points or arguments for why the book should be kept in the classroom or in the library.

- Tell them *your* story. You are a teenager. You know the kinds of things real teens deal with every day. If you can include personal information about how one of these books changed (or saved) your life AND/OR changed your opinion of reading, it will be much more powerful. You don't have to give too many personal details, but it wouldn't hurt to give them a little background about yourself.

- Tell them who misses out when these books get removed from schools.

- Offer some concrete alternatives or suggestions about ways to keep the book available for kids who would like to read it.

- Tell them why censorship is a danger to us as Americans.

- Be clear and to the point. You don't need to sound like a college professor, just be yourself.

- Ask someone to proofread your letter before you send it so you can be sure it makes sense and to check for errors. Also, write out all the words—no "texting talk."

From Commando Classics: A Field Manual for Helping Teens Understand (and Maybe Even Enjoy) Classic Literature
by Daria Plumb. Bowie, MD: VOYA Press, an imprint of E L Kurdyla Publishing, LLC. Copyright 2012

IDENTIFYING THOSE WHO HAVE BEEN MISTREATED:
NATIVE AMERICANS TEXT SET

NOVELS
- *The Absolutely True Diary of a Part-Time Indian* by Sherman Alexie. Little Brown, 2007.
- *Morning Girl* by Michael Dorris. Hyperion Books for Children, 1992.

ILLUSTRATED BOOKS
- *Chief Joseph 1840-1904* by Mary Englar. Blue Earth Books/Capstone Press, 2004.
- *Red Hawk's Account of Custer's Last Battle* by Paul Goble. University of Nebraska Press, 1992.

FILMS /VIDEOS
- *Broken Rainbow.* Docurama: New Video Works, 1985.
- "How Hollywood Stereotyped Native Americans" *http://www.youtube.com/watch?v=_hJFi7SRH7Q&feature=channel_video_title*
- "Indian Boarding School Abuse" *http://www.youtube.com/watch?v=p1tiQB8gt5g&feature=related*
- "Our Sprits Don't Speak English: Indian Boarding Schools" *http://www.youtube.com/watch?v=qDshQTBh5d4&NR=1*
- Rich Heape Films *http://www.richheape.com/*

POEMS
- "The Cry of the Native American" by Albert Gazeley
- "Dear John Wayne" by Lois Erdrich
- "Ghost Warriors" by Donald Hook
- "The Indian Problem" by Greta Hogan (Moon Child)
- "The Never Ending Trail" by Del "Abe" Jones
- "The Powwow at the End of the World" by Sherman Alexie
- "The Trail of Tears" by Brian Childers
- "Treaty One 1871" by Wayne Scott
- "A Tribute to Chief Joseph" by Duane Niatum

INTERNET SOURCES
- *American Indians in Children's Literature* (AICL) by Debbie Reese *http://americanindiansinchildrensliterature.blogspot.com/*
- *History on the Net: American West* © Historyonthenet 2000-2011 *http://historyonthenet.com/American_West/americanwestmain.htm*

From *Commando Classics: A Field Manual for Helping Teens Understand (and Maybe Even Enjoy) Classic Literature* by Daria Plumb. Bowie, MD: VOYA Press, an imprint of E L Kurdyla Publishing, LLC. Copyright 2012

- *History on the Net: Native Americans* © Historyonthenet 2000-2011 *http://www.historyon-thenet.com/Native_Americans/nativeamericansmain.htm*

- *Indian Law Resource Center* © 2010 *http://www.indianlaw.org/*

SONGS

- "$20 Bill" by Corporate Avenger *http://www.youtube.com/watch?v=ZWPd69b6eNg&list=PL 27AC941A7215AA83*

HISTORIES

- "Blankets for the Dead" by Jim Carnes from *Us and Them: A History of Intolerance in America.* Southern Poverty Law Center, 1995.

- "Ghost Dance at Wounded Knee" from *Us and Them: A History of Intolerance in America* by Jim Carnes. Teaching Tolerance, 1995.

- "Indian Removal." *Oklahoma Historical Society's Encyclopedia of Oklahoma History & Culture http://digital.library.okstate.edu/encyclopedia/entries/I/IN015.html*

- *Scholastic Encyclopedia of the American Indian* by James Ciment. Scholastic, 1996.

SPEECHES

- "I Will Fight No More Forever" by Chief Joseph

- "The Indians' Night Promises to Be Dark" by Chief Seattle

ESSAYS / ARTICLES

- "American Indian Boarding Schools Haunt Many" by Charla Bear for National Public Radio, May 12, 2008. *http://www.npr.org/templates/story/story.php?storyId=16516865&ps=rs*

- "The North American Indian Holocaust" by Kahentinetha Horn, *MNN Mohawk Nation News* Wake *http://www.caledoniawakeupcall.com/news/hitler.html*

- "A Sorry Saga: Obama Signs Native American Apology Resolution; Fails to Draw Attention to It" by Rob Capriccioso for *Indian Country Today*, Jan. 13, 2010 © 2010 Indian Law Resource Center *http://www.indianlaw.org/node/529*

- "Soul Wound: The Legacy of Native American Schools" by Andrea Smith for *Amnesty International Magazine* © 2007 *http://amnestyusa.org/amnestynow/soulwound.html*

- "Statement on the Causes of Wounded Knee" by Red Cloud

MISCELLANEOUS

- *The Declaration of Indian Purpose*, June 20, 1961

IDENTIFYING THOSE WHO HAVE BEEN MISTREATED:
AFRICAN AMERICANS TEXT SET

NOVELS

Slavery
- *Nightjohn* by Gary Paulsen. Delacorte Press, 1993.
- *Roots* by Alex Haley. Doubleday, 1976.
- *The Slave Dancer* by Paula Fox. Aladdin Paperbacks, 1973.

Emmett Till
- *Mississippi Trial, 1955* by Chris Crowe. Speak, 2002.

16th Street Baptist Church Bombing
- *The Watsons Go to Birmingham, 1963* by Christopher Paul Curtis. Bantam Doubleday Dell Books for Young Readers, 1997.

Other
- *Whale Talk* by Chris Crutcher. Greenwillow Books, 2001.

ILLUSTRATED BOOKS

Slavery
- *The Kidnapped Prince: The Life of Okaudah Equiano* by Olauduh Equiano, adapted by Ann Cameron. Random House, 1995.

Escape/Underground Railroad
- *Almost to Freedom* by Vaunda Micheaux Nelson. Carolrhoda Books, 2003.
- *Friend on Freedom River* by Gloria Whelan. Sleeping Bear Press, 2004.
- *Henry's Freedom Box: A True Story from the Underground Railroad* by Ellen Levine. Scholastic, 2007.
- *Minty: A Story of Young Harriet Tubman* by Alan Schroeder. Dial Books for Young Readers, 1996.
- *Passage on the Underground Railroad* by Stephen Marc. University Press of Mississippi, 2009.
- *The People Could Fly: The Picture Book* by Virginia Hamilton. Knopf Books for Young Readers, 2004.
- *A Picture Book of Harriet Tubman* by David Adler. Holiday House, 1992.

Lynching
- *Without Sanctuary: Lynching Photography in America* by James Allen et al. Twin Palms, 2000. *As suggested by the title, this book contains graphic photography. You can find a link to an online teachers' guide in the Miscellaneous section.

From *Commando Classics: A Field Manual for Helping Teens Understand (and Maybe Even Enjoy) Classic Literature* by Daria Plumb. Bowie, MD: VOYA Press, an imprint of E L Kurdyla Publishing, LLC. Copyright 2012

16th Street Baptist Church Bombing

- *Birmingham, 1963* by Carole Boston Weatherford. Wordsong, 2007.

FILMS / VIDEOS

Slavery

- *Roots: Breaking Kunta http://www.youtube.com/watch?v=H_A2o8lCclQ*
- *Slavery and the Making of America, Volumes 1-4.* Ambrose Video, 2005.

Lynching

- *Rosewood.* Warner Home Video, 2007.

Emmett Till

- *The Untold Story of Emmett Louis Till* by Till Freedom Come Productions. ThinkFilm, LLC, 2005.

16th Street Baptist Church Bombing

- *4 Little Girls.* HBO Home Video, 1998.

Other

- *A Class Divided.* Yale University Films, 2003.
- *The Jena 6* ESPN Outside the Lines *http://www.youtube.com/watch?v=3SrlEM8X0qA*
- *Little Rock Central: 50 Years Later.* HBO Home Video, 2007.
- *Miss Evers' Boys.* HBO Home Video, 2001.
- *Mississippi Burning.* MGM Home Entertainment, 1988.
- *Prom Night in Mississippi.* Docurama, 2009.

POEMS

Slavery

- "Bury Me in a Free Land" by Francis E.W. Harper
- "The Middle Passage" by Robert Hayden
- "The Slave Auction" by Francis E.W. Harper
- "The Slave Mother" by Francis E.W. Harper
- "The Slaves Complaint" by George Moses Horton

Escape/Underground Railroad

- "The Fugitive Slave" by Jones Very
- "Runagate Runagate" by Robert Hayden

Lynching

- "Biography" by Amiri Baraka (LeRoi Jones)
- "The Bitter River" by Langston Hughes
- "The Haunted Oak" by Paul Lawrence Dunbar
- "The Lynching" by Claude McKay
- "Song for a Black Girl" by Langston Hughes

Emmett Till

- "The Lovesong of Emmett Till" by Anthony Walton
- "Mississippi—1955" by Langston Hughes

16th Street Baptist Church Bombing

- "American History" by Michael Harper
- "Birmingham Sunday" by Langston Hughes
- "Coded Language" by Saul Williams *http://www.youtube.com/watch?v=jzY2-GRDiPM&feature=related*

Other

- "Dark Symphony" by Melvin B. Tolson
- "Incident" by Countee Cullen
- "Niggas, Niggers, and Niggaz" by Julian Curry *http://www.youtube.com/watch?v=wD-UpHlB9no&feature=related*
- "Super Negro" by Al B. *http://www.youtube.com/results?search_query=super+negro+al+b.&aq=o*

INTERNET SOURCES

Slavery

- *History on the Net: Black Peoples in America http://historyonthenet.com/Slave_Trade/slaverymain.htm*

From *Commando Classics: A Field Manual for Helping Teens Understand (and Maybe Even Enjoy) Classic Literature* by Daria Plumb. Bowie, MD: VOYA Press, an imprint of E L Kurdyla Publishing, LLC. Copyright 2012

IDENTIFYING THOSE WHO HAVE BEEN MISTREATED: AFRICAN AMERICANS TEXT SET (*Cont.*)

Escape/Underground Railroad

- "Myths and Codes of the Underground Railroad" *http://www.safepassageohio.org/resources/weblesson.pdf*
- *National Geographic Online* presents The Underground Railroad *http://www.nationalgeographic.com/railroad/*

Emmett Till

- *Emmett Till Legacy Foundation http://www.emmetttilllegacyfoundation.com*
- The Murder of Emmett Till *http://www.emmetttillmurder.com/*
- The Untold Story of Emmett Louis Till *http://emmetttillstory.com/*

Other

- *Africans in America by PBS and WGBH http://www.pbs.org/wgbh/aia/home.html*
- *Jim Crow Museum of Racist Memorabilia at Ferris State University http://www.ferris.edu/htmls/news/jimcrow/menu.htm*
- *National Underground Railroad Freedom Center http://freedomcenter.org/*
- *Southern Poverty Law Center http://www.splcenter.org/*
- "U.S. Public Health Service Syphilis Study at Tuskegee," *Centers for Disease Control and Prevention http://www.cdc.gov/tuskegee/index.html*

SONGS

Lynching

- "Strange Fruit" composed by Abel Meeropol, originally sung by Billie Holiday *http://www.youtube.com/watch?v=h4ZyuULy9zs&feature=related*

Emmett Till

- "The Death of Emmett Till" by Bob Dylan
- "The Money Mississippi Blues" by Langston Hughes

16th Street Baptist Church Bombing

- "Ballad of Birmingham" by Dudley Randall (listen to an amazing rendition by Tennessee State University students) *http://www.youtube.com/watch?v=cHxG2b4rAlA*
- "Bear It Away" by Kate Campbell
- "Birmingham Sunday" by Richard Farina
- "Mississippi Goddam" by Nina Simone *http://www.youtube.com/watch?v=TkcuNX4vrS8*
- "On Her Hand a Golden Ring" by Phil Ochs

IDENTIFYING THOSE WHO HAVE BEEN MISTREATED: AFRICAN AMERICANS TEXT SET (*Cont.*)

Other

- *Sing for Freedom: The Story of the Civil Rights Movement through Its Songs.* Washington, D.C.: Smithsonian Folkways Records, 1990.

BIOGRAPHIES / AUTOBIOGRAPHIES

Slavery

- *Biography: Need to Know: Frederick Douglass http://www.youtube.com/watch?v=Su-4JBEIhXY&feature=view_all&list=PL27AC941A7215AA83&index=48*

- *Biography: Need to Know: Harriet Tubman http://www.youtube.com/watch?v=XmsNGrkbHm4&feature=relmfu*

- *Narrative of the Life of Frederick Douglass* by Frederick Douglass. Dover Publishing, 1995.

- *To Be a Slave* by Julius Lester. Dial Press, 1968.

HISTORIES

Slavery

- "African Slave Trade and the Middle Passage" *Africans in America. http://www.pbs.org/wgbh/aia/part1/1narr4.html*

- *Great Slave Narratives* selected and introduced by Arna Bontemps. Beacon Press, 1969.

- "Living Africans Thrown Overboard" *Africans in America. http://www.pbs.org/wgbh/aia/part1/1h280.html*

- *The Slave Ship: A Human History* by Marcus Rediker. Viking/Penguin, 2007.

Escape/Underground Railroad

- "The Underground Railroad" from *Us and Them: A History of Intolerance in America* by Jim Carnes. Teaching Tolerance, 1995.

Lynching

- "Lynching Statistics" *The Charles Chestnut Digital Archive. http://faculty.berea.edu/browners/chesnutt/classroom/lynchingstat.html*

- "A Town Called Rosewood" from *Us and Them: A History of Intolerance in America* by Jim Carnes. Teaching Tolerance, 1995.

Emmett Till

- *Death of Innocence: The Story of the Hate Crime That Changed America* by Mamie Till-Mobley and Christopher Benson. Random House, 2003.
- *Getting Away with Murder: The True Story of the Emmett Till Case* by Chris Crowe. Phyllis Fogelman Books, 2003.
- *The Murder of Emmett Till* by David Robson. Lucent Books/Gale, Cengage Learning, 2010.
- *Simeon's Story: An Eyewitness Account of the Kidnapping of Emmett Till* by Simeon Wright, with Herb Boyd. Lawrence Hill Books, 2010.

MISCELLANEOUS

Slavery

- *Slave Ship, Part I* by Amiri Baraka *http://www.youtube.com/watch?v=UgNiczXgbjg&feature=related*

Escape/Underground Railroad

- *The Underground Railroad for Kids: From Slavery to Freedom with 21 Activities* by Mary Kay Carson. Chicago Review Press, 2005.

Lynching

- *Without Sanctuary: Lynching Photography in America Teachers' Guide* by *National Underground Railroad Freedom Center http://freedomcenter.org/without-sanctuary/WithoutSanctuaryTeacherGuide.pdf*

Other

- Active U.S. Hate Groups, *Southern Poverty Law Center http://www.splcentr.org/get-informed/hate-map*
- Hate Crime Statistics
    - "Incidents, Offenses, Victims, and Known Offenders by Bias Motivation" table *http://www2.fbi.gov/ucr/hc2009/data/table_01.html*
    - "Incidents, Offenses, Victims, and Known Offenders by Offense Type" table *http://www2.fbi.gov/ucr/hc2009/data/table_02.html*
- "Literacy Tests" *Veterans of the Civil Rights Movement. http://www.crmvet.org/info/lithome.htm*

IDENTIFYING THOSE WHO HAVE BEEN MISTREATED:
AFRICAN AMERICANS TEXT SET (*Cont.*)

ESSAYS / ARTICLES

Escape/Underground Railroad

- "When Special Delivery Meant Deliverance for a Fugitive Slave" by Alison Leigh Cowen for *The New York Times City Room*, Feb. 26, 2010 *http://cityroom.blogs.nytimes.com/2010/02/26/when-special-delivery-meant-deliverance-for-a-fugitive-slave/*

16th Street Baptist Church Bombing

- "16th Street Baptist Church Bombing Forty Years Later, Birmingham Still Struggles with Violent Past" *NPR* September 15, 2003 *http://www.npr.org/templates/story/story.php?storyId=1431932*

Other

- "Investigations Force Feds to Revisit Murders of Civil Rights Era" by Benjamin Greenberg for *Colorlines.com*, Jan. 12, 2011 *http://colorlines.com/archives/2011/01/civil_rights_era_murders_reopened_in_mississippi.html*

- "Remembering Tuskegee: Syphilis Study Still Provokes Disbelief, Sadness" *National Public Radio http://www.npr.org/programs/morning/features/2002/jul/tuskegee*

- "What Gabby Sidibe's Cover Tells Us About 'Looking Good' in Print" by Ayana Bird for *Colorlines.com*, Sept. 25, 2010 *http://colorlines.com/archives/2010/09/gabby_sidibe_elle_and_fashion_industry_editing.html*

From *Commando Classics: A Field Manual for Helping Teens Understand (and Maybe Even Enjoy) Classic Literature* by Daria Plumb. Bowie, MD: VOYA Press, an imprint of E L Kurdyla Publishing, LLC. Copyright 2012

IDENTIFYING THOSE WHO HAVE BEEN MISTREATED: JAPANESE INTERNMENT TEXT SET

NOVELS

- *A Boy No More* by Harry Mazer. Simon & Schuster, 2004.
- *Farewell to Manzanar* by Jeanne Wakatsuki Houston. Houghton Mifflin, 1973.
- *The Fences Between Us: The Diary of Piper Davis* by Kirby Larson. Scholastic, 2010.
- *The Journal of Ben Uchida, Citizen #13559, Mirror Lake Internment Camp* by Barry Denenberg. Scholastic, 1999.
- *Missing in Action* by Dean Hughes. Atheneum Books for Young Readers, 2010.
- *Thin Wood Walls* by David Patneaude. Houghton Mifflin, 2004.
- *Weedflower* by Cynthia Kadohata. Atheneum Books for Young Readers, 2006.

ILLUSTRATED BOOKS

- *Baseball Saved Us* by Ken Mochizuki. Live Oak Media, 2004.
- *The Bracelet* by Yoshiko Ushida. Philomel, 1993.
- *I Am an American: A True Story of Japanese Internment* by Jerry Stanley. Crown Publishers, 1994.
- *A Place Where Sunflowers Grow* by Amy Lee-Tai. Children's Book Press, 2006.
- *So Far from the Sea* by Eve Bunting. Sandpiper, 2009.

FILMS / VIDEOS

- *American Pastime*. Warner Home Video, 2007.
- *Beyond Barbed Wire*. Kit Parker Films, 2001.
- *George Takei in Japanese Concentration Camps*. http://www.youtube.com/watch?v= oUr-pIFp7EMA
- *Japanese Relocation* Produced by Office of War Information—Bureau of Motion Pictures. http://www.youtube.com/watch?v=_OiPIdKsM5w
- *Most Honorable Son*. PBS Home Video, 2007.
- *A Nisei Story*. http://www.youtube.com/watch?v=QqlNthzBU2l
- *Passing Poston: An American Story*. New Video Group, 2008.
- *PBS Home Video's Time of Fear*. PBS Home Video, 2004.
- *Pearl Harbor Day Attack*. http://www.youtube.com/watch?v=Nt13c3olXkU

IDENTIFYING THOSE WHO HAVE BEEN MISTREATED:
JAPANESE INTERNMENT TEXT SET (*Cont.*)

ARTWORK

- *American Memory Gallery of Japanese Internment http://memory.loc.gov/learn/lessons/99/fear/gallery.html*

- *Ansel Adams's Photographs of Japanese-American Internment at Manzanar.* The Library of Congress *http://memory.loc.gov/ammem/collections/anseladams/*

- *The Art of Gaman: Arts and Crafts from the Japanese American Internment Camps 1942-1946* by Delphine Hirasuna. Ten Speed Press, 2005.

- Ben Sakoguchi *Postcards from Camp* paintings *http://www.bensakoguchi.com/series_post-cards_from_camp.html*

- *Born Free and Equal: The Story of Loyal Japanese Americans* by Ansel Adams. Spotted Dog Press, Inc., 2002.

- *Impounded: Dorothea Lange and the Censored Images of Japanese American Internment* edited by Linda Gordon. W.W. Norton & Company, 2008.

- *Topaz Moon: Chiura Obata's Art of the Internment* by Chiura Obata. Heyday Books, 2000.

POEMS

- "In Response to Executive Order 9066: All Americans of Japanese Descent Must Report to Relocation Center" by Dwight Okida

- "Manzanar" by Michiko Mizumoto

- "My Mom, Pop, and Me" by Itsuko Taniguchi

- "The Nice Thing about Counting Stars" by Dwight Okida

- "That Damned Fence" by Anonymous

INTERNET SOURCES

- *The Children of the Camps: The Documentary http://www.pbs.org/childofcamp/*

- *Exploring the Japanese Internment through Film & the Internet* © National Asian American Transcommunications Association *http://caamedia.org/jainternment/*

- *InternmentArchives.com http://www.internmentarchives.com/index.php*

- *Life in Japanese Internment Camps http://library.thinkquest.org/TQ0312008/bhjic.html*

- *A More Perfect Union: Japanese Americans & the U.S. Constitution http://americanhistory.si.edu/perfectunion/experience/index.html*

- *National Archives Documented Rights: Relocation http://www.archives.gov/exhibits/documented-rights/exhibit/section3/relocation.html*

From *Commando Classics: A Field Manual for Helping Teens Understand (and Maybe Even Enjoy) Classic Literature* by Daria Plumb. Bowie, MD: VOYA Press, an imprint of E L Kurdyla Publishing, LLC. Copyright 2012

IDENTIFYING THOSE WHO HAVE BEEN MISTREATED:
JAPANESE INTERNMENT TEXT SET (*Cont.*)

- "Nothing to Fear but Fear Itself" lesson plan by Gail Desler *http://memory.loc.gov/learn/lessons/99/fear/intro.html*

- *WWII Japanese Internment: An Interactive Lesson Plan Using Primary Sources* by Deanna Olson *http://www.wisconsinhistory.org/teachers/lessons/secondary/internment.asp*

SONGS

- "Kenji" by Fort Minor *http://www.youtube.com/watch?v=3Ckvmc_486U*

BIOGRAPHIES

- *The Invisible Thread: An Autobiography* by Yoshiko Uchida. J. Messner, 1991.

HISTORIES

- *And Justice for All: An Oral History of the Japanese American Detention Camps* compiled by John Tateishi. Random House, 1984.

- *Dear Miss Breed : True Stories of the Japanese American Incarceration during World War II and a Librarian Who Made a Difference* by Joanne Oppenheim. Scholastic Nonfiction, 2006.

- *"Home Was a Horse Stall"* from *Us and Them: A History of Intolerance in America* by Jim Carnes. Teaching Tolerance, 1995.

- *Japanese American Internment Camps* by Gail Sakurai. Children's Press/Scholastic, 2002.

- *Japanese-American Internment in American History* by David K. Fremon. Enslow, 1996.

MISCELLANEOUS

- Cartoon supporting the internment of the Japanese in California, from the Sacramento Bee. 1942. *http://bad.eserver.org/issues/2004/71/expulsion.gif/view?searchterm=internment*

- *The History Channel's History's Mysteries: Italian-American Internment: A Secret Story.* A&E Home Video, 2000.

- Japanese Internment Curriculum – Posters from World War II. Anti-Japanese propaganda. *http://bss.sfsu.edu/internment/postersower.html*

- *Transcript of Executive Order 9066: Resulting in the Relocation of Japanese. 1942. http://www.ourdocuments.gov/doc.php?flash=false&doc=74&page=transcript*

ESSAYS / ARTICLES

- "Can It Happen Again? Postwar & Impact Today" from *Exploring the Japanese Internment through Film & the Internet* © National Asian American Transcommunications Association *http://caamedia.org/jainternment/postwar/index.html*

- "A Civil Rights Hero Gets His Day" by Maria L. La Ganga for the *Los Angeles Times*, Jan. 31, 2011 *http://articles.latimes.com/2011/jan/31/local/la-me-0131-korematsu-20110131*

IDENTIFYING THOSE WHO HAVE BEEN MISTREATED:
WOMEN TEXT SET

ILLUSTRATED BOOKS

- *A Is for Abigail: An Almanac of Amazing American Women* by Lynne Cheney. Simon & Schuster Books for Young Readers, 2003.
- *Elizabeth Leads the Way: Elizabeth Cady Stanton and the Right to Vote* by Tanya Lee Stone. Henry Holt, 2008.
- *Independent Dames: What You Never Knew about the Women and Girls of the Revolution* by Laurie Halse Anderson. Simon & Schuster Books for Young Readers, 2008.
- *Patriots in Petticoats: Heroines of the American Revolution* by Shirley Raye Redmond. Random House, 2004.
- *Rabble Rousers: 20 Women Who Made a Difference* by Cheryl Harness. Dutton Children's Books, 2003.
- *Women's Right to Vote* by Elaine Landau. Children's Press/Scholastic, 2005.

FILMS /VIDEOS

- "Abigail Adams Was a Brilliant" (from the miniseries *John Adams*) *http://www.youtube.com/watch?v=WXQZlo6JN2Q*
- "Ain't I a Woman" by Sojourner Truth performed by Alfre Woodard *http://www.youtube.com/watch?v=4vr_vKsk_h8*
- "The Birth Control Revolution" *http://www.youtube.com/watch?v=KmYSNOEsukM*
- *Equality: A History of the Women's Movement in America.* Schlessinger Media, 2007.
- *Iron Jawed Angels.* Warner Home Video/HBO Films, 2004. *http://iron-jawed-angels.com/*
- "Life of Sojourner Truth: Ain't I a Woman?" *http://www.youtube.com/watch?v=Fy0z3egS7L4*
- "Roe v. Wade in PBS' The Supreme Court" *http://www.youtube.com/watch?v=1q5AgCzPluA*
- "School House Rock—Sufferin' Till Sufferage" *http://www.youtube.com/watch?v=3dPF0SGh_PQ*
- "Seneca Falls" *http://www.youtube.com/watch?v=yXdr7q3jVck*
- "This Is What a Feminist Looks Like" *http://www.youtube.com/watch?v=3YA13GNT8Mc*

ARTWORK

- "Women's History Primary Source Sets: Women's Suffrage" from the Library of Congress *http://www.loc.gov/teachers/classroommaterials/themes/womens-history/set.html*

POEMS

- "Phenomenal Woman" by Maya Angelou *http://www.youtube.com/watch?v=IEz6BsYP5vc*
- "Right to Life" by Marge Pearcy
- "Still I Rise" by Maya Angelou *http://www.youtube.com/watch?v=JqOqo50LSZ0*
- "Suffrage Songs and Verses" by Charlotte Perkins Gilman *http://digital.library.upenn.edu/women/gilman/suffrage/suffrage.html*
- "What Women Deserve" by Sonya Renee Taylor *http://www.youtube.com/watch?v=BoLL6Zqc-Qo*

From *Commando Classics: A Field Manual for Helping Teens Understand (and Maybe Even Enjoy) Classic Literature* by Daria Plumb. Bowie, MD: VOYA Press, an imprint of E L Kurdyla Publishing, LLC. Copyright 2012

IDENTIFYING THOSE WHO HAVE BEEN MISTREATED: WOMEN TEXT SET (*Cont.*)

- "Women's Rights" by Anna Louisa Walker
- "Women's Suffrage" by William Topaz McGonagall

INTERNET SOURCES

- "Women's History" from *The Liz Library* *http://www.thelizlibrary.org/site-index/site-index-frame.html#soulhttp://www.thelizlibrary.org/undelete/library.html*
- *Women's History Month for Teachers* from Library of Congress *http://www.womenshistory-month.gov/teachers.html*

SONGS

- "Because We're Women" by Joyce Stevens *http://unionsong.com/u420.html*
- "Bread and Roses" by James Oppenheim *http://unionsong.com/u159.html*
- "For Women" by Talib Kweli *http://www.youtube.com/watch?v=0qkjtK3O15Q*
- "Four Women" by Nina Simone *http://www.youtube.com/watch?v=qCwME6Jpn3s&feature=related*
- "I Am Woman" by Helen Reddy

BIOGRAPHIES

- "First Lady Biography: Abigail Adams" © National First Ladies' Library *http://www.firstladies.org/biographies/firstladies.aspx?/biography=2*

HISTORIES

- *33 Things Every Girl Should Know about Women's History: From Suffragettes to Skirt Lengths to the E.R.A.* edited by Tonya Bolden. Crown Books for Young Readers, 2002.
- *Almost Astronauts: 13 Women Who Dared to Dream* by Tanya Lee Stone. Candlewick Press, 2009.

MISCELLANEOUS

- "Ain't I a Woman?" by Sojourner Truth
- *Declaration of Sentiments*, Seneca Falls Convention
- Letters between Abigail Adams and Her Husband John *http://www.thelizlibrary.org/suffrage/abigail.htm*
- "Letter to John Adams, March 31, 1776" by Abigail Adams

ESSAYS / ARTICLES

- "Ads Tell Women: 'Abortion Changes You': A Dishonest Abortion Campaign Premieres in New York City's Subway" by Tracy Clark-Flory for *Salon*. March 9, 2010. *http://www.salon.com/life/broadsheet/2010/03/09/abortion_changes_you/index.html*
- "I'd Rather be Black than Female" by Shirley Chisolm
- "Poor Jane's Almanac" by Jill Lepore for *The New York Times*, April 23, 2011 *http://www.nytimes.com/2011/04/24/opinion/24lepore.html?_r=1*

From *Commando Classics: A Field Manual for Helping Teens Understand (and Maybe Even Enjoy) Classic Literature* by Daria Plumb. Bowie, MD: VOYA Press, an imprint of E L Kurdyla Publishing, LLC. Copyright 2012

IDENTIFYING THOSE WHO HAVE BEEN MISTREATED:
WORKERS TEXT SET

NOVELS

Triangle Shirtwaist Fire

- *Ashes of Roses* by Mary Jane Auch. Henry Holt, 2002.
- *Threads and Flames* by Esther N. Friesner. Viking/Penguin, 2010.
- *Uprising* by Margaret Peterson Haddix. Simon & Schuster Books for Young Readers, 2007.

Farmworkers

- *The Circuit: Stories from the Life of a Migrant Child* by Francisco Jimenez. University of New Mexico Press, 1997.

ILLUSTRATED BOOKS

Farmworkers

- *A Picture Book of Cesar Chavez* by David Adler. Holiday House, 2010.

FILMS / VIDEOS

Triangle Shirtwaist Fire

- *Triangle Fire.* PBS Video, 2011.

Farmworkers

- "Harvest of Shame" *http://www.youtube.com/watch?v=vyrJClHzxig&list=PL27AC941A721 5AA83*
- Viva La Causa. Video and Teachers' Guide. Available from *Teaching Tolerance http://www. tolerance.org/kit/viva-la-causa*

Coal Miners

- *Harlan County, USA.* First Run Features Home Video, 2006.

ARTWORK

Triangle Shirtwaist Fire

- "Remembering the Triangle Factory Fire 100 Years Later: Photos and Illustrations" *http:// www.ilr.cornell.edu/trianglefire/primary/photosIllustrations/index.html*

IDENTIFYING THOSE WHO HAVE BEEN MISTREATED: WORKERS TEXT SET (*Cont.*)

POEMS

Triangle Shirtwaist Fire

- *Fragments from the Fire: The Triangle Shirtwaist Factory Fire of March 25, 1911* by Chris Llewellyn. Viking Penguin, Inc., 1987.
- "Labor Pains Have Been Intense" by Safiya Henderson
- "Memorial to Triangle Shirtwaist Victims" by Morris Rosenfeld
- "Shirt" by Robert Pinsky *http://www.youtube.com/watch?v=YI8DvfM0VCs&list=PL27AC94 1A7215AA83*
- "Sisters in the Flames" by Carol Tarlen

Farmworkers

- "Napa, California" by Ana Castilo

Fair Wages / Unions

- "Forced Overtime" by David G. Hurlburt
- "What is a Union?" by David G. Hurlburt

INTERNET SOURCES

Triangle Shirtwaist Fire

- *Remembering the Triangle Factory Fire 100 Years Later*, Cornell University *http://www.ilr. cornell.edu/trianglefire/index.html*

Fair Wages / Unions

- *Union Songs…*online collection by Mark Gregory *http://unionsong.com/*

Other

- "Paying with Their Health" activity from *Teaching Tolerance http://www.tolerance.org/activity / paying-their-health*

SONGS

Triangle Shirtwaist Fire

- "Ballad of the Triangle Fire" by Ruth Rubin
- "Mournful Song of the Great Fire" by Yehuda Horvitz
- "My Little Shirtwaist" by Rasputina
- "The Uprising of the Twenty Thousand: Dedicated to the Waistmakers of 1909" by Ladies' Garment Workers' Union

IDENTIFYING THOSE WHO HAVE BEEN MISTREATED:
WORKERS TEXT SET (*Cont.*)

Farmworkers

- "Corrido de Cesar Chavez." ("Ballad of Cesar Chavez"). by Rumel Fuentes
- "El Corrido de Cesar Chavez by El Teatro Campesino
- "Si Se Puede" by Linda Allen

Coal Miners

- "Canaries in the Mine" by Linda Allen
- "Come All You Coal Miners" by Sarah Ogan Dunning
- "Dark as a Dungeon" by Merle Travis
- "The Death of Mother Jones" by Unknown

Fair Wages / Unions

- "I Hate the Company Bosses" by Sarah Ogan Gunning
- "The Living Wage" by Kristin Lems
- "Union ABC's" by Kristin Lems
- "Union Maid" by Woody Guthrie
- "Union Town" by Tom Morello: The Nighwatchmen *http://www.youtube.com/watch?v=a5ZT 71DxLuM&list=PL27AC941A7215AA83*
- "We're AFL-CIO" by Julius Margolin
- "You Gotta Go Down and Join the Union" adapted by Woody Guthrie

MISCELLANEOUS

Farmworkers

- "Prayer of the Farm Worker's Struggle" by Cesar Chavez
- "Speech to Striking Grape Workers" by Cesar Chavez

From *Commando Classics: A Field Manual for Helping Teens Understand (and Maybe Even Enjoy) Classic Literature*
by Daria Plumb. Bowie, MD: VOYA Press, an imprint of E L Kurdyla Publishing, LLC. Copyright 2012

IDENTIFYING THOSE WHO HAVE BEEN MISTREATED:
LGBT TEXT SET

FILMS /VIDEOS

- *The Laramie Project.* HBO Home Video, 2002.

- "10 Years after Matthew Shepard's Murder", *Rocky Mountain News http://www.youtube. com/watch?v=So5RAanecsg&feature=related*

POEMS

- "Autumn in Maine (for Charlie Howard)" by David E. Patton

- "At 13" by Keith Morrison *http://www.youtube.com/watch?v=BzfX1HWlW4w&list=PL27AC 941A7215AA83*

- "Charlie Howard's Descent" by Mark Doty

- "Dive" by Andrea Gibson *http://www.youtube.com/watch?v=GqKORO5XIHw&list=PL27AC 941A7215AA83*

INTERNET SOURCES

- *Freedom to Marry http://www.freedomtomarry.org/*

- *Give a Damn Campaign http://www.wegiveadamn.org/*

- *Human Rights Campaign http://www.hrc.org/*

- *The Matthew Shepard Foundation http://www.matthewshepard.org/our-story*

- *The Trevor Project http://www.thetrevorproject.org/*

SONGS

- "Above the Clouds" by Jed Leiber, Jeff Beck, and Cyndi Lauper

- "American Triangle" by Elton John and Bernie Taupin *http://www.youtube.com/watch?v=S9IM_ T4yEaM&feature=related*

- "Scarecrow" by Melissa Etheridge *http://www.youtube.com/watch?v=NUX3rglSRJ0*

- "The Ballad of Mathew Shepherd" by Russell Henderson and Aaron McKinney

- "The Fence (Mathew Shepard's Song)" by Peter Katz

IDENTIFYING THOSE WHO HAVE BEEN MISTREATED:
LGBT TEXT SET (*Cont.*)

HISTORIES

- "A Rose for Charlie" from *Us and Them: A History of Intolerance in America* by Jim Carnes. Teaching Tolerance, 1995.

MISCELLANEOUS

- Hate Crime Statistics

  - "Incidents, Offenses, Victims, and Known Offenders by Bias Motivation" table *http://www2.fbi.gov/ucr/hc2009/data/table_01.html*

  - "Incidents, Offenses, Victims, and Known Offenders by Offense Type" table *http://www2.fbi.gov/ucr/hc2009/data/table_02.html*

ESSAYS / ARTICLES

- "26th Annual Charlie Howard Memorial Held in Bangor" by Judy Harrison for *Bangor Daily News*, July 11, 2010

- "Asking For It: Judges and Juries May Go Easy on Gay Bashers Who Blame Their Victims" by Jeff Stryker for *SALON*, Oct. 23, 1998 *http://www.salon.com/news/1998/10/23news.html*

- "Federal LGBT Legislation: An Economic Empowerment Agenda" from *Human Rights Campaign http://www.hrc.org/documents/EconomicEmpowerment.pdf*

- "Gay Rights" from *SpeakOut.com http://speakout.com/activism/gayrights/*

- "La. Student Sent Home for Gay T-Shirt" by *Advocate.com* Editors, March 23, 2011 *http://www.advocate.com/News/Daily_News/2011/03/23/La_Student_Sent_Home_for_Gay_TShirt/*

- "Should Anti-Discrimination Laws Be Enforced to Protect Gays from Discrimination?" by Barbara McCuen for *SpeakOut.com*, April 26, 2000 *http://www.speakout.com/activism/gayrights/*

- "Should Crimes against Gays Be Considered Hate Crimes?" by Jenny Murphy for *SpeakOut.com,* April 26, 2000 *http://www.speakout.com/activism/issue_briefs/1202b-1.html*

- "Should *South Park* Get Away with Using the F-Word?" by Michael Jones for *Change.org*, Nov. 6, 2009 *http://news.change.org/stories/should-south-park-get-away-with-using-the-f-word*

- "When Words Can Kill: 'That's So Gay'" by Susan Donaldson James for ABC News *http://abcnews.go.com/m/story?id=7328091&sid=26*

- "Where are Charlie Howard's Killer's?" by Judy Harrison for *Bangor Daily News*, July13, 2009

From *Commando Classics: A Field Manual for Helping Teens Understand (and Maybe Even Enjoy) Classic Literature* by Daria Plumb. Bowie, MD: VOYA Press, an imprint of E L Kurdyla Publishing, LLC. Copyright 2012

AFRICAN AMERICAN PROTEST AND RESISTANCE TEXT SET

NOVELS

Civil Rights Era

- *The Rock and the River* by Kekla Magoon. Aladdin, 2009.

ILLUSTRATED BOOKS

Slavery

- *No More! Stories and Songs of Slave Resistance* by Doreen Rappaport. Candlewick Press, 2002.

Civil Rights Era

- *Freedom Walkers: The Story of the Montgomery Bus Boycott* by Russell Freedman. Holiday House, 2006.

FILMS / VIDEOS

Civil Rights Era

- "1968 King Assassination Report (CBS News)" *http://www.youtube.com/watch?v=cmOBbx gxKvo&feature=related*
- "Black Panthers Distribute Free Groceries" CBS5 KPIX-TV, March 28, 1972 *https://diva. sfsu.edu/collections/sfbatv/bundles/190199*
- *A History of the Civil Rights Movement* Schlessinger Media, 2007
- "Malcolm X's Death (Spike Lee's Most Powerful Scene)" *http://www.youtube.com/ watch?v=53IvBoGf8-s&feature=view_all&list=PL27AC941A7215AA83&index=92*
- "Malcolm X, Hospital Scene" *http://www.youtube.com/watch?v=5Uoy6xy5AFM&feature=vi ew_all&list=PL27AC941A7215AA83&index=146*
- "Malcolm X: 'My Father Was Killed by the Ku Klux Klan'" *http://www.youtube.com/watch?v= izy6BiCV3Nw&feature=view_all&list=PL27AC941A7215AA83&index=71*
- "Malcolm X on Dr. Martin Luther King" *http://www.youtube.com/watch?v=kctEXjAeOKA&fe ature=view_all&list=PL27AC941A7215AA83&index=84*
- "Malcolm X: We've Never Bombed Any Churches" *http://www.youtube.com/watch?v=r3WM fAmg3Bo&feature=autoplay&list=PL27AC941A7215AA83&index=73&playnext=1*
- *March On! The Day My Brother Martin Changed the World . . . And More Stories about African American History.* New Video, 2010.
- "Martin Luther King, Jr. on Malcolm X" *http://www.youtube.com/watch?v=MwKIUMbi9Jk&f eature=related*
- "Robert Kennedy Announces Death of Martin Luther King, Jr." *http://www.youtube.com/ watch?v=MyCWV_N0EsM&feature=related*
- "Selma 1965—Edmund Pettis Bridge" *http://www.youtube.com/watch?v=s00-OoZAWno& feature=view_all&list=PL27AC941A7215AA83&index=93*

POEMS

- "African American Protest Poetry" from *National Humanities Center Teacher Serve http://nationalhumanitiescenter.org/tserve/freedom/1917beyond/essays/aaprotestpoetry.htm*
- "Ballad of the Landlord" by Langston Hughes
- "Dream Deferred" by Langston Hughes (Nike Commercial, narrated by Danny Glover) *http://www.youtube.com/watch?v=PiL2znfkvFk&feature=view_all&list=PL27AC941A7215AA83&index=105*
- "Dreams Are Illegal in the Ghetto" by Twin Poets *http://www.youtube.com/watch?v=Yj1MNl3Bqoc&feature=view_all&list=PL27AC941A7215AA83&index=103*
- "If We Must Die" by Claude McKay
- "Malcolm Is 'bout More Than Wearing a Cap" by Michael Warr
- "Strong Men" by Sterling Brown
- "Why Is We Americans?" by Amiri Baraka *http://www.youtube.com/watch?v=7ziRjhAgTO8&feature=view_all&list=PL27AC941A7215AA83&index=63*
- "The X Is Black" by Amiri Baraka *http://www.youtube.com/watch?v=4cOSMGzdZf8&feature=view_all&list=PL27AC941A7215AA83&index=64*

INTERNET SOURCES

Slavery

- *The Schomburg Center for Research in Black Culture: The Abolition of the Slave Trade* for the New York Public Library *http://abolition.nypl.org/essays/african_resistance*
- "Slave Resistance" worksheet from *History on the Net.com http://www.historyonthenet.com/Lessons/worksheets/black_peoples.htm*

Civil Rights Era

- *Black Panther.org http://www.blackpanther.org/index.html*
- *Civil Rights Movement Veterans.* © 1999-2009. *http://www.crmvet.org/index.htm*
- *The Complete Malcolm X: Speeches and Interviews 1960-1965 http://malcolmxfiles.blogspot.com/*
- *Free at Last: The U.S. Civil Rights Movement http://www.america.gov/publications/books-content/free-at-last.html*

SONGS

Civil Rights Era

- *Sing for Freedom: The Story of the Civil Rights Movement through Its Songs.* Smithsonian/Folkways Records, 1990)

Other

- "15 Songs Inspired by Martin Luther King, Jr." for *Spinner*, Jan. 14, 2010 *http://www.spinner.com/2010/01/14/mlk-day-songs/*

AFRICAN AMERICAN PROTEST AND RESISTANCE TEXT SET (*Cont.*)

- "Black Panther" by Mason Jennings *http://www.youtube.com/watch?v=9I0AQaW8ais*
- "I Have a Dream" by Common *http://www.youtube.com/watch?v=r_2cwhJndKY&feature= view_all&list=PL27AC941A7215AA83&index=88*
- "Revolution" by Arrested Development *http://www.youtube.com/watch?v=SDF8Evb_ jQw&feature=view_all&list=PL27AC941A7215AA83&index=67*

BIOGRAPHIES

Civil Rights Era

- *Biography: Rosa Parks http://www.youtube.com/watch?v=v8A9gvb5Fh0&feature=relmfu*

HISTORIES

Slavery

- "Harriet Jacobs Owns Herself" from *Us and Them: A History of Intolerance in America* by Jim Carnes. Teaching Tolerance, 1995.
- "Part I: Largest Slave Rebellion in U.S. History" by J.B. Bird, June 5, 2005 *http://www.john-horse.com/highlights/essays/largest.htm*

MISCELLANEOUS

Civil Rights Era

- *Mighty Times: The Children's March* teaching kit from *Teaching Tolerance http://www. tolerance.org/kit/mighty-times-childrens-march*

SPEECHES

Slavery

- "What to the Slave Is the Fourth of July?" by Frederick Douglass (read by James Earl Jones) *http://www.youtube.com/watch?v=8tTkHJWxfP0&feature=view_all&list=PL27AC94 1A7215AA83&index=47*

Civil Rights Era

- "The Ballot or the Bullet" by Malcolm X *http://www.youtube.com/watch?v=kjEO05mrLdQ&f eature=view_all&list=PL27AC941A7215AA83&index=86*
- "The Black Panther Party's Ten Point Program" by Bobby Seale *http://www.youtube.com/ watch?v=LPP0hiLuxdQ&feature=view_all&list=PL27AC941A7215AA83&index=85* "By Any Means Necessary" by Malcolm X *http://www.youtube.com/watch?v=hhg6LxyTnY8*
- "I Have a Dream" by Dr. Martin Luther King, Jr. *http://www.youtube.com/watch?v=iEMXaTk tUfA&feature=view_all&list=PL27AC941A7215AA83&index=10*
- "I See the Promised Land" Dr. Martin Luther King, Jr. *http://www.youtube.com/ watch?v=x1L8y-MX3pg&feature=related*
- "See for Yourself, Listen for Yourself, Think for Yourself" by Malcolm X

PROTEST SONGS TEXT SET

SONGS

- *Classic Protest Songs.* Smithsonian Folkways Recordings, 2009.
- My "Protest Songs" playlist on YouTube. *http://www.youtube.com/playlist?list=PLBD44DCA 0119DF97C&feature=mh_lolz*

INTERNET SOURCES

- "20 Protest Songs That Matter" for *Spinner* July 13, 2007. *http://www.spinner. com/2007/07/13/20-protest-songs-that-mattered-no-20/*
- "Best Classic Anti-War Protest Songs" by Kim Ruehl, *About.com* Guide. *http://folkmusic. about.com/od/toptens/tp/Top10Protest.htm*
- "Best Social & Political R&B/Soul Songs: Sing It Loud!" by Mark Edward Nero, *About.com* Guide. *http://randb.about.com/od/top5lists/tp/Protest_Songs.htm*
- "Civil Rights Songs: Some of the Most Notable Songs of the Civil Rights Movement" by Kim Ruehl, *About.com* Guide. *http://folkmusic.about.com/od/toptens/tp/CivilRightsSong.htm*
- *Protest Records. http://www.protest-records.com/index.html#*
- "Strange Fruit" for PBS: Independent Lens. © 2011 Independent Television Service. *http:// www.pbs.org/independentlens/strangefruit/protest.html*
- "Top 10 Best Labor Songs" by Kim Ruehl, *About.com* Guide. *http://folkmusic.about.com/ od/toptens/tp/BestLaborSongs.htm*

ESSAYS / ARTICLES

- "Beasties, Audioslave Say Protest Songs AN Important Part of Our Culture" by Corey Moss for *MTV News*, March 20, 2003. *http://www.mtv.com/news/articles/1470658/beasties-system-talk-protest-songs.jhtml*
- "Hip-Hop's Socially Conscious Side" by Jeff Chang and Dave Zirin for *Los Angeles Times*, April 23, 2007. *http://www.latimes.com/news/opinion/la-oe-zirin23apr23,0,3088270.story*
- "Protest Song Is Back—With a Vengeance" by Christopher Blagg for *The Christian Science Monitor*, June 4, 2004. *http://www.csmonitor.com/2004/0604/p11s01-almp.html*
- "Rock's Voices of Protest Finally Wake up—And It's About Time" by John Noris for *MTV News*, June 29, 2007
- "Why So Few Protest Songs? Chuck D, Tom Morello Have Ideas" by Gil Kaufman for *MTV News*, May 10, 2006. *http://www.mtv.com/news/articles/1531529/where-all-protest-songs. jhtml*

From *Commando Classics: A Field Manual for Helping Teens Understand (and Maybe Even Enjoy) Classic Literature* by Daria Plumb. Bowie, MD: VOYA Press, an imprint of E L Kurdyla Publishing, LLC. Copyright 2012

PROTEST SONG ANALYSIS

SONG TITLE:

ARTIST:

YEAR:

What is this song about? What specific issues, problems, or events are discussed in the song?

Is the song written in response to a specific event? What were the circumstances at the time the song was released?

What point of view, attitudes, or emotions does the songwriter/performer seem to have about the subject matter in the song? What is the tone (angry, sad, hopeful, sarcastic, ironic, etc.)?

Does this song suggest any solutions to the problems it is addressing?

Do you think this song would be effective as a form of social protest? In other words, would it inspire you to act? Why or why not?

MOVING BEYOND PROTEST TO VIOLENCE: WAR TEXT SET

NOVELS

- *April Morning* by Howard Fast. Bantam, 1962.
- *Bull Rider* by Suzanne Morgan Williams. Margaret K. McElderry Books, 2009.
- *Fallen Angels* by Walter Dean Myers. Scholastic, 1988.
- *The Last Mission* by Harry Mazer. Dell Publishing, 1992.
- *A Soldier's Heart: Being the Story of the Enlistment and Due Service of the Boy Charley Goddard in the First Minnesota Volunteers : A novel of the Civil War* by Gary Paulsen. Dell-Laurel Leaf, 2000.
- *Sunrise Over Fallujah* by Walter Dean Myers. Scholastic, 2008.
- *Things a Brother Knows* by Dana Reinhardt. Wendy Lamb, 2010.
- *Woods Runner* by Gary Paulsen. Wendy Lamb, 2010.

FILMS /VIDEOS

- *Johnny Got His Gun.* Shout! Factory, 2009.

ARTWORK

- "Reflections" by Lee Teter

POEMS

- "At the Vietnam Memorial" by George Bilgere
- "Belleau Wood" by Paul Engle
- "Come Up from the Field Father" by Walt Whitman
- "The Death of a Soldier" by Wallace Stevens
- "The Death of the Ball Turrett Gunner" by Randall Jarrell
- "Grass" by Carl Sandburg
- "In Flanders Fields" by John McCrae
- "Losses" by Randall Jarrell
- "The March into Virginia, Ending on the First Manassas. July 1861" by Herman Melville
- "A Mark in the Ranks Hard-Prest and the Road Unknown" by Walt Whitman
- "A Sight in Camp in the Daybreak Gray and Dim" by Walt Whitman
- "Snookie Johnson Goes Down to the Recruiter's Office Near Benning Road and Starts Some Shit" by Kenneth Carroll
- "War Is Kind" by Stephen Crane
- "A Warning to America" by Phillip Freneau
- "The Wound Dresser" by Walt Whitman

From *Commando Classics: A Field Manual for Helping Teens Understand (and Maybe Even Enjoy) Classic Literature* by Daria Plumb. Bowie, MD: VOYA Press, an imprint of E L Kurdyla Publishing, LLC. Copyright 2012

SONGS

- "One" by Metallica
- "War Pigs" by Black Sabbath

MISCELLANEOUS

- "Chapter 5: A Night" from *Hospital Sketches* by Louisa May Alcott
- "Military Statistics Service Age and Obligation (Most Recent) by Country by NationMaster. com *http://www.nationmaster.com/graph/mil_ser_age_and_obl-military-service-age-and-obligation*
- "Serving the Country: Military Service around the World" published by Nystrom a Division of Herff Jones, Inc. *http://www.worldatlases.com/gi/cltr_MS.pdf*

SHORT STORIES

- *A Horseman in the Sky* by Ambrose Bierce

"It's Alive!" (and Still Relevant): British Literature

"Why do we hafta learn British literature anyways? We live in America," Phillip complained one day at the end of the school year. Well, probably the most important reason (as Phillip's classmates and I pointed out) is that the good stories found in classic British literature remain extremely relevant today. The best example I can give is to point to the slew of recent feature films based on stories from British literature. According to *Internet Movie Database* (*http://www.imdb.com*), there are versions of *Paradise Lost, Hamlet, The Acts of King Arthur and His Noble Knights, Dracula, The Invisible Man, Dr. Jekyll and Mr. Hyde, Treasure Island, Great Expectations, Robin Hood,* and *Frankenstein* currently "in production." Movie versions of *Gulliver's Travels* and *Robin Hood* came out in 2010, *A Christmas Carol* and *Sherlock Holmes* in 2009, *Beowulf* in 2007, *The War of the Worlds* and *Oliver Twist* in 2005, *King Arthur* in 2004, and *The Time Machine* in 2002. Also several recent movies are related to, but not necessarily based on, British classics, such as *Van Helsing* (2004), which features the characters of Dracula and Frankenstein, and *The League of Extraordinary Gentlemen* (2003), which features the characters of Dr. Jekyll, Mr. Hyde, Dorian Grey, Captain Nemo, and the Invisible Man. There have been several recent hit movies based on classic and contemporary British fantasy novels, such as *The Lord of the Rings* trilogy by J.R.R. Tolkien, *The Lion, the Witch, and the Wardrobe* and *Prince Caspian* from C.S. Lewis' *The Chronicles of Narnia* series, J.K. Rowling's *Harry Potter* series, and *The Golden Compass* from Philip Pullman's *His Dark Materials* trilogy. If students still need proof that stories from British literature are specifically relevant to them today, consider the teen films *Clueless* (1995) based on Jane Austen's *Emma, She's All That* (1999) based on George Bernard Shaw's *Pygmalion, A Knight's Tale* (2001) based on Geoffrey Chaucer's "A Knight's Tale" from *The Canterbury Tales, She's the Man* (2006) based on Shakespeare's *Twelfth Night, 10 Things I Hate about You* (1999) based on Shakespeare's *Taming of the Shrew, Get Over It* (2001) based on Shakespeare's *A Midsummer Night's Dream,* and *O* (2001) based on Shakespeare's *Othello.* Some of these films are obviously better interpretations of the classics that inspired them than others, but they do provide students with some name recognition, and that gives us a doorway into the story.

Yes, the stories from British literature really are everywhere. And the only good reason for any story to hang around for one hundred years (i.e. *Dracula*) or four hundred years (i.e. Shakespeare's works) or even one thousand, two hundred, fifty years (i.e. *Beowulf*), is because it continues to appeal to people. English language arts teachers need to spend much more time driving that point home. Yes, these stories are also beautifully written and have literary merit, but if the plots weren't captivating they would fade into oblivion. My students respond really well to the *stories* being told, which supports my idea that, if we can make the plot accessible, then there is still something in these classics for contemporary teens.

British Literature is another class that could be interesting to teach thematically. You could study the limitations of science or the mad scientist by combining *Frankenstein, Dr. Jekyll and Mr. Hyde*, and *The Invisible Man* (see the Mad Scientists text set in the British Literature Arsenal) or to study the hero tale using *Beowulf*, the Arthurian legend, and *The Hobbit* (see the Heroes text set in the World Mythology and Folklore Arsenal). However, I always come back to teaching British literature chronologically (see Bakersfield College's *British Literature Timeline* for an outline/overview of each period *http://www2.bakersfieldcollege. edu/gdumler/English%205A/Periods%20&%20Timelines/british_literature_timeline.htm*). This approach makes sense to me because I'm always pointing out to students that all art, be it literature, music, painting, fashion, etc., builds upon what comes before it—that without *Beowulf* there is no King Arthur or *The Hobbit*.

In the upcoming pages I'll tell how Brit Lit becomes a commando class. Although I won't talk about all of them in depth, we do read many poems that are considered typical Brit Lit fare in their traditional forms, such as "The Pardoner's Tale" from *The Canterbury Tales* (Chaucer), "On His Blindness" (Milton), "The Lamb" and "The Tyger" (Blake), "To a Mouse" and "Auld Lang Syne" (Burns), "How Do I Love Thee?" (Browning), "The Lady of Shalott" (Tennyson), "The Highwayman" (Noyes), "Do Not Go Gentle into that Good Night" (Thomas), and more. Whenever possible, I pair these with a song, painting, or short video to help make them relevant to students, but generally I teach them in a pretty traditional way. It's when we get to the longer works—epic poems, novels, plays—that I zero in on getting students to know the entire plot of the story whenever possible. It would be incredibly difficult to have students read all of these works in their entirety in one school year, but we can give students a good plot overview and a general idea about the themes of all these works. In a best case scenario, they might actually choose to re-read these stories in their original forms in the future. In a worst case scenario, they will have a passing familiarity with the authors, themes, and characters of some important literary works. Although I hate the term, we *cover* many more classic works in my class than I did when I took advanced English in high school.

Old English Literature

The Old English epic *Beowulf* is a story that's been given short shrift in English classes over the years. It's a fantastically exciting story featuring a larger-than-life hero who kills monsters (he rips the arm off one and dives to the bottom of a lake to fight another) and battles a dragon. If students were asked if they'd like to play a video game or watch a movie based on that premise, the answer would be a resounding, "Yes!" Yet, before the animated movie version of the story came out in 2007, most high school students couldn't say who Beowulf was. If they did recognize his name, their response might have been something like, "Oh, that, we had to read that in my English class. It was boring/stupid/terrible." This, my friends, worries me. If we can't get teens excited about a bloody, action-packed adventure, what hope could we possibly have of selling them on Shakespearean sonnets or the romantic poets or *anything* else for that matter? From a teenager's standpoint, *Beowulf* pretty much has it all.

I think a lot of the problem is in the method of delivery. As I mentioned in Chapter 1, my British Literature anthology only gives us one hundred, twenty-three lines of the 3,182 line poem. That's kind of a problem, especially when they're taken from the middle of the poem. That's like taking someone to the middle twenty minutes of a movie and then expecting them to, not only know what the entire movie was about, but also to engage with it. This is just plain crazy with a story that's as good as *Beowulf*. Therefore, we spend two days of class time reading Kevin Crossley-Holland's prose version of the poem (Oxford University Press, 1999). Students do understand the story when they read this version; consider my student Marvin's statement that *Beowulf* is a rip-off of *The Lord of the Rings*. Although he didn't verbalize it, Marvin was responding to the striking similarities between two epic hero stories written more than one thousand years apart. This is why I would argue that this commando approach is effective. No, we're not reading the original version (or technically, a translation) in its entirety, but the students do have the opportunity to appreciate the story. For my money, that's a better use of time than reading part of the original text and having students disengage.

Consider also using Gareth Hinds' graphic novel, *The Collected Beowulf* (*thecomic.com, 2000*) as another way to present the story and/or to help students envision the characters and setting (for example, what does a mead hall or a moor look like?). Or share some scenes from John Gardner's novel *Grendel* (Vintage Books, 1989), told from the point-of-view of the monster. Read the scene in which Beowulf rips off Grendel's arm from the viewpoints of both characters. First read this:

> Now Beowulf twisted Grendel's right arm behind his neck. He locked it and turned it, putting terrible pressure on Grendel's shoulder.
>
> The monster bellowed and dropped to one knee. He jerked and his whole body shuddered and trembled. With superhuman strength he jerked again as he tried to escape Beowulf's grip, he jerked and all at once, his right shoulder ripped. A ghastly tearing of muscle and sinew and flesh; a spurting of hot blood: the monster's arm came apart from his body. Grendel howled. He staggered away from Beowulf, and reeled out of the hall. (Crossley-Holland, p.18)

And then read this:

> The room goes suddenly white, as if struck by lightning. I stare down, amazed. He has torn off my arm at the shoulder! Blood pours down where the limb was. I cry, I bawl like a baby. He stretches his blinding white wings and breathes out fire. I run for the door and through it. I move like the wind. I stumble and fall, get up again. I'll die! I howl. The night is aflame with winged men. *No, no! Think!* I come suddenly awake once more from the nightmare. Darkness. I really will die! Every rock, every tree, every crystal of the snow cries out cold-blooded objectness. Cold, sharp outlines, everything around me: distinct, detached as dead men. I understand. "Mama!" I bellow. "Mama, Mama! I'm dying!" But her love is history. (Gardner, pp. 172-173)

Does the scene from Gardner's story change the way students view Grendel? Does it make their reaction to the story different when they "hear" his version of the tale? This could also make for an interesting lesson on how authors use point-of-view.

Medieval Literature

Following *Beowulf*, it's on to one of my favorites . . . the Arthurian legend. I had an English teacher in high school who absolutely loved these stories, so I think that's part of the reason I love them today. From a teaching standpoint, there is so much going on in this story because it offers something for everyone—love, betrayal, battles, quests, magic—which means that it's not a terribly hard sell to high school students. A logical segue between Beowulf and Arthur is a mini-unit on heroes, consisting of Lord Raglan's scale and Joseph Campbell's hero's journey (information about these is in Chapter 6). Arthur's life story scores a nineteen out of twenty-two on Lord Raglan's scale, for example. This is something to start and finish with; I say this because students won't necessarily be aware of how Arthur's life aligns with Raglan's scale until after they've read the story, but at the same time, they should be watching for examples as they read the legends. This could become another bingo game.

When beginning the study of Arthur, be sure to introduce the many incarnations of Arthur. There is the historical Arthur of the Middle Ages who may have been an actual chieftain living sometime during the late 5th and early 6th Centuries. This Arthur would have worn leather protective clothing, rather than chainmail and armor, and would have lived in a hill fort, rather than a stone castle. It is a decidedly less romantic version of the tale. Archaeologists and historians are still searching for proof of the existence of this Arthur; there is evidence to connect him to the area around Cadbury Hill, Glastonbury, and the River Cam, for example. Then there is the mythical Arthur of Celtic mythology. Many of the main characters from the Arthurian legend—Arthur, Merlin, Nimue (the Lady of the Lake), Morgan le Fay, and Guinevere—can be traced to Celtic mythology. The story also features magical/supernatural objects, like Excalibur and its sheath. The fact that upon Arthur's death, he is taken to a magical island from which he may return in a time of England's great need, suggests that he may actually be immortal (more god than mortal man).

Finally, there is the literary Arthur of medieval legend with whom most of us are familiar. This is where the early stories and ballads (that were probably loosely based on historical Arthur) picked up the romantic elements many of us identify with the story of King Arthur: the castle of Camelot; the love triangle between Arthur, Guinevere, and Lancelot; the knights of the Round Table; the search for the Holy Grail; and the ideas of chivalry, justice, and courtly manners.

MYTHICAL CHARACTERS IN THE ARTHURIAN LEGEND

Arthur	Celtic bear god, Artaios
Morgan le Fay	Celtic goddesses Morgan, Matrona, and Morrigan
Merlin	Druid wizard
Nimue	Shape-changer
Guinevere	Celtic goddess Gwynhwfar

MYTHICAL ELEMENTS IN ARTHURIAN LEGEND

Excalibur	Magical sword
Excalibur's sheath	Healing powers
Isle of Avalon	Otherworld

COMMANDO LIBRARIANS

Six Activities for a Medieval Themed Program

(Courtesy of RoseMary Honnold, Coshocton Public Library, Coshocton, OH)

1. Invite the Society for Creative Anachronisms to perform sword fights in costume. Your group may also know someone who will do a program about Medieval life or the life of a knight.

2. Host a series of chess nights and end with a tournament of champions.

3. Create personalized coat of arms. Precut shields can be decorated with colored paper cutouts, clip art (sports, music, school, movies, books, etc.) and calligraphy markers. Hang up in the YA room to decorate.

4. Cover the YA room walls with tan or gray Kraft paper. Use a black marker and yardstick to create stone walls and cut out crenulations along the top edges.

5. Play Castle Clue (*http://www.cplrmh.com/clue.html*) modeled after the Clue board game. Your library becomes a castle and teens move from room to room collecting clues. Use my version or have your teens create a variation.

6. If you have a movie license, there are several Arthurian films teens would like and *A Knight's Tale* or *Monty Python and the Holy Grail* are very funny.

Find six more ideas here: *http://www.cplrmh.com/medievalteens.html*
©2011, 2005 RoseMary Honnold

This is the version of the story that I share with my students, but because I also want them to be aware of how the legend has grown and changed, we begin with the 2002 BBC documentary *Arthur: King of the Britons*, narrated by the late Richard Harris (who played Arthur in the movie version of *Camelot*, but who most of students will recognize as Dumbledore from the first two *Harry Potter* movies). This fantastic documentary helps to delineate historical Arthur from literary Arthur and uses computer graphics to show what Arthur's world might have looked like. During this time we also use the Dorling Kindersley's Eyewitness Guides *Knight* and *Medieval Life* (Dorling Kindersley Publishers, 1993 and 1996, respectively) to study the time period and living conditions. Then we jump into the legends. Daniel and Ronne Randall's *Tales of Arthur* (Armadillo, 2002) provides us with the bulk of the legend, but we also look at a few extra tales from Rosalind Kerven's Eyewitness Classics *King Arthur* (DK Publishing, 1998). Using two different sources serves to illustrate that there are many different versions (or variants) of these tales.

I want students to really know the legend because later we watch the movie *Monty Python and the Holy Grail* to reinforce the idea that, "If you're

COMMANDO LIBRARIANS

Making chain mail will surely attract teen boys to your library. There are wikis, *YouTube* videos and more on the Internet with instructions on how to make basic chain mail and elaborate costumes, such as "How to Make Chainmail" at *Wiki How: http://www.wikihow.com/Make-Chainmail*. Wire, pliers, and time are the main ingredients! Combine with a movie showing of *A Knight's Tale* or *Monty Python and the Holy Grail*.

Also, consider bringing in a blacksmith to demonstrate/explain how weapons and armor would have been forged. Check with the Artist Blacksmith Association of North America (*http://www.abana.org/affiliates/affiliate_list.shtml*) for a list of affiliate organizations in many states across the country.

smart, you can get the jokes." Usually a handful of students have already seen this movie, but watching it immediately after reading the legend makes it funnier. The killer rabbit scene will always be funny, but characters (like Sir Robin and the Black Knight) or scenes (like Sir Lancelot's attempt to rescue Prince Herbert from Swamp Castle or Arthur describing to the peasants how he became their king) are even funnier when it is understood how they play off the original legend. This film also provides a perfect opportunity to talk about postmodernism. The scenes with the historian and the police or the characters screaming, "Get on with it!" at the narrator or the use of coconut shells to replicate the sound of galloping horses, are just some wonderful examples of the departure from a traditional telling of the Arthurian legend.

Studying the Arthurian legend leads us to a project that has been a student favorite over the years. Using Rosemary Chorzempa's *Design Your Own Coat of Arms: An Introduction to Heraldry* (Dover Publications, 1987) as our primary source, each student creates his/her own medieval coat of arms (see Coat of Arms Rubric in the British Literature Arsenal). We begin with the vocabulary of heraldry (see the Coat of Arms Vocabulary Key and Coat of Arms Vocabulary Worksheet in the British Literature Arsenal). Then I give students a rubric outlining the requirements for the project (see Coat of Arms Rubric in the British Literature Arsenal). The expectation is that each shield will contain typical medieval colors, shapes, and elements (I am not as particular about the charges they select because I want them to be able to personalize it with their own interests). However, a student who chooses to veer away from the traditional design can still get a decent grade on the project if s/he is mindful of the scoring scale.

COAT OF ARMS RESOURCES

- *Armorial Gold: Family and Heraldic Mottoes* © 2001-2010 http://www.heraldryclipart.com/mottoes.html

- *Clipart ETC.: An Online Service of Florida's Educational Technology Clearinghouse: Heraldry, Charges*, Florida Center for Instructional Technology, College of Education, University of South Florida http://etc.usf.edu/clipart/galleries/designs/heraldry_charges.php

- *Fleur-de-Lis Designs: Custom Crests, Logos, and Coats of Arms Design Services* http://www.fleur-delis.com/

- *Free Translation and Professional Translation Services from SDL* © 2000-2009 http://www.freetranslation.com/

- "PDF List of Mottoes" from *Mottoes* compiled by Baron Modar Neznanich © 1998-2007 Ron Knight http://www.modaruniversity.org/Motto-1.pdf

- University of Notre Dame's *Heraldic Dictionary* © 2005 http://www.rarebooks.nd.edu/digital/heraldry/index.html

Because I am aware that not everybody is particularly artistic, this project is set up in the least threatening way possible. Students begin with tracing paper and are allowed to trace or freehand the shield and its elements onto the paper. We use many Internet sources to find heraldic symbols, headgear, and mottoes (which can be written in English or translated to a different language). Some students even choose to look up their family's coat of arms and to copy it. Once their sketches are complete, students bring them to me for approval, then they trace over their design with a pen or a marker. Each student gets a full-size poster board and signs up for a time to use the opaque projector so that their original sketch can be enlarged and traced onto the poster board. Then, they color. We do all of this as part of class because my students don't necessarily have access to the materials and information at home. I also like to see the students working together and helping one another and, since I usually make one, too, we're all participating and interacting with it at the same time, which (I think) makes it more fun.

Next, we spend a few days on medieval ballads. Ballads are fun reading and they aren't terribly threatening to students (and poetry is always met with resistance by my students); they are fairly easy to understand, tell a good story, have a strong rhyme and rhythm, and are about love, outlaws, revenge, envy, superstitions, the supernatural, etc. My anthology only has two examples of medieval ballads, *Robin Hood and Allen-a-Dale* and *Barbara Allen*, so I supplement with several more ballads, including those on the Medieval Ballads handout (see the British Literature Arsenal) and from Charles Vess' graphic novel *The Book of Ballads* (Tor, 2006). More ballads are on Lesley Nelson-Burns' website *Folk Music of England, Scotland, Ireland, Wales, and America* (*http://www.contemplator.com/folk.html*) and at *Mostly Medieval: Exploring the Middle Ages* (*http://www.mostly-medieval.com/explore/ballads.htm*). Consider exploring the folklore of typical ballad characters like fairies, witches, demons, or ghosts during this unit, as well.

While studying the ballad, we also examine another legendary character whose story has been told and preserved through ballads, Robin Hood. Like King Arthur, Robin Hood was probably based on a real person, but the stories that make up the lore of Robin Hood are, for the most part, just stories. Allen W. Wright's website, *Robin Hood: Bold Outlaw of Barnsdale and Sherwood* (*http://www.boldoutlaw.com/*), has a myriad of resources about the Robin Hood legend, including the history behind the legend, ballads featuring Robin and his Merry Men (we read "The Bold Peddlar and Robin Hood," "Robin Hood and the Bishop of Hereford," and "Robin Hood and Allen-a-Dale"), artwork featuring Robin Hood, and photographs of the area in which the Robin Hood legends are set. There is also a section of FAQs for students, and a section for teachers about using the website as a classroom resource, so take some time to explore the site.

Ask students to compare the numerous film representations of the Robin Hood character; he has been portrayed on film nearly every decade since the 1910s. Use *YouTube* to show video clips of some of the more famous actors to play Robin Hood, or assign pairs or groups of students a particular version and have them find clips to share with the class (see my *YouTube* channel—Brit Lit playlist—for some short clips/trailers *http://www.youtube.com/user/daridoo*). How is Douglas Fairbanks' (*Robin Hood*, 1922) silent film Robin Hood different from or similar to Errol Flynn's (*The Adventures of Robin Hood*, 1938), Frank Sinatra's (*Robin and the 7 Hoods*, 1964), Sean Connery's (*Robin and Marian*, 1976), Kevin Cost-

BRITISH MYTHS, LEGENDS, AND FOLKLORE

(from England, Ireland, Scotland, and Wales)

- *A Dictionary of English Folklore*, edited by Jacqueline Simpson and Steve Roud, Oxford University Press on *Answers.com* © 2011 Answers Corporation. *http://www.answers.com/library/ English+Folklore*

- *Folklore and Mythology Electronic Texts http:// www.pitt.edu/~dash/folktexts.html* ©D.L. Ashliman, University of Pittsburgh, 1996-2011

- *The Illustrated Book of Fairy Tales: Spellbinding Stories from Around the World* retold by Neil Philip (D.K. Publishing, 1997)

- *The Illustrated Book of Myths: Tales and Legends of the World* retold by Neil Philip (Dorling Kindersley, 1999)

- *The Kingfisher Book of Mythology: Gods, Goddesses, and Heroes from Around the World* edited by Peter Casterton, Catherine Headlam, & Cynthia O'Neal (Kingfisher, 2001)

- *Mysterious Britain & Ireland: Mysteries, Legends, and the Paranormal. http://www.mysteriousbritain.co.uk/*

- *Orkneyjar: The Heritage of the Orkney Islands* © 1996-2011 Sigurd Towrie. *http://www.orkneyjar.com/*

ner's (*Robin Hood: Prince of Thieves*, 1991), or Russell Crowe's (*Robin Hood*, 2010) version? What about spoofs of the character like Carey Elwes' (*Robin Hood Men in Tights*, 1993) or Robin "the Hood" (*Shrek*, 2001)? The Disney version (*Robin Hood*, 1973)? Can the class come up with a standard/consistent definition or image of the Robin Hood character? Is Robin Hood a hero or is he an anti-hero?

The Renaissance

Obviously one of the most important British writers of the Renaissance era was Shakespeare. Because I find that students are more intimidated by Shakespeare than by anything else, including poetry, I take about a month of class to present his life and his work in ways that are accessible to students. This is why an entire chapter in this book is devoted to teaching Shakespeare's plays. What isn't mentioned in that chapter is that we do a few days on fairy folklore prior to reading *A Midsummer Night's Dream*. The lore of fairies can also be included with the study of medieval ballads, as mentioned earlier, or later during the Victorian era when you study Sir Arthur Conan Doyle because of his interest (and belief) in the case of the Cottingley Fairies.

During the Renaissance unit we also read several short poems, such as Christopher Marlowe's "The Passionate Shepherd to His Love" and Sir Walter Raleigh's response "The Nymph's Reply to the Shepherd"; John Donne's "The Bait"; Ben Johnson's "Song: To Celia" and "Still to Be Neat"; Richard Lovelace's "To Lucasta, on Going to the Wars"; and several Shakespearean sonnets (18, 75, 116, and 130). Several of these are "love" poems, which reminds me of a line from the movie *Dead Poets Society* (1989) in which Mr. Keating (played by Robin Williams) tells his students that the purpose of language is not to communicate, but rather to "woo women" (find this on my *YouTube* playlist).

A perfect example of this is the poem "To His Coy Mistress" by Andrew Marvell. I often use Marvin Gaye's song "Let's Get it On" to introduce students to this poem. Though Gaye is not a recent artist, most teens know this song and, when it is played at the beginning of a class period, it grabs their attention immediately. How could a song recorded in 1973 possibly have anything to do with a poem that was written in 1646? Because people are people are people—some things never change. Isn't the speaker in Marvell's poem basically saying the same thing in lines 37-44 as Gaye's song is saying (albeit in a "prettier" way)?

FAIRY LORE

- *Changeling Legends from the British Isles* edited by D.L. Ashliman © 1998-2002. *http://www.pitt.edu/~dash/britchange.html*

- "Changelings: An Essay" by D.L. Ashliman © 1997. *http://www.pitt.edu/~dash/changeling.html*

- "Cottingley: At Last the Truth" by Joe Cooper for *The Unexplained*, No. 117, pp. 2338-40, 1982. *http://www.lhup.edu/~dsimanek/cooper.htm*

- "Fairy Art Collections" from *ArtPassions.net*. *http://www.artpassions.net/fairies/fairy.html*

- Library, *The Case of the Cottingley Fairies* by the James Randi Educational Foundation © 2001-2006

- *Poems of Fairy*. *http://members.tripod.com/poems_of_fairy/index.html*

- *Puck: That Shrewd and Knavish Sprite Called Robin Goodfellow* by Allen W. Wright © 1997-2004. *http://www.boldoutlaw.com/puckrobin/puck.html*

- *The UnMuseum: The Case of the Cottingley Fairies* © Lee Krystek 2000. *http://www.unmuseum.org/fairies.htm*

Now let us sport us while we may,

And now, like amorous birds of prey,

Rather at once our time devour

Than languish in this slow-chapped power.

Let us roll all our strength, and all

Our sweetness, up into one ball,

and tear our pleasures with rough strife

Thorough the iron gates of life:

Students won't necessarily understand Marvel's words, but when paired with Gaye's song, they will. They might even be able to come up with new songs that share the same theme. After we've read and discussed the other poems about love, I ask students to choose the poem that best captures their attitude towards love and relationships.

The other theme that emerges with this set of poems is the idea that time passes quickly; that youth is fleeting and we should make the most of the time we have. Another clip from *Dead Poets Society* can help to introduce that theme. In the scene probably most often associated with this film, Mr. Keating introduces his students to the notion of *carpe diem* (seize the day) using Robert Herrick's poem "Counsel to Girls"/"To the Virgins to Make Much of Time." This is a theme that teenagers can relate to, as they often seem to think about and live only for the present (for a bigger list of poems with this theme, see "Carpe Diem: Poems for Making the Most of Time" from *Poets.org http://www.poets.org/viewmedia.php/prmMID/20258*).

Next, we tackle one of the most important epic poems in the English language, John Milton's *Paradise Lost*. Though *Paradise Lost* was technically published after the Renaissance period ended, Milton is considered to be a Renaissance poet. This is a challenging poem and, if I had to teach it in its original form someone probably wouldn't make it out of my room alive (and that someone would probably be me). I do want to expose my students to this poem, though, because it's got a good story line and interesting characters. So I use the character list and plot overview from *Sparknotes* (*http://www.sparknotes.com*) to give students a rough idea of what the poem is about. I pair this with Gustave Dore's haunting black and white illustrations (find them on *Art Passions.net http://www.artpassions.net/dore/dore.html*) and other illustrations featuring Adam and Eve, Satan, the Garden of Eden, and angels (see Don Ulin's "Paradise Lost Illustrated" page *http://www.pitt.edu/~ulin/Paradise/* for some examples). The reference to Hell as a lake of fire reminds me of the Nirvana song "Lake of Fire," so I play that for the students. We also watch film clips from *The Prophecy* (1995), a film about a second war in Heaven between the angels. This overview gave my students enough background to draw comparisons between Othello and Iago's relationship in *Othello*, and God and Lucifer's relationship in *Paradise Lost*.

ARTWORK FOR USE WITH *PARADISE LOST*

- *Abdiel Leads Good Angels into the Fight with Satan* by J. Huyot
- *Adam and Eve* by Lucas Cranach the Elder
- *Adam and Eve* by Jan Scovel
- *Adam and Eve Banished from Paradise* by Tommaso Masaccio
- *The Archangel Michael Defeating Satan* by Guido Reni
- *The Creation of Adam* by Michelangelo Buonarroti
- *Eden* by Lila Rose Kennedy
- *Eva Prima Pandora* by Jean the Elder Cousin
- *The Fall of Man* by Hugo Van Der Goes
- *Fall of Satan and the Rebel Angels from Heaven* by Jakob Isaaksz
- *The Garden of Earthly Delights* triptych by Hieronymous Bosch
- *The Garden of Eden, in the Background the Temptation* by Jan Bruegel the Elder
- Gustave Dore's illustrations (*http://dore.artpassions.net/*)
- *Paradise* by Lucas Cranach the Elder
- *Satan Shown as the Fallen After Having Been Smitten by Michael* by Piaud
- *Satan, Sin, and Death: Satan Comes to the Gates of Hell* by William Blake
- *The Sistine Chapel Ceiling: The Fall of Man and the Expulsion from the Garden of Eden* by Michelangelo Buonarroti
- *St. Michael* by Carlo Crivelli
- *St. Michael Archangel* by Denys Calvaert
- *The Temptation and Fall of Eve* by William Blake

The Neoclassical Period

We spend a few days on Jonathon Swift's *Gulliver's Travels*. We read the Now Age Illustrated version of the story, which takes about two class periods to read. Though students are most familiar with Gulliver's trip to the land of Lilliput (they associate the image of a giant Gulliver tied down on the beach with the story), this version of the story also includes his trips to Brobdingnag, Laputa, Glubbdubdrib, and the land of the Houyhnhnms. On each stop, Gulliver learns something about human nature and eventually returns to his home, only to discover that he longs for the company of the Houyhnhnms. When we finish the reading, I ask students to adopt the persona of Lemeul Gulliver and to imagine that, rather than returning home, he has decided to stay in (or return to) one of the lands he has visited. They then write a letter to his family explaining where he has decided to stay and why (see *Gulliver's Travels* Writing Assignment in the British Literature Arsenal). It's interesting to me to see what the students choose. It's pretty clear from the story that Gulliver would choose to return to the land of the Houyhnhnms, but that's not always what the students choose; some choose to stay in Lilliput so that they can be of help to the people; some go to Laputa to lend their building skills; and some do go to the land of the Houyhnhnms because that's where Gulliver was happiest. This demonstrates to me that students are able to move beyond the simple image of a giant Gulliver tied down on a beach to a deeper understanding of the story.

Romantic Era

We begin our study of the early Romantic period with poetry by Robert Burns (Scotland's national poet) and William Blake. Several of both Burns' and Blake's poems were often sung, and musical versions of these (including "Auld Lang Syne" and "A Red, Red Rose" by Burns and "The Tyger" and "The Lamb" by Blake) are available on *YouTube*. Blake was also an accomplished artist who illustrated not only his own works, but the works of others, including The Book of Job from the *Bible* and Milton's *Paradise Lost* (see *The William Blake Page http://www.gailgastfield.com/Blake.html*).

Also in this unit, we read a summary of Coleridge's *The Rime of the Ancient Mariner* from *Sparknotes*. I can't think of a more perfect way to introduce this poem and to pique students' interest than to play Iron Maiden's song "Rime of the Ancient Mariner." Much like we did with *Paradise Lost*, I pair the summary with the Gustave Dore illustrations of the poems. I use the site *Artsy Craftsy* (*http://www.artsycraftsy.com/dore_mariner.html*) for the illustrations this time because each print is accompanied by two couplets from the original poem. This gives students the opportunity to see the action of the story unfolding and also to "hear" some of Coleridge's original text. Again, the idea here is to give students a general overview of the basic plot and themes of the poem. Because it's still not uncommon to hear someone describe their struggle by referring to it as an "albatross" or to say, "Water, water everywhere, but not a drop to drink," I want students to understand that these terms and phrases are referencing Coleridge's poem, written more than two hundred years ago.

The majority of the poems that we read from the early romantics are by William Wordsworth. Our anthology features his poem "Daffodils," but I've found that it doesn't play all that well to a 21ˢᵗ century teenage audience; my students think it's really strange for a grown man to write about how happy the sight of daffodils makes him. To be honest, I don't particularly care for the poem either, so I found five poems that we all seem to like better: "Simon Lee: The Old Huntsman," "She Dwelt Among the Untrodden Ways," "There Was a Boy," "To Sleep," and "We Are Seven" (see More Wordsworth Poems in the British Literature Arsenal). By far the students' favorite (and mine) is the poem "We Are Seven" in which the speaker argues with an eight-year-old girl about how many children are in her family. She insists that there are seven, while the speaker argues that, since two are dead, there are only five. Despite his arguments, the girl remains steadfast in her claim that there are seven. Use the website *Visit Cumbria* (*http://www.visitcumbria.com/amb/windermere-lake.htm*) to show students the area in which Wordsworth lived and wrote; this will help them to visualize the settings of the poems.

My favorite poets of the Romantic era are Byron, Keats, and Shelley. When introducing these poets to my students I describe them as rock stars—larger-than-life characters who lived fast and died young (Byron was the only one to make it into his 30s). Though we do read several of each poet's shorter poems, we actually spend more time on their lives because their biographies read like soap opera scripts, rife with drug use, children born out of wedlock, adultery, and suicides (see the website *Neurotic Poets* to read about Byron and Shelley *http://www.neuroticpoets.com/*). Byron was a notorious womanizer, Shelley was a bigamist, and Keats' short life was filled with tragedy and a strange premonition about his own death. In addition to their huge contributions to English poetry, Byron and Shelley are also indirectly linked to the creation of what is arguably one of the most famous British novels (and probably also one of the most famous "monsters"), *Frankenstein.*

It was a challenge from Lord Byron to see who could write the best ghost story that led to Mary Shelley's (wife of Percy Shelley) novel *Frankenstein.* When we study *Frankenstein,* one point that I continuously drive into my students' heads is that, though people often refer to him as such, the monster is *not* Frankenstein. If they don't remember anything else, I want them to remember that. *Frankenstein* is obviously a story that still has relevance today. As mentioned earlier, this novel could be paired with others featuring mad scientists who push the moral boundaries of science; as long as science continues to advance, this will always be a timely subject. This is another novel for which you could study all of the incarnations the story and its characters have taken on over the years, as it has been captured on film since the early 1900s. We read the Now Age Illustrated Classic, watch the 1994 film *Mary Shelley's Frankenstein,* and read news articles about current scientists who are striving to clone humans and to allow parents to choose the gender of their unborn child (see the *Frankenstein* Text Set in the British Literature Arsenal). I then ask students to adopt the persona of Victor Frankenstein and to write a letter to one of the doctors from the articles giving them some advice (see *Frankenstein* Writing Assignment in the British Literature Arsenal). Again, this gives students a chance to demonstrate their understanding of the larger themes of the novel; most advise the doctors not to "play God," and warn them using examples from Victor Frankenstein's life.

Victorian Era

The Victorian era provides us with some of the most enduring and well-known stories and characters in British literature: Charles Dickens' *Oliver Twist* and *A Christmas Carol*; Lewis Carroll's *Alice in Wonderland*; Robert Louis Stevenson's *Treasure Island* and *The Strange Case of Dr. Jekyll and Mr. Hyde*; H.G. Well's *The Time Machine* and *War of the Worlds*; Bram Stoker's *Dracula*; and Sir Arthur Conan Doyle's Sherlock Holmes mysteries. These are stories that have been told and re-told over the years and most students already have some basic familiarity with them (whether they know it or not). For example, nearly every television sitcom has played upon Dickens' ghosts of Christmas past, present, and future; most Halloween parties will have at least one Dracula costume; and, as mentioned earlier in this chapter nearly all of these stories have recently been (or will be soon) the basis for a feature film. As will be particularly evident from this section, using illustrated versions of these novels not only allows us to see an overview of the plot and characters of numerous classic stories, but also frees up some class time to do other related reading, thereby giving students a broader view of the time period and folklore, and to make modern-day connections to the stories.

Because of the recent popularity of Disney's *Pirates of the Caribbean* movies, I built an entire unit on pirate and sea lore around Robert Louis Stevenson's *Treasure Island* (see the *Treasure Island* text set in the British Literature Arsenal). We begin with some background on pirates from the website *Pirates! Fact and Legend* (*http://www.piratesinfo.com/History_of_Piracy.asp*). We read about pirate life (both at sea and on land), pirate codes of conduct and insurance, different types of pirates and ships, the symbolism of pirate flags, real-life historical pirates (men and women), and even modern day pirates. To prepare for our reading of the Now Age Illustrated Classic *Treasure Island*, we also read background information about Robert Louis Ste-

---

COMMANDO LIBRARIANS AND TEACHERS

- Arrrrrr... September 19th is International Talk Like a Pirate Day (*http://www.talklikeapirate.com/piratehome.html*). Teens can celebrate their inner pirates with a program in the library and classroom. Students can generate their pirate names, learn how to talk like a pirate, and find a booklist of pirate titles.

- Divide the group into teams that choose pirate names and ship names and create a pirate flag for their ship. Engage in a Pirate Insult War using their new pirate vocabulary.

- Pair a reading of *Treasure Island* by Robert Louis Stevenson with activities. See *http://www.tamrootbeer.com/teacherstuff/* for printable crossword puzzles and a ship parts worksheet.

---

venson. Following the story, students create their own treasure maps and pirate flags. Also closely tied to pirates (and referenced in both *Treasure Island* and the *Pirates of the Caribbean* movies) are sea songs or shanties, so we spend a couple of days reading about and listening to examples of these work songs (some of which are pretty racy). As seamen are a superstitious bunch, and because there are references in the shanties to mermaids, we use that to segue into the folklore of the sea. In addition to reading about merpeople, we also read about selkies (shapeshifting seals), the finfolk, the kraken, sea monsters, and freshwater monsters (like the Loch Ness monster, Jenny Greenteeth, and the water horse). So, as to leave no stone unturned, we also read about ghost ships. Phew!

Three years after *Treasure Island*, Stevenson published *The Strange Case of Dr. Jekyll and Mr. Hyde*. Not only does this story comment on the limitations of science (see the Mad Scientists text set in the British Literature Arsenal), it also asks the question of whether humans are inherently good or evil. After reading the Now Age Illustrated Classic *Dr. Jekyll and Mr. Hyde*, we take a look at information from Joan Pere Roselló and Oscar Sabato's website *Study of Doctor Jekyll and Mr. Hyde* (*http://www.usefulweb.org/jekyll/*), which provides analysis of the symbolism, Dr. Jekyll's sins, and Mr. Hyde's role in the story. In addition to the many film interpretations of this novel, there is also a musical version, which enables us to use song lyrics to better understand Henry Jekyll's motivation. To help make the pop culture link, there are several songs that reference Dr. Jekyll and Mr. Hyde ("Dr. Jekyll and Mr. Hyde" by The Damned, "Dr. Jekyll and Mr. Hyde" by The Who, "Jekyll & Hyde" by GTR, and "The Shadow" by Devo), and even a couple of examples of cartoon portrayals (find these on my *YouTube* playlist). Since we're already on the topic of good vs. evil, we also spend a little time reading up on the case of Jack the Ripper, which has its own folklore attached to it. The website *Casebook: Jack the Ripper* (*http://www.casebook.org/index.html*) has tons of information on the case, everything from information on the victims, witnesses, and suspects to press reports to links to blogs, wikis, and podcasts.

If students aren't sufficiently creeped out by Mr. Hyde and Jack the Ripper, we follow with Bram

Stoker's *Dracula* (see the *Dracula* Text Set in the British Literature Arsenal). As an introduction, we begin with the folklore surrounding vampires—students may be surprised to learn that not all vampires "sparkle." Again, we read the Now Age Illustrated Classic version of *Dracula*. There are several documentaries available about the real Vlad Dracul, as well as about Transylvania and also the search for real vampires. Vampires are definitely a hot topic right now, and with the *Twilight* phenomena, students can compare modern film and literary depictions of vampires with the folklore or to examine the portrayal of vampires and Dracula throughout the history of film.

20th Century

We generally wrap up our year of British literature with a unit on fantasy. British fantasy writers have produced some of the best-loved and most well known children's classics, such as Lewis Carroll's *Alice's Adventures in Wonderland*, J.M. Barrie's *Peter Pan*, Beatrix Potter's *Peter Rabbit*, P.L. Travers' *Mary Poppins*, Kenneth Grahame's *Wind in the Willows*, and C.S. Lewis's *The Chronicles of Narnia*, to name just a few. Again, largely thanks to the motion picture industry, many teens already have some familiarity with these stories, so I utilize that knowledge to teach them about the structure of this genre. We begin with an overview of some of the subgenres of fantasy literature: science fiction; low fantasy; and high fantasy. If we had time (which we usually don't by this point in the year), we could take some time to talk more about science fiction, although we do touch on that when we read *Frankenstein*, *The Strange Case of Dr. Jekyll and Mr. Hyde*, *The War of the Worlds*, and *The Invisible Man*. We zero in on the difference between low fantasy (it involves magic, such as personified toys or talking animals, but takes place in this world) and high fantasy (which takes place in another, often "medieval-type" world and focuses on the conflict between good and evil). High fantasy draws a lot of its influence from epic hero stories, legends, and mythology, so it brings us full circle to where we began the year. The video *Rings, Kings, and Things: Swords and Sorcery* (Cerebellum Corporation, 2001) by the Standard Deviants outlines the three Ms of high fantasy: magic, myth, and medievalism. Admittedly, this video is pretty corny, and is intended for a much younger audience, but I like it because it makes several references to *Beowulf* and to other fantasy classics that we have talked or will talk about in this unit. It also introduces a new kind of hero—the small-but-spunky hero, who is different from the epic hero we've already studied, and who students will encounter when we conclude our unit and our school year by watching the animated version of *The Hobbit*.

Of the four English classes I teach, this is the one that still has the most "traditional" approach and content. This approach can be adapted to other literature classes, as well. I think the idea that I'd like to leave with the reader is that, even if you can't/aren't willing to/don't want to totally change up the curriculum, these are ways to connect students with the classics.

British Literature Arsenal

MAD SCIENTISTS TEXT SET

(or Just Because You *Can*, Does it Mean You *Should*?)

For use with *Dr. Jekyll and Mr. Hyde, The Tragical History of Doctor Faustus, The Birthmark, Rappacini's Daughter, Frankenstein, The Invisible Man, The Island of Doctor Moreau, Daedelus Myth,* etc.

NOVELS

- *Double Helix* by Nancy Werlin. Dial Books, 2004.
- *Dr. Franklin's Island* by Ann Halam. Wendy Lamb Books, 2002.
- *The Goodness Gene* by Sonia Levitin. Dutton Children's Books, 2005.
- *The House of the Scorpion* by Nancy Farmer. Atheneum Books for Young Readers, 2002.
- *Maximum Ride: The Angel Experiment* by James Patterson. Little, Brown, 2005.

FILMS /VIDEOS

- *Dr. Jekyll and Mr. Hyde.* Warner Home Video, 1989.
- *Dr. Jekyll and Ms. Hyde.* HBO Home Video, 1995.
- *Edward Scissorhands.* CBS/FOX Video, 1994.
- *The Fly.* 20th Century Fox Home Entertainment, 2002.
- *Hollow Man.* Columbia TriStar Home Video, 2000.
- *The Incredible Hulk: How the Legend Began.* Universal, 2003.
- *Jurassic Park.* MCS Universal Home Video, 1994.
- *The Nutty Professor.* MCA Universal Home Video, 1998.
- *The Nutty Professor.* Paramount Home Entertainment, 2004.
- *The Stepford Wives.* Harper Torch, 2004.
- *Weird Science.* MCA Home Video, 1986.

GRAPHIC NOVELS

- *The League of Mad Scientists* © 2008 Courtney Davis. *http://leagueofmadscientists.com/*
- *Naoki Urasawa's Monster: Volume 1: Herr Dr. Tenma* by Naoki Urasawa. VIZ Media, 1995.

TV SHOWS

- "The Island of Dr. Hibbert." *The Simpsons' Treehouse of Horror XIII.* Writ. Kevin Curran. Dir. David Silverman. Season 14, episode 292. FOX. 3 Nov 2002. Watch it: *http://watch-thesimpsonsonline.com/movie/329-The_Simpsons_1401_Treehouse_of_Horror_XIII.htm.l http://watchthesimpsonsonline.com/movie/329-The_Simpsons_1401_Treehouse_of_Horror_XIII.html.*

INTERNET SOURCES

- "For Science." *TV Tropes Wiki. http://tvtropes.org/pmwiki/pmwiki.php/Main/ForScience*
- "List of Mad Scientists." *Wikipedia. http://en.wikipedia.org/wiki/List_of_mad_scientists*

From *Commando Classics: A Field Manual for Helping Teens Understand (and Maybe Even Enjoy) Classic Literature* by Daria Plumb. Bowie, MD: VOYA Press, an imprint of E L Kurdyla Publishing, LLC. Copyright 2012

MAD SCIENTISTS TEXT SET (*Cont.*)

- "Mad Scientist." *TV Tropes Wiki. http://tvtropes.org/pmwiki/pmwiki.php/Main/MadScientist*
- "Morally Ambiguous Doctorate." *TV Tropes Wiki. http://tvtropes.org/pmwiki/pmwiki.php/Main/MorallyAmbiguousDoctorate*
- "Science Is Bad." *TV Tropes Wiki. http://tvtropes.org/pmwiki/pmwiki.php/Main/ScienceIsBad*

SONGS

- "About Science" by Mekong Delta.
- "Now There Is No Choice" and "This Is the Moment" *Jekyll & Hyde—The Musical.*
- "She Blinded Me with Science" by Thomas Dolby.
- "Weird Science" by Oingo Boingo.
- "When Silence Fails" by Nasum.

BIOGRAPHIES

- *Guinea Pig Scientists: Bold Self-Experimenters in Science and Medicine* by Leslie Dendy and Mel Borin. Henry Holt, 2005.

HISTORIES

- *Great Scientists, Mad Science: Incredible Inventions and Absurd Ideas from the Most Brilliant Minds in History* by Joel Levy. Vision, 2008.

MISCELLANEOUS

- *Different Engines: How Science Drives Fiction and Fiction Drives Science* by Mark L. Brake and Neil Hook. Macmillan, 2007.
- *From Faust to Strangelove: Representations of the Scientist in Western Literature* by Roslynn D. Haynes. The Johns Hopkins UP, 1994.
- *Introducing Mad Scientists (Famous Movie Monsters)* by Betty Burnette and Ross Watton. Rosen Publishing Group, 2006.
- *Mad, Bad and Dangerous? The Scientist and the Cinema* by Christopher Frayling. Reaktion Books, 2006.
- *Mad Scientist Hall of Fame: Muwahahahaha!* by Daniel H. Wilson and Anna C. Long. Citadel, 2008.
- *The Mad Scientist's Notebook: Warning! Dangerously Wacky Experiments Inside* by Elizabeth Snoke Harris, Rain Newcomb, and Ian Nagy. Lark Books, 2008.
- *Science on Stage: From "Doctor Faustus" to "Copenhagen"* by Kirsten Sheperd-Barr. Princeton University Press, 2006.

SHORT STORIES

- *Mad Scientists: An Anthology of Fantasy and Horror* edited by Stuart David Schiff. Doubleday, 1980.

ARTHURIAN LEGEND TEXT SET

NOVELS

- *Arthur, High King of Britain* by Michael Morpurgo. Harcourt Brace, 1995.
- *Avalon High* by Meg Cabot. Harper Collins, 2006.
- *The Book of Mordred* by Vivian Vande Velde. Houghton Mifflin, 2005.
- *A Connecticut Yankee in King Arthur's Court* by Mark Twain. Bantam Books, 1981.
- *Damosel: In Which the Lady of the Lake Renders a Frank and Often Startling Account of Her Wondrous Life and Times* by Stephanie Spinner. Alfred A. Knopf, 2008.
- *Here Lies Arthur* by Philip Reeve. Scholastic, 2008.
- *King Arthur and the Knights of the Round Table* by Howard Pyle, adapted by Joshua E. Hanft. Baronet Books, 1993.
- *The Road to Camlann* by Rosemary Sutcliff. Dutton, 1982.
- *The Seeing Stone* by Kevin Crossley-Holland. Arthur A. Levine Books/Scholastic, 2001.
- *Song of the Sparrow* by Lisa Ann Sandell. Scholastic, 2007.
- *The Sword and the Circle: King Arthur and the Knights of the Round Table* by Rosemary Sutcliff. Puffin, 1994.

ILLUSTRATED BOOKS

- *How to Be a Medieval Knight* by Fiona Macdonald. National Geographic, 2005.
- *The Kitchen Knight: A Tale of King Arthur* by Margaret Hodges. Holiday House, 1990.
- *Merlin and the Making of the King* retold by Margaret Hodges. Holiday House, 2004.
- *Sabuda and Reinhart Present Castle: Medieval Days and Knights* by Kyle Olmon. Orchard Books, 2006.
- *The Usborne Official Knight's Handbook* by Sam Taplin. EDC Publishing, 2006.
- *Young Merlin* by Robert D. Sans Souci. Doubleday, 1990.

FILMS / VIDEOS

- *Arthur: King of the Britons.* British Broadcasting Corporation, 2002.
- *A&E Ancient Mysteries: Camelot.* A&E Home Video, 2005.
- *A&E Ancient Mysteries: The Quest for the Holy Grail.* A&E Home Video, 2000.
- *Biography: King Arthur His Life and Legends.* A&E Home Video, 2005.
- *Camelot.* Acorn Media, 2007.
- *Excalibur.* Warner Home Video, 1999.
- *First Knight.* Sony Pictures Home Entertainment, 2008.
- *The History Channel: In Search of History: The Holy Grail.* A&E Home Video, 2005.
- *The History Channel: Knights and Armor.* A&E Home Video, 2004.
- *A Kid in King Arthur's Court.* Buena Vista Home Video, 1995.
- *King Arthur.* Touchstone Home Entertainment, 2004.
- *King Arthur: The Truth Behind the Legend.* Delta Entertainment, 2004.
- *King Arthur's Britain.* Acorn Media, 2005.

From *Commando Classics: A Field Manual for Helping Teens Understand (and Maybe Even Enjoy) Classic Literature* by Daria Plumb. Bowie, MD: VOYA Press, an imprint of E L Kurdyla Publishing, LLC. Copyright 2012

ARTHURIAN LEGEND TEXT SET (*Cont.*)

- *Knights of Camelot.* A&E Home Video, 2000.
- *The Legend of Arthur: In Search of Camelot.* Kultur Video, 2002.
- *The Legend of King Arthur: In Search of King Arthur.* Kultur Video, 2002.
- *The Legend of King Arthur: In Search of Merlin.* Kultur Video, 2002.
- *Merlin.* Lionsgate, 2004.
- *The Mists of Avalon.* Warner Home Video, 2001.
- *Monty Python and the Holy Grail.* Columbia Tri-Star Home Video, 2001.
- *The Sword in the Stone.* Walt Disney Studios Home Entertainment, 2008.
- *Times Medieval.* Discovery Communications, 2001.
- *TLC & Discovery Channel School's Great Books: Le Morte d'Arthur: Legend of the King.* Discovery Communications, 1993.

GRAPHIC NOVELS

- *Excalibur: The Legend of King Arthur: A Graphic Novel* written by Tony Lee. Candlewick, 2011.

ARTWORK

- *The Camelot Project,* The University of Rochester © Alan Lupack and Barbara Tepa Lupack *http://www.lib.rochester.edu/camelot/mainmenu.htm*
- *The Death of King Arthur* by James Archer
- *God Speed* by Edmund Leighton
- *Guinevere* by Marcel Lorange
- *The Holy Grail Is Achieved* by Aubrey Beardsley
- *How Four Queens Found Lancelot Sleeping* by Aubrey Beardsley
- *King Arthur and Sir Lancelot* by Howard Johnson
- *King Arthur and the Holy Grail* by Howard Johnson
- *King Arthur's Round Table Hanging in the Great Hall, Winchester, England, UK.* Photograph by Roy Rainford
- *The Knight, Death and the Devil* by Albrecht Durer
- *Knights and Castles: Exploring History through Art* by Alex Martin. Creative Publishing International, 2005.
- *The Knights of the Round Table* French School
- *Knights of the Round Table* by Newel Wyeth
- *Lancelot and Guinevere* by Donato Giancola
- *Lancelot and Guinevere* by Herbert Draper
- *Lancelot Rescues Guinevere* by Newell Wyeth
- *Parsifal in Quest of the Holy Grail* by Ferdinand Leeke
- *Sir Galahad Is Introduced to the Round Table* by Walter Crane

ARTHURIAN LEGEND TEXT SET (*Cont.*)

- *Sir Galahad's Vision of the Holy Grail* by Joseph Paton
- *Sir Lancelot Challenges Sir Tarquin Who Has Imprisoned King Arthur's Knights* by Newell Wyeth

INTERNET SOURCES

- *Arthurian Literature & Art*, Pittsburg State University, Pittsburg, Kansas. *http://faculty.pitt-state.edu/~knichols/labelle2.html#recent*

BIOGRAPHIES

- *King Arthur* by Paul Doherty. Chelsea House, 1987.

FOLKLORE AND LEGENDS

- *Bulfinch's Medieval Mythology: The Age of Chivalry* by Thomas Bulfinch. Dover Publishing, 2004.
- *The Great Deeds of Superheroes* retold by Maurice Saxby. P. Bedrick Books, 1990.
- *King Arthur* retold by Rosalind Kerven. DK Publishing, 1998.
- *The Legend of King Arthur* retold by Robin Lister. Doubleday, 1990.
- *Tales of King Arthur* retold by Daniel and Ronne Randall. Armadillo Books, 2002.
- *Tales of King Arthur by Sir Thomas Malory* edited and abridged, with an introduction by Michael Senior. Schocken Books, 1981.

HISTORIES

- *King Arthur* by Norma Lorre Goodrich. F. Watts, 1986.
- *King Arthur: Hero and Legend* by Richard Barber. Boydell, 1990.
- *King Arthur in Fact and Legend* by Geoffrey Ashe. T. Nelson, 1971.
- *The Landscape of King Arthur* by Geoffrey Ashe. Henry Holt, 1988.
- *Pendragon: Arthur and His Britain* by Joseph P. Clancy. Praeger Publishers, 1971.
- *The Search for King Arthur* by Christopher Hibbert. Harper and Row, 1969.

MISCELLANEOUS

- *Britain's Medieval Castles* by Lisa E. Hull. Praeger, 2006.
- *Castle* by David Macaulay. Houghton Mifflin, 1977.
- *The King Arthur Companion* by Phyllis Ann Karr. Reston Publishing Company, 1983.
- *Knight* by Christopher Gravett. DK Publishing, 2007.
- *Knights* by Stewart Ross. Copper Beech Books, 1996.
- *Medieval Life* by Andrew Langley. DK Publishing, 2011.
- *Yours Truly, King Arthur: How Medieval People Wrote, and How You Can, Too* by Marc Drogin. Taplinger Publishing Company, 1982.

From *Commando Classics: A Field Manual for Helping Teens Understand (and Maybe Even Enjoy) Classic Literature* by Daria Plumb. Bowie, MD: VOYA Press, an imprint of E L Kurdyla Publishing, LLC. Copyright 2012

COAT OF ARMS VOCABULARY KEY

Blazon – to describe heraldic bearing in technical terms

Charge / Device – the symbols and figures used to decorate shields

Compartment – a base on which the shield and the supporters stand

Crest – a design above the headgear in a coat of arms

Ermine – a weasel with a white winter coat with black on the tail

Escutcheon – shield-shaped surface on which a coat of arms is shown

Headgear – usually a helmet or crown that sits on top of the shield and represents the person's rank or title

Heraldry – the art or science of tracing a person's family history and determining its coat of arms

Mantle – the cloth that hangs from the wreath and protected the back of the head and neck

Motto – a short expression, guiding principle, or battle cry

Partition – the act of parting or dividing the shield

Rampant – rearing up on one or both hind legs with the front legs suspended

Supporters – animal, human, or fantastic figures placed on each side of the shield as if they are supporting it

Tincture – a substance, the colors, dyes, or stains

Vair – the bluish-gray and white fur of a squirrel

Wreath – a rope of six parts, which sits on top of the headgear

COAT OF ARMS VOCABULARY

Blazon –

Charge / Device –

Compartment –

Crest –

Ermine –

Escutcheon –

Headgear –

Heraldry –

Mantle –

Motto –

Partition –

Rampant –

Supporters –

Tincture –

Vair –

Wreath –

From *Commando Classics: A Field Manual for Helping Teens Understand (and Maybe Even Enjoy) Classic Literature*
by Daria Plumb. Bowie, MD: VOYA Press, an imprint of E L Kurdyla Publishing, LLC. Copyright 2012

COAT OF ARMS CHECKLIST AND RUBRIC

Tinctures / 10
1 color (black, blue, red, green, purple, orange, or blood red)
1 metal (gold or silver)

Shield Shape / 10
(lozenge, heater, Polish jousting, oval, half-round Spanish,
European, Russian, or German jousting)

Parting the Field / Ordinaries and Sub-Ordinaries / 10

Lines of Partition / 10

Appropriate use of Charges (2 minimum) / 10

Headgear / 10

Mantling / 10

Scroll / 10

Motto / 10

Neatness / 10

---

100 points possible

Optional (for Extra Credit):

    Supporters / 5

    Crest / 5

    Wreath / 5

*I realize that not everyone is artistically inclined, but this project is designed so that
everyone **can** do a nice job on it. If you have all of the required elements
and it is neatly done, then you will get a good grade.*

"The Cruel Mother"

There was a lady dwelt in York:
Fal the dal the di do,
She fell in love with her father's clerk,
Down by the green wood side.

She laid her hand against a stone,
Fal the dal the di do,
And there she made most bitter moan,
Down by the green wood side.

She took a knife both long and sharp,
Fal the dal the di do,
And stabb'd her babes unto the heart,
Down by the green wood side.

As she was walking home one day,
Fal the dal the di do,
She met those babes all dress'd in white
Down by the green wood side.

She said, "Dear children, can you tell,
Fal the dal the di do,
Where shall I go? To heav'n or hell?"
Down by the green wood side.

"O yes! dear mother, we can tell,
Fal the dal the di do,
For it's we to heav'n and you to hell."
Down by the green wood side.

From *Commando Classics: A Field Manual for Helping Teens Understand (and Maybe Even Enjoy) Classic Literature* by Daria Plumb. Bowie, MD: VOYA Press, an imprint of E L Kurdyla Publishing, LLC. Copyright 2012

"Lady Isabel and the Elf Knight"

Fair lady Isabel sits in her bower sewing,
Aye as the gowans grow gay
There she heard an elf-knight blawing his horn.
The first morning in May

"If I had yon horn that I hear blawing,
An yon elf-knight to sleep in my bosom."

This maiden had scarcely these words spoken,
Till in at her window the elf-knight has luppen

"It's a very strange matter, fair maiden," said he,
"I canna blaw my horn but ye call on me.

"But will ye go to yon greenwood side?
If ye canna going, I will cause you to ride,"

He leapt on a horse, and she on another,
And they rode on the greenwood together.

"Light down, light down, lady Isabel," said he,
"We are come to the place where ye are to die."

"Hae mercy, hae mercy, kind sir, on me,
Till ance my dear father and mother I see."

"Seven king's-daughters here hae I slain,
And ye shall be the eight o them."

"O sit down a while, lay your head on my knee,
That we may hae some rest before I die."

She stroak'd him sae fast, the nearer he did creep,
Wi a sma charm she lulld him fast asleep.

Wi his ain sword-belt sae fast as she ban him
Wi his ain dag-durk sae sair as she dang him

"If seven king's-daughters here ye hae slain,
Lye ye here, a husband to them a.'"

"Lord Randall"

"O where ha you been, Lord Randall, my son?
And where ha you been, my handsome young man?"
"I ha been at the greenwood; mother, mak my bed soon,
For I'm wearied wi hunting, and fain wad lie down."

"An wha met ye there, Lord Randal, my son?
And wha met ye there, my handsome young man?"
"O I met wi my true-love; mother, mak my bed soon,
For I'm wearied wi huntin, and fain wad lie down."

"And what did she give you, Lord Randal, My son?
And wha did she give you, my handsome young man?"
"Eels fried in a pan; mother, mak my bed soon,
For I'm wearied wi huntin, and fein wad lie down."

"And what gat your leavins, Lord Randal my son?
And wha gat your leavins, my handsome young man?"
"My hawks and my hounds; mother, mak my bed soon,
For I'm wearied wi huntin, and fein wad lie down."

"And what becam of them, Lord Randal, my son?
And what becam of them, my handsome young man?'
"They stretched their legs out and died; mother mak my bed soon,
For I'm wearied wi huntin, and fain wad lie down."

"O I fear you are poisoned, Lord Randal, my son!
I fear you are poisoned, my handsome young man!"
"O yes, I am poisoned; mother, mak my bed soon,
For I'm sick at the heart, and fain wad lie down."

"What d'ye leave to your mother, Lord Randal, my son?
What d'ye leave to your mother, my handsome young man?"
"Four and twenty milk kye; mother, mak my bed soon,
For I'm sick at the heart, and I fain wad lie down."

From *Commando Classics: A Field Manual for Helping Teens Understand (and Maybe Even Enjoy) Classic Literature*
by Daria Plumb. Bowie, MD: VOYA Press, an imprint of E L Kurdyla Publishing, LLC. Copyright 2012

"What d'ye leave to your sister, Lord Randal, my son?
What d'ye leave to your sister, my handsome young man?"
"My gold and my silver; mother mak my bed soon,
For I'm sick at the heart, an I fain wad lie down."

"What d'ye leave to your brother, Lord Randal, my son?
What d'ye leave to your brother, my handsome young man?"
"My houses and my lands; mother, mak my bed soon,
For I'm sick at the heart, and I fain wad lie down."

"What d'ye leave to your true-love, Lord Randal, my son?
What d'ye leave to your true-love, my handsome young man?"
"I leave her hell and fire; mother mak my bed soon,
For I'm sick at the heart, and I fain wad lie down."

From *Commando Classics: A Field Manual for Helping Teens Understand (and Maybe Even Enjoy) Classic Literature*
by Daria Plumb. Bowie, MD: VOYA Press, an imprint of E L Kurdyla Publishing, LLC. Copyright 2012

"The Unquiet Grave"

Cold blows the wind to my true love,
And gently drops the rain,
I never had but one sweetheart,
And in greenwood she lies slain,
And in greenwood she lies slain.

I'll do as much for my sweetheart
As any young man may;
I'll sit and mourn all on her grave
For a twelvemonth and a day

When the twelvemonth and one day was past,
The ghost began to speak;
"Why sittest here all on my grave,
And will not let me sleep?"

"There's one thing that I want, sweetheart,
There's one thing that I crave
And that is a kiss from your lily-white lips—
Then I'll go from your grave"

"My breast it is as cold as clay,
My breath smells earthly strong
And if you kiss my cold clay lips,
Your days they won't be long."

"Go fetch me water from the desert,
And blood from out of a stone;
Go fetch me milk from a fair maid's breast
That a young man never had known."

"O down in yonder grove, sweetheart,
Where you and I would walk,
The first flower that ever I saw
Is wither'd to a stalk"

"The stalk is wither'd and dry, sweetheart,
And the flower will never return
And since I lost my own sweetheart,
What can I do but mourn?"

"When shall we meet again, sweetheart?
When shall we meet again?"
"When the oaken leaves that fall from trees
Are green and spring up again
Are green and spring up again."

From *Commando Classics: A Field Manual for Helping Teens Understand (and Maybe Even Enjoy) Classic Literature*
by Daria Plumb. Bowie, MD: VOYA Press, an imprint of E L Kurdyla Publishing, LLC. Copyright 2012

"The Wife of Usher's Well"

There lived a wife at Usher's Well,
And a wealthy wife was she;
She had three stout and stalwart sons,
And sent them o'er the sea.

They hadna been a week from her,
A week but barely ane,
Whan word came to the earline wife
That her three sons were gane.

They hadna been a week from her,
A week but barely three,
Whan word came to the carlin wife
That her sons she'd never see.

"I wish the wind may never cease,
Nor (fashes) in the flood,
Till my three sons come home to me,
In earthly flesh and blood,"

It fell about the Martinmass,
When nights are lang and mirk,
The carlin wife's three sons came hame,
And their hats were o' the birk.

It neither grew in syke nor ditch,
Nor yet in ony sheugh;
But at the gates o Paradise,
That birk grew fair enough

"Blow up the fire, my maidens!
Bring water from the well!
For a' my house hall feast this night,
Since my three sons are well."

And she has made to them a bed,
She's made it large and wide
And she's ta'en her mantle her about,
Sat down at the bed-side.

Up then crew the red, red cock,
And up and crew the gray;
The eldest to the youngest said,
"'Tis time we were away."

From *Commando Classics: A Field Manual for Helping Teens Understand (and Maybe Even Enjoy) Classic Literature* by Daria Plumb. Bowie, MD: VOYA Press, an imprint of E L Kurdyla Publishing, LLC. Copyright 2012

"The Wife of Usher's Well"

The cock he hadna craw'd but once,
And clapp'd his wings at a,'
When the youngest to the eldest said,
"Brother, we must awa."

"The cock doth craw, the day doth daw,
The channerin' worlm doth chide;
Gin we be mist out o' our place,
A sair pain we maun bide."

"Fare ye weel, my mother dear!
Fareweel to barn and byre!
And fare ye weel, the bonny lass
That kindles my mother's fire."

From *Commando Classics: A Field Manual for Helping Teens Understand (and Maybe Even Enjoy) Classic Literature*
by Daria Plumb. Bowie, MD: VOYA Press, an imprint of E L Kurdyla Publishing, LLC. Copyright 2012

"Kemp Owyne"

Her mother died when she was young,
Which gave her cause to make great moan;
Her father married the warst woman
That ever lived in Christendom.

She served her with foot and hand,
In every thing that she could dee,
Till once, in an unlucky time,
She threw her in ower Craigy's sea.

Says, "Lie you there, dove Isabel,
And all my sorrows lie with thee;
Till Kemp Owyne come ower the sea,
And borrow you with kisses three,
Let all the warld do what they will,
Oh borrowed shall you never be!"

Her breath grew strang, her hair grew lang,
And twisted thrice about the tree,
And all the people, far and near,
Thought that a savage beast was she.

These news did come to Kemp Owyne,
Where he lived, far beyond the sea;
He hasted him to Craigy's sea,
And on the savage beast lookd he.

Her breath was strang, her hair was lang,
And twisted was about the tree,
And with a swing she came about:
"Come to Craigy's sea, and kiss with me."

"Here is a royal belt," she cried,
"That I have found in the green sea;
And while your body it is on,
Drawn shall your blood never be;
But if you touch me, tail or fin,
I vow my belt your death shall be."

He stepped in, gave her a kiss,
The royal belt he brought him wi;
Her breath was strang, her hair was lang,
And twisted twice about the tree,
And with a swing she came about:
"Come to Craigy's sea, and kiss with me."

From *Commando Classics: A Field Manual for Helping Teens Understand (and Maybe Even Enjoy) Classic Literature*
by Daria Plumb. Bowie, MD: VOYA Press, an imprint of E L Kurdyla Publishing, LLC. Copyright 2012

"Here is a royal ring," she said,
"That I have found in the green sea;
And while your finger it is on,
Drawn shall your blood never be;
But if you touch me, tail or fin,
I swear my ring your death shall be."

He stepped in, gave her a kiss,
The royal ring he brought him wi;
Her breath was strang, her hair was lang,
And twisted ance about the tree,
And with a swing she came about:
"Come to Craigy's sea, and kiss with me."

"Here is a royal brand," she said,
"That I have found in the green sea;
And while your body it is on,
Drawn shall your blood never be;
But if you touch me, tail or fin,
I swear my brand your death shall be."

He stepped in, gave her a kiss,
The royal brand he brought him wi;
Her breath was sweet, her hair grew short,
And twisted nane about the tree,
And smilingly she came about,
As fair a woman as fair could be.

From *Commando Classics: A Field Manual for Helping Teens Understand (and Maybe Even Enjoy) Classic Literature*
by Daria Plumb. Bowie, MD: VOYA Press, an imprint of E L Kurdyla Publishing, LLC. Copyright 2012

MEDIEVAL BALLADS (*Cont.*)

"Lady Margaret"

(variant of Sweet William's Ghost)

Lady Margaret sitting in her own lone home,
Alone, O all alone,
When she thought she heard a dismal cry,
She heard a deadly moan.

"Is it my father Thomas?" she said,
"Or is it my brother John?
Or is it my love, my own dear Willie
Come home to me again?"

"I am not your father Thomas," he said,
"Nor am I your brother John,
But I am your love, your own dear Willie,
Come home to you again."

"Then where are the red and rosy cheeks
That even in winter bloom?
And where is the long and yellow hair
Of the love I lost too soon?"

"The ground have rotten them off, my dear,
For the worms are quick and free,
And when you're so long lying in your grave,
The same will happen thee."

He took her by the lily-white hand
And begged her company;
He took her by her apron band,
Says, "Follow, follow me."

She took her underskirts one by one
And wrapped them above her knee,
And she's over the hills on a winter's night
In a dead man's company.

They walked, they walked to the old churchyard,
Where the grass grow grassy-green:
"Here's the home where I live now,
The bed I do lie in."

From Commando Classics: A Field Manual for Helping Teens Understand (and Maybe Even Enjoy) Classic Literature
by Daria Plumb. Bowie, MD: VOYA Press, an imprint of E L Kurdyla Publishing, LLC. Copyright 2012

"Is there any room at your head, my love,
Is there any room at your feet?
Is there any room about you at all
For me to lie down and sleep?"

"My father is at my head, dear girl,
My mother is at my feet,
Upon my heart are three hell-hounds
Bound my soul to keep.

One is for my drunkenness
And another is for my pride,
And one is for promising a pretty fair girl
That she should be my bride."

She took the cross from all on her bosom
And smoted him on the breast,
"Here's your token I kept so long:
God send you a happy rest."

"Goodnight, goodnight, goodnight, my love,
Farewell, dear girl," said he;
"If ever the dead may pray for the living,
My love, I'll pray for thee."

From *Commando Classics: A Field Manual for Helping Teens Understand (and Maybe Even Enjoy) Classic Literature*
by Daria Plumb. Bowie, MD: VOYA Press, an imprint of E L Kurdyla Publishing, LLC. Copyright 2012

GULLIVER'S TRAVELS WITING

Imagine that you are Lemuel Gulliver. You have decided to stay in or return to one of the lands that you have visited (Lilliput, Brobdingnag, Laputa, Glubbdubdrib, or the land of the Houyhnhnms). Write a letter to your family explaining your decision.

Your letter should:

- describe the island and the people who live there

- tell why you have decided to stay

- tell what you plan to do while you are there

This may be the last letter you write home, so say your goodbyes and tell your family anything you want them to know. This should be written in the form of a letter and should be at least 8 sentences long.

MORE WILLIAM WORDSWORTH POEMS

"Simon Lee: The Old Huntsman"

With an incident in which he was concerned

1   In the sweet shire of Cardigan,
     Not far from pleasant Ivor-hall,
     An old Man dwells, a little man,—
     'Tis said he once was tall.
5   For five-and-thirty years he lived
     A running huntsman merry;
     And still the centre of his cheek
     Is red as a ripe cherry.

     No man like him the horn could sound,
10   And hill and valley rang with glee
     When Echo bandied, round and round
     The halloo of Simon Lee.
     In those proud days, he little cared
     For husbandry or tillage;
15   To blither tasks did Simon rouse
     The sleepers of the village.

     He all the country could outrun,
     Could leave both man and horse behind;
     And often, ere the chase was done,
20   He reeled, and was stone-blind.
     And still there's something in the world
     At which his heart rejoices;
     For when the chiming hounds are out,
     He dearly loves their voices!

25   But, oh the heavy change!—bereft
     Of health, strength, friends, and kindred, see!
     Old Simon to the world is left
     In liveried poverty.
     His Master's dead—and no one now
30   Dwells in the Hall of Ivor;
     Men, dogs, and horses, all are dead;
     He is the sole survivor.

From *Commando Classics: A Field Manual for Helping Teens Understand (and Maybe Even Enjoy) Classic Literature* by Daria Plumb. Bowie, MD: VOYA Press, an imprint of E L Kurdyla Publishing, LLC. Copyright 2012

And he is lean and he is sick;
His body, dwindled and awry,
35   Rests upon ankles swoln and thick;
His legs are thin and dry.
One prop he has, and only one,
His wife, an aged woman,
Lives with him, near the waterfall,
40   Upon the village Common.

Beside their moss-grown hut of clay,
Not twenty paces from the door,
A scrap of land they have, but they
Are poorest of the poor.
45   This scrap of land he from the heath
Enclosed when he was stronger;
But what to them avails the land
Which he can till no longer?

Oft, working by her Husband's side,
50   Ruth does what Simon cannot do;
For she, with scanty cause for pride,
Is stouter of the two.
And, though you with your utmost skill
From labour could not wean them,
55   'Tis little, very little—all
That they can do between them.

Few months of life has he in store
As he to you will tell,
For still, the more he works, the more
60   Do his weak ankles swell.
My gentle Reader, I perceive,
How patiently you've waited,
And now I fear that you expect
Some tale will be related.

From *Commando Classics: A Field Manual for Helping Teens Understand (and Maybe Even Enjoy) Classic Literature* by Daria Plumb. Bowie, MD: VOYA Press, an imprint of E L Kurdyla Publishing, LLC. Copyright 2012

65 O Reader! had you in your mind
Such stores as silent thought can bring,
O gentle Reader! you would find
A tale in every thing.
What more I have to say is short,
70 And you must kindly take it:
It is no tale; but, should you think,
Perhaps a tale you'll make it.

One summer-day I chanced to see
This old Man doing all he could
75 To unearth the root of an old tree,
A stump of rotten wood.
The mattock tottered in his hand;
So vain was his endeavour,
That at the root of the old tree
80 He might have worked for ever.

"You're overtasked, good Simon Lee,
Give me your tool," to him I said;
And at the word right gladly he
Received my proffered aid.
85 I struck, and with a single blow
The tangled root I severed,
At which the poor old Man so long
And vainly had endeavoured.

The tears into his eyes were brought,
90 And thanks and praises seemed to run
So fast out of his heart, I thought
They never would have done.
—I've heard of hearts unkind, kind deeds
With coldness still returning;
95 Alas! the gratitude of men
Hath oftener left me mourning.

From *Commando Classics: A Field Manual for Helping Teens Understand (and Maybe Even Enjoy) Classic Literature*
by Daria Plumb. Bowie, MD: VOYA Press, an imprint of E L Kurdyla Publishing, LLC. Copyright 2012

"She Dwelt among the Untrodden Ways"

1   She dwelt among the untrodden ways
Beside the springs of Dove,
A Maid whom there were none to praise
And very few to love:

5   A violet by a mossy stone
Half hidden from the eye!
—Fair as a star, when only one
Is shining in the sky.

She lived unknown, and few could know
10   When Lucy ceased to be;
But she is in her grave, and, oh,
The difference to me!

From *Commando Classics: A Field Manual for Helping Teens Understand (and Maybe Even Enjoy) Classic Literature*
by Daria Plumb. Bowie, MD: VOYA Press, an imprint of E L Kurdyla Publishing, LLC. Copyright 2012

"There Was a Boy (1799)"

THERE was a Boy; ye knew him well, ye cliffs
And islands of Winander!—many a time,
At evening, when the earliest stars began
To move along the edges of the hills,
Rising or setting, would he stand alone,
Beneath the trees, or by the glimmering lake;
And there, with fingers interwoven, both hands
Pressed closely palm to palm and to his mouth
Uplifted, he, as through an instrument,
Blew mimic hootings to the silent owls,
That they might answer him.—And they would shout
Across the watery vale, and shout again,
Responsive to his call,—with quivering peals,
And long halloos, and screams, and echoes loud
Redoubled and redoubled; concourse wild
Of jocund din! And, when there came a pause
Of silence such as baffled his best skill:
Then, sometimes, in that silence, while he hung
Listening, a gentle shock of mild surprise
Has carried far into his heart the voice
Of mountain-torrents; or the visible scene
Would enter unawares into his mind
With all its solemn imagery, its rocks,
Its woods, and that uncertain heaven received
Into the bosom of the steady lake.
This boy was taken from his mates, and died
In childhood, ere he was full twelve years old.
Pre-eminent in beauty is the vale
Where he was born and bred: the churchyard hangs
Upon a slope above the village-school;
And, through that church-yard when my way has led
On summer-evenings, I believe, that there
A long half-hour together I have stood
Mute—looking at the grave in which he lies!

From *Commando Classics: A Field Manual for Helping Teens Understand (and Maybe Even Enjoy) Classic Literature*
by Daria Plumb. Bowie, MD: VOYA Press, an imprint of E L Kurdyla Publishing, LLC. Copyright 2012

"To Sleep"

A flock of sheep that leisurely pass by
One after one; the sound of rain and bees
Murmuring; the fall of rivers, winds, and seas,
Smooth fields, white sheets of water, and pure sky; —

I've thought of all by turns, and still I lie
Sleepless; and soon the small birds' melodies
Must hear, first utter'd from my orchard trees,
And the first cuckoo's melancholy cry.

Even thus last night, and two nights more I lay,
And could not win thee, Sleep! by any stealth:
So do not let me wear to-night away:

Without Thee what is all morning's wealth?
Come, blessed barrier between day and day,
Dear mother of fresh thoughts and joyous health!

From *Commando Classics: A Field Manual for Helping Teens Understand (and Maybe Even Enjoy) Classic Literature*
by Daria Plumb. Bowie, MD: VOYA Press, an imprint of E L Kurdyla Publishing, LLC. Copyright 2012

MORE WILLIAM WORDSWORTH POEMS (*Cont.*)

"We Are Seven"

—A simple child,
That lightly draws its breath,
And feels its life in every limb,
What should it know of death?

I met a little cottage girl:
She was eight years old, she said;
Her hair was thick with many a curl
That clustered round her head.

She had a rustic, woodland air,
And she was wildly clad;
Her eyes were fair, and very fair;
—Her beauty made me glad.

"Sisters and brothers, little maid,
How many may you be?"
"How many? Seven in all," she said,
And wondering looked at me.

"And where are they? I pray you tell."
She answered, "Seven are we;
And two of us at Conway dwell,
And two are gone to sea.

"Two of us in the churchyard lie,
My sister and my brother;
And in the churchyard cottage, I
Dwell near them with my mother."

"You say that two at Conway dwell,
And two are gone to sea,
Yet ye are seven! — I pray you tell,
Sweet maid, how this may be."

Then did the little maid reply,
"Seven boys and girls are we;
Two of us in the churchyard lie,
Beneath the churchyard tree."

"You run about, my little maid,
Your limbs they are alive;
If two are in the churchyard laid,
Then ye are only five."

From *Commando Classics: A Field Manual for Helping Teens Understand (and Maybe Even Enjoy) Classic Literature*
by Daria Plumb. Bowie, MD: VOYA Press, an imprint of E L Kurdyla Publishing, LLC. Copyright 2012

"Their graves are green, they may be seen,"
The little maid replied,
"Twelve steps or more from my mother's door,
And they are side by side.

"My stockings there I often knit,
My kerchief there I hem;
And there upon the ground I sit,
And sing a song to them.

"And often after sunset, sir,
When it is light and fair,
I take my little porringer,
And eat my supper there.

"The first that died was sister Jane;
In bed she moaning lay,
Till God released her of her pain;
And then she went away.

"So in the churchyard she was laid;
And, when the grass was dry,
Together round her grave we played,
My brother John and I.

"And when the ground was white with snow,
And I could run and slide,
My brother John was forced to go,
And he lies by her side."
"How many are you, then," said I,
"If they two are in heaven?"
Quick was the little maid's reply,
"O master! We are seven."

"But they are dead; those two are dead!
Their spirits are in heaven!"
'T was throwing words away; for still
The little maid would have her will,
And say, "Nay, we are seven!"

FRANKENSTEIN; OR THE MODERN PROMETHEUS TEXT SET

NOVELS

- *Angelmonster* by Veronica Bennett. Candlewick Press, 2006.
- *Bernie Wrightson's Frankenstein.* Charles F. Miller, 1994.
- *Clay* by David Almond. Delacorte Books for Young Readers, 2008.
- *A Dark Endeavor: The Apprenticeship of Victor Frankenstein* by Kenneth Oppel. Simon & Schuster Children's Publishing, 2011.
- *Dean Koontz's Frankenstein, #1-5* by Dean Koontz. Bantam Doubleday, 2005-2011.
- *Frankenstein: The Shadow of Frankenstein, Volume 1* by Stefan Petrucha. DH Press, 2006.
- *I Am Frankenstein* by C. Dean Andersson. Zebra Books, 1996.
- *The Memoirs of Elizabeth Frankenstein* by Theodore Roszak. Bantam,1995.
- *The Monsters: Mary Shelley and the Curse of Frankenstein* by Dorothy and Thomas Hoobler. Back Bay Books, 2007.

ILLUSTRATED BOOKS

- *The Diary of Victor Frankenstein* by Timothy Basil Ering. DK INK, 1997.
- *Frankenstein* adapted by Larry Weinberg. Random Housem, 1993.
- *Golem* by David Wisniewski. Clarion Books, 1996.

FILMS / VIDEOS

- *Abbot and Costello Meet Frankenstein.* Universal Studios, 2006.
- *The Bride.* Sony Pictures Home Entertainment, 2001.
- *The Bride of Frankenstein.* MCA Home Video, 1986.
- *Decoding the Past: In Search of the Real Frankenstein.* A&E Home Video, 2008.
- *Frankenstein.* Universal Home Video, 2004.
- *Frankenstein Meets the Space Monster.* Dark Sky Films, 2006.
- *Frankenstein Meets the Wolf Man.* Universal Studios, 1992.
- *I Was a Teenage Frankenstein.* Sony Pictures Home Entertainment, 1993.
- *Gothic.* Lions Gate, 2002.
- *Great Books: Frankenstein: The Making of the Monster.* Discovery Communications, 1993.
- *Haunted Summer.* MGM, 2011.
- *In Search of History: Frankenstein.* A&E Home Video, 2000.
- *Mary Shelley's Frankenstein.* Sony Pictures Home Entertainment, 1998.
- *Mr. Magoo's Literary Classics: Sherlock Holmes/Dr. Frankenstein.* Paramount, 1998.
- *The Rocky Horror Picture Show.* 20th Century Fox Home Entertainment, 2000.

From *Commando Classics: A Field Manual for Helping Teens Understand (and Maybe Even Enjoy) Classic Literature* by Daria Plumb. Bowie, MD: VOYA Press, an imprint of E L Kurdyla Publishing, LLC. Copyright 2012

FRANKENSTEIN; OR THE MODERN PROMETHEUS TEXT SET (*Cont.*)

- *Transylvania 6-5000.* Starz/Anchor Bay, 2002.
- *Van Helsing.* Universal Home Video, 2004.
- *Weird Science.* Universal Studios, 2009.
- *Young Frankenstein.* 20th Century Fox Home Entertainment, 2004.
- Find more at *IMDB. http://us.imdb.com/M/title-substring?frankenstein*

GRAPHIC NOVELS

- *Doc Frankenstein* by Andy and Larry Wachowski. Betascript Publishing, 2011.
- *Frankenstein: The Graphic Novel* by Mary Shelley. Lucent Books, 2010.
- *Frankenstein: The Graphic Novel* by Mary Shelley. Classical Comics, 2008.
- *Graphic Revolve: Frankenstein.* Stone Arch Books, 2007.
- *Great Illustrated Classics: Frankenstein* by Mary Shelley. Playmore Publishers, 1993.
- *The League of Extraordinary Gentlemen, Volume 1* by Alan Moore. Wildstorm, 2002.
- *Mary Shelley's Frankenstein: The Graphic Novel* adapted by Gary Reed and Frazer Irving. Puffin, 2005.
- *The Monster of Frankenstein* by Dick Briefer, Alicia Jo Rabins, David Jacobs, and Edward Robinson. BookSurge Publishing, 2006.
- *Now Age Books: Frankenstein* by Mary Shelley. Pendulum Press, 1973.

ARTWORK

- Artwork of Mary Shelley's *Frankenstein*: Drawings, Paintings, Illustrations, Sculptures, etc. *http://www.geocities.com/orbofnight1816/*
- Nino Carbé's Illustrations from *Frankenstein* by Mary Wollstonecraft Shelley. *http://www.ninocarbe.com/illustration.html*

TV SHOWS

- "Frankenbone" episode of *Wishbone.* Season 1. PBS. 1996.
- "Frinkenstein" episode of *The Simpsons' Treehouse of Horror XIV.* Season 15, episode 314. FOX. 2 Nov 2003.
- *The Munsters.* CBS 1964-1966.
- *Saturday Night Live* – played by Phil Hartman in the early 1990s.
- "Some Assembly Required" episode of *Buffy the Vampire Slayer.* Season 2, episode 14. WB. 22 Sept 1997.
- "Post-Modern Prometheus" episode of *The X-Files.* Season 5, episode 102. FOX. 30 Nov 1997.

INTERNET SOURCES

- "Frankenstein." *Book-A-Minute Classics. http://www.rinkworks.com/bookaminute/b/shelley.frankenstein.shtml*
- *Frankenstein: The Art and Legends. http://frankensteinweb.com/*
- *Frankenstein: Penetrating the Secrets of Nature. http://www.nlm.nih.gov/hmd/frankenstein/frankhome.html*
- *Mary Shelley and Frankenstein. http://www.kimwoodbridge.com/maryshel/maryshel.shtml*

SONGS

- "All Along the Watchtower" by Bob Dylan
- "Behind Blue Eyes" by The Who
- "Boulevard of Broken Dreams" by Green Day
- "Chemistry" by Carey & Brubaker
- "Desperado" by the Eagles
- "Frankenstein" by Edgar Winter
- "Frankenstein" by Iced Earth
- "Jesse James Meets Frankenstein's Daughter" by Space Mandino
- "Mr. Lonely" by Akon
- "Over at the Frankenstein Place" from *The Rocky Horror Picture Show*. Broadway version.
- "The Siege and Investiture of Baron von Frankenstein's Castle at Weisseria" by Blue Oyster Cult
- "Teenage Frankenstein" by Alice Cooper

BIOGRAPHIES

- *Child of Light: Mary Shelley* by Muriel Spark. Welcome Rain Publishers, 1976.
- *Mary Shelley* by Miranda Seymour. Grove Press, 2002.

FOLKLORE and LEGENDS

- *The Golem: A Jewish Legend* edited by D.L. Ashliman. *http://www.pitt.edu/~dash/golem.html*
- *In Search of Frankenstein: Exploring the Myths behind Mary Shelley's Monster* by Radu Florescu. Robson Books,1975.
- "Prometheus," *Encyclopedia Mythica. http://www.pantheon.org/articles/p/prometheus.html*

HISTORIES

- *Frankenstein* by Steve Parker. Cooper Beach Books, 1995.
- *Frankenstein: A Cultural History* by Susan Tyler Hitchcock. W.W. Norton, 2007.

From *Commando Classics: A Field Manual for Helping Teens Understand (and Maybe Even Enjoy) Classic Literature* by Daria Plumb. Bowie, MD: VOYA Press, an imprint of E L Kurdyla Publishing, LLC. Copyright 2012

MISCELLANEOUS

- "The Biography of Dr. Victor Frankenstein" *http://www.trivia-library.com/b/biography-of-dr-victor-frankenstein-part-1.htm*

- *The Body of Frankenstein's Monster: Essays in Myth and Medicine* by Cecil Helman. W.W. Norton, 1992.

- *The Dead that Walk: Dracula, Frankenstein, the Mummy, and Other Favorite Movie Monsters* by Leslie Halliwell. Continuum, 1988.

- *Frankenstein* by Ian Thorne. Crestwood House, 1977.

- *Frankenstein* by Stephen Krensky. Lerner, 2006.

- *Frankenstein Meets Woldman* by Ian Thorne. Prentice Hall & IBD, 1981.

- *Frankenstein: Penetrating the Secrets of Nature* edited by Susan E. Lederer, Elizabeth Fee, and Patricia Tuohy. Rutgers University Press, 2002.

- *It's Alive: The Classic Cinema Saga of Frankenstein* by Gregory W. Mank. A.S. Barnes, 1981.

- *Mary Shelley's Frankenstein: A DVD Study Guide.* Rocketbook, 2005.

- *The Secret Laboratory Journals of Dr. Victor Frankenstein* by Jeremy Kay. Overlook, 1996.

- *Stage Plays from the Classics: One-Act Adaptations from Famous Short Stories, Novels, and Plays* by Joellen Bland. Plays, 2001.

NEWSPAPER ARTICLES

- "'It's a boy!' or 'It's a girl!' Choosing Getting Easier" by Susan Stevens, *Daily Herald*, Feb. 1, 2004.

- "Kentucky Cloning Doctor Says First Attempt Fails" by Reuters, Feb. 4, 2004. *http://cmbi.bjmu.edu.cn/news/0402/29.htm*

SHORT STORIES

- *Frankenstein: The Monster Wakes* by Martin H. Greenberg. DAW, 1993.

GAMES

- Frankenstein: The Monster Returns!. NES.

- Frankenstein's Monster. Atari 2600.

- Mary Shelley's Frankenstein. Super Nintendo, Sega Genesis, Sega CD.

- Promethean: The Created. Role playing game.

- Through the Eyes of the Monster – A Cinematic Adventure Starring Tim Curry. PC.

POEMS

- *Making Friends with Frankenstein: A Book of Monstrous Poems and Pictures* by Colin McNaughton. Candlewick, 2002.

From *Commando Classics: A Field Manual for Helping Teens Understand (and Maybe Even Enjoy) Classic Literature* by Daria Plumb. Bowie, MD: VOYA Press, an imprint of E L Kurdyla Publishing, LLC. Copyright 2012

Frankenstein Writing

Imagine that you are Dr. Victor Frankenstein. Respond to the articles "'It's a boy' or 'It's a girl!' Choosing Getting Easier and Kentucky Cloning Doctor Says First Attempt Fails." Consider the following quote from Dr. Michael Hickey: "Just because you can do something doesn't mean that you should."

- Would Victor Frankenstein agree or disagree with Dr. Hickey? Why or why not?
- What might Frankenstein say to the doctors that have created MicroSort?
- What might Frankenstein say to Dr. Panos Zavos (the "Kentucky Cloning Doctor")?
- What warnings might he give them (think back to his conversation with Robert Walton)?

Be sure to include examples from the story of *Frankenstein* to support your statements.

_____

_____

_____

_____

_____

_____

_____

_____

_____

_____

_____

_____

_____

_____

_____

From *Commando Classics: A Field Manual for Helping Teens Understand (and Maybe Even Enjoy) Classic Literature*
by Daria Plumb. Bowie, MD: VOYA Press, an imprint of E L Kurdyla Publishing, LLC. Copyright 2012

Treasure Island Text Set

(Also, Pirate Lore and Sea Lore)

NOVELS

- *Bloody Jack: Being an Account of the Curious Adventures of Mary "Jacky" Faber, Ship's Boy* by L.A. Meyer. Harcourt, 2002.
- *Pirates: The True and Remarkable Adventures of Minerva Sharpe and Nancy Kington, Female Pirates* by Celia Rees. Bloomsbury USA Children's Books, 2003.
- *Silver: My Own Tale as Written by Me with a Goodly Amount of Murder* by Edward Chupack. St. Martin's Press, 2008.
- *To Catch a Pirate* by Jade Parker. Point/Scholastic, 2007.
- *Treasure Island from the Story by Robert Louis Stevenson* retold by Henry Brook. Usborne, 2006.

ILLUSTRATED BOOKS

- *Eyewitness Books: Pirates* by Richard Platt. Alfred A. Knopf, 1994.
- *How I Became a Pirate* by Melinda Long and David Shannon. Harcourt, 2003.

FILMS / VIDEOS

- *History's Mysteries Ghost Ships*. A&E Home Video, 2001.
- *History's Mysteries: Monsters of the Sea*. A&E Home Video, 2008.
- *MonsterQuest*, Season 1. A&E Home Video, 2008.
  - "America's Loch Ness Monster"
  - "Giant Squid Found?"
- *MonsterQuest*, Season 2. A&E Home Video, 2009.
  - "Giant Squid Ambush"
  - "Lake Monsters of the North"
- *MonsterQuest*, Season 3. A&E Home Video, 2009.
  - "Death of Loch Ness"
  - "Gigantic Killer Fish II"
  - "Killer Jellyfish"
  - "Sea Monsters"
- "Monsters of the Deep" Animal X, Series 3, Episode 7. *http://www.animalx.net*
- *Muppet Treasure Island*. Buena Vista Home Video,1996.
- *Pirates of the Caribbean*
  - *At World's End*. Buena Vista Home Entertainment, 2007.
  - *The Curse of the Black Pearl*. Buena Vista Home Entertainment, 2003.
  - *Dead Man's Chest*. Buena Vista Home Entertainment, 2006.
- *Treasure Island*. Warner Home Video, 2006.
- *Treasure Island*. Cambium Film & Video, Ltd., 1986.

- *Treasure Planet*. Buena Vista Home Entertainment, 2002.
- *True Caribbean Pirates*. A&E Dod., 2009.

GRAPHIC NOVELS

- *Graphic Classics: Robert Louis Stevenson* edited by Tom Pomplun. Eureka Productions, 2004.
- *Robert Louis Stevenson's Treasure Island: The Graphic Novel* adapted by Tim Hamilton. Puffin Books/Penguin, 2005.
- *Treasure Island* by Robert Louis Stevenson. Atheneum Books for Young Readers, 2003.

ARTWORK

- Pirate Images. *http://beej.us/pirates/index.html*
- *Visions of Adventure: N.C. Wyeth and the Brandywine Artists* edited by John Edward Dell in association with Walt Reed. Watson-Guptill Publications, 2000.
- "Way to Treasure Island" by Harold Farnsworth

POEMS

- *The New England Pirate Museum: Pirate Poetry. http://www.piratemuseum.com/edpoems.htm*

INTERNET SOURCES

- "Modern High Seas Piracy." *http://www.cargolaw.com/presentations_pirates.html*
- *Pirates! http://www.nationalgeographic.com/pirates/*
- *Pirates Theme Page. http://webtech.kennesaw.edu/jcheek3/pirates.htm*
- *Rob Ossian's Pirate Cove. http://www.thepirateking.com/index.htm*
- *Talk Like a Pirate Day—September 19th. http://www.talklikeapirate.com*

SONGS

- *Disney's Pirates of the Caribbean: Swashbuckling Sea Songs*. Disney, 2006.
- Hal Willner's *Rogue's Gallery: Pirate Ballads, Sea Songs and Chanteys*. ANTI-, 2006.
- "Songs of the Sea: Tunes, Lyrics and Information" *http://www.contemplator.com/sea/index.html*

BIOGRAPHIES

- "Into the Mountains of the Moon." *Lives of the Writers: Comedies, Tragedies (and What the Neighbors Thought)* by Kathleen Krull. Sandpiper, 2011.
- *Lives of the Pirates: Swashbucklers, Scoundrels, (Neighbors Beware!)* by Kathleen Krull. Harcourt Children's Books, 2010.
- *Sea Queens: Women Pirates from Around the World* by Jane Yolen. Charlesbridge, 2008.

FOLKLORE AND LEGENDS

- *Arthur Spiderwick's Field Guide to the Fantastical World Around You* by Tony DiTerlizzi and Holly Black. Simon & Schuster, 2008.

Treasure Island Text Set (*Cont.*)

- "Davy Jones: The Folklore of the Devil that Ruled the Sea." © Dana Tierney. June 12, 2007. *http://folktales.suite101.com/article.cfm/davy_jones*
- "The Flying Dutchman." © Trevor Mendham 2004 – 2008. *http://www.wyrdology.com/other/flying-dutchman.html*
- "Ghost Ships" © Jamie Molyneaux. *http://www.gettysburgghosts.net/ghostships.htm*
- "The Legendary Kraken" *The UnMuseum. http://unmuseum.mus.pa.us/kraken.htm*
- "Sea Monster Tales." *The UnMuseum. http://www.unmuseum.org/tales.htm*
- "The Selkie Folk." *http://www.orkneyjar.com/folklore/selkiefolk/index.html*
- "The Sorcerous Finfolk and Mermaids." *http://www.orkneyjar.com/folklore/finfolk/index.html*

HISTORIES

- *The Book of Pirates: A Guide to Plundering, Pillaging, and Other Pursuits* by Jamaica Rose and Michael MacLeod. Gibbs Smith, 2010.
- *Piratepedia* by Alisha Niehaus and Alan Hecker. DK Publishing, 2007.
- *Pirates* by John Matthews. Atheneum Books for Young Readers, 2006.
- *Pirates of the Caribbean: The Curse of the Black Pearl.* Disc Two. Buena Vista Home Entertainment, 2003.
- *Pirates! Fact and Legend. http://www.piratesinfo.com/about.php*
- *Pirate Secrets Revealed* by Anna Claybourne. Capstone Press, 2009.
- *You Wouldn't Want to Be a Pirate's Prisoner!: Horrible Things You'd Rather Not Know* by John Malam. F. Watts/Scholastic, 2002.

MISCELLANEOUS

- *The Great Pirate Activity Book* by Deri Robbins and George Buchanan. Kingfisher, 1995.
- *The New England Pirate Museum:* Class Handouts and Lesson Plans. *http://www.pirate-museum.com/ec.html*
- *The Pirate Dictionary* by Teri Breverton. Pelican Publishing, 2004.
- *The Pirate Primer: Mastering the Language of Swashbuckler's and Rogues* by George Choundas. Writer's Digest Books, 2010.
- *Pirates: Facts, Things to Make, Activities* by Rachel Wright. F. Watts, 1991.
- *Pirattitude!: So You Wanna Be a Pirate": Here's How* by John "Chumbucket" Baur and Mark "Cap'n Slappy" Summers. NAL Trade, 2005.

ESSAYS / ARTICLES

- "Modern Pirates Terrorize Seas with Guns and Grenades" by Stefan Lovgren for *National Geographic News*, July 6, 2006 *http://news.nationalgeographic.com/news/2006/07/060706-modern-pirates.html*

SHORT STORIES

- *The Big Book of Pirates* by Joan and Albert Vinyoli. Sterling Pub., 2011.

DRACULA TEXT SET

NOVELS

- *Bloodline #1 and 2* by Kate Cary. Razorbill, 2005-2007.
- *Blue Bloods, Volumes 1-7* by Melissa de la Cruz. Hyperion, 2006-2013
- *Bunnicula: A Rabbit Tale of Mystery* by James Howe. Avon Books, 1979.
- *The Chronicles of Vladimir Tod, Volumes 1-5* by Heather Brewer. Dutton Children's Books, 2008-2010.
- *High School Bites: The Lucy Chronicles* by Liza Conrad. NAL Trade, 2006.
- *The Historian* by Eizabeth Kostova. Little, Brown and Co., 2005.
- *The Saga of Darren Shan, Volumes 1-12* by Darren Shan. Little, Brown, 2000-2004.
- *Sherlock Holmes vs. Dracula: Or the Adventure of the Sanguinary Count* by John H. Watson as edited by Loren D. Estelman. Penguin, 1979.
- *Tantalize, Volumes 1-3* by Cynthia Leitich Smith. Candlewick, 2007-2011.
- *The Twilight Saga* by Stephenie Meyer. Little, Brown and Co., 2005-2008.
- *The Vampyre* by John Polidori. Forgotten Books, 2008.
- *Vampirates, Volumes 1-6* by Justin Somper. Little, Brown Books for Young Readers, 2005-2011.
- *Vampire Academy, #1-6* by Richelle Mead. Razorbill, 2007-2010.
- *Vampire Kisses, #1-8* by Ellen Schreiber. HarperTeen, 2003-2011.
- *Vlad the Undead* by Hanna Lutzen. Groundwood Books, 2001.

ILLUSTRATED BOOKS

- *Castle Dracula: Romania's Vampire Home* by Barbara J. Knox. Bearport, 2005.
- *Trapped in Transylvania: Dracula* by Tony Abbott. Volo/Hyperion, 2002.
- *Vampyre: The Terrifying Lost Journal of Dr. Cornelius Van Helsing* by Gustav De Wolff. HarperCollins Children's Books, 2007.
- *Van Helsing: The Junior Novel* by Carla Jablonski. HarperFestival, 2004.

FILMS / VIDEOS

- *30 Days of Night*. Sony Pictures Home Entertainment, 2008.
- *The Batman vs. Dracula*. Warner Home Video, 2005.
- "Bela Lugosi Dracula." *http://www.youtube.com/watch?v=IVPxAgy7lBA&feature=PlayList&p=A02304B271D243CB&index=21*
- *Blade*. New Line Cinema and Amen Ra Productions, 1998.
- *Bram Stoker's Dracula*. Sony Pictures Home Entertainment, 2007.

From *Commando Classics: A Field Manual for Helping Teens Understand (and Maybe Even Enjoy) Classic Literature* by Daria Plumb. Bowie, MD: VOYA Press, an imprint of E L Kurdyla Publishing, LLC. Copyright 2012

- *Dracula.* Universal Home Entertainment, 2006.
- *Dracula: Dead and Loving It.* Columbia TriStar Home Video, 1996.
- "Dracula … on 60 Minutes." *Yahoo! News. http://60minutes.yahoo.com/segment/107/dracula*
- *Interview with the Vampire.* Warner Home Video, 2000.
- *The Lost Boys.* Warner Home Video, 2004.
- *The Monster Squad.* Lionsgate, 2007.
- *Nosferatu: A Symphony of Horror.* Kino International, 2007.
- *The Real Dracula.* FilmRoos Inc. and A&E Television Networks, 1998.
- *Salem's Lot.* Warner Home Video, 2004.
- *Underworld.* Columbia TriStar Home Entertainment, 2004.
- *Van Helsing.* Universal Home Video, 2004.

GRAPHIC NOVELS

- *Bram Stoker's Dracula: The Graphic Novel* adapted by Gary Reed. Puffin Books/Penguin Young Readers Group, 2006.
- *The Complete 30 Days of Night* by Steve Niles. IDW Publishing, 2004.
- *Graphic Classics 7: Bram Stoker, 2nd Edition* by Bram Stoker, Rich Rainey, and Gerry Alanguilan. Eureka Productions, 2007.
- *The Saga of Darren Shan, Volumes 1-12* by Darren Shan. Yen Press, 2009-2012.
- *Tantalize: Kieran's Story* by Cynthia Leitich Smith and Ming Doyle. Candlewick, 2011.
- *Vampire Hunter D, Volumes 1-15* by Hideyuki Kikuchi. Dark Horse, 2007-2010.
- *Vampire Knight, Volumes 1-13* by Matsui Hino. VIZ Media LLC, 2007-2010.
- *Vampire Loves* by Joann Sfar. First Second, 2006.

POEMS

- *Dracula Spectacula* by John Goldthwaite. Harlan Quist, 1975.

TV SHOWS

- *Buffy the Vampire Slayer.* The WB, 1997-2001; UPN, 2001-2003.
- *Dark Shadows.* ABC, 1988-1971.
- *Moonlight.* CBS, 2007-2008.
- *The Munsters.* CBS 1964-1966.
- "Vampire Beasts," *MonsterQuest*, Season 2. A&E Television Networks, 2008.

DRACULA TEXT SET (*Cont.*)

INTERNET SOURCES

- "Counting on the Count" by Rebecca Leung for *60 Minutes*, Feb. 11, 2009. *http://www. cbsnews.com/stories/2005/05/27/60minutes/main698273.shtml?tag=contentMain;content Body*

- *Dracula's Castle. http://draculascastle.com/*

- *Dracula's Homepage* © Dr. Elizabeth Miller. *http://www.ucs.mun.ca/~emiller/index.html*

- *Dracula Info: Dracula between Hero and Vampire. http://www.draculas.info/*

- "Forget *Twilight*, Here's the Real Dracula." *60 Minutes Overtime*, Oct. 31, 2010. *http://www. cbsnews.com/8301-504803_162-20021189-10391709.html*

SONGS

- "Dracula" by Gorillaz

- "Dracula" by Iced Earth

- "Vampires Are Alive" by DJ Bobo

- "Vampires Will Never Hurt You" by My Chemical Romance

BIOGRAPHIES

- *Bram Stoker: A Biography of the Author of Dracula* by Barbara Belford. Random House, 1996.

FOLKLORE AND LEGENDS

- *The Dead Travel Fast: Stalking Vampires from Nosferatu to Count Chocula* by Eric Nuzem. St. Martin's Griffin, 2008.

- *Encyclopedia Horrifica: The Terrifying Truth! About Vampires, Ghosts, Monsters, and More* by Joshua Gee. Scholastic, 2007.

- *Ghosts, Werewolves, Witches, and Vampires* by Jo-Anne Christensen. Lone Pine Publishing, 2001.

- *Monsters* by Bernard Brett. Wanderer Books, 1983.

- *Out of the Dark: The Complete Guide to Beings from Beyond* by Brad Steiger. K Trade Paper, 2001.

- *The Science of Vampires* by Kathleen Ramsland. Berkley Trade, 2002.

- *Vampires* by Stephen Krensky. Lerner Classroom, 2007.

- *Vampires: A Field Guide to the Creatures that Stalk the Night* by Bob Curran. New Page Books, 2005.

From *Commando Classics: A Field Manual for Helping Teens Understand (and Maybe Even Enjoy) Classic Literature* by Daria Plumb. Bowie, MD: VOYA Press, an imprint of E L Kurdyla Publishing, LLC. Copyright 2012

DRACULA TEXT SET (*Cont.*)

HISTORIES

- *Dracula, Prince of Many Faces: His Life and Times* by Radu R. Florescu and Raymond T. McNally. Little, Brown, 1989.

- *Hollywood Gothic: The Tangled Web of Dracula from Novel to Stage to Screen* by David J. Skal. Faber & Faber, 2004.

- *In Search of Dracula: A True History of Dracula and Vampire Legends* by Raymond T. McNally. New York Graphic Society, 1972.

- *Vlad the Impaler: The Real Count Dracula (A Wicked History)* by Enid A. Goldberg and Norman Itzkowitz. Franklin Watts, 2008.

MISCELLANEOUS

- *The Dead That Walk: Dracula, Frankenstein, the Mummy, and Other Favorite Movie Monsters* by Leslie Halliwell. Continuum, 1988.

- *The Dracula Book* by Donald F. Glut. Scarecrow Press, 1975.

- *Dracula: The Conoisseur's Guide* by Leonard Wolf. Broadway Books, 1997.

- *Dracula: The Musical Adapted from Bram Stoker's Classic Gothic Novel.* Copyright © 2000 - 2008 by Gareth Evans and Christopher J. Orton. *http://www.dracula-uk.com/*

- *Edward Gorey's Dracula: A Toy Theatre: Die Cut, Scored and Perforated Foldups and Foldouts* by Edward Gorey. Pomegranate, 2007.

- *V is Vampire: The A-to-Z Guide to Everything Undead* by David J. Skal. Plume, 1996.

SHORT STORIES

- *Blood Thirst: 100 Years of Vampire Fiction* edited by Leonard Wolf. Oxford University Press, 1997.

- *The Dracula Book of Great Vampire Stories* edited by Leslie Shepard. Citadel Press, 1977.

- *The Many Faces of Van Helsing* edited by Jeanne Cavelos. Berkley, 2004.

THE HOUND OF THE BASKERVILLES TEXT SET

NOVELS

- *The Adventures of Sherlock Holmes* retold from the Arthur Conan Doyle original by Chris Sasaki; illustrated by Lucy Corvino. Sterling Publishing, 2005.
- Enola Holmes Mysteries by Nancy Springer:
  - *The Case of the Missing Marquess.* Sleuth/Philomel, 2006.
  - *The Case of the Left-Handed Lady.* Sleuth/Philomel, 2007.
  - *The Case of the Bizarre Bouquets.* Philomel, 2008.
- *Goosebumps: The Barking Ghost* by R.L. Stine. Scholastic, 1995.
- *The Hound of the Baskervilles* by Sir Arthur Conan Doyle; illustrated by Pam Smy. Candlewick Press, 2006.
- *Thursday Next: First Among Sequels* by Jasper Fforde. Thorndike Press, 2007.

FILMS / VIDEOS

- *The Hound of the Baskervilles.* Tiger Aspect Productions, 2002.
- *The Hound of the Baskervilles.* Universal TV, 1972.
- *The Hound of the Baskervilles.* Hammer Film Productions, 1959.
- *The Hound of the Baskervilles.* Twentieth Century Fox Film Corporation, 1939.
- *The Hound of the Baskervilles-Trailer (1959). http://www.youtube.com/watch?v=l4p5yJVbnvQ&feature=PlayList&p=A02304B271D243CB&index=22*
- *Martin Shaw in "The Hound of the Baskervilles" (1983) http://www.youtube.com/watch?v=aXIM-ybUaNo&feature=PlayList&p=A02304B271D243CB&index=23*
- *Mr. Magoo's Literary Classics: Sherlock Holmes/Dr. Frankenstein.* Paramount, 1998.

GRAPHIC NOVELS

- *The Hound of the Baskervilles.* Illustrated Classic Book Club. Pendulum Press, 1977.

ARTWORK

- *The Hound of the Baskerville* by Diana Bryan
- *The Hound of the Baskervilles* by Sidney Paget
- Hound of the Baskervilles. UK postage stamp. *http://www.ianpollock.co.uk/portraits/baskervilles.html*

POEMS

- "Black Shuck" by Martin Newell. Jardine Press, 1999.

TV SHOWS

- "Ghostly Creatures: Black Dogs." Animal X Natural Mystery Unit. Series 1, Episode 1. *http://www.animalx.net/ghostly_creatures.html*

From *Commando Classics: A Field Manual for Helping Teens Understand (and Maybe Even Enjoy) Classic Literature* by Daria Plumb. Bowie, MD: VOYA Press, an imprint of E L Kurdyla Publishing, LLC. Copyright 2012

THE HOUND OF THE BASKERVILLES TEXT SET (*Cont.*)

INTERNET SOURCES

- *Baskerville Hall Hotel. http://www.baskervillehall.co.uk/*
- *Masterpiece Theatre: The Hound of the Baskervilles. http://www.pbs.org/wgbh/masterpiece/hound/essays.html*
- *The Official Website of the Sir Arthur Conan Doyle Literary Estate. http://www.sherlockholmesonline.org/*
- *The Sherlock Holmes Museum. http://www.sherlock-holmes.co.uk/*
- *The Strand Magazine: The Magazine for Mystery and Short Story Lovers. http://www.strandmag.com/*
- *Yorkshire Moors and Coast Travel and Tourism. http://www.yorkshiremoorsandcoast.com/*

BIOGRAPHIES

- *Arthur Conan Doyle: Beyond Baker Street* by Janet B. Pascal. Oxford University Press, 2000.
- *The Real World of Sherlock Holmes: The True Crimes Investigated by Arthur Conan Doyle* by Peter Costello. Carroll & Graf, 1991.

FOLKLORE & LEGENDS

- *Apparitions of Black Dogs. http://nli.northampton.ac.uk/ass/psych-staff/sjs/blackdog.htm*
- *At the Edge: Exploring New Interpretations of Past and Place in Archaeology, Folklore and Mythology http://www.indigogroup.co.uk/edge/bdogfl.htm*
- "Chapter 1: Guises of the Reaper." *The Enchanted World: Ghosts.* Time-Life Books, 1984.

MISCELLANEOUS

- *The Science of Sherlock Holmes: From Baskerville Hall to the Valley of Fear, the Real Forensics Behind the Great Detective's Greatest Cases* by E.J. Wagner. John Wiley & Sons, 2006.
- *The Sherlock Holmes Encyclopedia* by Orlando Park. Citadel Press, 1981.
- *The Sherlock Holmes Quiz Book* by Albert J. Menendez. Drake, 1975.
- *Sherlock Holmes: The Man and His World; With 136 Illustrations* by Henry Reymond Fitzwalter Keating. Charles Scribner's Sons, 1979.
- *Sherlock Holmes's London: Following the Footsteps of London's Master Detective* by Tsukasa Kobayashi, Akane Higashiyama, and Masaharu Uemura. Chronicle Books, 1986.
- *The World of Sherlock Holmes* by Michael Harrison. Dutton, 1975.

ESSAYS / ARTICLES

- "The War of the Baskervilles" by Guy Saville. *The Independent*, July 11, 2001

EDUCATIONAL VIDEOS: BRITISH LITERATURE

Channel	Series	Title	Length	Unit/Text Set
A&E	ANCIENT MYSTERIES	Camelot	50 minutes	Arthurian Legend
A&E	ANCIENT MYSTERIES	The Quest for the Holy Grail	50 minutes	Arthurian Legend
TLC & Discovery Channel School	GREAT BOOKS	Le Morte d'Arthur: Legend of the King	50 minutes	Arthurian Legend
The History Channel	IN SEARCH OF HISTORY	The Holy Grail	50 minutes	Arthurian Legend
The History Channel	IN SEARCH OF HISTORY	The Knights of Camelot	50 minutes	Arthurian Legend
The History Channel	n/a	Knights and Armor	100 minutes	Arthurian Legend
The History Channel	n/a	The Quest for King Arthur	100 minutes	Arthurian Legend
A&E	BIOGRAPHY	Robin Hood: Outlaw of the Forest	50 minutes	Ballads & Legends
A&E	ANCIENT MYSTERIES	Vampires	50 minutes	Dracula
A&E	BIOGRAPHY	Bram Stoker	50 minutes	Dracula
The History Channel	CITIES OF THE UNDERWORLD	Dracula's Underground	50 minutes	Dracula
TLC & Discovery Channel School	GREAT BOOKS	Dracula	50 minutes	Dracula
The History Channel	HAUNTED HISTORY	The Real Dracula	50 minutes	Dracula
The History Channel	LOST WORLDS	The Real Dracula	50 minutes	Dracula
The History Channel	MONSTERQUEST	Vampire Beast	50 minutes	Dracula
The History Channel	n/a	Vampire Secrets	100 minutes	Dracula
The History Channel	TIME MACHINE	Bloodlines: The Dracula Family Tree	50 minutes	Dracula
A&E	BIOGRAPHY	H.G. Wells: Time Traveler	50 minutes	Fantasy
TLC & Discovery Channel School	GREAT BOOKS	Alice in Wonderland	50 minutes	Fantasy
TLC & Discovery Channel School	GREAT BOOKS	The War of the Worlds	50 minutes	Fantasy
Standard Deviants School	SDS FANTASY LITERATURE	Module 1: Intro	26 minutes	Fantasy
Standard Deviants School	SDS FANTASY LITERATURE	Module 2: Heroes and Hocus Pocus	26 minutes	Fantasy
Standard Deviants School	SDS FANTASY LITERATURE	Module 3: Monsters and Myth	26 minutes	Fantasy
Standard Deviants School	SDS FANTASY LITERATURE	Module 4: Grendel, Dragons, & Meanies	26 minutes	Fantasy
The History Channel	DECODING THE PAST	In Search of the Real Frankenstein	50 minutes	Frankenstein

From *Commando Classics: A Field Manual for Helping Teens Understand (and Maybe Even Enjoy) Classic Literature* by Daria Plumb. Bowie, MD: VOYA Press, an imprint of E L Kurdyla Publishing, LLC. Copyright 2012

EDUCATIONAL VIDEOS: BRITISH LITERATURE (*Cont.*)

Channel	Series	Title	Length	Unit/Text Set
TLC & Discovery Channel School	GREAT BOOKS	Frankenstein: The Making of the Monster	50 minutes	Frankenstein
The History Channel	IN SEARCH OF HISTORY	Frankenstein	50 minutes	Frankenstein
A&E	ANCIENT MYSTERIES	Lost Castles of England	50 minutes	Miscellaneous
TLC & Discovery Channel School	GREAT BOOKS	The Origin of Species	50 minutes	Miscellaneous
The History Channel	MODERN MARVELS	Castles and Dungeons	50 minutes	Miscellaneous
The History Channel	n/a	The Dark Ages	94 minutes	Miscellaneous
The History Channel	n/a	The Plague	100 minutes	Miscellaneous
The History Channel	HISTORY'S MYSTERIES	Bloody Tower of London	50 minutes	Mythology & Folklore
The History Channel	IN SEARCH OF HISTORY	Enduring Mystery of Stonehenge	50 minutes	Mythology & Folklore
The History Channel	IN SEARCH OF HISTORY	Haunted London	50 minutes	Mythology & Folklore
The History Channel	MONSTERQUEST	Black Beast of Exmoor	50 minutes	Mythology & Folklore
TLC & Discovery Channel School	GREAT BOOKS	Gulliver's Travels	50 minutes	Neoclassical
A&E	BIOGRAPHY	Adam & Eve	50 minutes	Paradise Lost
The History Channel	DECODING THE PAST	Mysteries of the Garden of Eden	50 minutes	Paradise Lost
The History Channel	HAUNTED HISTORY	The Pirate's Lost City	50 minutes	Pirates
The History Channel	HISTORY'S MYSTERIES	Ghost Ships	50 minutes	Pirates
The History Channel	HISTORY'S MYSTERIES	Monsters of the Sea	50 minutes	Pirates
The History Channel	LOST WORLDS	Pirates of the Caribbean	50 minutes	Pirates
The History Channel	MONSTERQUEST	Giant Squid Found?	50 minutes	Pirates
The History Channel	MONSTERQUEST	Gigantic Killer Fish	50 minutes	Pirates
TLC & Discovery Channel School	GREAT BOOKS	Lord of the Flies	50 minutes	Postmodern
Channel	Series	Title	Length	Unit/Text Set
A&E	BIOGRAPHY	The Bronte Sisters	50 minutes	Romantic
TLC & Discovery Channel School	GREAT BOOKS	Pride and Prejudice	50 minutes	Romantic
PBS Home Video	MASTERPIECE	Miss Austen Regrets: The Life and Loves of Jane Austen	90 minutes	Romantic

EDUCATIONAL VIDEOS: BRITISH LITERATURE (*Cont.*)

Channel	Series	Title	Length	Unit/Text Set
A&E	BIOGRAPHY	Queen Elizabeth: The Reluctant Queen	50 minutes	Shakespeare
A&E	BIOGRAPHY	William Shakespeare: Life of Drama	50 minutes	Shakespeare
PBS Home Video	FRONTLINE	Much Ado About Something	90 minutes	Shakespeare
The History Channel	IN SEARCH OF HISTORY	England's Theatres of Blood	50 minutes	Shakespeare
Standard Deviants School	SDS SHAKESPEARE	Module 1: Intro to Shakespeare	26 minutes	Shakespeare
Standard Deviants School	SDS SHAKESPEARE	Module 10: The Characters of Macbeth	16 minutes	Shakespeare
Standard Deviants School	SDS SHAKESPEARE	Module 11: King Lear Basics	14 minutes	Shakespeare
Standard Deviants School	SDS SHAKESPEARE	Module 12: Approaches to King Lear	15 minutes	Shakespeare
Standard Deviants School	SDS SHAKESPEARE	Module 2: What Is Tragedy?	21 minutes	Shakespeare
Standard Deviants School	SDS SHAKESPEARE	Module 3: Titus Andronicus	20 minutes	Shakespeare
Standard Deviants School	SDS SHAKESPEARE	Module 4: Romeo and Juliet	29 minutes	Shakespeare
Standard Deviants School	SDS SHAKESPEARE	Module 5: Hamlet Basics	16 minutes	Shakespeare
Standard Deviants School	SDS SHAKESPEARE	Module 6: Hamlet Themes	19 minutes	Shakespeare
Standard Deviants School	SDS SHAKESPEARE	Module 7: Othello Basics	20 minutes	Shakespeare
Standard Deviants School	SDS SHAKESPEARE	Module 8: Othello as a Tragedy	21 minutes	Shakespeare
The Discovery Channel	UNSOLVED HISTORY	Who Killed Julius Caesar?	42-45 minutes	Shakespeare
A&E	BIOGRAPHY	Charles Dickens: A Tale of Ambition and Genius	50 minutes	Victorian
A&E	BIOGRAPHY	Oscar Wilde-Wit's End	50 minutes	Victorian
The History Channel	HISTORY'S MYSTERIES	The Hunt for Jack the Ripper	50 minutes	Victorian
The History Channel	LOST WORLDS	Jekyll and Hyde	50 minutes	Victorian
The Discovery Channel	UNSOLVED HISTORY	Jack the Ripper	42-45 minutes	Victorian

Methinks Thou Dost Protest Too Much: Shakespeare

William Shakespeare represents the Holy Grail, the apex, the supreme challenge for teachers of literature. That's why he gets an entire chapter all to himself. Anyone can teach the romantic poets and *Beowulf* and even the newest teacher can teach King Arthur, but only the most remarkable can succeed in making students understand and lo, maybe even love, Shakespeare. Of course, I'm being facetious, but there is a certain aura that surrounds Shakespeare's work, not only in the classroom, but in our society as well. This impression is that only the truly educated and cultured can appreciate and understand Shakespeare's genius.

This may explain why many students come to English class absolutely terrified of Shakespeare. They won't admit they're scared; they're more likely to claim that Shakespeare is stupid, boring, or outdated. Of course, we know that Shakespeare is none of those things, but we need to let students in on the secret. Just because Shakespeare has been around for four hundred years doesn't mean we have to teach his work in the same stale, old way it has been taught for the last half century! We must go to students instead of expecting them to come to us, and Shakespeare's continued relevance makes it extremely easy to do if we are just willing to think outside the box.

The first thing I always point out to my students is that they already like Shakespeare, they just don't know it. This comment always receives a lot of "Oh, yeah, right" type responses and eye rolls from my students until I ask them to raise their hands if they've seen the movies *She's the Man* (based on *Twelfth Night*), *10 Things I Hate About You* (based on *Taming of the Shrew*), or *O* (based on *Othello*)— all teen movie adaptations of Shakespeare. Most of them raise their hands at least once, some all three times. "Shakespeare, Shakespeare, Shakespeare," I

CHECK OUT THESE RESOURCES

- "2B? NT2B? It's the Short Version of Hamlet . . ." *Independent Online*. November, 11 2005.

- Mendez, Teresa. "Hamlet Too Hard? Try a Comic Book." *The Christian Science Monitor*. October 12, 2004.

- Milburn, Michael. "Selling Shakespeare." *English Journal*. September 2002, pp. 74-79.

- Ross, Shmuel. "Shakespeare on Film." *Information Please® Database*, © 2006 Pearson Education, Inc. *http://www.infoplease.com/spot/shakespeareonfilm*.html

- Tabers-Kwak, Linda and Timothy U. Kaufman. "Shakespeare through the Lens of a New Age." *English Journal*. September 2002, pp. 69-73.

say. They're shocked. How can it be possible that this stupid, boring, outdated guy who wore tights, talked funny, and lived four hundred years ago is responsible for movies that are able to make them laugh and cry in the 21st century? The answer is that his stories speak to what makes us human; they deal with the full range of human emotions, from greed, hatred, and jealousy to love and happiness, and experiences, like falling in love, to the death of a parent, to thoughts of suicide.

COMMANDO LIBRARIANS

Create a bulletin board titled "Think You Hate Shakespeare? Think Again!" Display images from teen movies based on Shakespearean plays, like *O, Ten Things I Hate About You, She's the Man,* and *Get Over It,* along with YA books featuring Shakespearean characters or themes (see The Shakespeare Arsenal).

Undoubtedly the biggest barrier to Shakespeare's work is the language. I'll admit that even after watching a number of plays and taking a Shakespeare class as an undergrad, there are still things I just don't get when reading and watching Shakespeare. That's why I rely on the actors to convey the meaning of the text through their body language and tone of voice. Unfortunately, I've been to a couple of performances in which only two or three of the actors actually knew what their lines meant and the rest of them delivered the lines like they were reading a list of ingredients from the side of a cereal box. If the people performing the parts don't know what the words *mean*, they can't act them. It makes for a miserable theater experience. The same is true in the classroom. So why is it, then, that one of the most popular ways to teach Shakespeare's plays is to assign parts to students and to have them read the original text of the play out loud? They're new to this Shakespeare stuff and they definitely don't know what all those old words mean, but we're willing to ask them to come in blind on their first reading of Shakespeare and get it right? That's an awful lot of pressure.

Also, don't forget that the idea is to present the basic plot of the entire play and the more plays to which we can expose students, the better. I cram *Hamlet, Othello, A Midsummer Night's Dream,* and *Macbeth* into about a month of class—this commando stuff isn't for the weak. Most students read only two or three of Shakespeare's plays in their entire high school career: *Romeo and Juliet* in ninth grade, and *Julius Caesar* and/or *Macbeth* in their junior or senior year. That's pretty heavy on the tragedy. With thirty-seven plays in all, it would be impossible to get to every one of them, but how about throwing in a comedy or two? There is nothing that warms an English teacher's heart more than hearing students laughing out loud at Shakespeare, like mine do when Bottom turns into a donkey or when the craftsmen perform "Pyramus and Thisbe" in *A Midsummer Night's Dream.*

COMMANDO LIBRARIANS

Help students become more comfortable with Shakespearean language. Create a Shakespeare vocabulary game modeled after Balderdash, a commercial definitions game. Write a word from Shakespeare on a card with the correct definition on the back. One player reads the word aloud and all players get 3 minutes to write a definition on cards with their initials and pass to the first player. All definitions are read aloud and voted on. The students with the correct definition get a point, every definition that "balderdashed" someone (the definition seemed real enough to earn a vote) earns a point. The player to the right reads the next word. Clever players will write believable definitions even if they don't know the word!

Shakespeare on Film

Shakespeare wrote plays. That means that the only people who *read* what he wrote were the actors. Everyone else *watched* his words being acted out. Not only were books expensive and not readily available to most people during his lifetime, but many of the people who attended his plays were illiterate. That didn't keep fifteen thousand people a week from going to the theater in the 1590s. I tell my students that if Shakespeare was alive today he wouldn't be a novelist, he'd be a screenwriter—not Stephen King, but Steven Spielberg— who would be writing in "regular English" and he'd be incredibly popular. I also tell them that Shakespeare is probably spinning in his grave at the thought of high school students being forced to read his plays out loud in class for a grade. In order to really hook them, I also mention that there are tons of dirty jokes in the plays, but that they've really got to be paying attention if they want to catch them. Then, I fire up the SMARTboard and we do Shakespeare the way it was meant to be done—we *watch* it.

The play I like to start with is *Hamlet*. It's my favorite of the tragedies. Who can resist a story that starts out with a guy's dad dying, the dead father's brother marrying the mourning widow, a meeting with a ghost, and half of the characters dying before the final curtain? Besides, as my students pointed out, Hamlet—dressed all in black, moping around feeling misunderstood and pondering suicide—is the quintessential goth/emo guy; the only thing missing is the black eyeliner and a few piercings. We watch Franco Zeffirelli's 1990 version starring Mel Gibson

> ### COMMANDO LIBRARIANS
>
> Provide teachers with lists of Shakespearean movies. See http://www.infoplease.com/spot/shakespeareonfilm.html for suggestions.
>
> Also, consider showing a Shakespearean film at the library to coincide with the play being taught in English class. If it's a tragedy, don't forget to have them play "Death Bingo" for prizes (see The Shakespeare Arsenal).

as Hamlet, Glenn Close as Gertrude, and Helena Bonham Carter as Ophelia. I tell the students not to stress out if they don't understand every single word or line, but to watch the actors' body language and facial expressions and to listen to the tone of voice in order to decipher the overall meaning of the words. It doesn't take long for them to figure out what's going on.

After Act I, scene v, in which Hamlet meets the ghost of his father, I stop the video and ask students to write about and discuss the following questions: Is the ghost a reliable source of information? What do you think Hamlet should do next? What would you do if you were in Hamlet's place? Ray wrote, "I think Hamlet will hire someone to kill his uncle, because I think he's too weak to do it himself." Other students suggest that Hamlet try to get Claudius drunk and trick him into admitting the murder. They all seem to realize that it would be dangerous for Hamlet to make accusations or to kill Claudius without some proof of his treachery. It is clear from their responses that they understand the plot and are gathering insight into the characters' personalities. We also have discussions about Hamlet's "madness" (be sure to explain that *mad* means crazy, not angry)—whether it's real or invented and why it would be beneficial for him to pretend to be crazy. They notice that Hamlet doesn't act crazy when he and Horatio are alone and that he's able to concoct elaborate schemes in order to try to trick Claudius, so he can't possibly be insane. We also talk about his relationship with Ophelia. Alicia asked, "Does Ophelia know that he really does love her and he's just pretending to hate her?" I said, "No." She then expressed how horrible Ophelia must feel to think that Hamlet actually hates her. I had honestly never looked at it from Ophelia's perspective before, and for the first time, in six or seven viewings of the movie, I found my eyes welling up in Act IV, scene v, when Ophelia's sanity is gone and Gertrude asks Horatio to look after her. Of course, they love the final scene, Act V, scene ii, in which pretty much every major character dies.

When we finish Zeffirelli's version, we look at some of the crucial scenes in Michael Almereyda's modernized version of *Hamlet* set in the year 2000 in New York City and starring Ethan Hawke as Hamlet, Julia Stiles as Ophelia, and Bill Murray as Polonius. I thought my students would prefer the updated version, even though it kept the Elizabethan language, but I was surprised to find that they hated it. Their reaction may have been different if we had watched this version first, but I don't think so. Their biggest problem was with the juxtaposition of the old language and the modern setting—Hamlet delivers his "To be or not to be" soliloquy in a video store. Something about that doesn't feel quite right to me, but I was surprised to hear my students say that, if they were going to keep the "old language," then the story should be set in "old times." While some of them liked the fact that Hamlet, Laertes, and Claudius all die as a result of gunshot wounds (because "it's bloodier"), they could also appreciate the fact that using a gun is not quite as personal as stabbing someone with a sword.

Despite their less-than-enthusiastic reaction to a modernized version of Shakespeare, we forged ahead with the illustrated classic version of *Othello* and Tim Blake Nelson's movie *O* (rated R for sexual content, drug use, and language, so be sure to cover the bases if you're going to use it in the classroom). They loved it. This version is completely updated, in both language and setting, which I think makes a big difference. It is also set in a boarding school and stars high profile young stars like Mekhi Phifer as Odin (Othello), Josh Hartnett as Hugo (Iago) and Julia Stiles as Desi (Desdemona). The students were really into the story and were invested in what happens to the characters. For example, even after reading the illustrated classic and knowing that the title character in a Shakespearean tragedy always dies, Jenny and Cailyn said to me near the end of the movie, "Please tell us he doesn't kill her and then kill himself." I laughed and said, "You already know how this ends." Afterward, we discuss whether this story, with its jealousy, scheming, and betrayal, seems more realistic with teens or with adults as the main characters. On this point, the students are divided, but they can and do back up their opinions with support from the "real world."

The final movie I use in its entirety is Michael Hoffman's *William Shakespeare's A Midsummer Night's Dream,* starring Michelle Pfeiffer as Titania, Stanley Tucci as Puck, Rupert Everett as Oberon, and Kevin Kline as Bottom. I love this version—it is beautifully done and has a very magical feel to it. Most of the girls like it too, but many of the boys are not big fans; it is a little too flowery for their tastes and nobody dies at the end. They do manage to follow the story line, though, with Puck's mistake turning the lovers' pairings all topsy-turvy and there are always some laughs when Hermia and Helena mud wrestle in Act III, scene ii. But, by far their favorite scene (and mine) is when the craftsmen perform for the wedding party in Act 5, scene i. This scene is loaded with slapstick comedy and silliness and the students find it hilarious. I think it's important for them to understand that Shakespeare's work was and still is laugh-out-loud funny (see the *A Midsummer Night's Dream* text set in the Shakespeare Arsenal).

Shakespeare Adaptations

Despite what I said earlier, I'm not totally against asking students to read the plays aloud or to act out scenes in class. I don't personally like to ask them to do it in the original Shakespearean language, but there are other ways to do it. I know that some people have groups of students modernize a scene and act it out; I did this when I was a student teacher. Some of the groups were terrific, creative, and funny and some were absolutely clueless. What I learned was that the bright students can update Shakespeare to modern English straight from the text, but for the majority of them it's just frustrating; if they already knew what the original text meant, they wouldn't have a problem reading it in the first place. Besides, there are some really fantastic adaptations of Shakespeare's plays presented in modern English or with a modern "translation" side-by-side with the original text. One example is Classroom Theater for Schools' Classroom Classics. Between 1986 and 1988, teacher Annabelle Howard along with five other writers updated seventeen different classics for use in schools complete with stage directions, a board game titled "Break a Leg," background information, and a discussion of themes in the play. I use Howard's adaptation from Classroom Classics to teach *Macbeth.* Another example is *No Fear Shakespeare* from *Sparknotes* (*http://nfs.sparknotes.com/*). There are currently nineteen plays available in this format, which shows the original text on the left hand side and an updated version of that text on the right-hand side.

Another way to present adaptations is with picture books or graphic novels. Beverly Birch's *Shakespeare's Tales* (*Hamlet, Antony and Cleopatra, Othello*, and *The Tempest*) and Bernard Miles' *Well-loved Tales from Shakespeare* (*The Tempest, As You Like It, Othello, The Merry Wives of Windsor*, and *Julius Caesar*) retell the stories for children. Lisl Weil's *Donkey Head* is a picture book retelling of *A Midsummer Night's Dream.* Marcia Williams' *Tales from Shakespeare* (*Hamlet, Romeo and Juliet, Macbeth, The Winter's Tale, Julius Caesar, A Midsummer Night's Dream*, and *The Tempest*) and *More Tales from Shakespeare* (*As You Like It, Twelfth Night, The Merchant of Venice, Much Ado About Nothing, Antony and Cleopatra, Richard III*, and *King Lear*) both present the plays in four to six comic book style pages.

As for graphic novels, Puffin Graphics has *William Shakespeare's Macbeth: The Graphic Novel* adapted by Arthur Byron Cover and Tony Leonard Tamai. Classical Comics, Ltd. offers the following titles as graphic novels: *Henry V, Macbeth, Richard III, Romeo and Juliet*, and *The Tempest*. Shakespeare Graphic Library has the titles *King Lear* and *Macbeth.* And for the manga fans, there's even Self-Made Hero's Manga Shakespeare series featuring *Hamlet, Romeo and Juliet, A Midsummer Night's Dream, Julius Caesar*, and *Richard III.* More graphic novel adaptations are in Illustrated Shakespeare in the Shakespeare Arsenal. As educators begin to realize the usefulness of graphic novels in the classroom, look for these series to grow in years to come.

Shakespeare in Pop Culture

If Shakespeare wasn't still relevant in the 21st century, would he be referenced on both *South Park* AND *The Simpsons*? Absolutely not. In the *South Park* episode "To Be or Not To Be, Buddy," Terrance and Phillip perform the death scene of *Hamlet.* In *The Simpsons* episode "The Regina Monologues" (watch it at *http://www.wtso.net/movie/265-The_Simpsons_1504_The_Regina_Monologues.html* [12:05-13:11]), the

Simpson family encounters Ian McKellen outside a London theater where he is playing the title role in "the Scottish play." Here's the script of the scene (from *http://www.tv.com/the-simpsons/the-regina-monologues/ episode/223791/trivia.html#quotes*):

> **Ian McKellen:** Please, take these free tickets to my play!
>
> **Homer:** What? What play?
>
> **Ian McKellen:** We thespians believe it's bad luck to mention the name of this particular play out loud.
>
> **Homer:** You mean 'MacBeth'? *(A car splashes Ian McKellen.)*
>
> **Ian McKellen:** Quiet, you plundering fool! You'll curse us all!
>
> **Homer:** What, by saying 'MacBeth'? *(An anvil falls on Ian McKellen's foot.)*
>
> **Ian McKellen:** OW! Stop saying it!
>
> **Homer:** Saying what?
>
> **Ian McKellen:** 'MACBETH'!! Oh, now I've said it. *(McKellen is hit by lightning.)*
>
> **Bart:** This is cool! 'MacBeth', 'MacBeth', 'MacBeth'. *McKellen is hit by lightning each time Bart says 'MacBeth'.)*
>
> **Marge:** Bart, stop saying 'MacBeth'! *(McKellen is hit by lightning.)*
>
> **Lisa:** Mom, you said 'MacBeth'. *(McKellen is hit by lightning.)*
>
> **Homer:** Mr. 'MacBeth', I'm really sorry. *(McKellen is hit by lightning.)*
>
> **Ian McKellen:** That's quite alright. You didn't know.

If students don't know about the curse of Macbeth, then during this scene they are wondering, "What's so funny about that?," but as I always say, "If you're smart, you can get the joke." As luck would have it, we had just finished reading about the curse when this episode originally aired. My students who had seen it on Sunday night had all managed to get the joke and were excited to tell me about it on Monday morning.

Then of course, there is the new litmus test of pop culture popularity—*YouTube*. A search on *YouTube* for "Shakespeare" netted 89,000 results. Need I say more? Shakespeare has gone viral and he's in every form imaginable— cartoon, rap, comedy, drama, musical, and TV sitcom. Here's just a sampling of just some of the results:

- "Shakespeare Sketch" featuring Hugh Laurie as William Shakespeare and comedian Rowan Atkinson as his producer trying to cut down the length of *Hamlet*, particularly the "To be or not to be" soliloquy.

- British rapper Akala's video of his song "Shakespeare" (from the album *It's Not a Rumour*), in which he claims to be a modern version of Shakespeare and says, "It's like Shakespeare with a little twist."

- The Animaniacs (Warner Brothers cartoon characters) translating Puck's final speech from *A Midsummer Night's Dream*. They also translate the graveyard scene from *Hamlet* in another skit.

- The Beatles performing the "Pyramus and Thisbe" scene from *A Midsummer Night's Dream* on a 1964 British television show.

- John Barrymore performing a soliloquy from *King Henry VI, Part III*.

- The Reduced Shakespeare Company performing a brief (2:18 to be exact), albeit incorrect, comic biography of William Shakespeare.

- David Foubert and Jay Leibowitz performing an Elizabethan version of the famous Abbot and Costello skit "Who's on First."

- The song "Brush Up Your Shakespeare" from the 2001 Broadway revival of the musical *Kiss Me Kate*.

- The wedding scene from the *Moonlighting* episode "Atomic Shakespeare" with Bruce Willis playing Petruchio and Cybill Shephard playing Katarina from *The Taming of the Shrew*.

- Marcus Sykes performing a piece titled "Shakespeare in the Ghetto, *Othello*."

As my student Mitch pointed out, Shakespeare is truly everywhere. Another example I use is Penny Marshall's movie *Renaissance Man*. We watch clips from this movie, in which Danny DeVito's character, Bill Rago, teaches "academically challenged" army recruits, the Double Ds (which stands for dumber than dogshit), to read *Hamlet*. In the course of their class, the Double Ds create a *Hamlet* rap, which outlines the plot of the play (see Hamlet Rap and Cadence in the Shakespeare Arsenal: Hamlet Rap and Cadence), and their drill sergeant, Sergeant Cass (played by Gregory Hines), turns *Hamlet* into a marching cadence:

> Hamlet's mother, she's the queen
>
> Buys it in the final scene
>
> Drinks a glass of funky wine
>
> Now she's Satan's valentine.

Shakespeare Background Information

Before starting the unit on Shakespeare, make sure to cover the requisite background material. I have created a PowerPoint about Shakespeare's life and works that can be found on "The Play's the Thing" Shakespeare Activities page of my website, *Get 'Em Reading* (*http://www.getemreading.com/shakespeare.ppt*). Shakespeare's life, world, and works are also in a plethora of books, educational videos, and Internet sources.

Books

- *Bard of Avon: The Story of William Shakespeare* by Diane Stanley and Peter Vennema (Morrow Junior Books, 1992)
- "Cursed Be He That Moves My Bones: William Shakespeare" from *Lives of the Writers (Comedies, Tragedies, and What the Neighbors Thought)* by Kathleen Krull (Harcourt Brace, 1995)

COMMANDO LIBRARIANS

A fencing demonstration is an exciting attraction for teens in the library. Search the *United States Fencing* site for a club at *http://usfencing.org/clubs/find-a-club*.

The Society for Creative Anachronism (*http://www.sca.org/*) will dress in costume and talk about life in the Middle Ages and demonstrate sword play. Search *http://www.sca.org/geography/findsca.html* to find a kingdom near you.

- *Eyewitness: Shakespeare* by Peter Chrisp (DK Publishing, 2002)
- *Look Inside: A Shakespearean Theater* by Peter Chrisp and Adam Hook (Hodder Wayland, 1998)
- *Shakespeare A to Z: The Essential Reference to His Plays, His Poems, His Life and Times* by Charles Boyce (Laurel, 1990)
- *Shakespeare, A Pictorial Biography* by F.E. Halliday (Viking, 1964)
- *Shakespeare: His Work & His World* by Michael Rosen (Candlewick, 2001)
- *Welcome to the Globe: The Story of Shakespeare's Theater* by Peter Chrisp (DK Publishing, 2000)
- *William Shakespeare & the Globe* by Aliki (HarperCollins, 1999)

Videos / Films

- A&E Biography—*William Shakespeare: Life of Drama* (A&E Home Video, 2004)
- *Shakespeare in Love* (Miramax, 1999) Scenes to show Elizabethan England, the theaters, and the final scene of *Romeo and Juliet*: Chapters 1-3 (0:00 – 7:00); Chapter 11 (32:05 – 38:05); Chapter 23 (1:24:20 – 1:26:55); and Chapter 25 (1:32:00 – 1:50:20)
- Teaching Systems *Shakespeare Module: Intro to Shakespeare* (Cerebellum Corporation, 2008)

Websites

- *Absolute Shakespeare, the Essential Resource for William Shakespeare's Plays, Sonnets, Poems, Quotes, Biography and the Legendary Globe Theatre* (http://absoluteshakespeare.com/index.htm)
- *Mr. William Shakespeare and the Internet* (http://shakespeare.palomar.edu/)
- *Shakespeare Resource Center* (http://www.bardweb.net/)
- *Stratford-Upon-Avon* (http://www.stratford-upon-avon.co.uk/wslife.htm)

Rather than bringing in every resource listed above, have students pair up in groups, give them the list, and have them create their own PowerPoint presentations based on the information they gather. Or give each group a book, video, or Internet source to use as research, and then regroup in order to create one PowerPoint presentation with the entire class—let the students decide what information is important enough to include.

Fun Shakespeare Activities (No, that shouldn't be an oxymoron)

There are lots of great activities to use with Shakespeare. I haven't "field tested" all of them, yet, but I am working on it. The one I like best came to me as we were finishing *Hamlet* a few years ago. For lack of a better term, I call it "*Hamlet* Death Bingo" (see *Hamlet* Death Bingo in the Shakespeare Arsenal), but it could really be adapted for use with any Shakespearean tragedy. The idea started one year as I was keeping a running "body count" on the board while we were watching *Hamlet*. A day before we finished the movie, I asked the students to guess how many of the main characters would be dead by the end. The next day, I gave out prizes for those who guessed correctly. Then, it occurred to me that I could create a bingo card and students could not only guess who was going to die, but they could predict the order in which it happens. If they pay attention to all of the background information, they should know that the main title character(s) will definitely die, but because this is probably their first experience with Shakespearean tragedy, they don't necessarily realize that the title character(s) will likely be the last to die. With *Hamlet*, I do let them count King Hamlet (or The Ghost), since he's already dead when the play opens. Once they get three, four, or five dead characters in a row (depending on the story and the number of characters who die) they yell out, "Bingo!" and receive a prize (don't forget to plan for possible ties). The website, *Shakespeare's Den: Smart Gifts for Intelligent People* (*http://www.shakespearesden.com/*), has all kinds of cool, relatively cheap stuff that can be used as prizes, such as "After Shakespeare Mints," "Shakespeare Insult Gum," or "Shakespeare Cachous Mint Candy." This game definitely kept my students awake and paying attention to find out which characters (if any) were going to die each day. It also helped to reinforce the names of the characters and their relationships to one another.

Another terrific idea came from my local librarian (and former English teacher), Jennifer Grudnoski. When she was teaching, she had her students duel in Shakespeare Insult Wars. The idea was for students to face off and hurl Shakespearean insults at one another with the goal being to get an opponent to laugh. The book *Thy Father Is a Gorbellied Codpiece: Create Over 1,000 of Your Own Shakespearean Insults* by Barry Craft has pages that are split in thirds so the reader can mix and match to create all kinds of hilarious insults. The website *The Elizabethan Insult and Curses of an Elizabethan Nature or, How to Cuss Like an Elizabethan Sailor* (*http://www.museangel.net/insult.html*) provides a Shakespeare Insult Generator, as well as instructions on how to use such words and phrases as "Zounds," "God's teeth," "Fie," "Tush," and "Go to." The books *Shakespeare: The Bard's Guide to Abuses and Affronts* from Running Press Miniature Editions and *Shakespeare's Insults: Educating Your Wit* by Wayne F. Hill and Cynthia J. Ottchen, both feature actual Shakespearean insults from his plays.

> ### COMMANDO LIBRARIANS
>
> Stage a Shakespearean Insult War tournament. Allow teams to sign-up ahead of time and set up tournament brackets and rules. Don't forget to offer prizes (see Shakespeare's Den *http://www.shakespearesden.com* for more ideas).

Another idea I like, but haven't tried yet, is to have my students write their own ultra-condensed version of the plays *a la* the website *Book-A-Minute Classics*. *Book-A-Minute Classics*, by RinkWorks online entertainment, offers "ultra-condensed" versions of classic works because, "English teachers have the inconsiderate habit of assigning mammoth-sized works of literature to read and then actually expecting you to do it. This wouldn't be so bad except that invariably the requisite reading is as boring as fly fishing in an empty lake. Half those books don't even have discernible plots. And let's face it—the Cliff's Notes are pretty time consuming too." Here's an example of the ultra-condensed version of *Hamlet* written by Adrian Arnold:

Hamlet:

Whine whine whine . . . To be or not to be . . . I'm dead.

THE END

Here is David J. Parker and Samuel Stoddard's version of *A Midsummer Night's Dream*:

Hermia, Lysander, Demetrius, and Helena:

We're all in love with each other the wrong way around.

(Everyone goes into the woods. They have wacky experiences, pair off correctly, and live happily ever after.)

THE END

Teens can have a lot of fun trying to be as succinct as possible, while still demonstrating that they have a grasp of the story. In addition to the plays listed above, there are also versions of *Julius Caesar*, *King Lear*, *Othello*, *Richard III*, *Romeo and Juliet*, *The Taming of the Shrew*, and *The Tempest* (as well as many other classic works by other authors).

SCAVENGER HUNT

Use Shakespearean titles (or other classic titles) to create a Book-A-Minute Scavenger Hunt. Give students a list of summaries from the website *Book-A-Minute Classics* (*http://www.rinkworks.com/bookaminute/classics.shtml*), remove pertinent details (such as character names) and see who can correctly identify the most titles in the fastest amount of time.

Every class has students who are hams and who would love to get up and act out a death scene or a sword fight. Give them the chance, but don't forget that for every one who isn't afraid to do that, there are three or four who are terrified of getting up in front of their peers. Give students the option to do something else a little less public. If students are acting out scenes, don't make everybody have a speaking part. Let the shy, but smart, students write the script.

COMMANDO LIBRARIANS

How to Perform Shakespeare

(Courtesy of Diane Tuccillo, Poudre River Public Library District, Fort Collins, CO)

"How to Perform Shakespeare" was a program offered when I worked at the City of Mesa Library (Mesa, AZ). It was done in partnership with the teen theater troupe active at the Mesa Arts Center (*http://www.mesaartscenter.com/*).

The library offered the program and promoted it to teachers so they could offer extra credit (and we did get good turnouts for these sessions). We used pre-made extra credit slips we would fill out and sign for the students to give to their teachers whenever they attended a program that required proof they were there.

The East Valley Children's Theater (*http://www.evct.org/_New/audition.html*) and the Southwest Shakespeare Company (*http://www.swshakespeare.org/*) are active theater groups in this area.

Find contact information for your local Shakespeare Company at "Shakespeare Festivals and Theatres," *Shakespeare Fellowship* (*http://www.shakespearefellowship.org/linksfestivals.htm*).

Artistic students can design and make costumes or scenery. Your students with good technical skills can create a PowerPoint presentation or a video interpretation of the play. The musical students can develop a soundtrack of songs that share the themes of the play or that represent each character's personality and/or development throughout the play.

If there is time, or if there is sustained silent reading time, try choosing three or four of the young adult novels featuring Shakespearean characters or themes (see Shakespearean Characters and Themes in Young Adult Literature in the Shakespeare Arsenal) for students to read in literature circles. If possible, select a variety of books and allow students to choose the one they'd like to read. In their groups they can write about or discuss how the novels are related to the plays they have read as a class. Then each group can share their reactions with the entire class or complete a project (see Final Projects).

The Internet is a great place to look for fun activities. If there is a SMARTboard in the classroom (or other technology that allows projecting things from the computer for the entire class), go to the following sites or assign the students to visit them in order to gain information.

> **COMMANDO LIBRARIANS**
>
> Offer to visit language arts classes to booktalk YA books featuring Shakespearean characters or themes. See the list Shakespearean Characters and Themes in Young Adult Literature in The Shakespeare Arsenal.

- To research the curse surrounding *Macbeth*, go to *The Straight Dope* (*http://www.straightdope.com/mailbag/mmacbeth.html*). Also read "The Curse of *Macbeth*: Is there an evil spell on this ill-starred play?" by Dina Tritsch for *Showbill*, April 1984. (*http://pretallez.com/onstage/theatre/broadway/macbeth/macbeth_curse.html*)

- To watch clips of the one man show performed by Rick Miller doing all of the characters from *Macbeth* in voices from *The Simpsons*, go to *MacHomer.* (*http://www.machomer.com*)

- For legends and ballads about the fairy Puck, go to *Puck—That Shrewd and Knavish Sprite Called Robin Goodfellow.* (*http://www.boldoutlaw.com/puckrobin/puck.html*)

- To view paintings based on *A Midsummer Night's Dream*, go to *A Midsummer Night's Dream Paintings.* (*http://www.english.emory.edu/classes/Shakespeare_Illustrated/MidsummerPaintings.html*)

- To view a number of links about *Hamlet*, go to *William Shakespeare's Hamlet.* (*http://classroom.jc-schools.net/hendersonn/hamlet.html*)

- To find a list of movies based on Shakespeare, go to *Shakespeare on Film.* (*http://www.infoplease.com/spot/shakespeareonfilm.html*)

- For crazy and interesting short videos, go to the Shakespeare playlist on my *YouTube* channel. (*http://www.youtube.com/user/daridoo/videos*)

References

10 Things I Hate About You. Touchstone Home Video: Buena Vista Home Entertainment, 1999.

A&E Biography—William Shakespeare: Life of Drama. VHS. A&E Home Video, 1997.

Classical Comics, Ltd. Towcester, Classical Comics, Limited

———. *Henry V* by William Shakespeare (2007)

———. *Macbeth* by William Shakespeare (2008)

———. *Richard III* by William Shakespeare (2009)

———. *Romeo and Juliet* by William Shakespeare (2009)

———. *The Tempest* by William Shakespeare (2009)

Cover, Arthur Byron and Tony Leonard Tamai. *William Shakespeare's Macbeth.* Puffin Books, 2005.

Craft, Barry. *Thy Father Is a Gorbellied Codpiece: Create Over 1,000 of Your Own Shakespearean Insults.* Smithmark Publishers, 1998.

Hamlet. Warner Home Video, 1991.

Hamlet. Miramax Home Entertainment, 2001.

Hill, Wayne F., and Cynthia J. Ottchen. *Shakespeare's Insults: Educating Your Wit.* Three Rivers Press, 1995.

Howard, Annabelle. *Classroom Classics Macbeth.* NY: Classic Theatre for Schools, 1986.

Manga Shakespeare. SelfMadeHero.

———. *As You like It* (2008)

———. *Hamlet* (2007)

———. *Julius Caesar* (2008)

———. *Macbeth* (2008)

———. *A Midsummer Night's Dream* (2008)

———. *Othello* (2008)

———. *Richard III* (2007)

———. *Romeo and Juliet* (2007)

———. *The Tempest* (2007)

"No Fear Shakespeare." *Sparknotes. http://www.nfs.sparknotes.com*

O. Lions Gate Home Entertainment, 2001.

"Othello." *Lake Illustrated Classics.* Lake Education, 1980.

"The Regina Monologues." *The Simpsons*. Aired: November, 16, 2003.

Renaissance Man. Touchstone, 1994.

SDS Shakespeare Module: Intro to Shakespeare. VHS. Cerebellum, 2003.

Shakespeare in Love. Miramax Home Entertainment: Beuna Vista Home Entertainment, 1999.

Shakespeare Graphic Library. Black Dog and Leventhal Publishers, Inc.

————. *King Lear* (1984)

————. *Macbeth* (1982)

Shakespeare's Tales by Beverley Birch. Hodder Children's Books, 2002.

Shakespeare: The Bard's Guide to Abuses and Affronts. Running Press Miniature Editions, 2001.

She's the Man. DreamWorks Pictures and Lakeshore Entertainment, 2006.

"To Be or Not To Be Buddy?." *South Park*. Aired: July, 17, 2001.

Weil, Lisl. *Donkey Head.* Atheneum, 1977.

Well-loved Tales from Shakespeare by Bernard Miles. Rand McNally, 1986.

William Shakespeare's A Midsummer Night's Dream. 20th Century Fox Home Entertainment, 1999.

Williams, Marcia. *More Tales from Shakespeare.* Candlewick Press, 2005.

————. *Tales from Shakespeare.* Candlewick Press, 1998.

The Shakespeare Arsenal

HAMLET WRITING

1. If you were Hamlet, what would you do next? Be specific.

2. Do you think that the Ghost is a reliable source of information? Explain.

3. Predict what you think Hamlet will do next.

From *Commando Classics: A Field Manual for Helping Teens Understand (and Maybe Even Enjoy) Classic Literature*
by Daria Plumb. Bowie, MD: VOYA Press, an imprint of E L Kurdyla Publishing, LLC. Copyright 2012

A MIDSUMMER NIGHT'S DREAM TEXT SET

NOVELS

- *Celtic Night: A Fifteen Year Old Girl's Modern Retelling of Shakespeare's A Midsummer Night's Dream* by Bridget O'Dwyer. Fresh Writers Group, 2006.
- *Mid-Semester Night's Dream* by Margaret Meacham. Holiday House, 2004.
- *This Must be Love* by Tui T. Sutherland. HarperCollins, 2004.
- *A Winter Night's Dream* by Andrew Matthews. Delacorte Books for Young Readers, 2004.

ILLUSTRATED BOOKS

- *Donkey Head* by Lisl Weil. Atheneum, 1977.
- *A Midsummer Night's Dream* by Philip Page and Marilyn Petit. Barron's Educational Series, 2005.
- *A Midsummer Night's Dream for Kids* by Lois Burdett. Firefly Books, 1997.
- *Shakespeare's Stories: Comedies* by Beverley Birch. P. Bedrick Books, 1988.
- *Tales from Shakespeare* by Marcia Williams. Candlewick Press, 1998.
- *William Shakespeare & the Globe* by Aliki. HarperCollins, 1999.

FILMS / VIDEOS

- *Get Over It*. Miramax Home Entertainment, 2001.
- *A Midsummer Night's Dream*. Miramax Home Entertainment, 2000.
- *A Midsummer Night's Dream*. MGM, 1998.
- *A Midsummer Night's Dream*. Royal Shakespeare Company. Water Bearer Films, 1968.
- *Mr. Magoo's Literary Classics: Cyrano de Bergerac/A Midsummer Night's Dream*. Paramount Home Video, 1991.
- *Standard Deviants Shakespeare Module: Intro to Shakespeare*. Cerebellum Corp., 2003.
- *William Shakespeare's A Midsummer Night's Dream*. 20th Century Fox Home Entertainment, 1999.

GRAPHIC NOVELS

- *The Sandman: Dream Country* by Neil Gaiman. DC Comics, 1991.

ARTWORK

- MSND Paintings. *http://www.english.emory.edu/classes/Shakespeare_Illustrated/Midsummer Paintings.html*
- *Pyramus and Thisbe* by Hans Balding
- *Thisbe, or The Listener* by John William Waterhouse

POEMS

- "The Fairy Kingdom" and "Rushen Glen" by Frances Jenkins Olcott from *Wonder Tales from Fairy Isles: England, Cornwall, Wales, Scotland, Man and Ireland*. Longmans, Green and Co., 1929.

A MIDSUMMER NIGHT'S DREAM TEXT SET (Cont.)

- "The Mad Merry Pranks of Robin Goodfellow" (early 17th c. broadside – thought to be the work of Ben Jonson).
- "Puck of Pook's Hill" by Rudyard Kipling
- "Robin Goodfellow" (ancient ballad)

TV SHOWS

- *BBC Television Shakespeare A Midsummer Night's Dream*. BBC, 1981.
- *Shakespeare: The Animated Tales*. Ambrose Video Production, 2004.
- *Shakespeare Retold*. BBC Warner, 2007.

INTERNET SOURCES

- *Absolute Shakespeare. http://absoluteshakespeare.com/index.htm*
- "A Midsummer Night's Dream." *Book-A-Minute Classics. http://www.rinkworks.com/bookaminute/b/shakespeare.midsummer.shtml*
- *Mr. William Shakespeare and the Internet. http://shakespeare.palomar.edu/*
- *Puck – That Shrewd and Knavish Sprite Called Robin Goodfellow. http://www.boldoutlaw.com/puckrobin/puck.html*
- *Shakespeare Resource Center. http://www.bardweb.net/*
- *Stratford-Upon-Avon. http:// www.stratford-upon-avon.co.uk/wslife.htm*

SONGS

- *The Fairy-Queen* (semi-opera) by Henry Purcell.
- Felix Mendelssohn's *A Midsummer Night's Dream* London Symphony Orchestra, Andre Previn, conductor.
- *A Midsummer Night's Dream* (opera) by Benjamin Britten.
- *William Shakespeare's A Midsummer Night's Dream: Original Motion Picture Soundtrack* by Renee Fleming and Simon Boswell.

BIOGRAPHIES

- *A & E Biography: William Shakespeare: Life of Drama*. A&E Home Video, 1997.
- "Cursed Be He That Moves My Bones: William Shakespeare" from *Lives of the Writers (Comedies, Tragedies, and What the Neighbors Thought)* by Kathleen Krull. Harcourt Brace, 1994.
- *Frontline: Much Ado About Something*. PBS Home Video, 2008.
- *In Search of Shakespeare*. PBS Home Video, 2004.
- *Shakespeare: His Work & His World* by Michael Rosen. Candlewick Press, 2001.
- *Shakespeare, A Pictorial Biography* by F.E. Halliday. Viking, 1964.
- *Teaching Systems Shakespeare Module 1: Intro to Shakespeare*. Cerebellum Corporation, 2008.
- *William Shakespeare* by Dorothy Turner. Bookwright Press, 1985.

From *Commando Classics: A Field Manual for Helping Teens Understand (and Maybe Even Enjoy) Classic Literature* by Daria Plumb. Bowie, MD: VOYA Press, an imprint of E L Kurdyla Publishing, LLC. Copyright 2012

A MIDSUMMER NIGHT'S DREAM TEXT SET (*Cont.*)

FOLKLORE AND LEGENDS

- *Arthur Spiderwick's Field Guide to the Fantastical World Around You* by Tony DiTerlizzi and Holly Black. Simon and Schuster Children's Publishing, 2005.
- *Faeries* by Brian Froud and Alan Lee. Abrams, 1978.
- *Fairy Island: An Enchanted Tour of the Homes of the Little Folk* by Laura Martin and Cameron Martin. Black Dog and Leventhal Publishers, 2005.
- *Folklore of Shakespeare* by T. F. Thiselton Dyer. Kessinger Publishing, 2004.
- *The Great Encyclopedia of Faeries* by Pierre Dubois, Claudine Sabatier, and Roland Sabatier. Simon and Schuster, 2000.

HISTORIES

- *A & E Biography Queen Elizabeth: The Reluctant Monarch*. A&E, 2009.
- *The History Channel's In Search of History: England's Theatres of Blood*. A&E Television Networks, 2009.

MISCELLANEOUS

- *Essential Shakespeare Handbook* by Leslie Downer. DK Publishing, 2004.
- *Eyewitness: Shakespeare* by Peter Chrisp. DK Publishing, 2002.
- *What Would Shakespeare Do?: Personal Advice from the Bard* by Jess Winfield. Seastone, 2000.
- *Look Inside: A Shakespearean Theater* by Peter Chrisp and Adam Hook. Raintree, 2000.
- *No Fear Shakespeare: A Midsummer Night's Dream* from Sparknotes.com. *http://nfs.sparknotes.com/msnd/*
- *Shakespeare A to Z: The Essential Reference to His Plays, His Poems, His Life and Times* by Charles Boyce. Delta, 1991.
- *Shakespeare for Kids: His Life and Times: 21 Activities* by Colleen Aagesen. Chicago Review Press, 1999.
- *Shakespeare's Den: Smart Gifts for Intelligent People*. *http://www.shakespearesden.com/*
- *Thy Father Is a Gorbellied Codpiece: Create Over 1,000 of Your Own Shakespearean Insults* by Barry Craft. Smithmark Publishers, 1998.
- *Welcome to the Globe: The Story of Shakespeare's Theater* by Peter Chrisp. DK Children, 2000.
- *The Young Person's Guide to Shakespeare: With Performances on CD by the Royal Shakespeare Company* by Anita Ganeri. Harcourt Brace, 1999.

SHORT STORIES

- *The Faery Reel Stories from the Faery Realm* edited by Eileen Datlow and Terri Windling. Penguin, 2004.

ILLUSTRATED SHAKESPEARE

SHAKESPEARE'S LIFE AND WORLD

- *Bard of Avon: The Story of William Shakespeare* by Diane Stanley and Peter Vennema. Morrow Junior Books, 1992.
- "Cursed Be He That Moves My Bones: William Shakespeare" from *Lives of the Writers (Comedies, Tragedies, and What the Neighbors Thought)* by Kathleen Krull. (Harcourt Brace & Co., 1994.
- *Essential Shakespeare Handbook* by Leslie Downer. DK Publishing, 2004.
- *Eyewitness: Shakespeare* by Peter Chrisp. DK Publishing, 2002.
- *Shakespeare A to Z: The Essential Reference to His Plays, His Poems, His Life and Times* by Charles Boyce. Delta, 1991.
- *Shakespeare: His Work & His World* by Michael Rosen. Candlewick Press, 2001.
- *William Shakespeare* by Dorothy Turner. Bookwright Press, 1985.

THE GLOBE THEATER

- *Look Inside: A Shakespearean Theater* by Peter Chrisp and Adam Hook. Raintree, 2000.
- *Shakespeare's Globe: An Interactive Pop-Up Theater* by Toby Forward. Candlewick, 2005.
- *Shakespeare's Theater* by Jacqueline Morley. P. Bedrick Books, 1994.
- *Welcome to the Globe: The Story of Shakespeare's Theater* by Peter Chrisp. DK Children, 2000.
- *William Shakespeare & the Globe* by Aliki. HarperCollins, 1999.

RETELLINGS FOR CHILDREN

- *All the World's a Stage* by Rebecca Piatt Davidson. Greenwillow Books/HarperCollins, 2003.
- *Donkey Head* by Lisl Weil. Atheneum, 1977.
- *More Tales from Shakespeare* by Marcia Williams. Candlewick Press, 2005.
- Picture This! Shakespeare Series. Barron's Educational Series.
    - *Hamlet* by Christina Lacie
    - *Julius Caesar* by Christina Lacie. 2006.
    - *Macbeth* by Philip Page and Marilyn Petit. 2005.
    - *A Midsummer Night's Dream* by Philip Page and Marilyn Petit. 2005.
    - *Romeo and Juliet* by Philip Page and Marilyn Petit. 2005.
    - *Twelfth Night* by Philip Page and Marilyn Petit. 2005.
- Shakespeare Can Be Fun Series by Lois Burdett. Firefly Books.
    - *A Child's Portrait of Shakespeare.* 1995.
    - *Hamlet for Kids.* 2000.
    - *MacBeth for Kids.* 1996.
    - *A Midsummer Night's Dream for Kids.* 1997.
    - *Much Ado About Nothing for Kids.* 2002.

From *Commando Classics: A Field Manual for Helping Teens Shakespearean (and Maybe Even Enjoy) Classic Literature* by Daria Plumb. Bowie, MD: VOYA Press, an imprint of E L Kurdyla Publishing, LLC. Copyright 2012

- *Romeo and Juliet for Kids*. 1998.
- *The Tempest for Kids*. 1999.
- *Twelfth Night for Kids*. 1994.
- *Shakespeare's Stories: Comedies* by Beverley Birch. P. Bedrick Books, 1988.
- *Shakespeare's Stories: Histories* by Beverley Birch. P. Bedrick Books, 1988.
- *Shakespeare's Stories: Tragedies* by Beverley Birch. P. Bedrick Books, 1988.
- *Shakespeare's Tales* by Beverley Birch. Hodder Children's Books, 2002.
- *Tales from Shakespeare* by Marcia Williams. Candlewick Press, 1998.
- *Well-loved Tales from Shakespeare* by Bernard Miles. Rand McNally, 1986.

MISCELLANEOUS

- *The Boy, the Bear, the Baron, the Bard* by Gregory Rogers. Roaring Brook Press, 2004.
- *Midsummer Knight* by Gregory Rogers. Roaring Brook Press, 2007.
- *Shakespeare for Kids: His Life and Times: 21 Activities* by Colleen Aagesen. Chicago Review Press, 1999.
- *A Treasury of Shakespeare's Verse* by Gina Pollinger. Kingfisher, 2000.
- *What Would Shakespeare Do?: Personal Advice from the Bard* by Jess Winfield. Seastone, 2000.

GRAPHIC NOVELS

- Cartoon Shakespeare. Can of Worms Enterprises. *http://www.graphicshakespeare.com*
  - *Othello*
  - *Twelfth Night*
  - *King Lear*
  - *Macbeth*
- Classical Comics, Ltd.. Classical Comics, Limited. *http//www.classicalcomics.com*
  - *Henry V* by William Shakespeare. 2007.
  - *Macbeth* by William Shakespeare. 2008.
  - *Richard III* by William Shakespeare. 2009.
  - *Romeo and Juliet* by William Shakespeare. 2009.
  - *The Tempest* by William Shakespeare. 2009.
- Graphic Shakespeare by Graphic Planet
  - *Hamlet* by Rebecca Dunn and Ben Dunn. 2008.
  - *King Lear* by Brian Farrens and Chris Allen. 2008.
  - *Macbeth* by Joeming Dunn and David Hutchison. 2008.
  - *A Midsummer Night's Dream* by Daniel Conner and Rod Espinoza. 2008.
  - *Othello* by Vincent Goodwin and Chris Allen. 2008.
  - *Romeo and Juliet* by Joeming Dunn and Rod Espinosa. 2008.
  - *The Tempest* by Daniel Conner and Cynthia Martin. 2008.
  - *Twelfth Night* by Vincent Goodwin and Cynthia Martin. 2008.

From *Commando Classics: A Field Manual for Helping Teens Understand (and Maybe Even Enjoy) Classic Literature* by Daria Plumb. Bowie, MD: VOYA Press, an imprint of E L Kurdyla Publishing, LLC. Copyright 2012

ILLUSTRATED SHAKESPEARE (*Cont.*)

- Lake Illustrated Classics: Shakespeare Collection. Lake Education, 1994.
  - *As You Like It*
  - *Hamlet*
  - *Julius Caesar*
  - *Macbeth*
  - *The Merchant of Venice*
  - *A Midsummer Night's Dream*
  - *Othello*
  - *Romeo and Juliet*
  - *The Taming of the Shrew*
  - *The Tempest*
  - *Twelfth Night*
- Manga Shakespeare. SelfMadeHero. *http://www.mangashakespeare.com*
  - *As You Like It*. 2008.
  - *Hamlet*. 2007.
  - *Julius Caesar*. 2008.
  - *Macbeth*. 2008.
  - *A Midsummer Night's Dream*. 2008.
  - *Othello*. 2008.
  - *Richard III*. 2007.
  - *Romeo and Juliet*. 2007.
  - *The Tempest*. 2007.
- Shakespeare Graphic Library. Black Dog and Leventhal Publishers, Inc..
  - *King Lear*. 1984.
  - *Macbeth*. 1982.
- *William Shakespeare's Macbeth* by Arthur Byron Cover and Tony Leonard Tamai. Puffin Books, 2005.

TEACHER RESOURCES

- *Instant Shakespeare: A Proven Technique for Actors, Directors, and Teachers* by Louis Fantasia. Ivan R. Dee, 2003.
- *Irresistible Shakespeare* by Carol Rawlings Miller. Scholastic Professional Books, 2001.
- *Practical Approaches to Teaching Shakespeare* by Peter Reynolds. Oxford School Shakespeare, 1992.
- *Shakespeare: To Teach or Not to Teach: Teaching Shakespeare Made Fun from Elementary to High School* by Cass Foster and Lynn G. Johnson. Five Star Publications, 1992.
- *Teaching Shakespeare: A Handbook for Teachers* by Rex Gibson. Cambridge University Press, 1998.

From *Commando Classics: A Field Manual for Helping Teens Understand (and Maybe Even Enjoy) Classic Literature* by Daria Plumb. Bowie, MD: VOYA Press, an imprint of E L Kurdyla Publishing, LLC. Copyright 2012

HAMLET RAP AND CADENCE

From *Renaissance Man*

[All] They gotta know, they gotta know,
We gotta flow, they gotta know, they gotta know, ho
They gotta know, they gotta know,
We gotta flow, they gotta know, they gotta know, ho
They gotta know, they gotta know,
We gotta flow, they gotta know, they gotta know, ho
They gotta know, they gotta know,
We gotta flow, they gotta know, they gotta know, ho
To be or not to be
The Double D MCs are letting it be
Let be, to be or not to be

[Montgomery] MC Hobbs on the job
Ripping rhymes like the mob

[Hobbs] The sh*t's iller than Cape Fear, the Shakespeare saga
Started with this Prince kid, his moms and his father
His pops got took for his props undercover by his brother, man [damn]
Now his brother's king lover, man
Actin' real trite he took his brother's life
For his green and to sex up his queen
But the prince, he ain't goin' for it, he's out for revenge
His pop's ghost comes and then

[Montgomery] Dammit, Hamlet, those are your ends!
So just chill and cool for now
Play the fool until you take him out
Cuz all eyes is on you, so the one way or another,
It's a kamikaze style, or do it undercover
But either way, ya gotta say-ah, so what the hey-ah
Strap on your black and get set for the payback

[Benitez] Ain't got no gat, but he's sportin' a tool
Strap on the sword for the Laertes duel

Renaissance Man. Dir. Penny Marshall. Perf. Danny DeVito, Gregory Hines. Touchstone, 1994.

[Leroy] Cuz he's tryin' to blame Hamlet for his sister's death
But she took her own last breath, she ain't got shhh left

[Melvin] Never heard yet
A more absurd set
Of circumstances
Murder and romances so

[Montgomery] Incest, we had to put it to rest
We had time to manifest, he stuck the dagger in the king's
chest

[All] To be or not to be
The Double D MCs is letting it be
Let be, To be or not to be
The Double D MCs is letting it be
Let be, To be or not to be [Ophelia]
The Double D MCs is letting it be
Let be, To be or not to be
The Double D MCs is letting it be
Go Hamlet, go Hamlet, go Hamlet, go Hamlet.

HAMLET CADENCE

From *Renaissance Man*

Hamlet's momma she's the queen
Buys it in the final scene
Drinks a glass of funky wine
Now she Satan's valentine

Renaissance Man. Dir. Penny Marshall. Perf. Danny DeVito, Gregory Hines. Touchstone, 1994.

From *Commando Classics: A Field Manual for Helping Teens Understand (and Maybe Even Enjoy) Classic Literature*
by Daria Plumb. Bowie, MD: VOYA Press, an imprint of E L Kurdyla Publishing, LLC. Copyright 2012

HAMLET DEATH BINGO

Fill in each square with the name of a character from *Hamlet*. You may use King Hamlet, even though he is already dead when the play begins. **HINT:** If you've been paying attention, you should be able to guarantee the death of at least one other character. As they die off, cross them off with an "X." The first person (or people) to get 5 in a row wins.

From *Commando Classics: A Field Manual for Helping Teens Understand (and Maybe Even Enjoy) Classic Literature* by Daria Plumb. Bowie, MD: VOYA Press, an imprint of E L Kurdyla Publishing, LLC. Copyright 2012

SHAKESPEARE WRITING

So far we have studied three of Shakespeare's tragedies (*Hamlet*, *Macbeth*, and *Othello*) and four of his sonnets. We have also studied the Globe Theater. Use any information from the movies, reading, movie clips, etc. to answer the following questions.

1. Tell me two things (facts, not opinions) that you have learned about Shakespeare's life and/ or his plays:

    1)

    2)

2. Is your opinion of Shakespeare's work (plays and/or poems) now the same or different from your opinion of his work before we started studying it? **Explain**.

    _____

    _____

    _____

    _____

    _____

    _____

    _____

3. Try to imagine Shakespeare's plays written in "regular" English and without the tights. Do you think Shakespeare would be a popular writer/producer today? Do you think his themes and plots are still relevant today? Explain and **give one example** to support your opinion.

    _____

    _____

    _____

    _____

    _____

    _____

    _____

From *Commando Classics: A Field Manual for Helping Teens Understand (and Maybe Even Enjoy) Classic Literature* by Daria Plumb. Bowie, MD: VOYA Press, an imprint of E L Kurdyla Publishing, LLC. Copyright 2012

SHAKESPEAREAN CHARACTERS AND THEMES
IN YOUNG ADULT LITERATURE

SHAKESPEARE'S LIFE AND WORLD

- *King of Shadows* by Susan Cooper. Margaret K. McElderberry Books, 1999.
- *Loving Will Shakespeare* by Carolyn Meyer. Harcourt, 2006.
- *My Father Had a Daughter: Judith Shakespeare's Tale* by Grace Tiffany. Berkley, 2003.
- *Shakespeare and Me* by Cynthia Mercati. Perfection Learning Corp., 2001.
- *Shakespeare's Scribe* by Gary Blackwood. Dutton Juvenile, 2000.
- *Shakespeare's Spy* by Gary Blackwood. Dutton Children's Books, 2003.
- *The Shakespeare Stealer* by Gary Blackwood. Dutton Children's Books, 1998.
- *Swan Town: The Secret Journal of Susanna Shakespeare* by Michael J. Ortiz. HarperCollins, 2006.
- *The Two Loves of Will Shakespeare* by Laurie Lawlor. Holiday House, 2006.
- *Will* by Grace Tiffany. Penguin Putnam, 2005.

MISCELLANEOUS

- *Shakespeare Bats Clean-Up* by Ron Koertge. Candlewick, 2003.
- *The Wednesday Wars* by Gary Schmidt. Clarion Books, 2007.

AS YOU LIKE IT

- *The Flip Side* by Andrew Matthews. Delacorte Press, 2003.

HAMLET

- *Dating Hamlet* by Lisa Fiedler. Henry Holt, 2002.
- *The Dead Father's Club* by Matt Haig. Viking Adult, 2007.
- *Joker* by Ranulfo. HarperTeen, 2006.
- *Ophelia: A Novel* by Lisa Klein. Bloomsbury USA Children's Books, 2006.
- *Something Rotten: A Horatio Wilkes Mystery* by Alan Gratz. Dial, 2007.
- *Thursday Next in Something Rotten* by Jasper Fforde. Penguin, 2004.

MACBETH

- *Enter Three Witches* by Caroline Cooney. Scholastic Press, 2007.
- *Enter Three Witches* by Kate Gilmore. Houghton Mifflin, 1990.
- *Macbeth: A Retelling* by Adam McKeown. Sterling Publishing, 2004.

A MIDSUMMER NIGHT'S DREAM

- *As Puck Would Have It: An Original Novel* by Paul Ruditis. Simon Spotlight Entertainment, 2006.

- *Celtic Night : A Fifteen Year Old Girl's Modern Retelling of Shakespeare's A Midsummer Night's Dream* by Bridget O'Dwyer. Fresh Writers Group, 2006.
- *Mid-Semester Night's Dream* by Margaret Meacham. Holiday House, 2004.
- *This Must Be Love* by Tui T. Sutherland. HarperCollins, 2004.
- *A Winter Night's Dream* by Andrew Matthews. Delacorte Books for Young Readers, 2004.

OTHELLO

- *Othello: A Novel* by Julius Lester. Scholastic, 1995.

ROMEO AND JULIET

- *Romeo and Juliet Together (and Alive!) at Last* by Avi. Orchard Books, 1987.
- *Romeo's Ex: Rosaline's Story* by Lisa Fiedler. Henry Holt and Co., 2006.
- *Romiette & Julio* by Sharon Draper. Atheneum Books for Young Readers, 1999.

THE TAMING OF THE SHREW

- *Pretty Things* by Sara Manning. Dutton Books, 2005.

THE TEMPEST

- *Ariel* by Grace Tiffany. HarperCollins, 2005.
- *Shakespeare's Secret* by Elise Broach. Henry Holt, 2005.
- *The Sweet, Terrible, Glorious Year I Truly, Completely Lost It* by Lisa Shanahan. Delacorte, 2007.
- *Undine* by Penni Russon. HarperTeen, 2006.

ELIZABETHAN ENGLAND

- *The Black Canary* by Jane Louise Curry. Margaret K. McElderberry Books, 2005.
- *Raleigh's Page* by Alan Armstrong. Random House, 2007.
- *The Secret of the Rose* by Sarah L. Thomson. Greenwillow Books, 2006.
- *Ship of Fire* by Michael Cadnum. Penguin, 2003.

For Graphic Novels, see Illustrated Shakespeare List.

From *Commando Classics: A Field Manual for Helping Teens Understand (and Maybe Even Enjoy) Classic Literature* by Daria Plumb. Bowie, MD: VOYA Press, an imprint of E L Kurdyla Publishing, LLC. Copyright 2012

Final Projects

These projects are designed to show that you have gained a thorough understanding of the novel (its characters, plots, and themes) without necessarily writing a book report or taking a test.

* * *

Your assignment is to complete a combination of the following projects (your choice) that will total 100 points.

The point values are listed.

* * *

*IF YOU HAVE AN IDEA FOR AN ASSIGNMENT THAT IS NOT INCLUDED ON THIS LIST, THEN **WRITE** THE IDEA AND TURN IT IN TO ME. YOUR PROPOSAL MUST BE **IN WRITING** IN ORDER TO BE CONSIDERED. I WILL DECIDE THE POINT VALUE.*

* * *

100 Point Assignments—these demonstrate a thorough knowledge of the entire novel.

- Create a word and/or picture collage representing the entire novel (main characters, major events, turning point, etc.). This must be done on a large sheet of drawing paper or poster board (8" x 11" paper is too small). This must be accompanied by a one page written explanation of why you selected the certain words and/or pictures. This must be neat and aesthetically pleasing.

- Create a newspaper about the entire novel that includes such things as classified ads, obituaries, news items, sports articles, cartoons, etc.

- Create a board game in which the game pieces represent the characters and the board shows the plot sequence/main events of the entire novel. This must include rules and be "playable." You might want to consider games like Life, Monopoly, Clue, or Taboo.

- Re-write the entire novel in comic book form. You should remain true to any physical or setting descriptions.

- Keep a diary from a main character's point of view (your gender doesn't matter). This should include her/his thoughts and feelings, actions, and significant events from the entire novel.

- Take an open book essay test about the entire novel (this option may only be available for teacher-selected texts).

- Write a series of letters that two main characters in the novel might have written to one another during the course of the entire novel.

- Make puppets, finger puppets, or masks representing the main characters of the novel. Then, act out the plot of the entire novel for the class.

- Do several pieces of art about the novel. Be sure to include the major themes and characters. These should be accompanied by written pieces explaining them.

- Create a PowerPoint presentation/book report. This should include a minimum of fifteen slides, which have clipart, animations, and sounds. The following information must be included: title, author, main characters, minor characters, protagonist(s), antagonist(s), setting, three major events, conflict, and resolution. You will present the presentation to the class.

50 Point Assignments

- Using the alphabet (you may skip two letters), write a word for each letter (noun, verb, adverb, or adjective) that is relevant to the book. Write at least one sentence that tells why this word is significant.

- Select (from an outside source) or write ten poems and/or songs that you feel say something about the theme, mood, characters, or settings of the novel. Explain why you selected or wrote each poem/song.

- Write a new ending for the story, a new adventure for the main character, or the beginning of a sequel. The tone and format should be the same as the original novel. If you get rid of old characters, then tell what happened to them; if you invent new characters, then describe them. This should be at least two chapters long.

- Compile a list of five other novels that have similar themes. This must include a brief summary of each book (you may find these online, in magazines or book catalogs, at the library, etc.) and the name of the author. The summaries do not need to be written by you, but you must tell why you think the books are similar. It is not necessary that you read the five books, but you must be familiar with the basic storyline of each.

- If the novel you read was made into a movie, then watch the movie. Write a two page essay comparing and contrasting the book and the movie. How are they different? Which one did you like best?

- Explain how you'd make your book into a movie. Write up a cast of characters and tell who would play each one. Where would you film it? What parts might you change/omit? Why? Be sure to explain all of your choices.

25 Point Assignments—these demonstrate a knowledge of certain events or characters from the novel.

- Make paper dolls of the main character(s). Research the types of clothing worn during the era (if the story is set in a different time period) or check for clothing descriptions in the book and make a wardrobe for them. The dolls and their garments should be true to the physical descriptions given in the book.

- Make a diorama in which you show the scene that you feel is the most significant in the story. This must be accompanied by one written page explaining why you selected this scene.

- Select a character from the book. Then select ten quotations from the text that you feel reveals the character's personality. You must explain what each quotation/sentence tells you about the character. You must also tell which page the quotation/sentence came from.

- Select (from an outside source) or write five poems or songs that you feel one of the characters from your novel would either like to read or that relate to her/his life. Explain why you selected or wrote each poem or song.

- Story Bag: Put together a bag that contains at least ten items that would be useful to or significant to a character in your novel. Include a description of each item and its relevance to the story.

- Select one of the characters in the novel and imagine what would happen if you brought her/him to your school or to your home for a day. You should consider things like: how would s/he fit in with the other students/family members; how s/he might react to the rules, teachers/parents, assignments/chores, etc.; how would s/he dress and how would people react to that; what might s/he find interesting? This may either be written from your point of view or from the character's point of view.

- Create a tri-fold brochure or pamphlet with drawings, pictures, and text that advertise or promote something in the novel.

- Select a character from the novel and "interview" her/him. What kinds of things would you like to ask her/him and how would s/he respond? Write this up in an interview format.

- Make a "wanted" poster for one of the main characters. Give a physical description and picture, what s/he has done, what the reward is, and who to contact. Also indicate whether s/he is wanted dead or alive.

- Write a book review for the novel. Briefly outline the main characters, setting, plot, and theme. Also tell whether or not you would recommend this novel to someone your own age and specify who might enjoy it.

- Compare and contrast two of the main characters from the book. You may use a Venn diagram for this, but you must explain what makes the characters different from one another and how they are similar.

- Research the author of the novel. Tell where s/he is from, where s/he went to school, where s/he lives now, her/his family, etc. You should also include the names of other books that s/he has written, what awards/honors s/he has received. This must be in your own words.

- Use the Story Pyramid format (get it from me) for the novel.

- Find and get copies of summaries of five other books written by the author of the novel that you just finished.

- List fifteen interesting words from your novel. Tell why each word is interesting or significant.

- Make a crossword puzzle using words from your novel. Be sure to include character names, setting, and main ideas or terms from the book.

- Draw a map of where the story takes place. Label all of the places that were important in the story. Write one page about how the places were used in the novel.

- Write an obituary or a eulogy for one character in the novel. Give all the pertinent information-- birthplace, schooling, accomplishments, career, etc. How do you think that person would want to be remembered?

- Compare your novel with several TV shows that are similar. Describe the ways in which they are similar and the ways in which they are different.

- If the story takes place in an actual city/town, research the setting. Where is it located? Climate? Population? Main language and religion? Provide a map of the place and surrounding areas. How many miles is it from your home? Include a map showing how you'd travel to get there from where you live. Tell what mode of transportation you'd use to get there.

- Find ten recipes that relate to your story in some way. For example, if the story takes place in a particular region, then include recipes that tell what kinds of foods are served there. If the story deals with a certain time period or socio-economic group, then tell what kinds of foods would be served in that era or to that group of people.

- Have a character from your book endorse or sell a product (like a TV commercial). Tell what product it is and why people should buy it. Write a one paragraph dialogue for your character to say. The item you select should relate to the story.

- Select (from an outside source) or write a "theme song" for at least five characters from the novel. Explain why you selected or wrote each song.

- Choose three songs that might become a score for the book; for example, choose the three most important scenes in the novel and select the music that might be playing in the background while these scenes are taking place. Explain why you selected each song.

- Choose a character from the novel and select five songs that might illustrate her/his development throughout the course of the story. Explain why you selected each song.

Index

About the Author

Daria Plumb has taught English and social studies at Riverside Academy (formerly Dundee Alternative High School) since 1994. She has also taught survey classes in children's literature at Washtenaw Community College and Eastern Michigan University. Plumb is actively involved in the National Council of Teachers of English (NCTE) and the Assembly on Literature for Adolescents of the NCTE (ALAN), and serves on the editorial review board for *The ALAN Review*. Her 2007 article for *English Leadership Quarterly*, "New Rules for Old Lit: Connecting At-Risk Kids to the Classics, 'Commando Style,'" was named honorable mention for Best Article of the Year. Plumb shares many of her strategies for working with at-risk teens and reluctant readers on her website *Get 'Em Reading* at *http://www.getemreading.com*.

CPSIA information can be obtained at www.ICGtesting.com
Printed in the USA
LVOW09s1700140414

381646LV00016B/507/P